ler Siege

ONE WEEK LOAN

D1388689

STEPHEN GRAHAM is Professor of Cities and Society at Newcastle University and previously taught at Durham and MIT, among other universities. He is the author of several books, including *Disrupted Cities*; *Cities, War and Terrorism*; *The Cybercities Reader*; and (with Simon Marvin) *Splintering Urbanism*.

Cities Under Siege:
The New Military Urbanism

Stephen Graham

VERSO
London • New York

First published by Verso 2010
This paperback edition first published by Verso 2011
© Stephen Graham 2011

The moral rights of the author have been asserted

1 3 5 7 9 10 8 6 4 2

Verso
UK: 6 Meard Street, London W1F 0EG
US: 20 Jay Street, Suite 1010, Brooklyn, NY 11201
www.versobooks.com

Verso is the imprint of New Left Books

ISBN-13: 978-1-84467-762-7

British Library Cataloguing in Publication Data
A catalogue record for this book is available from the British Library

Library of Congress Cataloging-in-Publication Data
A catalog record for this book is available from the Library of Congress

Typeset in Minion Pro by Hewer Text UK Ltd, Edinburgh
Printed in the US by Maple Vail

For Doreen and Margaret

Political struggles are not fought on the surface of geography but through its very fabrication.

Steve Pile,
'The Troubled Spaces of Frantz Fanon'

Today, wars are fought not in trenches and fields, but in living rooms, schools and supermarkets.

Sultan Barakat,
'City War Zones'

Contents

Acknowledgements

During my time at Durham University's geography department, I was fortunate to be surrounded by an extraordinary range of friends and scholars who address the politics of geography with verve, power and creativity. I have learned an immeasurable amount from working amongst them, and they have been immensely important to the genesis of this book. Many have been especially kind commenting on drafts and providing ideas. Thanks, in particular, to Ash Amin, Louise Amoore, Harriet Bulkeley, Ben Anderson, David Campbell, Mike Crang, Angharad Closs Stephens, Stuart Elden, Alex Hall, Paul Harrison, Kathrin Hörschelmann, everyone at IBRU, Francisco Klauser, Colin McFarlane, John Mendel, Christine McEwan, Gordon McLeod, Rachel Pain, Marcus Power, Joe Painter and Divya Tolia-Kelly.

Further afield, I have received vital long-term encouragement from colleagues who have done much to open up the agendas that this book has taken up. I have also benefited from a wide range of critical feedback, which is especially important to a book of this breadth. My debts here are too numerous to list in full. But thanks, in particular, to Rowland Atkinson, John Armitage, Kirstie Ball, John Beck, Zygmunt Bauman, Ryan Bishop, Alastair Bonnett, Neil Brenner, Judit Carrera, Bob Catterall, Greg Clancey, Jon Coaffee, Deborah Cowen, Jordan Crandall, Lieven De Cauter, Simon Dalby, Mike Davis, Ashley Dawson, Volker Eick, Keller Easterling, Ulrike Engel, Derek Gregory, James Harkin, Ken Hewitt, Bryan Finoki, Omar Jabary Salamanca, Caren Kaplan, Maria Kaika, Roger Keil, Stephen Legg, Patrick LeGalès, Setha Low, David Lyon, Peter Marcuse, Eduardo Mendietta, Deborah Natsios, Clive Norris, Vyjayanthi Rao, Neil Smith, Michael Sorkin, Eric Swyngedouw, Nigel Thrift, Nick Turse, Robert Warren, Eyal Weizman, David Wood, Elvin Wyly, Alison Williams, Rachel Woodward, Steve Wright, Charles Zerner and Elia Zureik. Grateful thanks also to the support of New York University's department of sociology – especially to Neil Brenner and Harvey Molotch – which allowed me to visit in November 2007. I must emphasize, of course, that all mistakes and weaknesses of the current work remain my own.

Grateful appreciation is due to the Economic and Social Research Council for supporting the 'Contested Borders' project (RES-155-25-0087) that provided many of the insights developed in Chapter 5.

The visual material in this book draws on the work of a large number of friends and colleagues. Many thanks to Lisa Benton-Short, Adam Broomberg, Oliver Chanarin, Ben Colebrook, Teddy Cruz, Keller Easterling, Ulrike Engel, Bryan Finoki, Mark Gillem, Francisco Klauser, Paula Levine, Deborah Natsios, Jereemy Nemeth, Clive Norris, Steve Rowell, Anne-Marie Schleiner, Elin O'Hara Slavick, John Young and Micah Ian Wright for kindly providing images. I am also extremely grateful to Michele Allan and Chris Orton for their excellent job preparing the line-drawn tables, maps and figures. Thanks also to Rayya Badran for suggesting the cover image.

Penultimately, I should note that previous versions of parts of this work have already been published as follows: Introduction as a paper in *City* (13:4, November 2009). Chapter 6 as an LSE *Crisis States* working paper, as an article in *City* (12: 1, April 2008), and in different forms in two books: Deborah Cowen and Emily Gilbert (eds), *War, Citizenship, Territory* (Routledge: New York, 2008); and David Lyon (ed.), *Theorizing Surveillance* (Willan: Cullompton, 2006). Chapter 7 (in very different form in *New Left Review* 2: 44, March/April 2006); Chapter 8 (in very different form in *New Left Review* 2: 19, January/ February 2003); and, finally, Chapter 9 (as an article in *City* 9: 2, July 2005, and in different forms as chapters in two books: Allan Pred and Derek Gregory, *Violent Geographies* (New York: Routledge, 2006), and Eric Swyngedouw, Nick Heynen and Maria Kaika (eds), *In the Nature of Cities* (London: Routledge, 2005).

Finally, thanks to Simon Marvin for the Haifa beers in 2002 that got this started; to Tom Penn and Mark Martin at Verso for perfect encouragement; to Avis Lang and Noah Eber-Schmid for, respectively, superb copy-editing and fact-checking; to Palma, Lynn and Sally for the time to finish; and, above all, to Annette, Ben and Oliver, for the light and love that allowed me to get to the other side.

Stephen Graham, Newcastle

Introduction: 'Target Intercept . . .'

On 14 November 2007, Jacqui Smith, then the UK's home secretary, announced one of the most ambitious attempts by any state in history for the systematic tracking and surveillance of all persons entering or leaving British territory. The highly controversial e-Borders programme aims to deploy sophisticated computer algorithms and data-mining techniques to identify 'illegal' or threatening people or behaviour before they threaten the UK's territorial limits. The programme utilizes technology developed by the Trusted Borders consortium, led by the massive Raytheon defence corporation.

The e-Borders project is based on a dream of technological omniscience: to track everyone flowing across the UK's borders, using records of past activity and associations to identify future threats before they materialize. Smith promised that when the system is finally functional in 2014 – although many argue that it is unworkable – border control and security will be reinstated for the UK in a radically mobile and insecure world. 'All travellers to Britain will be screened against no-fly lists and intercept target lists,' she predicted. 'Together with biometric visas, this will help keep trouble away from our shores . . . As well as the tougher double check at the border, ID cards for foreign nationals will soon give us a triple check in country.'[1]

Smith's language here – 'target lists', 'screening', 'biometric visas' and so on – reveals a great deal. The massive global proliferation of deeply technophiliac state surveillance projects like the e-Border programme signals the startling militarization of civil society – the extension of military ideas of tracking, identification and targeting into the quotidian spaces and circulations of everyday life. Indeed, projects like this one are more than a state's responses to changing security threats. Rather, in a world marked by globalization and

---

1 Nicole Kobe, 'Government announces that half of £1.2 billion in funding for technology to boost border security will go to Raytheon-led Trusted Borders consortia for a screening system,' *IT Pro,* 14 Nov. 2007, at http://www.itpro.co.uk/139053/650-million-e-borders-contract-to-raytheon-group. In a rich irony, another sort of surveillance – a record of the pay-per-view bills – almost forced Smith to resign in late March 2009, when it was discovered that she tried to claim for the costs of her husband's pornographic viewing habits as a parliamentary expense. In the same month, a later exposé of MPs abusing such expenses also put her, and many of her colleagues, under pressure. Smith eventually resigned in June 2009.

increasing urbanization, they represent dramatic attempts to translate long-standing military dreams of high-tech omniscience and rationality into the governance of urban civil society.

With both security and military doctrine within Western states now centred on the task of identifying insurgents, terrorists and an extensive range of ambient threats from the chaos of urban life, this fact becomes clearer still. Moreover, whether in the queues of Heathrow, the tube stations of London or the streets of Kabul and Baghdad, the latest doctrine stresses that ways must be found to identify such people and threats before their deadly potential is realized, at a point when they are effectively indistinguishable from the wider urban populace. Hence the parallel drive in cities within both the capitalist heartlands of the global North and the world's colonial peripheries and frontiers to establish high-tech surveillance systems which mine data accumulated about the past to identify future threats.

THEIR SONS AGAINST OUR SILICON

At the root of such visions of war and security in the post–Cold War world are fantasies in which the West harnesses its unassailable technological power to reinstate its waning military, economic and political supremacy. 'At home and abroad,' wrote US security theorists Mark Mills and Peter Huber in the right-wing *City Journal*, a year after the 9/11 attacks, 'it will end up as their sons against our silicon. Our silicon will win.'[2]

Huber and Mills foresee a near future straight out of *Minority Report*. In their vision, a whole suite of surveillance and tracking systems emerge on the back of high-tech modes of consumption, communication and transportation to permeate every aspect of life in Western cities. Continually comparing individuals' current behaviour with vast databases recording past events and associations, these tracking systems – so the argument goes – will automatically signal when the city's bodies, spaces, and infrastructure systems are about to come under terrorist attack. Thus, what Huber and Mills call 'trustworthy' or 'cooperative targets' are continually separated from 'non-cooperators' and their efforts to use postal, electricity, Internet, finance, airline and transport systems as the means to project resistance and violence. In effect, Huber and Mills's vision calls for an extension of airport-style security and surveillance systems to encompass entire cities and societies utilizing, at its foundation, the

---

2 Mark Mills and Peter Huber, 'How Technology Will Defeat Terrorism,' *City Journal*, Winter 2002.

high-tech means of consumption and mobility that are already established in Western cities.

As for the resistant colonial frontiers, Huber and Mills, like many US military and security theorists, dream of continuous, automated and robotized counter-insurgency warfare. Using systems similar to those deployed in US cities, but this time granted the sovereign power to kill autonomously, they imagine that US troops might be spared from the dirty job of fighting and killing on the ground in rapidly urbanizing frontier zones. Swarms of tiny, armed drones, equipped with advanced sensors and communicating with each other, will thus be deployed to loiter permanently above the streets, deserts and highways. Huber and Mills dream of a future where such swarms of robotic warriors work tirelessly to 'project destructive power precisely, judiciously, and from a safe distance – week after week, year after year, for as long as may be necessary.'[3]

Such fantasies of high-tech omnipotence are much more than science fiction. As well as constructing the UK's e-Borders programme, for example, Raytheon is also the leading manufacturer of both cruise missiles and the unmanned drones used regularly by the CIA to launch assassination raids across the Middle East and Pakistan since 2002. Raytheon is also at the heart of a range of very real US military projects designed to use computer software to allow robotic weapons to target and kill their foes autonomously without any human involvement whatsoever, as Huber and Mills have envisioned.

THE NEW MILITARY URBANISM

The crossover between the military and the civilian applications of advanced technology – between the surveillance and control of everyday life in Western cities and the prosecution of aggressive colonial and resource wars – is at the heart of a much broader set of trends that characterize the new military urbanism. Of course, the effects observed in the urban Western setting differ wildly from those seen in the war-zone. But, crucially, whatever the environment, these hi-tech acts of violence are predicated on a set of shared ideas.

Fundamental to the new military urbanism is the paradigmatic shift that renders cities' communal and private spaces, as well as their infrastructure – along with their civilian populations – a source of targets and threats. This is manifest in the widespread use of war as the dominant metaphor in describing the perpetual and boundless condition of urban societies – at war against

---

3 Mills and Huber, 'How Technology Will Defeat Terrorism'.

drugs, against crime, against terror, against insecurity itself. This development incorporates the stealthy militarization of a wide range of policy debates, urban landscapes, and circuits of urban infrastructure, as well as whole realms of popular and urban culture. It leads to the creeping and insidious diffusion of militarized debates about 'security' in every walk of life. Together, once again, these work to bring essentially military ideas of the prosecution of, and preparation for, war into the heart of ordinary, day-to-day city life.

The insidious militarization of urban life occurs at a time when humankind has become a predominantly urban species for the first time in its 150,000-year history. It gains its power from multiple circuits of militarization and securitization which, thus far, have not been considered together or viewed as a whole. It is this task to which the current book is devoted.

By way of introduction, and to give a flavour of the remarkable range of political, social and cultural circuits currently being colonized by the new military urbanism, it is worth introducing its five key features.

URBANIZING SECURITY

As with Huber and Mills's prescriptions for the future, the new military urbanism, in all its complexity and reach, rests on a central idea: militarized techniques of tracking and targeting must permanently colonize the city landscape and the spaces of everyday life in both the 'homelands' and domestic cities of the West as well as the world's neo-colonial frontiers. To the latest security and military gurus, this is deemed imperative, the only adequate means to address the new realities of what they call 'asymmetric' or 'irregular' war.

Such wars pitch non-state terrorists or insurgents against the high-tech security, military and intelligence forces of nation-states and their burgeoning array of private and corporate affiliates-in-arms. Non-uniformed and largely indistinguishable from the city populace, non-state fighters, militia, insurgents and terrorists lurk invisibly thanks to the anonymity offered by the world's burgeoning cities (especially the fast-growing informal districts). They exploit and target the spiralling conduits and arteries which link modern cities: the Internet, YouTube, GPS technology, mobile phones, air travel, global tourism, international migration, port systems, global finance, even postal services and power grids.

The terrorist outrages in New York, Washington, Madrid, London and Mumbai (to name but a few sites of attack), along with state military assaults on Baghdad, Gaza, Nablus, Beirut, Grozny, Mogadishu and South Ossetia, demonstrate that asymmetric warfare is the vehicle for political violence across transnational spaces. More and more, contemporary warfare takes place in supermarkets, tower blocks, subway tunnels, and industrial districts rather than open fields, jungles or deserts.

All this means that, arguably for the first time since the Middle Ages, the localized geographies of cities and the systems that weave them together are starting to dominate discussions surrounding war, geopolitics and security. In the new military doctrine of asymmetric war – also labelled 'low-intensity conflict', 'netwar', the 'long war', or 'fourth-generation war' – the prosaic and everyday sites, circulations and spaces of the city are becoming the main 'battlespace'[4] both at home and abroad.

In such a context, Western security and military doctrine is being rapidly reimagined in ways that dramatically blur the juridical and operational separation between policing, intelligence and the military; distinctions between war and peace; and those between local, national and global operations. Increasingly, wars and associated mobilizations cease to be constrained by time and space and instead become both boundless and more or less permanent. At the same time, state power centres increasingly expend resources trying to separate bodies deemed malign and threatening from those deemed valuable and threatened within the everyday spaces of cities and the infrastructures that lace them together. Instead of legal or human rights and legal systems based on universal citizenship, these emerging security politics are founded on the profiling of individuals, places, behaviours, associations, and groups. Such practices assign these subjects risk categories based on their perceived association with violence, disruption or resistance against the dominant geographical orders sustaining global, neoliberal capitalism.

In the West, this shift threatens to re-engineer ideas of citizenship and national boundaries central to the concept of the Western nation-state since the mid-seventeenth century. An increasing obsession with risk profiling may use the tools of national security to unbundle ideas that feed into the conception of universal national citizenship. For example, the United States is already pressuring Britain to bring in a special visa system for UK citizens who want to visit America with close links to Pakistan. In other words, such developments threaten to establish border practices *within* the spaces of nation-states – challenging the definition of the geographical and social 'insides' and 'outsides' of political communities. This process parallels, in turn, the eruption of national border points within the territorial limits of nations at airports, cargo ports, Internet terminals and the railway stations of express trains.

---

4 See Tim Blackmore, *War X: Human Extensions in Battlespace,* Toronto: University of Toronto Press, 2005.

Meanwhile, the policing, security and intelligence arms of governments are also reaching out beyond national territorial limits as global surveillance systems are created to monitor the world's airline, port, trade, finance and communications systems. Electronic border programmes, for example – like Raytheon's in the UK – are being integrated into transnational systems so that passengers' behaviour and associations can be data-mined before they attempt to board planes bound for Europe and the US. Policing powers are also extending beyond the borders of nation-states. The New York Police Department, for example, has recently established a chain of ten overseas offices as part of its burgeoning anti-terror efforts. Extra-national policing proliferates around international political summits and sporting events. In a parallel move, refugee and asylum camps are increasingly being 'offshored' to keep them beyond the territorial limits of rich capitalist nations so that human bodies deemed malign, unworthy or threatening can be stored and dealt with invisibly and at a distance.

The expansion of police powers beyond national borders occurs just as military forces are being deployed more regularly within Western nations. The United States recently established a military command for North America for the first time: the Northern Command.[5] Previously, this was the only part of the world not covered in this way. The US Government has also gradually reduced long-standing legal barriers to military deployment within US cities. Urban warfare training exercises now regularly take place in American cities, geared towards simulations of 'homeland security' crises as well as the challenges of pacifying insurgencies in the cities of the colonial peripheries in the global south. In addition, in a dramatic convergence of doctrine and technology, high-tech satellites and drones developed to monitor far-off Cold War or insurgent enemies are increasingly being used within Western cities.

FOUCAULT'S BOOMERANG

The new military urbanism feeds on experiments with styles of targeting and technology in colonial war-zones, such as Gaza or Baghdad, or security operations at international sports events or political summits. These operations act as testing grounds for technology and techniques to be sold on through the world's burgeoning homeland security markets. Through such processes of imitation, explicitly colonial models of pacification, militarization and control, honed on the streets of the global South, are spread to the cities of capitalist

5   See www.northcom.mil/.

heartlands in the North. This synergy, between foreign and homeland security operations, is the second key feature of the new military urbanism.

International studies scholar Lorenzo Veracini has diagnosed a dramatic contemporary resurgence in the importation of typically colonial tropes and techniques into the management and development of cities in the metropolitan cores of Europe and North America. Such a process, he argues, is working to gradually unravel a 'classic and long-lasting distinction between an outer face and an inner face of the colonial condition.'[6]

It is important to stress, then, that the resurgence of explicitly colonial strategies and techniques amongst nation-states such as the US, UK and Israel in the contemporary 'post-colonial' period[7] involves not just the deployment of the techniques of the new military urbanism in foreign war-zones but their diffusion and imitation through the securitization of Western urban life. As in the nineteenth century, when European colonial nations imported fingerprinting, panoptic prisons and Haussmannian boulevard-building through neighbourhoods of insurrection to domestic cities after first experimenting with them on colonized frontiers, colonial techniques today operate through what Michel Foucault termed 'boomerang effects.'[8] 'It should never be forgotten', Foucault wrote,

> that while colonization, with its techniques and its political and juridical weapons, obviously transported European models to other continents, it also had a considerable boomerang effect on the mechanisms of power in the West, and on the apparatuses, institutions, and techniques of power. A whole series of colonial models was brought back to the West, and the result was that the West could practise something resembling colonization, or an internal colonialism, on itself.[9]

In the contemporary period, the new military urbanism is marked by – and, indeed, comprises – a myriad of startling Foucauldian boomerang

---

6 Lorenzo Veracini, 'Colonialism Brought Home: On the Colonization of the Metropolitan Space,' *Borderlands*, 4:1, 2005, available at www.borderlands.net.au.

7 See Derek Gregory, *The Colonial Present*, Oxford: Blackwell, 2004; David Harvey, *The New Imperialism*, Oxford: Oxford University Press, 2005.

8 Michel Foucault, *Society Must Be Defended: Lectures at the Collège de France, 1975–6*, London: Allen Lane, 2003, 103. On the panopticon, see Tim Mitchell, 'The stage of modernity', in Tim Mitchell (ed), *Questions of Modernity*, Minneapolis; University of Minnesota Press, 2000, 1–34. On Hausmannian planning, see Eyal Weizman, interview with Phil Misselwitz, 'Military Operations as Urban Planning', *Mute Magazine*, August 2003 at www.metamute.org. And, on fingerprinting, see Chandak Sengoopta, *Imprint of the Raj: How Fingerprinting Was Born in Colonial India*, London: Pan Books, 2003.

9 Foucault, *Society Must Be Defended*, ibid.

effects, which this book spends much of its length elaborating in detail. For example, Israeli drones designed to vertically subjugate and target Palestinians are now routinely deployed by police forces in North America, Europe and East Asia. Private operators of US 'supermax' prisons are heavily involved in running the global archipelago organizing incarceration and torture that has burgeoned since the start of the 'war on terror'. Private military corporations heavily colonize reconstruction contracts in both Iraq and New Orleans. Israeli expertise in population control is sought by those planning security operations for international events in the West. And shoot-to-kill policies developed to combat suicide bombings in Tel Aviv and Haifa have been adopted by police forces in Europe and America – a process which directly led to the state killing of Jean Charles de Menezes by London anti-terrorist police on 22 July 2005.

Meanwhile, aggressive and militarized policing at public demonstrations and social mobilizations in London, Toronto, Paris and New York are now starting to utilize the same 'non-lethal weapons' as Israel's army in Gaza or Jenin. The construction of 'security zones' around the strategic financial cores and government districts of London and New York directly import the techniques used at overseas bases and green zones. Finally, many of the techniques used to fortify enclaves in Baghdad or permanently lockdown civilians in Gaza and the West Bank are being sold around the world as cutting-edge and combat-proven 'security solutions' by corporate coalitions linking Israeli, US and other companies and states.

Crucially, such boomerang effects that meld security and military doctrines in the cities of the West with those on colonial peripheries is backed up by the cultural geographies which underpin the political right and far-right, along with hawkish commentators within Western militaries themselves. These tend to deem cities per se to be intrinsically problematic spaces – the main sites concentrating acts of subversion, resistance, mobilization, dissent and protest challenging national security states both at home and abroad.

Bastions of ethno-nationalist politics, the burgeoning movements of the far right are often heavily represented within the police and the state military. They tend to see rural or exurban areas as the authentic and pure spaces of white nationalism, associated with Christian and traditional values. Examples here range from US Christian fundamentalists, through the British National Party to Austria's Freedom Party, the French National Front and Italy's Forza Italia. The fast-growing and sprawling cosmopolitan neighbourhoods of the West's cities, meanwhile, are often cast by such groups in the same Orientalist terms as the mega-cities of the Global South, as places radically external to the vulnerable nation – territories every bit as foreign as Baghdad or Gaza.

Paradoxically, however, the geographical imagination which underpins the new military urbanism tends to treat colonial frontiers and Western 'homelands' as fundamentally separate domains – two sides in a clash of civilizations, in Samuel Huntington's incendiary and highly controversial hypothesis.[10] This imaginative separation coexists uneasily with the ways in which the security, military and intelligence doctrines addressing both increasingly fuse together into a seamless whole. Such conceptions work to deny the ways in which the cities in both domains are increasingly linked by migration and investment.

The rendering of *all* such cities as problematic spaces beyond the rural or exurban heartlands of authentic national communities creates a peculiar consonance between the colonial peripheries and the capitalist heartlands. The construction of sectarian enclaves modelled on Israeli practice by US forces in Baghdad from 2003, for example, was widely described by US security personnel as the development of US-style gated communities in Iraq. In the aftermath of the devastation of New Orleans by Hurricane Katrina in late 2005, US Army Officers talked of the need to 'take back' the city from Iraqi-style 'insurgents.'

As ever, then, the way in which urban life in colonized zones is imagined reverberates powerfully in the cities of the colonizers. Indeed, the projection of colonial tropes and security exemplars into postcolonial metropoles in capitalist heartlands is fuelled by a new 'inner city Orientalism.'[11] This relies on the widespread depiction amongst rightist security, military, and political commentators of immigrant districts within the West's cities as 'backward' zones threatening the body politic of western cites or nations. In France, for example, post-war state planning worked to conceptualize the mass, peripheral housing projects of the *banlieues* as 'near peripheral' reservations attached to, but distant from, the country's metropolitan centres.[12] Bitter memories of the Algerian and other anti-colonial wars saturate the French far-right's discourse about waning 'white' power and the 'insecurity' caused by the banlieues – a process that has led to a dramatic mobilization of state security forces in and around the main immigrant housing complexes following the *banlieues* riots in 2005.

Discussing the shift from external to internal colonization in France, Kristin

---

10 See Samuel Huntington, *The Clash of Civilizations and the Remaking of World Order*, Simon and Schuster: New York, 1998.

11 See Sally Howell and Andrew Shryock, 'Cracking Down on Diaspora: Arab Detroit and America's "War on Terror" ', *Anthropological Quarterly* 76, 443–62.

12 Stefan Kipfer and with Kanishka Goonewardena, 'Colonization and the New Imperialism: On the Meaning of Urbicide Today', *Theory and Event* 10: 2, 2007, 1–39.

Ross points to the way in which France now 'distances itself from its (former) colonies, both within and without.' This functions, she continues, through a 'great cordoning off of the immigrants, their removal to the suburbs in a massive reworking of the social boundaries of Paris and other French cities.'[13] The 2005 riots were only the latest in a long line of reactions to the increasing militarization and securitization of this form of internal colonization and enforced peripherality within what Mustafa Dikeç has called the 'badlands' of the contemporary French Republic.[14]

Indeed, such is the contemporary right's conflation of terrorism and immigration that simple acts of migration are now often being deemed little more than acts of warfare. This discursive shift has been termed the 'weaponization' of migration[15] – shifting the emphasis from moral obligations to offer hospitality and asylum towards criminalizing or dehumanizing migrants as weapons against purportedly homogeneous and ethno-nationalist bases of national power.

Here the latest debates about asymmetric, irregular or low-intensity war – where nothing can be defined outside of boundless and never-ending definitions of political violence – blur uncomfortably into the growing clamour of demonization by right and far-right commentators of the West's diasporic and increasingly cosmopolitan cities. Samuel Huntington, taking his clash of civilizations thesis further, now argues that the very fabric of US power and national identity is under threat not just because of global Islamist terrorism but because non-white and especially Latino groups are colonizing, and dominating, US metropolitan areas.[16]

Adopting such Manichaean visions of the world, US military theorist William Lind has argued that prosaic acts of immigration from the global South to the North's cities must now be understood as acts of warfare. 'In Fourth Generation war,' Lind writes, 'invasion by immigration can be at least as dangerous as invasion by a state army.' Under what he calls the 'poisonous ideology of multiculturalism,' Lind argues that migrants within Western nations can now launch 'a homegrown variety of Fourth Generation war, which is by far the most dangerous kind.'[17]

---

13 Kristin Ross, *Fast Cars, Clean Bodies: Decolonization and the Reordering of French Culture,* Cambridge, MA: MIT Press, 1996. 12.

14 Mustafa Dikeç, *Badlands of the Republic: Space, Politics and Urban Policy,* Oxford: Blackwell, 2007. See also Ross, *Fast Cars, Clean Bodies.*

15 See Cato, 'The Weaponization of Immigration', Center for Immigration Studies, February 2008, at www.cis.org.

16 See Samuel Huntington, *Who Are We: The Challenges to America's National Identity,* Simon & Schuster: New York, 2005; and Huntington, *Clash of Civilizations.*

17 William Lind, 'Understanding Fourth Generation War,' *Military Review,* Sept–Oct 2004, 16, available at www.au.af.mil/au/awc/awcgate/milreview/lind.pdf.

Given the two-way movement of the exemplars of the new military urbanism between Western cities and those on colonial frontiers, fuelled by the instinctive anti-urbanism of national security states, it is no surprise that cities in both domains are starting to display startling similarities. In both, hard, military-style borders, fences and checkpoints around defended enclaves and 'security zones', superimposed on the wider and more open city, are proliferating. Jersey-barrier blast walls, identity check-points, computerized CCTV, biometric surveillance and military styles of access control protect archipelagos of fortified social, economic, political or military centres from an outside deemed unruly, impoverished or dangerous. In the most extreme examples, these encompass green zones, military prisons, ethnic and sectarian neighbourhoods and military bases; they are growing around strategic financial districts, embassies, tourist and consumption spaces, airport and port complexes, sports arenas, gated communities and export processing zones.

In both domains, efforts to profile urban populations are linked with similar systems which observe, track, and target dangerous bodies amid the mass of urban life. We thus see parallel deployments of high-tech satellites, drones, 'intelligent' CCTV, 'non-lethal' weaponry, data mining and biometric surveillance in the very different contexts of cities at home and abroad. And in both domains, finally, there is a similar sense that new doctrines of perpetual war are being used to treat all urban residents as perpetual targets whose benign nature, rather than being assumed, now needs to be continually demonstrated to complex architectures of surveillance or data-mining technology as the subject moves around the city. Such developments are backed by parallel legal suspensions targeting groups deemed threatening with special restrictions, pre-emptive arrests, or a priori incarceration within globe-straddling extra-legal torture camps and gulags.

While these various archipelagos function in a wide variety of ways, they all superimpose on urban traditions of open access security systems that force people to prove their legitimacy if they want to move freely. Urban theorists and philosophers now wonder whether the city as a key space for dissent and collective mobilization within civil society is being replaced by complex geographies made up of various systems of enclaves and camps which are linked together and withdrawn from the urban outside beyond the walls or access-control systems.[18] In such a context one wonders whether urban securitization might reach a level in the future which would effectively decouple the strategic

---

18 See Bülent Diken and Carsten Bagge Laustsen, *The Culture of Exception: Sociology Facing the Camp*, London: Routledge, 2005, 64; Stephen Graham and Simon Marvin, *Splintering Urbanism*, London: Routledge, 2001.

economic role of cities as the key drivers of capital accumulation from their historic role as centres for the mobilization of democratic dissent.

SURVEILLANT ECONOMY

Turning to our third key starting point – the new military urbanism's political economy – it is important to stress that the colonization of urban thinking and practice by militarized ideas of 'security' does not have a single source. In fact, it emanates from a complex range of sources. These encompass sprawling, transnational industrial complexes that stretch beyond the military and security sectors to span the technology, surveillance and entertainment industries; a wide range of consultants, research labs and corporate universities who sell security solutions as silver bullets to solve complex social problems; and a complex mass of security and military thinkers who now argue that war and political violence centre overwhelmingly on the everyday spaces and circuits of urban life.

Though vague and all-encompassing, ideas about security infect virtually all aspects of public policy and social life,[19] so these emerging industrial-security complexes work together on the highly lucrative challenges of perpetually targeting everyday activities, spaces and behaviours in cities, as well as the conduits that link conurbations. Amid global economic collapse, markets for security services and technologies are booming like never before.

Crucially, as the Raytheon example again demonstrates, the same constellations of security companies are often involved in selling, establishing and overseeing the techniques and practices of the new military urbanism in both war-zone and homeland cities. Often, as with the EU's new Europe-wide security policies, states or supranational blocks are not necessarily bringing in high-tech and militarized means of tracking illegal immigrants because they are the best means to address their security concerns. Rather, many such policies are intended to help build local industrial champions by developing their own defence, security or technology companies so they can compete in booming global markets for security technology.

In this lucrative export market, the Israeli experience of locking down cities and turning the Occupied Territories into permanent, urban prison camps is proving especially influential. It is the ultimate source of 'combat-proven' techniques and technology. The new high-tech border fence between the United States and Mexico, for example, is being built by a consortium linking

---

19   See Giorgio Agamben, 'Security and Terror,' *Theory and Event*, 5: 4, 2002, 1–2.

Boeing to the Israeli company Elbit, whose radar and targeting technologies have been developed in the permanent lockdown of Palestinian urban life. It is also startling how much US counterinsurgency strategies in Iraq have explicitly been based on efforts to emulate the Israeli treatment of the Palestinians during the Second Intifada.

The political economies sustaining the new military urbanism inevitably focus on the role of an élite group of so-called 'global' cities as the centres of neoliberal capitalism as well as the main arenas and markets for rolling out the new security solutions. The world's major financial centres, in particular, orchestrate global processes of militarization and securitization. They house the headquarters of global security, technology and military corporations, provide the locations for the world's biggest corporate universities – which dominate research and development in new security technologies – and support the global network of financial institutions which so often work to erase or appropriate cities and resources in colonized lands in the name of neoliberal economics and 'free trade'.

The network of global cities through which neoliberal capitalism is primarily orchestrated – London, New York, Paris, Frankfurt, and so on – thus helps to produce new logics of aggressive colonial acquisition and dispossession by multinational capital, which works closely with state militaries and private military contractors.

With the easing of state monopolies on violence and the proliferation of acquisitive private military and mercenary corporations, the brutal 'urbicidal' violence and dispossession that so often helps bolster the parasitic aspects of Western city economies, as well as feeding contemporary corporate capitalism, is more apparent than ever.[20] In a world increasingly haunted by the spectre of imminent resource exhaustion, the new military urbanism is thus linked intimately with the neocolonial exploitation of distant resources in an effort sustain the richer cities and wealthy urban lifestyles. New York and London provide the financial and corporate power through which Iraqi oil reserves have been appropriated by Western oil companies since the 2003 invasion. Neocolonial land-grabs to grow biofuels for cars or food for increasingly precarious urban populations of the rich North are also organized through global commodity markets centred on the world's big financial cities. Finally, the rapid global growth in markets for high-tech security is itself providing a major boost to these cities in a time of global economic meltdown.

---

20 See Kipfer and Goonewardena, 'Colonization and the New Imperialism'.

URBAN INFRASTRUCTURE, URBAN WAR

The very nature of the modern city – its reliance on dense webs of infrastructure, its density and anonymity, its dependence on imported water, food and energy – create the possibility of violence against it, and *through* it. Thus, the city is increasingly conceived of as the primary means of waging war by both state and non-state fighters alike.

Many recent examples demonstrate how non-state actors gain much of their power by appropriating the technical infrastructure necessary to sustain modern, globalized urban life in order to project, and massively amplify, the power of their political violence. Insurgents use the city's infrastructure to attack New York, London, Madrid or Mumbai. They disrupt electricity networks, oil pipelines, or mobile phone systems in Iraq, Nigeria and elsewhere. Somalis systematically hijacking global shipping routes have even used spies in London's shipping brokers to provide intelligence for their attacks. In doing so, such actors can get by with the most basic of weapons, transforming airliners, metro trains, cars, mobile phones, electricity and communications grids, or small boats, into deadly devices.

However, such threats of infrastructural terrorism, while very real, pale beside the much less visible efforts of state militaries to target essential city infrastructures. The US and Israeli forces, for example, have worked systematically to 'demodernize' entire urban societies through the destruction of the infrastructure of Gaza, the West Bank, Lebanon, and Iraq since 1991. States have replaced total war against cities with the systematic destruction of water and electricity supplies with weapons – such as bombs which rain down millions of graphite spools to short-circuit electricity stations – designed specially for this task.

Though sold to the media as a way to bring inexorable political pressure on adversary regimes, such purportedly humanitarian modes of war end up killing the most vulnerable members of society as effectively as carpet bombing, but beyond the capricious gaze of the cameras. Such assaults are engineered through the deliberate generation of public health crises in highly urbanized societies where no alternatives to modern water, sewerage, power, or medical and food supplies exist.

The devastating Israeli siege of Gaza since Hamas was elected in 2006 is a powerful example. This has transformed a dense urban corridor, with 1.5 million people squeezed into an area the size of the Isle of Wight, into a vast prison camp. Within these confines, the deaths of the weak, old, young and sick are invisible to the outside world. The stronger individuals are forced to live something approaching what Giorgio Agamben has called 'bare life' – a biological existence that can be sacrificed at any time by a colonial power that maintains the right to kill with impunity but has withdrawn all moral, political or human responsibilities from the population.[21]

Increasingly, the goals of such formal infrastructural war, as a means of political coercion, blur seamlessly into the structure of economic competition and energy geopolitics. A resurgent Russia, for example, gains much of its strategic power these days not through formal military deployments but through its continued threats to switch off the energy supplies of Europe's cities at a stroke.

CITIZEN SOLDIERS

The fifth key trait of the new military urbanism is the way its claims to legitimacy are fused with militarized veins of popular, urban, electronic and material culture. Very often, for example, the military tasks of tracking, surveillance and targeting do not require completely new technological systems. Instead, they simply appropriate the systems that operate in cities to sustain the latest means of digitally organized travel and consumption. Thus, as in central London, congestion-charging zones quickly morph into security zones. Internet interactions and transactions provide the basis for data-mining in efforts to root out supposedly threatening behaviours. Dreams of smart cars help bring into being robotic weapons systems. Satellite imagery and GPS support new styles of civilian urban life based on the use of the very US Air Force structures that facilitate 'precision' urban bombing. And, as in the new security initiative in Lower Manhattan, CCTV cameras designed to make shoppers feel secure are transformed into 'anti-terrorist' surveillance systems.

Perhaps the most powerful series of civilian–military crossovers at the heart of the new military urbanism are being forged within cultures of virtual and electronic entertainment and corporate news. Here, to tempt the nimble-fingered recruits best able to control the latest high-tech drones and weaponry, the US military produces some of the most popular urban warfare video games. Highly successful games like the US Army's *America's Army* or US Marines' *Full Spectrum Warrior*[22] allow players to slay terrorists in fictionalized and Orientalized cities in frameworks based directly on those of the US military's own training systems. To close the circle between virtual entertainment and remote killing, control panels for the latest US weapons systems – such as the latest control stations for the pilots of armed Predator drones, manufactured by

---

21   See Giorgio Agamben, *Homo Sacer: Sovereign Power and Bare Life*, Stanford: Stanford University Press.
22   See for example, www.americasarmy.com.

our old friends Raytheon – now imitate the consoles of PlayStations, which are, after all, very familiar to recruits.

A final vital circuit of militarization linking urban and popular culture in domestic cities to colonial violence in occupied ones centres on the well-established but intensifying militarization of car-culture. The most powerful symbol of this is the popularity of the explicitly military Sports Utility Vehicle, a phenomenon most notable in the United States. The rise and fall of the Hummer is an especially pivotal example. Here, as we shall see, US military vehicles for urban warfare have been converted into hyper-aggressive civilian vehicles marketed as the patriotic embodiment of the War on Terror. Modified civilian SUVs, in turn, have been the vehicle of choice for Blackwater's mercenaries on the streets of Iraq, as well as the recent focus of US recruitment drives targeting urban ethnic minorities. In addition, tentative shifts towards computerized civilian cars crossover heavily with the US military's impatient efforts to build fully robotic ground vehicles geared towards urban warfare. Embracing all these connections, of course, are the insecurities and violence perpetuated by US oil profligacy, which is forcing US military forces into a tawdry scramble to access and control rapidly diminishing reserves and supplies.

AIMS

This is the context in which *Cities Under Siege* aims to present a wide-ranging exploration and critique of the contours of the new military urbanism. Contrary to conventional debates within international politics, political science, and history, *Cities Under Siege* does not view the spaces, infrastructures and cultural aspects of city life as a mere passive backdrop to the imagination and propagation of violence or the construction of 'security'. Rather, the way cities and urban spaces are produced and restructured are seen actually to help constitute these strategies and fantasies, as well as their effects (and vice versa).

To achieve this, *Cities Under Siege* deliberately works across an unusually wide range of geographical scales. The book emphasizes how the new military urbanism works by constituting urban life in both metropolitan cores of the West, and the burgeoning cities on the global South's colonial frontiers. It reveals, moreover, how this is done through processes and connections which demand that transnational, national, urban and bodily scales be kept in view at the same time.[23]

---

23   See Michael Peter Smith, *Transnational Urbanism: Locating Globalization*, New York: Blackwell, 2001.

The book aims in particular to unite two very different, and usually separate, discourses on cities and urban life: the growing debate within security studies and international politics on the urbanization of security; and the generally more critical debates within urban studies, geography, architecture, anthropology and cultural studies as to how these changes are challenging the politics of cities and urban life in a time of rapid urbanization.

The writing of this book is partly motivated by the absence of an accessible and critical analysis exploring how resurgent imperialism and colonial geographies characteristic of the contemporary era umbilically connect cities within metropolitan cores and colonial peripheries.[24] Such neglect is the result of the stark division of labour within the academy. This has meant that, broadly speaking, foreign policy, military, legal and international relations scholars have had the task of addressing the new imperial wars at the international scale. At the same time, an almost completely separate body of urban, legal and social scholars has worked to explore the new politics of Western cities which have surrounded the homeland security drive at the urban and national scales within Western nations. But these debates have remained stubbornly separated by their different theoretical traditions, and the geographical and scalar orientations, of the two.

This analytical failure is in part explicable in terms of the way dominant, conservative, and realist investigations into the link between globalization and security split contemporary reality into the 'home' civilization of the rich, modern North and a separate civilization in the global South, characterized largely by backwardness, danger, pathology and anarchy.[25] Indeed, as we shall see, such Manichaean views of the world are themselves a driving force behind the new military urbanism. Such perspectives tend to demonize an Orientalized South as the source of all contemporary insecurity. They also actively work to deny the ways in which urban and economic life in the global North fundamentally relies on, and is constituted through, links to the postcolonial – and in some cases, newly colonial – South. In the process such discourses play a key role in producing the symbolic violence necessary to allow states to launch real violence and war.

By obsessing about the geopolitical rivalries of nation-states or transnational non-state movements, moreover, such realist, conservative perspectives completely ignore how cities and urbanization processes also provide crucial

---

24 See Gregory, *The Colonial Present*.

25 Robert Kaplan's writings are key examples here. See Kaplan, 'The Coming Anarchy,' *Atlantic Monthly*, February 1994; Kaplan *The Coming Anarchy: Shattering the Dreams of the Post–Cold War World*, New York: Random House, 2000.

territorial forms of domination, hyper-inequality, and insecurity and help to propogate violence. 'One of the fundamental determinants of the modern experience,' cultural theorist Fredric Jameson wrote in 2003, 'can be found in the way imperialism masks and conceals the nature of the system. For one thing, the imperial powers of the older system do not want to know about their colonies or about the violence and exploitation on which their prosperity is founded.'[26]

Perhaps surprisingly, academic disciplines which purportedly deal with urban issues are themselves struggling to overcome the legacies of their own colonial histories. This dramatically inhibits their ability to understand the new military urbanism. The Manichaean vision that characterizes conservative writings about globalization are also perceptible in the work of many urban theorists. In particular, the concept of a world partitioned into two hermetically sealed zones – 'developed' cities addressed through urban geography or sociology, and 'developing' cities addressed through 'development studies' – remains remarkably pervasive.

This means that, too often, cities in the West and the so-called developing world remain artificially separated, with theoretical attention centring overwhelmingly on the former. This leaves the burgeoning and pivotal cities of the South categorized as a mere Other, outside of Western culture, a status which makes it all but impossible for theorists to grasp how both sets of cities mutually constitute each other within imperial, neo-colonial or postcolonial geographies.[27]

The field of urban studies has been particularly slow to address the central role of cities within the new imperialism – the resurgence of aggressive, colonial militarism focusing on the violent appropriation of land and resources in the South.[28] Indeed, the prosperous cities of the North are today often idealized by liberal commentators and theorists as centres of migration and laboratories of cosmopolitan integration, characteristics construed as vital to their high-tech economic futures as the key nodes of the 'global knowledge economy'. Such integration is deemed by influential urban policy gurus, such as Richard Florida, to be a key engine of economic creativity within technologically advanced capitalism.[29]

---

26 Fredric Jameson, 'The End of Temporality', *Critical Inquiry*, 29(4), 2003, 700, cited in Kipfer and Goonewardena 'Colonization and the New Imperialism'.

27 Jenny Robinson, 'Cities Between Modernity and Development', paper presented to the annual meeting of the Association of American Geographers, 2003, New Orleans, unpublished paper. See also her *Ordinary Cities*, London: Routledge, 2006.

28 See Kanishka Goonewardena and Stefan Kipfer, 'Postcolonial Urbicide: New Imperialism, Global Cities and the Damned of the Earth', *New Formations*, 59, Autumn 2006, 23–33.

29 See Richard Florida, *The Rise of the Creative Class*, New York: Basic Books, 2002.

These perspectives, however, systematically ignore the way the North's global cities often act as economic or ecological parasites, preying on the South, violently appropriating energy, water, land and mineral resources, relying on exploitative labour conditions in offshore manufacturing, driving damaging processes of climate change, and generating an often highly damaging flow of tourism and waste. Even less recognized are the ways in which the North's global cities act as the main sites for financing and orchestrating the control of the developing world that is at the heart of the extension of neoliberal capitalism.[30] The ways in which the rich cities of the advanced capitalist world profit from 'urbicidal' violence, which deliberately targets the city geographies of the Global South to sustain capital accumulation, have barely been acknowledged.[31] *Cities Under Siege* is an attempt to rectify this situation.

OUTLINE

Cities Under Siege comprises three broad, thematic chapters, followed by seven extended case studies. The first of the thematic chapters looks at how warfare, political violence and military and security imaginaries are now re-entering cities. This development follows a long period when Western military thought was preoccupied with planning globe-straddling nuclear exchanges between superpowers or massed tank engagements across rural plains. It examines, too, the ways in which the latest military and security doctrine is working to colonize the everyday environments of modern conurbations.

Chapter 2 moves on to look at how the various bastions of the political right increasingly work to demonize cities as intrinsically threatening or problematic places necessitating political violence, militarized control, or radical securitization. In Chapter 3, I detail the particular characteristics of the new military urbanism, and use some of the latest research in the social sciences to highlight key features of the deepening crossover between urbanism and militarism.

The next six case studies address the circuits through which the new military urbanism connects urban life in the West to existence on colonial frontiers. The first three look at, respectively, the proliferation of borders and surveillance systems within the fabric of urban life; the US military's ambitions for urban

---

30 See, for example, Saskia Sassen, *The Global City: New York, London, Tokyo*, Princeton: Princeton University Press, (2nd Edition) 2002; Peter Taylor, *World City Network: A Global Urban Analysis*, London: Routledge, 2003.

31 For an excellent discussion of this, see Kipfer and Goonewardena 'Colonization and the New Imperialism'; and Goonewardena and Kipfer, 'Postcolonial Urbicide'.

and counterinsurgency warfare based on the deployment of armed robots; and the connections between entertainment, simulation and US military and imperial violence. The final three explore the diffusion of Israeli technology and doctrine in urban warfare and securitization; the links between urban infrastructure and contemporary political violence; and the ways in which Sports Utility Vehicle (SUV) culture is embedded within a geopolitical and political-economic setting that links domestic and colonial cities and spaces.

There are ways to challenge the new military urbanism's ideologies, tactics, and technologies and to defend and rejuvenate democratic and non-militarized visions of modern urban existence. It is to these positive possibilities that I turn in the final chapter, looking at a variety of 'counter-geographic' activists, artists, and social movements, each seeking to challenge urban violence, as now constituted, in different ways, and attempting to mobilize radical concepts of security as the bases for new political movements. Rather than the machinations of national security states, these new movements must centre on the human, urban and ecological bases of security in a world of spiralling food, water and environmental crises, burgeoning cities, rapid climate and sea-level change, and fast-diminishing fossil fuels.

CHAPTER ONE

War Re-enters the City

URBAN PLANET

At the dawn of the twentieth century, one in ten of the Earth's 1.8 billion people lived in cities – an unprecedented proportion, even though humankind remained overwhelmingly rural and agricultural. A mere fraction of the urban population, overwhelmingly located in the booming metropoles of the global North, orchestrated the industrial, commercial and governmental affairs of an ever more interconnected colonial world. Meanwhile, in the colonized nations, urban populations remained relatively tiny, concentrated in provincial capitals and entrepôts: 'The urban populations of the British, French, Belgian and Dutch empires at the Edwardian zenith,' writes Mike Davis, 'probably didn't exceed 3 to 5 per cent of colonised humanity'.[1] All told, the urban population of the world in 1900 – some 180 million souls – numbered no more than the total population of the world's ten largest cities in 2007.

In the course of the next half-century, Earth's population grew steadily but unspectacularly, reaching 2.3 billion by 1950. While the urban population nearly tripled to over 500 million, it still formed less than 30 per cent of the whole. Developments in the following half-century, however, were astonishing: the greatest mass movement, combined with the greatest burst of demographic growth, in human history. Between 1957 and 2007, the world's urban population quadrupled. By 2007, half the world's 6.7 billion people could be classed as city-dwellers (Figure 1.1). *Homo sapiens* had precipitously become a predominantly urban species. It had taken almost ten thousand years – from 8000 BC to 1960 – for cities to house the world's first billion urbanites; it will take a mere fifteen for this figure to rise from three billion to four.[2] Dhakar, the capital of Bangladesh, a city of 400,000 in 1950, will by 2025 have mushroomed into a metropolitan area of some 22 million – a fiftyfold increase within only seventy-five years (Figure 1.2). Given the density of cities, more than half of humanity is currently squeezed onto just 2.8 per cent of our planet's land surface, and the squeeze is tightening day by day.[3]

---

1 Mike Davis, 'The Urbanization of Empire: Megacities and the Laws of Chaos', *Social Text* 22: 4, 2004, 4.

2 Humansecurity-cities.org., *Human Security for an Urban Century,* Vancouver, 2004, 9, available at humansecuritycities.org.

3 William M. Reilly, 'Urban Populations Booming', TerraDaily.com, 27 June 2007.

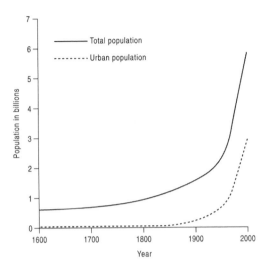

1.1   Total world population, and total urban population, 1600–2000.

As we move into what has been called the 'urban century', there appears to be no end to this headlong urbanization of our world. In 2007, 1.2 million people were added to the world's urban population each week. By 2025, according to current estimates, there could easily be five billion urbanites, two-thirds of whom will live in 'developing' nations. By 2030, Asia alone will have 2.7 billion; the Earth's cities will be packed with 2 billion more people than they accommodate today. Twenty years further on, by 2050, fully 75 per cent of the world's estimated 9.2 billion people will most likely be living in cities.[4]

In other words, within just over four decades the Earth will host seven billion urban dwellers – 4 billion more than in 2007. The overwhelming majority of these will be in the burgeoning cities and megacities of Asia, Africa and Latin America. To be sure, many cities in developed nations will still be growing, but their growth will be dwarfed by urban explosion in the global South.

As demographic, political, economic and perhaps technological centres of gravity emerge in the South, massive demographic and economic shifts will inexorably continue. As recently as 1980, thirteen of the world's thirty biggest

---

4   United Nations Habitat, *State of the World's Cities 2006/7*, United Nations Habitat: Nairobi, 2007, 4.

cities were in the 'developed world'; by 2010, this number will have dwindled to eight. By 2050, it is likely that only a few of the top thirty megacities will be located in the erstwhile 'developed' nations (Figure 1.2).

	1980		1990		2000		2010	
1	21.9	Tokyo	25.1	Tokyo	26.4	Tokyo	26.4	Tokyo
2	15.6	New York	16.1	New York	18.1	Mexico City	23.6	Bombay
3	13.9	Mexico City	15.1	Mexico City	18.1	Bombay	20.2	Lagos
4	12.5	Sao Paulo	15.1	Sao Paulo	17.8	Sao Paulo	19.7	Sao Paulo
5	11.7	Shanghai	13.3	Shanghai	16.6	New York	18.7	Mexico City
6	10.0	Osaka	12.2	Bombay	13.4	Lagos	18.4	Dhaka
7	9.9	Buenos Aires	11.5	Los Angeles	13.1	Los Angeles	17.2	New York
8	9.5	Los Angeles	11.2	Buenos Aires	12.9	Calcutta	16.6	Karachi
9	9.0	Calcutta	11.0	Osaka	12.9	Shanghai	15.6	Calcutta
10	9.0	Beijing	10.9	Calcutta	12.6	Buenos Aires	15.3	Jakarta
11	8.9	Paris	10.8	Beijing	12.3	Dhaka	15.1	Delhi
12	8.7	Rio de Janeiro	10.5	Seoul	11.8	Karachi	13.9	Los Angeles
13	8.3	Seoul	9.7	Rio de Janeiro	11.7	Delhi	13.9	Metro Manilla
14	8.1	Moscow	9.3	Paris	11.0	Jakarta	13.7	Buenos Aires
15	8.1	Bombay	9.0	Moscow	11.0	Osaka	13.7	Shanghai
16	7.7	London	8.8	Tianjin	10.9	Metro Manilla	12.7	Cairo
17	7.3	Tianjin	8.6	Cairo	10.8	Beijing	11.8	Istanbul
18	6.9	Cairo	8.2	Delhi	10.6	Rio de Janeiro	11.5	Beijing
19	6.8	Chicago	8.0	Metro Manilla	10.6	Cairo	11.5	Rio de Janeiro
20	6.3	Essen	7.9	Karachi	9.9	Seoul	11.0	Osaka
21	6.0	Jakarta	7.7	Lagos	9.6	Paris	10.0	Tianjin
22	6.0	Metro Manilla	7.7	London	9.5	Iatanbul	9.9	Seoul
23	5.6	Delhi	7.7	Jakarta	9.3	Moscow	9.7	Paris
24	5.3	Milan	6.8	Chicago	9.2	Tianjin	9.4	Hyderabad
25	5.1	Tehran	6.6	Dhaka	7.6	London	9.4	Moscow
26	5.0	Karachi	6.5	Istanbul	7.4	Lima	9.0	Bangkok
27	4.37	Bangkok	6.4	Teheran	7.3	Bangkok	8.8	Lima
28	4.6	St. Petersburg	6.4	Essen	7.2	Tehran	8.6	Lahore
29	4.6	Hong Kong	5.9	Bangkok	7.0	Chicago	8.2	Madras
30	4.4	Lima	5.8	Lima	6.9	Hong Kong	8.1	Tehran

1.2   World's largest thirty cities in 1980, 1990, 2000 and (projected) 2010.
Table illustrates the growing domination of 'mega-cities' in the global South.

POLARIZING WORLD

> We are now learning what countries across the developing world have experienced over three decades: unstable and inequitable neoliberal economics leads to unacceptable levels of social disruption and hardship that can only be contained by brutal repression.[5]

The rapid urbanization of the world matters profoundly. As the UN has declared, 'the way cities expand and organize themselves, both in developed and developing countries, will be critical for humanity.'[6]

While relatively egalitarian cities like those in continental Western Europe tend to foster a sense of security, highly unequal societies are often marked by fear, high levels of crime and violence, and intensifying militarization. The dominance of neoliberal models of governance over the past three decades, combined with the spread of punitive and authoritarian models of policing and social control, has exacerbated urban inequalities. As a result, the urban poor are often confronted with reductions in public services on the one hand, and a palpable demonization and criminalization on the other.

Neoliberalization – the reorganization of societies through the widespread imposition of market relationships – provides today's dominant, if crisis-ridden, economic order.[7] Within this framework, societies tend to sell off public assets (whether utilities or public spaces) and open up domestic markets to outside capital. Market-based strategies for the distribution of public services undermine and supplant social, health and welfare programmes.[8]

An extraordinary expansion of financial instruments and speculative mechanisms is also crucial to neoliberalization. Every area of society becomes marketized and financialized. States and consumers alike pile up drastic financial debt, securitized through arcane instruments of global stock markets. By 2006, just before the onset of the global financial crash, financial markets were trading more in a month than the annual gross domestic product of the entire world.[9]

In practice, the much-vaunted economic axioms of 'privatization', 'structural adjustment' and the 'Washington consensus' camouflage disturbing

---

5   Madeleine Bunting, 'Faith. Belief. Trust. This Economic Orthodoxy Was Built on Superstition', *Guardian*, 6 October 2008.

6   United Nations Population Fund, *The State of World Population 2007: Unleashing the Potential of Urban Growth*, United Nations, New York: Rensslaer Polytechnic Institute, 2007.

7   See Michael Pryke, 'City Rhythms: Neoliberalism and the Developing World', in John Allen, Doreen Massey and Michael Pryke, eds, *Unsettling Cities*, London: Routledge, 1999, 229–70.

8   Chris Wright and Samantha Alvarez. 'Expropriate, Accumulate, Financialise', *Mute Magazine*, 10 May 2007, available at www.metamute.org.

9   Randy Martin, 'Where Did The Future Go?', *Logos* 5: 1, 2006.

transformations. They serve as euphemisms for what Gene Ray has called 'the coordinated coercions of the global debtors' prison, for the pulverization of local labor and environmental protections, and for the breaking open of all markets to the uncontrolled operations of finance capital'.[10] Wealth has been stripped from poor and vulnerable economies through the flagrant predations of global capital, organized from a mere handful of megacities in the North. Structural adjustment policies (SAPs) imposed on the world's poor nations by the IMF and the World Bank between the late 1970s and the late 1990s re-engineered economies while ignoring issues of social welfare and human security. The result was enormous disruption, widespread insecurity, and massive, informal urbanization. Deteriorating conditions in increasingly marketized agricultural areas – often combined with the mandated withdrawal of welfare systems under the strictures of the SAPs[11] – forced many people to migrate to cities.

Invariably, then, 'liberalization' has meant a collapse in formal employment opportunities for marginal urban populations; a withering of fiscal, social, and medical safety-nets, public health systems, public utilities, and education services; and a massive growth of both consumer debt and the informal sector of economies. Such fiscal and debt regimes have often tended, as Mike Davis puts it, to 'strip-mine the public finances of developing countries and throttle new investment in housing and infrastructure.' SAPs have thus worked in many cases to 'decimate public employment, destroy import-substitution industries, and displace tens of thousands of rural producers unable to complete against the heavily subsidized agri-capitalism of the rich countries.'[12]

Such processes have been a key driving force behind the global ratcheting-up of inequality within the past three decades. Across the world, social fissures and extreme polarization – intensified by the global spread of neoliberal capitalism and market fundamentalism – have tended to concentrate most visibly and densely in burgeoning cities. The urban landscape is now populated by a few wealthy individuals, an often precarious middle class, and a mass of outcasts.

Almost everywhere, it seems, wealth, power and resources are becoming ever more concentrated in the hands of the rich and the super-rich, who increasingly sequester themselves within gated urban cocoons and deploy their own private security or paramilitary forces for the tasks of boundary enforcement and access control. 'In many cities around the world, wealth and

---

10 Gene Ray, 'Tactical Media and the End of the End of History', *Afterimage* 34: 1–2, 2006.
11 See Nigel Harris and Ida Fabricius, eds., *Cities and Structural Adjustment*, London: University College London Press, 1996.
12 Davis, 'Urbanization of Empire', 2.

poverty coexist in close proximity,' wrote Anna Tibaijuk, director of the UN's Habitat Programme, in October 2008. 'Rich, well-serviced neighbourhoods and gated residential communities are often situated near dense inner-city or peri-urban slum communities that lack even the most basic of services. [The divide is often] prominently marked by electrified fences and high walls, often patrolled by armed private security companies with killer dogs.'[13]

Such trends have two related dimensions. On the one hand, global neoliberalism has accentuated already yawning inequalities between rich nations and poor nations. As markets, speculative bubbles, and mergers add to the monopolistic power of dominant capital, so ever larger portions of wealth accrue to ever smaller numbers of people and to the urban enclaves in which they cluster. 'Gaps in income between the poorest and the richest countries have continued to widen,' confirms the United Nations. 'In 1960 the 20 per cent of the world's people in the richest countries had 30 times the income of the poorest 20 per cent in 1997, 74 times as much.'[14]

Even World Bank Economists noted with concern in 2002 that 'the richest 1 per cent of people in the world get as much income as the poorest 57 per cent.'[15] Startlingly, by 1988, the richest 5 per cent of the world's population had an average income seventy-eight times greater than that of the poorest 5 per cent; just five years later, this had risen to a multiple of 114. At the same time, the poorest 5 per cent of the world's population actually grew poorer, losing a full quarter of their real income.[16]

By 2006, an estimated 10.1 million individuals around the world had a net worth of more than $1 million, excluding the value of their homes. This was an increase of 6 per cent from the previous year. Each individual within this elite group owned assets totalling, on average, more than $4 million. This 'transnational capitalist class' now forms what Citigroup researchers have called 'the dominant drivers of demand' in many contemporary economies. They operate to skim the 'cream off productivity surges and technology monopolies, then spend . . . their increasing shares of national wealth as fast as possible on luxury goods and services.'[17] In the process, they generate enormous ecological and carbon footprints. Meanwhile, amid the turmoil of

---

13   Cited in 'UN-HABITAT unveils State of the World's Cities report', 23 October, 2008, available at www.unhabitat.org.

14   United Nations Development Project, *Human Development Report 1999*, United Nations: New York, 1999, 36.

15   Branco Milanovic, 'True World Income Distribution, 1988 and 1993: First Calculations Based on Household Surveys Alone', *The Economic Journal* 112, 2002, 88.

16   Ibid., 51–92.

17   Both quotes from Mike Davis and Daniel Bertrand Monk, eds, *Evil Paradises: Dreamworlds of Neoliberalism,* New York: New Press, 2007, xi–xii.

collapsing finance systems, 'most of the world watches the great binge on television.'[18]

On the other hand, and not surprisngly, social inequalities are also rising rapidly within nations, regions and cities. Many economists would concur with Giovanni Andrea Cornia when he argues that 'most of the recent surge in income polarization [within nations] would appear to be related to the policy drive towards domestic deregulation and external liberalization.'[19] This has tended to concentrate wealth within social classes, corporations and locations that are capable of profiting from privatization and the extension of finance capital, while undermining wages, wealth and security for more marginalized people and places.

In the US, for example, the Gini coefficient – the best measure of social inequality – rose from an already high level of 0.394 in 1970 to 0.462 in 2000. (A Gini score of 0 indicates perfect equality, with everyone having the the same income; a score of 1 represents perfect inequality, with one person collecting all the income and everyone else having an income of zero. A score above 0.3 implies an extremely unequal society.) Social polarization in the US is thus now exceeded by only a handful of very poor countries in Africa and Latin America.[20]

By 2007, the income of the wealthiest fifth of the US population averaged $168,170 a year, while the poorest fifth scraped by on an average of $11,352. It's been a feeding frenzy for a few dozen super-rich: the US had fifty-one billionaires in 2003 and 313 the next year.[21] In the United States, such extreme concentrations of wealth are combined with extraordinarily high levels of incarceration among poorer groups. As the world's pre-eminent 'penal democracy',[22] the US, with 5 per cent of the world's population, held fully 24 per cent of the world's prisoners (more than two million people) in 2007.[23]

The UK, meanwhile, is now the most polarized nation in Western Europe apart from Italy. Its income inequality – again measured by the Gini coefficient

18   Ibid., xiii.

19   Giovanni Andrea Cornia, 'The Impact of Liberalisation and Globalisation on Within-country Income Inequality', *CESifo Economic Studies* 49:4, 2003, 581.

20   Pat Murphy, 'Peak America – Is Our Time Up?', *New Solutions* 7, 2005, 2, available at www.communitysolution.org.

21   Holly Sklar, 'Boom Time for Billionaires', *ZNet Commentary*, 15 October 2004, cited in Henry Giroux, 'The Conservative Assault on America: Cultural Politics, Education and the New Authoritarianism', *Cultural Politics* 1:2, 143.

22   Joy James, ed., *Warfare in the American Homeland: Policing and Prison in a Penal Democracy*, Durham, NC: Duke University Press, 2007.

23   Ashley Seager, 'Development: US Fails to Measure Up on "Human Index"', *Guardian*, 17 July 2008.

– has risen dramatically since the early 1960s, with the remodelling of the economy through radical re-regulation, privatization and neoliberalization (Figure 1.3). For the richest 10 per cent of the UK population, incomes rose in real terms by 68 per cent between 1979 and 1995. Their collective income now matches that of the nation's poorest 70 per cent. During the same period, incomes for the poorest 10 per cent of UK households actually fell by 8 per cent (not considering housing costs). This rapidly reversed reductions in inequality achieved during the post-war Keynesian boom in the UK.

After housing costs, the UK's richest 10 per cent increased their share of the nation's marketable wealth from 57 per cent in 1976 to 71 per cent in 2003. At the same time, according to Philip Bond in the *Independent*, 'the speculative capital that could be deployed or invested by the bottom 50 per cent of the British population fell from 12 per cent to just 1 per cent'.[24]

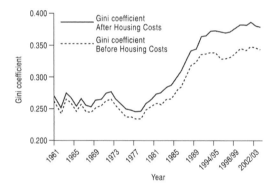

1.3   Radical growth in income inequality in the UK between 1961 and 2002/3 for income before housing costs (BHC) and after housing costs (AHC), as measured by the Gini coefficient.

The imposition of market fundamentalism had particularly spectacular effects on the ex-Communist Comecon block after the collapse of communism in the late 1980s. Not only did this create a handful of billionaires and oligarchs but, at the same time, it increased the number of people living in poverty and deep insecurity from three million in 1988 to 170 million in 2004.[25]

Globally, by 2007, well over a billion people – a third of all urban

24   Phillip Blond, 'Outside View: The End of Capitalism as We Know It?', *Independent*, 23 March 2008.

25   Davis, 'Urbanization of Empire', 12.

dwellers – were leading a highly precarious existence in fast-growing slums and informal settlements.[26] Increasingly, the developing world has come to be dominated by immiserized shanty-town populations whose daily insecurities encourage a receptivity to radical, violently anti-Western ideologies and movements. Most residents of informal settlements lead an especially precarious existence because they constitute what Mike Davis calls an 'outcast proletariat'. 'This is a mass of humanity', he writes, 'structurally and biologically redundant to global [capital] accumulation and the corporate matrix'.[27] Neither consumers nor producers, unintegrated into the dominant corporate system of globalization, they instead try to benefit indirectly, through 'black economies' and informal labour, from the urban cores they literally surround.

It is all too easy for political, corporate or military elites to portray the residents of informal settlements as existential, even sub-human, threats to the 'formal' neoliberal economy and its archipelago of privileged urban enclaves of residence, production, speculation, transportation, and tourism. Everywhere, the urban boundaries between the 'insides' and the 'outsides' of our planet's dominant economic order present sites of palpable militarization, as state and corporate security forces seek not only to police but also, often, to profit from the relations between the two.[28] Shanty settlements are frequently bulldozed by government planners, police forces or militaries, whether to clear the way for modern infrastructure or real-estate development, to address purported threats of crime or disease, or simply to push the marginalized populations out of sight of the enclaves.

Clearly, however, just as public, social, and health policies have proved ill-suited to deal with the insecurities created by massive informal settlements,[29] so the policies and doctrines of law enforcement and the military are ill-equipped to address their growth. Such places pose what Mike Davis terms 'unique problems of imperial order and social control that conventional geopolitics has barely begun to register'. He predicts, soberly, that 'if the point of the war against terrorism is to pursue the enemy into his sociological and cultural labyrinth, then the poor peripheries of developing cities will be the permanent battlefields of the twenty-first century'.[30]

---

26 Mike Davis, *Planet of Slums*, London: Verso, 2006.
27 Davis, 'Urbanization of Empire', 11.
28 See Loïc Wacquant, 'The Militarization of Urban Marginality: Lessons from the Brazilian Metropolis', *International Political Sociology* 2: 1, 2008, 56–74.
29 See Humansecurity-cities.org., *Human Security for an Urban Century*, 9.
30 Davis, 'Urbanization of Empire', 15.

At the same time, both national and international security policies centre on securing the rapidly merging archipelago of urban enclaves organized by and for the very groups that most benefit from neoliberalization. Yet the moorings of the super-rich are always tenuous, and this emerging class demonstrates the ultimate in transnational rootlessness. 'The people of the "upper tier" do not apparently belong to the place they inhabit', writes Zygmunt Bauman. 'Their concerns lie (or rather float) elsewhere.'[31]

Nevertheless, certain cities – most notably London – are becoming radically transformed, re-engineered as primary sites for the world's über-wealthy. Through grandiose city-planning, others – notably Dubai – are emerging as supercharged, hyperreal embodiments of global extremes, aimed primarily at luring the super-rich for vacations and possibly more. As Mike Davis writes, in Dubai developers 'are invited to plug into high-tech clusters, entertainment zones, artificial islands, glass-domed "snow mountains", *Truman Show* suburbs, cities within cities – whatever is big enough to be seen from space and bursting with architectural steroids.'[32]

OLD MILITARY URBANISMS

Looking at the urban landscapes of Dubai, one can readily forget that many of the world's cities originate, at least in part, as military constructions. The history of the imagination, construction and inhabitation of urban places cannot be told without considering the central role of such places as the critical sites of militarized power and control.[33] In premodern and early modern times, cities and city-states were the primary agents, as well as the main targets, of war. The sacking of fortified cities, together with the killing of their inhabitants, was the central event in war.[34] Partly allegorical stories of such acts make up a good part of the Bible – especially *Jeremiah* and *Lamentations* – as well as other ancient and classical texts. 'Myths of urban ruin grow at our culture's root', contends Marshall Berman.[35]

In the sixteenth and seventeenth centuries, the emerging modern European

---

31   Zygmunt Bauman, 'City of Fears, City of Hopes', London: Goldsmiths College, University of London, New Cross, 2003, 16, available at www.goldsmiths.ac.uk.

32   Mike Davis, 'Sand, fear and money in Dubai', in Denis and Monk, eds, *Evil Paradises*, New York: New Press, 2007, 51.

33   See Max Weber, *The City*, Glencoe, IL.: Free Press, 1958; Lewis Mumford, *The City in History*, New York: MJF Books, 1961.

34   See Christopher Gravett, *Medieval Siege Warfare*, Oxford: Osprey Publishing.

35   Marshall Berman, 'Falling Towers: City Life After Urbicide', in Dennis Crowe, ed., *Geography and Identity*, Washington: Maisonneuve Press, 1996, 172–192.

nation-states – 'bordered power containers' within the early systems of global imperial capitalism – began to seek a monopoly on political violence.[36] 'The states caught up with the forward gallop of the towns' as agents of war,' writes Fernand Braudel.[37] The expanding imperial and metropolitan cities that lay at the core of these nation-states no longer organized their own armies or defences, but they maintained political power and reach. Such cities directed violence, control, and repression, as well as the colonial acquisition of territory, raw materials, wealth, and labour power.[38]

Since then, cities have been central agents in the many forms of violence brought about by capitalist imperialism. A crucial element has been their capacity to '*centralise* military, political and economic activities and in so doing draw otherwise disparate social formations into hierarchical and exploitative structural relations at variously extensive spatial scales'.[39] But large-scale repressive violence was not always required within the colonial cities that served to organize the empires of Western powers; both middle and poorer classes were often integrated within, and dependent upon, exploitative colonial economies.[40] Yet war, erasure and the violent suppression of revolts – against rural revolutionary guerillas, against independence movements, against indigenous communities and industries, against demonized minorities – was equally indispensable to colonial conquest and exploitation. Indeed, as Pierre Mesnard y Méndez writes, the 'economic basis for the triumph of capitalism was colonial warfare-plunder from the 15th to the 18th and 19th centuries.'[41] More specifically, the construction of Europe's imperial empires was sustained by a wide spectrum of urban wars that lurched between the exploitation and the persistent struggles taking place in the colonies, and the equally volatile politics of imperial metropoles at the 'heart of empire'.[42]

Techniques and technologies of colonial urban warfare and repression

---

36   Anthony Giddens, *The Nation-State and Violence*, Los Angeles: The University of California Press, 1987.

37   Fernand Braudel, *Capitalism and Material Life,* New York: Harper Collins, 1973, 398.

38   See Felix Driver and David Gilbert, ed., *Imperial Cities*, Manchester: Manchester University Press, 2003.

39   Goonewardena and Kipfer, 'Postcolonial Urbicide'.

40   See Davis, 'Urbanization Of Empire', 9; Anthony King, *Urbanism, Colonialism and the World Economy*, London: Routledge, 1991.

41   Pierre Mesnard y Méndez, 'Capitalism Means/Needs War', *Socialism and Democracy* 16: 2, 2002.

42   See Henri Lefebvre, *The Critique of Everyday Life,* vol. 1, London: Verso, 1991; Kipfer and Goonewardena, 'Colonization and the New Imperialism'.

travelled back and forth between colonial frontiers and European metropolitan heartlands. (Foucault called such links 'boomerang effects, as discussed in the Introduction.)

European powers fought rebellions and insurgencies in the cities and rural areas that lay on their empires' fringes, while at the same time working to protect 'their exploding capital cities against homegrown rebellions and revolutions nourished by class struggles.'[43] In the process:

> The battleground shifted from the open fields to the city walls and further positioned itself within the heart of the city, as a fight for the city itself. If historical siege warfare ended when the envelope of the city was broken and entered, urban warfare started at the point of entering the city.[44]

Such colonial urban wars and boomerang effects provide contemporary reminders about the perils of attempting to placate guerilla resistance in occupied cities through superior military power, acts of brutal, urbicidal violence, or aggressive physical restructuring. Spatial experiments in the laboratory of the colonial city have often set the stage for the replanning of the colonial metropole. In the 1840s, for instance, after Marshall Thomas Robert Bugeaud[45] succeeded in quelling the insurrection in Algiers through the combination of atrocities and the destruction of entire neighbourhoods to make way for modern roads, his techniques of 'urban planning skipped over the Mediterranean, from the Algerian countryside, where they were experimented with, to the streets and alleyways of Paris.'[46] To undermine the revolutionary ferment of the poor of Paris, Bugeaud devised a plan for the violent reorganization of the city through the construction of wide military highways – a plan later implemented by his avid reader Baron Haussmann.[47]

By the late nineteenth and twentieth centuries, industrial cities in the global North had grown in synchrony with the killing power of technology. They provided the men and matériel to sustain the massive wars of the twentieth

---

43   Eyal Weizman and Phil Misselwitz, 'Military Operations as Urban Planning', *Mute Magazine*, August 2003.

44   Ibid.

45   In 1847 Bugeaud wrote perhaps the first Western manual of urban warfare, *La Guerre des Rues et des Maisons* [The War of Streets and Houses], republished in 1997 by Jean-Paul Rocher, Paris.

46   Eyal Weizman, introduction to 'The War of Streets and Houses', by Thomas Bugeaud, web exclusive, *Cabinet* 22, Summer 2006, available at www.cabinetmagazine.org.

47   Ibid.

century, while their (often female-staffed) industries and neighbourhoods emerged as the prime targets for total war. The industrial city thus became 'in its entirety a space for war. Within a few years . . . bombing moved from the selective destruction of key sites within cities to extensive attacks on urban areas and, finally, to instantaneous annihilation of entire urban spaces and populations.'[48]

Sometimes, exact replicas of the vernacular architecture of the cities to be bombed were built to facilitate the honing of the process. In Dugway Proving Grounds in Utah, for example, the US Army Air Force built exact replicas of Berlin tenements beside Japanese villages of wood and rice paper, and burned them repeatedly so as to perfect the design of its incendiary bombs.[49]

THE BOMBARDIER'S EYE

With the mutually assured destruction of the Cold War, such subtleties became less necessary. 'With the inter-continental missile', writes Martin Shaw, 'the capacity to simultaneously destroy *all* major centres of urban life became a symbol of the degeneration of war.'[50] Nevertheless, great efforts were made in the US during the Cold War to construct a bastion against both nuclear Armageddon and the Communist menace.[51] From these efforts emerged the nuclear family, the suburban house, and the nuclear state, fused into the political-cultural bastion of American life.

Right up to the start of the twenty-first century, the capture of strategic and politically important cities has remained 'the ultimate symbol of conquest and national survival'.[52] Moreover, ever since the demise of obvious systems of urban fortifications, the design, planning and organization of cities has been shaped by strategic and geopolitical concerns – a topic neglected in mainstream urban studies.[53] In addition to providing the famous 'machine for living' and bringing light and air to the

---

48 Martin Shaw, *War and Genocide*, Cambridge: Polity Press, 2003.

49 See Mike Davis, *Dead Cities, and Other Tales*, New York: New Press, 2003, chapter 3.

50 Martin Shaw, 'New Wars of the City: Relationships of "Urbicide" and "Genocide"', in Stephen Graham, ed., *Cities, War and Terrorism*, Oxford: Blackwell, 2004, 143.

51 Laura McEnaney, *Civil Defense Begins at Home*, Princeton: Princeton University Press, 2000.

52 Martin Shaw, 'New Wars of the City', unpublished manuscript, 2001, available at www.martinshaw.org.

53 Ryan Bishop and Greg Clancey, 'The City-as-Target, or Perpetuation and Death', in Graham, ed., *Cities, War and Terrorism*, 54–73.

urban masses, modernist planners and architects envisaged the situating of housing towers within parks as a means of reducing the vulnerability of cities to aerial bombing. Such towers were also designed to raise urbanites above the killer gas then expected to lie within the bombs.[54]

Along with the 'white flight' to the suburbs, early Cold War urban planning in the US sought to see US cities 'through the bombardier's eye',[55] and actively tried to stimulate decentralization and sprawl as means of reducing the nation's vulnerability to a pre-emptive Soviet nuclear attack.[56] And it is often forgotten that the massive US interstate highway system was initially labelled a 'defense highway' system and was partly designed to sustain military mobilization and evacuation in the event of global nuclear war. Announcing the plan in 1954, Vice President Richard Nixon argued that its prime raison d'être was to 'meet the demands of catastrophe or defense, should an atomic war come'.[57] Meanwhile bright, modernist new towns and new capitals were engineered across the world, both by Soviet and Western planners and by foreign aid programmes, as a means of shoring up geopolitical support on the globally stretched frontiers of the Cold War.[58]

Back in the United States, meanwhile, massive new high-tech districts such as California's Silicon Valley were forged as motors of a new 'knowledge economy' centred on emerging 'global' cities, as is well known. Much less recognized is the fact that such 'technopoles' were also the key foundries for the militarized control technologies which sustained the Cold War and were later mobilized as the basis for the transformation of US forces through the 'Revolution in Military Affairs'.[59] At the same time, the imperatives faced by the new military science of cybernetics quickly expanded from the remote control of missiles to the task of organizing new means of rebuilding US cities during

54   See José Luis Sert and International Congresses for Modern Architecture, *Can Our Cities Survive?: An ABC of Urban Problems, their Analysis, their Solutions; Based on the Proposals Formulated by the C.I.A.M.*, Cambridge, MA: Harvard University Press, 1942.

55   Peter Gallison, 'War against the Center', *Grey Room* 4, 2001, 29.

56   Gallison, 'War against the Center', 5–33; Michael Quinn Dudley, 'Sprawl as Strategy: City Planners Face the Bomb', *Journal of Planning Education and Research* 21: 1, 2001, 52–63; Matthew Farish, 'Another Anxious Urbanism: Simulating Defense and Disaster in Cold War America', in Graham, ed., *Cities, War and Terrorism*, 93–109.

57   Quoted in Dan McNichol, *The Roads That Built America: The Incredible Story of the US Interstate System*, New York: Sterling Publishing, 2006, 103.

58   Michelle Provoost, 'New towns on the Cold War frontier', *Eurozine*, June 2006, available at www.eurozine.com.

59   See Manuel Castells, 'High Technology and the Transition From the Urban Welfare State to the Suburban Warfare State', chapter 5 in *The Informational City*, Oxford: Blackwell, 1989; Anne Markusen, et al., *The Rise of the Gunbelt: The Military Remapping of Industrial America*, Oxford: Oxford University Press, 1991.

the years of mass 'slum' clearance in the 1950s and 1960s, as well as building early cable TV networks.[60] We should also not forget the more indirect geopolitical and international security implications of Cold War geographies and architectures of urbanization. State-sponsored suburbanization, for example, was the central axiom of the 'military Keynesianism' that sustained the US during the era of the Cold War. Together, as Andrew Ross has argued, Cold War militarization and technological research and rapid, state-sponsored suburbanization can in fact be considered 'the twin economic anchors of the Pax Americana, and, to the degree that they still are, present a clear and present danger to anyone unlucky enough to get in the way of the fuel that supplies their energy needs.'[61]

On colonial and imperial frontiers, meanwhile, the Cold War was characterized by a complex array of very 'hot' urban guerilla, independence and proxy wars. Brutal full-scale wars or low-intensity urban struggles in Seoul (1950), Algiers (1954–62), Hué (1968), Prague (1968), Northern Ireland (1968–1998), South Africa (1948–90), Israel-Palestine (1948–) and elsewhere fused with struggles within the imperial metropolitan cores of the North over the 'right of the city' – the civil rights movement; anti-racist, anti-war, environmental and post-colonial social movements; urban riots.[62]

For Western military theorists, though, these were always seen to be largely irrelevant side-shows to the main preoccupation: plans for planetary nuclear 'exterminism',[63] for the instant erasure of entire systems of cities from the face of the Earth, and for massed 'Air-Land' battles between Soviet and NATO forces across a European plain. It is fitting, then, that the physical legacies of Cold War military urbanism in the global North are dominated by extraordinary subterranean burrowings designed to ensure the survival of political elites and samples of the wider population in the Strangelovian worlds of the post-apocalyptic future.[64]

60 Jennifer Light, *From Warfare to Welfare: Defense Intellectuals and Urban Problems in Cold War America*, Baltimore: The Johns Hopkins University Press, 2003.

61 Andrew Ross, 'Duct Tape Nation', *Harvard Design Magazine* 20, 2004, 2.

62 See Kipfer and Goonewardena, 'Colonization and the New Imperialism: On the Meaning of Urbicide Today', 1–39.

63 See E. P. Thompson, 'Notes on exterminism: The last stage of civilization', in E. P. Thomson, ed., *Exterminism and Cold War*, London: NLB, 1982.

64 See, for example, Tom Vanderbilt, *Survival City: Adventures Among the Ruins of Atomic America*, New York: Princeton Architectural Press, 2002.

GLOBAL IMPLOSIONS

War has entered the city again – the sphere of the everyday.[65]

In the 'new' wars of the post–Cold War era – wars which increasingly straddle the 'technology gaps' that separate advanced industrial nations from informal fighters – the world's burgeoning cities are the key sites. Indeed, urban areas have become the lightning conductors for our planet's political violence.

Warfare, like everything else, is being urbanized. The great geopolitical contests – of cultural change, ethnic conflict and diasporic social mixing; of economic re-regulation and liberalization; of militarization, informatization and resource exploitation; of ecological change – are, to a growing extent, boiling down to violent conflicts in the key strategic sites of our age: contemporary cities. The world's geopolitical struggles increasingly articulate around violent conflicts over urban strategic sites, and in many societies the violence surrounding such civil and civic warfare strongly shapes quotidian urban life.

In the process, the distinctions between wars within nations and wars between nations radically blur, making long-standing military/civilian binaries increasingly unhelpful.[66] Indeed, what this book labels the new military urbanism tends to 'presume a world where civilians do not exist'.[67] All human subjects are thus increasingly rendered as real or potential fighters, terrorists or insurgents, legitimate targets.

Strategies for the deliberate attack of the systems and places that support civilian urban life have only become more sophisticated since the mass urban annihilation that characterized the twentieth century. The deliberate devastation of urban living spaces, by state and non-state actors alike, continues apace. Fuelling this are multiple, parallel transformations that characterise the post-colonial, post–Cold War world.

Here we must consider a veritable blizzard of factors : the unleashing of previously constrained ethnic hatreds since the end of the bipolar system of the Cold War; the proliferation of fundamentalist religious and ethno-nationalist political groups motivated by hatred of urban cosmopolitanism; the militarization of gangs, drug cartels, militias, corrupt political regimes and

---

65   Phillip Misselwitz and Eyal Weizman, 'Military Operations as Urban Planning', in *Territories: Islands, Camps and Other States of Utopia*, ed. Anselme Frankes, Berlin: KW, Institute for Contemporary Art, 272.

66   Arjun Appadurai, *Fear of Small Numbers: An Essay on the Geography of Anger*, Durham, NC: Duke University Press, 2006, 1.

67   Ibid., 31. See also Derek Gregory, 'Editorial: The Death of the Civilian?', *Environment and Planning D: Society and Space* 24: 5, 633–638.

law enforcement agencies, all effectively undermining the state's monopoly of violence; the collapse of certain national and local states; the urbanization of populations and geography; the increasing accessibility of heavy weapons; a crisis of increasing social polarization at all geographical scales already discussed; and the growing scarcity of many essential resources.

In Africa, for instance, there has been rapid urbanization, social hyper-inequality, a proliferation of wars over key global resources, and radical shifts in the political economy of states in the past quarter-century. With many states losing their monopoly on both violence and territory, coercion becomes a commodity to be bought and sold. 'Military manpower is bought and sold on a market in which the identity of suppliers and purchasers means almost nothing', writes Achille Mbembe. 'Urban militias, private armies, armies of regional lords, private security firms, and state armies all claim the right to exercise violence or to kill.'[68]

To this lethal cocktail we must add the destabilizing effects of structural adjustment policies, the United States' increasingly aggressive and violent interventions in a widening range of nations, and its long-term support for many a brutal regime. Added to this, the break-up of Communist or authoritarian states has often unleashed long-repressed ethno-nationalist aspirations and hatreds which often manifest themselves in the deliberate targeting of the sites and symbols of cosmopolitan mixing: cities and their architectural embodiments of collective memory. As in the Balkans during the early 1990s, contemporary genocidal violence is often shot through – if readers will pardon the pun – with deliberate attempts at urbicide: the killing of cities and the devastation of their symbols and architectures of pluralism and cosmopolitanism.[69] All too often, then, the heterogeneities and fluidities inherent in contemporary city life fall within the cross-hairs of a wide spectrum of cultural fundamentalisms seeking targets, scapegoats, certainties, and objects suitable for cultural or architectural erasure. Indeed, the calls to violence against cities must themselves be seen as attempts to form political communities based on certainty and simplicity. Stereotyping and othering the immense complexity of the city as a single, pure identity becomes a crucial prelude to calling for violence against it.[70]

Collectively, these factors are now forcing what the anthropologist Arjun

---

68 Achille Mbembe, 'Necropolitics', *Public Culture* 15:1, 2003, 32.

69 See Robert Bevan, *The Destruction of Memory: Architecture at War*, London: Reaktion Books, 2006.

70 Appadurai, *Fear of Small Numbers*, 7. See also Jean-Luc Nancy, 'In Praise of the Melee', in Jean-Luc Nancy *A Finite Thinking*, Stanford: Stanford University Press, 2003.

Appadurai has called an 'implosion of global and national politics into the urban world'[71] – a process which has led to a proliferation of bloody, and largely urban, wars. Many of these, in turn, have stimulated not only vast migrations but also the construction of city-scale refugee camps to accommodate the displaced populations, who already numbered some fifty million by 2002.[72]

The permiation of organized, political violence within and through cities and systems of cities is complicated by the fact that much 'planned' urban change, even in times of relative peace, itself involves warlike levels of violence, destabilization, rupture, forced expulsion and place annihilation.[73] Particularly within the dizzying peaks and troughs of capitalist and neoliberal urbanism or the implementation of programmes for large-scale urban 'renewal', 'regeneration' or 'renaissance', state-led planning often amounts to the legitimized clearance of vast tracts of cities in the name of the removal of decay, of modernization, improvement, or ordering, of economic competition, or of facilitating technological change and capital accumulation and speculation.[74]

While tracts of booming cities are often erased through state-engineered speculation, the many cities that are shrinking because of de-industrialization, global industrial relocation, and demographic emptying are also vulnerable to clean-sweep planning. 'The economically, politically and socially driven processes of creative-destruction through abandonment and redevelopment', suggests David Harvey, 'are often every bit as destructive as arbitrary acts of war. Much of contemporary Baltimore, with its 40,000 abandoned houses, looks like a war zone to rival Sarajevo.'[75]

WAR UNBOUND

In such a context, and given the increasingly extreme social inequalities, it is no surprise that Western military theorists and researchers are now particularly preoccupied with how the geographies of cities, especially the cities of the global South, are beginning to influence both the geopolitics and the technoscience of

71   Arjun Appadurai, *Modernity at Large: Cultural Dimensions of Globalization*, Minneapolis, MN: University of Minnesota Press, 1996, 152.

72   See Michel Agier, 'Between War and City: Towards an Urban Anthropology of Refugee Camps', *Ethnography* 3: 3, 2002, 317–341.

73   Berman, 'Falling Towers'.

74   For an excellent example, see Greg Clancey, 'Vast Clearings: Emergency Technology, and American De-Urbanization, 1930-1945', *Cultural Politics* 2: 1, 2006, 49–76.

75   David Harvey, 'The City as a Body Politic', in Jane Schneider and Ida Susser, eds, *Wounded Cities: Destruction and Reconstruction in a Globalized World*, eds. New York: Berg, 2003, 26.

post–Cold War political violence. After long periods of preaching the avoidance of urban conflict or, conversely, the annihilation of urban centres from afar through strategic bombing, military doctrine addressing the challenges of military operations within cities is rapidly emerging from under what a Canadian colonel, Jean Servielle, recently termed 'the dust of history and the . . . weight of nuclear deterrence'.[76]

Indeed, almost unnoticed within 'civil' urban social science, a shadow system of military urban research is rapidly being established, funded by Western military research budgets. As Keith Dickson, a US military theorist of urban warfare, puts it, the increasing perception within Western militaries is that 'for Western military forces, asymmetric warfare in urban areas will be the greatest challenge of this century . . . The city will be the strategic high ground – whoever controls it will dictate the course of future events in the world.'[77]

The consensus among the theorists pushing for this shift is that 'modern urban combat operations will become one of the primary challenges of the 21st century'.[78] In this vein, Major Kelly Houlgate, a US Marine Corps commentator, notes that between 1984 and 2004, 'of 26 conflicts fought over by US forces . . . 21 have involved urban areas, and 10 have been exclusively urban'.[79]

The widening adoption of urban-warfare doctrine follows centuries of Western military planners preaching a mantra articulated in 1500 BC by the Chinese philosopher Sun Tzu, that the 'worst policy is to attack cities'. It follows a Cold War marked by an obsession with massive, superpower-led Air-Land engagements centred on the northern European plain, within and above the spaces between intentionally by-passed European city-regions. Although Western forces fought numerous wars in cities of the developing world during the Cold War, as part of wider struggles against independence movements, terrorist movements and hot proxy wars, as already mentioned, such conflicts were seen by military theorists in the West as unusual side-shows to Air-Land and nuclear engagements, the imagined main events.

As well as the military and geopolitical catastrophe that is the overwhelmingly urban war in Iraq, there are iconic military operations such as the US 'Black Hawk Down' humiliations in Mogadishu in 1991,

---

76   Jean Servielle, 'Cities and War', *Doctrine* 3, 2004, 43–44.

77   Keith Dickson, 'The War on Terror: Cities as the Strategic High Ground', unpublished paper, 2002.

78   Defense Intelligence Reference Document (DIRC), *The Urban Century: Developing World Urban Trends and Possible Factors Affecting Military Operations*, MCIA-1586-003-9, Quantico, VA: United States Marine Corps, 1997, 11.

79   Kelly Houlgate, 'Urban Warfare Transforms the Corps', *The Naval Institute: Proceedings*, November 2004, available at www.military.com.

US operations in Kosovo in 1999 and Beirut in the 1980s, and various US operations in the Caribbean and Central America: Panama City (1989), Grenada (1983), Port-au-Prince (1994). Urban conflicts such as those in Grozny in Chechnya (1994), Sarajevo (1992–5), Georgia and South Ossetia (2008), and Israel-Palestine (1947–) also loom large in current military debates about the urbanization of warfare.

The US military's focus on operations within the domestic urban sphere is also being dramatically strengthened by the so-called War on Terror,[80] which designates cities – whether US or foreign – and their key infrastructures as 'battlespaces'. Viewed through such a lens, the Los Angeles riots of 1992; the various attempts to securitize urban cores during major sports events or political summits; the military response to Hurricane Katrina in New Orleans in 2005; the challenges of 'homeland security' in US cities – all become 'low-intensity' urban military operations comparable to conducting counter-insurgency warfare in an Iraqi city.[81] 'Lessons learned' reports drawn up after military deployments whose goal was to contain the Los Angeles riots in 1992, for example, credit the '"success" of the mission to the fact that "the enemy" – the local population – was easy to outmaneuver given their simple battle tactics and strategies'.[82] High-tech targeting practices such as unmanned drones and organized satellite surveillance programmes, previously used to target spaces beyond the nation to (purportedly) make the nation safe, are beginning to colonize the domestic spaces of the nation itself.[83] Military doctrine has also come to treat the operation of gangs within US cities as 'urban insurgency', 'fourth-generation warfare' or 'netwar', directly analogous to what takes place on the streets of Kabul or Baghdad.[84]

Importantly, then, the US military's paradigms of urban control, surveillance and violent reconfiguration now straddle the traditional inside/outside binary of cities within the US nation versus cities elsewhere. Instead, the 'security' concerns which until recently dominated abstract foreign-policy discussions now erupt within ordinary urban sites – spaces of the 'homeland'. What had previously been international security concerns are now 'penetrating . . . all

---

80   See Nathan Canestaro, 'Homeland Defense: Another Nail in the Coffin for *Posse Comitatus*', *Washington University Journal of Law & Policy* 12, 2003, 99–144.

81   See Phil Boyle, 'Olympian Security Systems: Guarding the Games or Guarding Consumerism?', *Journal for the Arts, Sciences, and Technology* 3: 2, 2005, 12–17.

82   Deborah Cowen, 'National Soldiers and the War on Cities', *Theory and Event* 10: 2, 2007, 1.

83   See, for example, Siobhan Gorman, 'Satellite-Surveillance Program to Begin Despite Privacy Concerns', *Wall Street Journal*, 1 October 2008.

84   Max Manwaring, *Street Gangs: The New Urban Insurgency*, Carlisle, PA: Strategic Studies Institute, US Army War College, 2005 available at www.strategicstudiesinstitute.army. mil.

levels of governance. Security is becoming more civic, urban, domestic and personal: security is coming home.'[85]

CITIES AS BATTLESPACE

The city [is] not just the site, but the very *medium* of warfare – a flexible, almost liquid medium that is forever contingent and in flux.[86]

Driving the military targeting of the ordinary sites and spaces of urban life across the world is a new constellation of military doctrine and theory. In it, the spectre of state-versus-state military conflict is seen to be in radical retreat. Instead, the new doctrine centres around the idea that a wide spectrum of transnational insurgencies now operate across social, technical, political, cultural and financial networks. These are deemed to provide existential threats to Western societies by targeting or exploiting the sites, infrastructure and control technologies that sustain contemporary cities. Such lurking threats are presumed to camouflage themselves within the clutter of cities for protection against traditional forms of military targeting. This situation, the argument goes, necessitates a radical ratcheting-up of techniques of tracking, surveillance and targeting, centred on both the architectures of circulation and mobility – infrastructure – and the spaces of everyday urban life.

The focus of this new body of military doctrine thus blurs the traditional separation of military and civil spheres, local and global scales, and the inside and outside of nations. In so doing, writes Jeremy Packer, 'citizens and non-citizens alike are now treated as an always present threat. In this sense, all are imagined as combatants and all terrain the site of battle.'[87] In the case of the United States, for example, this process allows the nation's military to overcome traditional legal obstacles to deployment within the nation itself.[88] As a consequence, the US military's PowerPoint presentations talk

---

85   David Murakami Wood and Jonathan Coaffee, 'Security Is Coming Home: Rethinking Scale and Constructing Resilience in the Global Urban Response to Terrorist Risk', *International Relations* 20:4, 2006, 503.

86   Eyal Weizman, 'Lethal theory', *LOG Magazine*, April 2005, 53.

87   Jeremy Packer, 'Becoming Bombs: Mobilizing Mobility in the War of Terror', *Cultural Studies* 20: 4–5, 2006, 378.

88   The US Posse Comitas act, for example, which explicitly forbade the domestic deployment of US troops within the US mainland. In addition a new US Strategic Command – Northcom – has been established covering North America. Previous to 2002, this was the only part of the world not so covered. US military forces also now regularly conduct exercises within US cities as part of their efforts to hone their 'urban warfare' skills.

of urban operations in Mogadishu, Fallujah or Jenin in the same breath as those during the Los Angeles riots, the anti-globalization confrontations in Seattle or Genoa, or the devastation of New Orleans by Hurricane Katrina. Such a paradigm permits a host of transnational campaigns and movements – for social justice or ecological sustainability, against state oppression or the devastating effects of market fundamentalism – to be rendered as forms of 'netwar', in effect turning the ideas of the Zapatistas into the equivalent of the radical and murderous Islamism of al-Qaeda.[89] Finally, this blurring means that the militarization and walling of national borders, such as that between the US and Mexico, not only involve the same techniques and technologies as the walling-off of neighbourhoods in Baghdad or Gaza, but sometimes actually involve lucrative contracts being awarded to the same military and technology corporations.

Thus it becomes imperative to continually connect the effects of US military aggression abroad with US domestic counterterrorist policies in what is now commonly called the homeland – policies which target, profile, map and incarcerate Arab and Asian Americans in particular. In a context where 'imperial power operates by obscuring the links between homeland projects of racial subordination and minority co-optation and overseas strategies of economic restructuring and political domination', as Sunaina Maira and Magid Shihade describe it, 'this link between the domestic and overseas fronts of imperial power helps us understand that the shared experiences of Asian and Arab Americans in the US, both those that are visible and those not so visible, are due to the workings of empire.'[90]

These radical and multiple blurrings have other manifestations as well. Civil law enforcement agencies, for example, are becoming remodelled along much more (para)militarized lines.[91] As well as reorganizing themselves to engage in highly militarized counterterrorist operations and the fortification of major conventions, sports events or political summits, they increasingly adopt the techniques and language of war to launch SWAT teams against a widening array of civilian events and routine call-outs.[92] 'There is something

---

89   John Arquilla and David Ronfeldt, *Networks and Netwars*, Santa Monica: RAND, 2001.

90   Sunaina Maira and Magid Shihade, 'Meeting Asian/Arab American Studies: Thinking Race, Empire, and Zionism in the US,' *Journal of Asian American Studies*, 9:2, 2006, 118.

91   See James Shepptycki, 'Editorial – Reflections on Policing: Paramilitarisation and Scholarship on Policing,' *Policing and Society* 9, 2000, 117–123.

92   See Radey Balko, 'Overkill: The Latest Trend in Policing', *Washington Post* 5 February 2006.

driving an attitudinal shift among police, en masse', states the *Signs of the Times* blog, which 'is prompting zealous overreaction even to minor disturbances'.[93] Peter Kraska has estimated that SWAT teams are called out in the US about forty thousand times a year, a rise from the three thousand annual call-outs of the 1980s.[94] Most of the call-outs, he notes, are executed to 'serve warrants on nonviolent drug offenders'.[95]

Explicitly military models thus increasingly sustain new ideas in penology and law enforcement doctrine and technology, as well as civilian surveillance, training, simulation, and disaster assistance.[96] Doctrines addressing urban warfare, military operations on urban terrain, or low intensity conflict – military concepts developed for the purpose of controlling urban masses on the global periphery – are quickly imitated 'to discipline groups and social movements deemed dangerous within the heartlands of the imperial metropolis'.[97]

Military-style command and control systems are now being established to support 'zero tolerance' policing and urban surveillance practices designed to exclude failed consumers or undesirable persons from the new enclaves of urban consumption and leisure.[98] What Robert Warren calls 'pop-up armies' are organized transnationally to pre-emptively militarize cities facing major anti-globalization demonstrations.[99] The techniques of high-tech urban warfare – from unmanned drones to the partitioning of space by walls and biometric check-points – increasingly provide models for the reorganization of domestic urban space.[100] In addition, the almost infinite metaphorization of 'war' – on crime, on drugs, on terror, on disease – solidifies wider shifts from social, welfarist and Keynesian urban paradigms to authoritarian and militarized notions of the state's role in sustaining order.

---

93 *Signs of the Times* Special Correspondent, 'Militarized Police, Overreaction and Overkill: Have You Noticed It In Your Town Yet?', *Signs of the Times*, 16 December 2007, available at ponerology.blogspot.com.

94 Cited in Balko, 'Overkill'.

95 Ibid.

96 See Peter Kraska, ed., *Militarizing the American Criminal Justice System*, Chicago: Northwestern University Press, 2001

97 Ashley Dawson, 'Combat in Hell: Cities as the Achilles' Heel of US Imperial Hegemony', *Social Text* 25: 2, 2007, 176.

98 Stephen Graham and Simon Marvin, *Splintering Urbanism*, London: Routledge, 2001.

99 Robert Warren, 'City streets – The War Zones of Globalization: Democracy and Military Operations on Urban Terrain in the Early 21st Century', in Graham, ed, *Cities, War and Terrorism*, 214–230.

100 Leonard Hopper and Martha Droge, *Security and Site Design*, New York: Wiley, 2005.

WHEN LIFE ITSELF IS WAR

The US military's search for new doctrine applicable to cities explicitly recognizes the similarities between urbanized terrain at home and abroad, notwithstanding the geographic differences. According to Maryann Lawlor, writing in the military magazine *Signal*, key personnel at the US Joint Forces Command (JFCOM) in Norfolk, Virginia, have used large-scale war games and simulations, such as one named Urban Resolve, to 'identif[y] several key concerns common to both areas'.[101] Among these concerns are the difficulty of separating 'terrorists' or 'insurgents' from the urban civilian population; the high density of infrastructure; the way cities interfere with old-style military surveillance and targeting systems; and the complex three-dimensional nature of the urban 'battlespace'.

All too easily, such a discourse slips into a world where 'life itself is war'.[102] It manifests a profound inability to deal with any notion of the other beyond placing that other in the cross-hairs of the targeting mechanism. If military thinking is allowed to run rampant, eventually there would be nothing left in the world that is not a target for the full spectrum of symbolic or actual violence. 'The truth of the continual targeting of the world as the fundamental form of knowledge production', writes media theorist Rey Chow, 'is xenophobia, the inability to handle the otherness of the other beyond the orbit that is the bomber's own visual path'. For the xenophobe, she adds, 'every effort needs to be made to sustain and secure this orbit – that is, by keeping the place of the other-as-target always filled'.[103]

This is where domestic and foreign conceptions of the city converge. Thus, on the one hand, US military officials have routinely talked on the walling-off of neighbourhoods within Baghdad as constructions analogous to the gated communities that encompass more than half of new homes in many Southern and Western cities in the US.[104] Not only military sales pitches but also right-wing media commentaries have blurred homeland and Iraqi cities into a single, demonized space requiring high-tech, heavy-handed assault. Nicole Gelinas, for instance, proposed in 2007 in the Manhattan Institute's

---

101   Maryann Lawlor, 'Military Lessons Benefit Homeland', *Signal Magazine,* February 2008, available at www.afcea.org/signal.

102   Phil Agre, 'Imagining the Next War: Infrastructural Warfare and the Conditions of Democracy', *Radical Urban Theory,* 14 September 2001.

103   Rey Chow, *The Age of the World Target: Self-Referentiatility in War, Theory, and Comparative Work*, Durham, NC: Duke University Press, 2006, 42.

104   Edward J. Blakely and Mary Gail Snyder, *Fortress America: Gated Communities in the United States,* Washington, DC: Brookings Institution Press, 1999.

City Journal that post-Katrina New Orleans was a 'Baghdad on the Bayou' and argued that the city required a similarly militarized response so as to introduce order and investment amid its supposed pathologies of crime and violence.[105]

A recent advertisement in a military magazine for helicopter infra-red sensors powerfully captures this blurring of domestic and distant (Figure 1.4). Surrounding the image of a two-sided helicopter – the military side with rockets, the police side with aerial cameras – the message reads, 'Every Night, All Night – From Baghdad to Baton Rouge – We've Got Your Back'.

The US response to Hurricane Katrina's devastation of the largely African-American city of New Orleans provides a pivotal example here.[106] Some US Army officers discussed their highly militarized response to the Katrina disaster as an attempt to 'take back' New Orleans from African-American 'insurgencies'.[107] Rather than organizing a massive humanitarian response that treated Katrina's victims as citizens who required immediate help, officials (eventually) executed a largely military operation. Such a response merely reinforced the idea that it is equally fitting to treat both external and internal geographies as the sites of state-backed wars against racialized and 'biopolitically disposable' others.[108] The Katrina operation dealt with those abandoned in the central city as a threat – to be contained, targeted and addressed as a means of protecting the property of the largely white suburban and exurban populations who had escaped in their own cars.[109] In the process, African-American citizens of New Orleans were made refugees within their own country. As Robert Stam and Ella Shohat contend, 'Katrina not only ripped the roofs off Gulf Coast houses but also ripped the façade off "the national security state."'[110]

---

105   See Nicole Gelinas 'Baghdad on the Bayou', *City Journal*, Spring 2007, 42–53.

106   See Stephen Graham '"Homeland" Insecurities? Katrina and the Politics of Security in Metropolitan America', *Space and Culture* 9: 1, 2006, 63–7.

107   Peter Chiarelli and Patrick Michaelis 'Winning the Peace: the Requirement for Full-Spectrum operation', *Military Review*, July–August, 2005.

108   See Henry Giroux , 'Reading Hurricane Katrina: Race, Class, and the Biopolitics of Disposability', *College Literature* 33: 3, 171–96.

109   Ibid.

110   Robert Stam and Ella Shohat, *Flagging Patriotism: Crises of Narcissism and Anti-Americanism*, New York: Routledge, 2007, 167.

1.4   A classic 'boomerang effect': Advert for helicopter infra-red sensors
symbolizing the blurring between the military's efforts to use high-
tech surveillance and targeting to dominate colonized cities 'outside'
the nation and the militarization of the police's 'urban operations'
in pervasive 'low-intensity conflict' within domestic cities.

URBANIZING MILITARY DOCTRINE

> In 1998, at the same time that urban geographers were writing that cities are places where identities form, social capital is built, and new forms of collective action emerge, the US Marine Corps explained the phenomenon a bit differently: 'cities historically are the places where radical ideas ferment, dissenters find allies and discontented groups find media attention' thereby making cities 'a likely source of conflict in the future.'[111]

The combination of racialized right-wing anti-urbanism and the new military doctrine is an incendiary one. It means that not only key domestic cities but also far-off cities at the heart of the War on Terror are conceived as troublesome or anarchic battlespaces, presenting stark contrasts to the putative order, security and harmony of the normalized zones of suburbia and exurbia – zones which require protection from the threats and contagions emanating from all cities everywhere. When the techniques of (attempted) urban control – cordoned-off security zones, walling, tracking, targeting, biometrics, ostensibly non-lethal weapons, data-mining – are similar in Gaza, Baghdad and New York, then blurring becomes inevitable, especially if backed by a generalized right-wing demonization of central cities.

The new military doctrine engenders a notion of war as a permanent, boundless exercise, pitting high-tech militaries and security operations – along with private-sector outsourcers and military corporations – against a wide array of non-state adversaries. All of this occurs within an environment marked by intense mediatizing, a high degree of mobility, and the rapid exploitation of new military technologies.

Thus, many military theorists speak of a 'fourth generation' of warfare – based, they argue, on 'unconventional' wars, 'asymmetric' struggles, 'global insurgencies' and 'low intensity conflicts' which pit high-tech state militaries against informal fighters or mobilized civilians.[112] Military theorist Thomas Hammes argues that the key characteristic of such conflicts is that 'superior political will, when properly employed, can defeat greater economic and military power'.[113] Relying on such a doctrine, US commanders in Baghdad have emphasized the need to coordinate the entire 'battlespace' of the city – addressing civilian infrastructure and the shattered economy, strengthening

---

111   Gan Golan, 'Closing The Gateways of Democracy: Cities and the Militarization of Protest Policing', Cambridge, MA: Massachusetts Institute of Technology, 69, available at dspace.mit.edu.

112   Thomas Hammes, *The Sling and the Stone*, New York: Zenith, 2006, p. 208.

113   Ibid., 2.

cultural awareness, and using 'the controlled application of violence' to try to secure the city.[114]

Such paradigms turn the prosaic social acts that collectively constitute urban life into existential, societal threats. As we saw in the Introduction, US military theorist William Lind – extending the US 'culture wars' debates of the 1980s and 1990s, and swallowing whole Huntington's 'clash of civilisations' binary – has argued that even urban immigration must now be understood as an act of warfare. 'In Fourth Generation war', Lind writes, 'invasion by immigration can be at least as dangerous as invasion by a state army'. Under what he calls the 'poisonous ideology of multiculturalism', Lind contends that immigrants within Western nations can now launch 'a homegrown variety of Fourth Generation war, which is by far the most dangerous kind'.[115]

Here we confront what the Center for Immigration Studies has called the 'weaponization' of immigration.[116] Such conceptions of political violence are particularly pernicious because they render all aspects of human life as nothing but war: nations are conceptualized in narrow ethno-nationalist terms, and diasporic cities emerge as cultural pollutants.[117] 'The road from national genius to a totalized cosmology of the sacred nation', writes Arjun Appadurai, 'and further to ethnic purity and cleansing, is relatively direct'.[118]

Other US military theorists and commanders, meanwhile, have generated a massive debate since the early 1990s of a purported revolution in military affairs (given the acronym RMA).[119] This debate considers how new technologies of surveillance, communications, and 'stealth' or 'precision' targeting through 'smart weapons' can be harnessed to sustain a globe-spanning form of US military omnipotence based on 'network-centric' warfare. In a unipolar, post–Cold War world, the dream of the RMA was that the United States' dauntingly high-tech 'military superiority would now signal the capacity to defeat the prospect of any challenge to the way the world was being ordered', as Randy Martin frames it.[120] With the 'fog of war'

---

114   Chiarelli and Michaelis, 'Winning the Peace'.

115   William Lind, 'Understanding Fourth Generation War', *Military Review* Sept–Oct 2004, 13–4.

116   See Cato, *The Weaponization of Immigration*, Center for Immigration Studies, Backgrounders and Reports, February 2008, available at www.cis.org.

117   Ibid.

118   Appadurai, *Fear of Small Numbers*, 2006, 4.

119   See Richard Ek, 'A Revolution in Military Geopolitics?', *Political Geography* 19, 2000, 841–74; Jerry Harris, 'Dreams of Global Hegemony and the Technology of War', *Race and Class* 45: 4, 2003, 54–67.

120   Randy Martin, 'Derivative Wars', *Cultural Studies* 20: 4–5, 2006, 459.

rendered historic by the perfect real-time sensing and killing capabilities of remote US military control technologies, dominance over any enemy was to be assured, even though numbers of troops as well as the sheer weight of armies were to be radically reduced. War, in other words, was to be a capital-intensive process of high-tech killing at a distance.

Such a vision of technological omnipotence was especially attractive, militarily and culturally, because, in Ashley Dawson's words, 'the big technostick sanitized the gory side of warfare through its pixellated displays of precision destruction'.[121] The technophilic fantasies of perfect power that drove RMA debates thus offered to 'absolve those who wielded it from moral responsibilities for their acts'.[122] Indeed, amongst many hawks and neocons,[123] the RMA helped to make American imperial wars a desirable means of forcing the 'pre-emptive' reordering of the world so as to extend US political and economic power within the framework of the clash of civilisations.[124] Marshalled by Donald Rumsfeld, the US secretary of defense between 2001 and 2006, these conceptualizations of war underpinned the Bush administration's strategy of using new military technology to sustain a new phase of US political hegemony and imperialism. The RMA thus provided 'an immense boon and alibi for hawks'.[125]

However, as the gurus of fourth generation warfare never tire of pointing out, and the bloody morass in Iraq's cities continues to demonstrate, RMA theorists' obsession with hardware has done little, in a rapidly urbanizing world, to make the US military invincible. In Iraq, as so often in urban and military history, the violent occupation of a far-off city seems to have rendered all dreams of conducting warfare at a distance – withdrawing the US soldier from risk whilst high-tech weapons annihilate the enemy – as little more than science fiction (or perhaps simply convenient PR for the military-industrial-security complex). Once again it has become clear that, as Edward Luttwak put it, 'the armed forces of the most advanced countries, and certainly of the United States, all formidable against enemies assembled

121   Dawson, 'Combat in Hell', 171.

122   Ibid.

123   See Christian Parenti, 'Planet America: The Revolution in Military Affairs as Fantasy and Fetish" in Ashley Dawson and Malini Johar Schueller, *Exceptional State: Contemporary US Culture and the New Imperialism,* eds, Durham, NC: Duke University Press, 2007, 101.

124   Susan Roberts, Anna Secor, and Matthew Sparke, 'Neoliberal Geopolitics', *Antipode* 35: 5, 2003; Huntington, *Clash of Civilizations*; Luiza Bialasiewicz, '"The Death of the West": Samuel Huntington, Oriana Fallaci and a New "Moral" Geopolitics of Births and Bodies', *Geopolitics* 11: 4, 2006, 1–36.

125   Dawson, 'Combat in Hell', 171.

in conveniently targetable massed formations, are least effective in fighting insurgents'.[126]

In the cities of Iraq, the US military has found it largely impossible to separate insurgents from civilians. The military's catastrophic linguistic and cultural ignorance of the places it has been fighting in has been a massive hindrance. In addition, the complex three-dimensional geometry of Iraqi cities has interfered with the sensing and networking systems meant to create military omniscience and a clear battlespace,[127] and the superior firepower and aggressive tactics of the US – often imposed with racist contempt for the lives of Iraq's urban inhabitants, who live in inescapable proximity to the point of impact – has been massively counterproductive. The resulting masses of maimed and dead Iraqi civilians have only added to the legitimacy and power of the Iraqi insurgencies.

Strangely, however, the cultural resilience of US military technophilia is such that 'the seductive mythology of high-tech, postmodern warfare still enshrined in the mythic active-combat phase of the invasion of Iraq has been kept carefully uncontaminated by the brutal, chaotic realities of the occupation'.[128] As we shall see later, dreams of high-tech omnipotence have simply migrated from the RMA's planet-straddling fantasies of domination from above, into fantasies of controlling the complex microgeographies of the urban realm through robotic warriors and ubiquitous sensors.

A third and final group of US military theorists now obsesses about the need to be concerned by 'effects-based operations' – the complex effects of military operations rather than the simple imperative of destroying or killing the enemy. In typically unsubtle language, one such theorist argues that warfare has become more than a matter of 'putting steel on the target'.[129] The control or manufacture of war imagery and information is thus considered as important as the dropping of bombs or the firing of missiles. Hence 'information warfare' may involve everything from dropping leaflets and bombing TV stations that depict civilian casualties, to efforts at political and social coercion that bring the entire infrastructure of urbanized nations to a sudden, grinding halt.

---

126   Edward Luttwak, 'Dead-end: Counterinsurgency Warfare as Military Malpractice', *Harper's Magazine*, February 2007, 33–42.

127   Tim Blackmore, 'Dead Slow: Unmanned Aerial Vehicles Loitering in Battlespace', *Bulletin of Science, Technology & Society* 25: 3, 2005, 195–214.

128   Patrick Deer, 'Introduction: The Ends of War and the Limits of War Culture', *Social Text* 25: 2, 2007, 1.

129   John W. Bellflower, 'The Indirect Approach', *Armed Forces Journal* January 2007, available at www.armedforcesjournal.com.

The key concept driving current military thinking and practice is 'battlespace'. It is crucial because, in essence, it sustains 'a conception of military matters that includes absolutely everything'.[130] Nothing lies outside battlespace, temporally or geographically. Battlespace has no front and no back, no start nor end. It is 'deep, high, wide, and simultaneous'.[131] The concept of battlespace thus permeates everything, from the molecular scales of genetic engineering and nanotechnology through the everyday sites, spaces and experiences of city life, to the planetary spheres of space and the Internet's globe-straddling cyberspace.[132]

With wars and battles no longer declared or finished, temporalities of war threaten to extend indefinitely. 'War is back and seemingly forever,' writes Patrick Deer.[133] No wonder Pentagon gurus convinced George W. Bush to replace the idea of the 'War on Terror' with the new Big Idea of the 'Long War' in 2004.[134]

Managing and manipulating the politics of fear through what the US military terms 'information operations' – propaganda – are central to these new constellations of military doctrine. As ever in warfare, the use of propaganda to convince domestic populations that only bold military action abroad can prevent them from being terrorized at home has been particularly important to the War on Terror. Indeed, fear-mongering permitted the catastrophic macroeconomic mismanagement of the US economy, and the resulting economic distress of the US population, to be glossed over – at least until the financial collapse of 2008–9. The fusion of entertainment, media and war into what James Der Derian calls the 'military-industrial-media-entertainment network' has been centrally important here.[135] 'With the advent of the so-called war on terror', wrote Andrew Ross in 2004, 'the US government's legitimacy no longer derives from its capacity or willingness

---

130   Agre, 'Imagining the Next War'.

131   Tim Blackmore, *War X: Human Extensions in Battlespace,* Toronto: University of Toronto Press, 2005.

132   Major David Pendall of the US Army writes,'Friendly cyber or virtual operations live on the same networks and systems as adversaries' networks and systems. In most cases, both use the same protocols, infrastructures, and platforms. They can quickly turn any space into a battlespace.' David Pendall, 'Effects-Based Operations Exercise of National Power', *Military Review,* Jan–Feb 2004, 26.

133   Deer, 'The Ends Of War', 1.

134   Dr. David H. McIntyre, 'Strategies for a New Long War: Analysis and Evaluation', Statement before the House Committee on Government Reform, Subcommittee on National Security, Emerging Threats, and International Relations, 3 February 2004, available at www. iwar.org.uk.

135   James Der Derian, *Virtuous War: Mapping the Military-Industrial-Media-Entertainment Network*, Boulder, CO: Westview, 2001.

to ensure a decent standard of living for those citizens; it depends, instead, on the degree to which they can be successfully persuaded they are on the verge of being terrorized.'[136] Even amid the chaos and devastation of the credit crunch, desperate Republican campaign managers widely depicted the Democratic presidential candidate, Barack Obama, as a lurking ally of that ultimate terrorist foe, Osama bin Laden.

'THE CITIES ARE THE PROBLEM'

> The future of warfare lies in the streets, sewers, high-rise buildings, industrial parks, and the sprawl of houses, shacks, and shelters that form the broken cities of our world.[137]

Urban sites and urban military operations increasingly take centre-stage in all these new conceptualizations of war. Anti-urban military theorists propagate the notion that urban sites concentrate, shelter and camouflage an array of anti-state agitators, insurgents and social movements. It is cities, they contend, where the high-tech advantages of Western militaries break down because it is no longer possible to use the weapons of the Revolution in Military Affairs to annihilate targets on desert plains conveniently and cheaply, as was done in Iraq in 1991. It is in the burgeoning cities that the vulnerabilities of Western state, economic and military power are most exposed. And it is cities that serve as camouflage against the vertical omniscience and omnipotence of US forces. After 1991, many theorists hypothesized that 'insurgent forces around the world, having witnessed the annihilation of Saddam's troops in the open desert by US "smart bombs," [during the first Gulf War], had realized that their only chance of survival lay in fighting future wars in the urban jungles of the underdeveloped world.'[138]

Such perspectives suggest, as Duane Schattle of the US Joint Forces Command's Joint Urban Operations Office puts it, that 'the cities are the problem'[139] for US military power. In the same vein, James Lasswell, head of the Office of Science and Technology at the Marine Corps Warfighting Laboratory, thinks that 'urban is the future' and that 'everything worth fighting for is in the urban environment'. And Wayne Michael Hall, advisor in the Joint Urban

---

136   Ross, 'Duct Tape Nation', 4.
137   Ralph Peters, 'Our Soldiers, Their Cities', *Parameters, US Army War College Quarterly* 26: 1, 1996, 43.
138   Dawson, 'Combat In Hell', 172.
139   Nick Turse , 'Slum Fights: The Pentagon Plans for a New Hundred Years' War', *Tom Dispatch,* 11 October 2007.

Operations Office, posits that US forces 'will be fighting in urban terrain for the next hundred years'.[140]

CULTURAL TURNS, WANING POWER

Strikingly, however, broad-brush discussions within the US military about urban warfare are now being supplemented by discussions about how to colonize the intimate inflections of urban culture within the main counterinsurgency cities. This 'cultural turn'[141] in military urban and counterinsurgency doctrine centres on what the Pentagon calls the 'Human Terrain System'[142] (see Figure 1.5). In the Long War, it seems, 'anthropologists are hot property'.[143]

As well as recruiting anthropologists, 'Pentagon budgets reflect an increasing commitment to so-called "cultural knowledge" acquisition', writes Roberto González.[144] The cultural specifics of cities and districts are thus now being modelled and simulated. US soldiers are being given rudimentary training in the appreciation of Iraqi cultural traditions, Islamic urbanism, Iraq's complex ethnic make-up, and local mores and customs. Specifically military studies of the Islamic city are being done, laden with Orientalist clichés.[145] The goal of collecting anthropological and ethnographic data about the human terrain of US counterinsurgency operations is apparently, as González puts it, 'to help win the "will and legitimacy" fights' (perhaps through propaganda), to 'surface the insurgent IED networks' (presumably for targeting), and to serve 'as an element of combat power' (i.e. as a weapon). The concern here, he notes, is that 'in the near future, agents might use cultural profiles for pre-emptive targeting of statistically probable (rather than actual) insurgents or extremists in Iraq, Afghanistan, Pakistan or other countries deemed to be terrorist havens'.[146]

---

140   Ibid.

141   See Derek Gregory, '"The Rush to the Intimate" Counterinsurgency and the Cultural Turn in Late Modern War', *Radical Philosophy* 150, 2008.

142   Not surprisingly, this trend has received vociferous criticism from many academic Anthropologists. See Roberto González '"Human Terrain": Past, Present and Future Applications', *Anthropology Today* 24: 1, 2008 21–6.

143   Laura McNamara, 'Culture, Critique and Credibility: Speaking Truth to Power during the Long War', *Anthropology Today* 23: 2, 2007, 20–1; and Roberto González, 'Towards Mercenary Anthropology? The New US Army Counterinsurgency Manual *FM 3-24* and the Military-Anthropology Complex', *Anthropology Today* 23: 3, 2007, 14–5.

144   González, '"Human Terrain"', 22.

145   See Louis DiMarco, *Traditions, Changes, and Challenges: Military Operations and the Middle Eastern City*, Global War On Terrorism Occasional Paper #1, Fort Leavenworth, KS: US Army Combat Studies Institute Press, 2006.

146   González, '"Human Terrain"', 21–6.

1.5   Culturally sensitive imperialism: A recruitment advert for US special forces.

The deployment of so-called cultural awareness as a weapon against Iraq's insurgencies is, however, completely fraudulent. In its attempt to reposition US forces as little more than innocent bystanders amidst the carnage on Baghdad's streets, it obfuscates and sanitizes the imperial violence and radical insecurity generated by the very presence of those forces,[147] and instead blames such conditions entirely on the pathologies created by intra-Iraq ethnic and sectarian divides. It obscures the provocative presence and murderous actions of US military personnel, along with their proxy forces and mercenary legions. It fails to take account of the complex ways in which myriad deals between the US military, their proxy regimes and militia, and a wide spectrum of private military contractors have massively amplified, and indeed exploited, sectarian tensions in Iraq and thereby fostered programmes of ethnic cleansing.

This failure is symptomatic of a much broader problem that pervades the urban and cultural turn in US military doctrine. It underpins a highly technocratic and technophilic discussion centred on what Ashley Dawson refers to as 'the increasing prominence of urban combat zones' combined with a complete inability 'to acknowledge the underlying economic and political forces that are driving urbanization in the megacities of the global South.'[148] In failing to address the root causes of the extreme polarization and violence generated by neoliberalization and the massive growth of informal settlements, urban military discourse simply echoes the catastrophic failure of the world's political and economic élites to 'question how to integrate the surplus humanity of the global South into the global economy'. Fantasies harboured by US military theorists of controlling the world's burgeoning cities and settlements are probably best interpreted as what Dawson calls 'an index of the waning hegemony of US imperial power rather than a sign of the empire's invincible might.'[149] In 2009, as one witnesses the rapidly waning power of the US economy, reeling under the current financial crash, one is hard pressed to disagree. This does not mean, of course, that these military fantasies are of no consequence. Rather, as becomes evident in the next chapter, they reflect deep-rooted and extremely problematic ways of thinking which turn our urbanizing world into a dangerously seductive geography of goodness versus enmity.

---

147 Gregory, "'The Rush to the Intimate'".
148 Dawson, 'Combat in Hell', 171.
149 Ibid., 174.

CHAPTER TWO

Manichaean Worlds

SPLITTING REALITY

> [T]he epistemological separation of colony from metropolis, the systematic occultation of the colonial labour on which imperial prosperity is based, results in a situation in which . . . the truth of metropolitan existence is not visible in the metropolis itself.[1]

This book argues that contemporary warfare and terror now largely boil down to contests over the spaces, symbols, meanings, support systems and power structures of cities. As has happened throughout the history of war, such struggles are fuelled by dichotomized, Manichaean[2] constructions of 'us' and an othered 'them' – the target, the enemy, the hated.

Programmes of organized, political violence have always been legitimatized and sustained through complex 'imaginative geographies' – a term that, following the work of Edward Said[3] and Derek Gregory,[4] denotes the ways in which imperialist societies construct binary generalizations about both 'foreign' and colonized territories and the 'home' spaces which sit at the 'heart of empire'.

Such imaginative geographies are crucial to the 'colonial splitting of reality'[5] that sustains all empires. Edward Said, for instance, argues that imaginative geographies have long been crucial in sustaining an Orientalist treatment of the Arab world as Other. As he stressed just before his death, the devaluation and demonization of far-off places and people as a targeted 'them' cannot operate without the parallel valorization of a righteous 'us', and thus, 'without a well-organized sense that these people over there were not like "us" and didn't

---

1 Fredric Jameson, 'The End of Temporality', *Critical Inquiry* 29: 4, 2003, 700.

2 'Manichaeanism' refers to a system of religious doctrine taught by Mani, a Persian prophet, in the third century AD. This was based 'on the supposed primordial conflict between light and darkness or goodness and evil' (Collins English Dictionary, London, 1995). In contemporary International Relations theory the term 'Manichean' is used to describe all renderings or imaginings of the world which split it into hermetic and purportedly self-evident 'good' and 'bad' peoples or places. This is the use adopted here.

3 Edward Said, *Orientalism*, London: Routledge and Kegan Paul, 1978.

4 Derek Gregory, 'Imaginative Geographies', *Progress in Human Geography* 19, 1995, 447–85.

5 Kipfer and Goonewardena, 'Colonization and the New Imperialism'.

appreciate "our" values – the very core of the Orientalist dogma – there would have been no war' in Iraq.[6]

By burying similarities or connections between 'us' and 'them', Orientalism deploys considerable symbolic violence and translates difference into the othering necessary to legitimatize and sustain violence against far-off people and places.[7] Crucially, this results in both the 'Third World' and 'the West',[8] or 'the West' and the 'Islamic world', being regarded as separate, and apparently unconnected, realms. In the process, the possibility of forging linkages between the lived experiences of people in both realms is systematically denied. 'One of the fundamental determinants of [modern] experience', suggests Fredric Jameson, 'can be found in the way imperialism masks and conceals the nature of its system'. Above all, Jameson stresses, 'the imperial powers of the older system do not want to know about their colonies or about the violence and exploitation on which their own prosperity is founded, nor do they wish to be forced into any recognition of the multitudinous others hidden away beneath the language and stereotypes, the subhuman categories, of colonial racism'.[9]

To undermine the separateness of separated civilizations, normalized categories – the faraway target versus the putatively homogenous and national community of 'home' – must be actively resisted and disturbed. In a fast-urbanizing world, forged from an abundance of unstable diasporas and urban circulations which continually transcend imaginative geographies, such a project is imperative. Amir Parsa, for example, suggests that 'there is no "Islamic world"! And there is, of course, no "West" – unless it's meant to depict a direction (geographic, at that)'.[10] Parsa asserts that 'most dichotomies [are] simplistic portrayals of much more complex phenomena and divisions [but] this one is particularly perturbing', and points out that 'this generalized concoction completely denies the vast complexes of individualities, subjectivities, communities, each with layers upon layers of differences and complexity and ambiguity within their own fabric, that exist and operate within all the strata of the "world".'[11]

6   Edward Said, *Orientalism*, 25th Anniversary ed., London: Penguin, 2003, xxiii.
7   Hugh Gusterson, 'Nuclear Weapons and the Other in the Western Imagination', *Cultural Anthropology* 14, 1999, 111–143.
8   Ibid.
9   Fredric Jameson, 'The End of Temporality', *Critical Inquiry* 29: 4, 2003, 700.
10 Amir Parsa, 'Division', *Under Fire 1. The Organization and Representation of Violence*, ed. Jordan Crandall, Rotterdam: Witte De Witte, 2004, 29.
11 Ibid.

PLACE ATTACHMENT

War discourse … operates as a strategy that partitions, separates, and compartmentalizes knowledge, offering a highly seductive, militarized grid through which to interpret the world.[12]

Imaginative geographies tend to be characterized by stark binaries of place attachment. Not surprisingly, these tend to be especially potent and uncompromising during times of war. War mobilizes a charged dialectic of attachment to place: the idea that 'our' places are the antithesis of those of the demonized enemy.[13] Often such polarization is manufactured and recycled through the discourses of the state, backed up by representations suited to popular culture. It sentimentalizes one's own place while stripping the humanity from the enemy's places. In building the political willingness to target and destroy the latter, binaried constructions are a crucial element.[14]

Since its inception, the United States' so-called War on Terror has relied on such two-sided constructions of place – especially urban place. These have been essential to achieving even minimal legitimation of the core idea that massive, globe-spanning, perpetual war is the appropriate response to urban terrorist attacks or threats. Since 11 September 2001, the discursive construction of the War on Terror has been marked by the reworking of imaginative geographies separating the cities of a putative US homeland from Arab cities purported to be the source of terrorist threats against US national interests. This involved the assignment of places to two mutually exclusive and mutually constitutive classifications: either 'with us' or 'against us', according to Bush's famous phrase. The war has thus been portrayed, especially in its earlier stages, as what Derek Gregory has called 'a conflict between a unitary and universal Civilization (epitomised by the United States) and multiple, swarming barbarisms that were its negation and nemesis'.[15] With the Christian and Zionist right seamlessly integrating Israel's treatment of Palestinians into the US War on Terror – all under the mandate of the Judaeo-Christian deity – such discursive techniques have set the stage for Saddam Hussein's Iraq, al-Qaeda and Palestinian refugee camps to be equated, and assaulted, in parallel.

---

12   Deer, 'The Ends Of War'.

13   Ken Hewitt, 'Place Annihilation: Area Bombing and the Fate of Urban Places', *Annals of the Association of American Geographers* 73, 1983, 258.

14   Ibid.

15   Derek Gregory, 'Geographies, Publics and Politics', essay derived from 'Raising Geography's Profile in the Public Debate', annual meeting of the Association of American Geographers, Philadelphia, PA, March 2004, 8, available at geography.berkeley.edu.

MANICHAEAN MIRRORS

> Hatred of relatively open, cosmopolitan forms of life (with often explicit anti-Semitic overtones) is an important aspect of the lived politics of American and Islamic theocrats.[16]

What is striking here is how fundamentalist and racist constructions of urban place are almost exactly mirrored in the charged representations of cities routinely disseminated by fundamentalist Islamist groups such as al-Qaeda.[17] Here, however, because the theological mandate derives from a different source, the targets are the 'infidel', 'Christian' or 'Zionist' cities of the West and of Israel, and the sentimentalized places of the Islamic homeland are to be violently purified of Western presence in order to forcibly create a transnational Islamic space, or *Ummah*, which systematically excludes all diversity and otherness through the continuous exercise of murderous force.

Rather than Huntington's 'clash of civilizations', then, what emerges here is Gilbert Achcar's 'clash of barbarisms'.[18] Indeed, in many ways, terrorism and counterterrorism are umbilically connected. So often in the end, tragically, they are self-perpetuating, sustained by their mirror-image imaginative geographies. This is especially so as both the War on Terror and radical Islamism tend to demonize the messy cosmopolitanism of cities, construing them as intrinsically amoral, sinful and unnatural places. It is no wonder that both barbarisms murderously target cities and their inhabitants. Or that both the neocon/ Christian and the Islamist fundamentalism share what Zillah Eisenstein terms a 'masculinist-militarist' mentality, in which violence is the path to the creative destruction of cities, nations or civilizations.[19]

The Manichaean mirrors of the two polarized fundamentalisms inevitably produce a duplication and reduplication of violence.[20] What results is a convergence between state terror and non-state terror. The 'ultimate catastrophe' of the War on Terror, as Joseba Zulaika points out, 'is that such a categorically ill-defined, perpetually deferred, simple-minded Good-versus-Evil war echoes and re-creates

---

16   Kipfer and Goonewardena, 'Colonization and the New Imperialism'.

17   Joseba Zulaika, 'The Self-Fulfilling Prophecies of Counterterrorism', *Radical History Review* 85, 2003, 191–9.

18   See Gilbert Achcar, *Clash of Barbarisms: September 11 and the Making of the New World Disorder*, New York: Monthly Review Press, 2002.

19   Zillah Eisenstein , 'Feminisms in the Aftermath of September 11', *Social Text* 20: 3, 2002, 81.

20   Emran Qureshi and Michael Sells, 'Introduction: Constructing the Muslim Enemy', in Emran Qureshi and Michael Sells, eds, *The New Crusades: Constructing the Muslim Enemy*, New York: Columbia University Press, 2003, 1–50.

the very absolutist mentality and exceptionalist tactics of the insurgent terrorists.' Zulaika further suggests that 'by formally adopting the terrorists' own game – one that by definition lacks rules of engagement, definite endings, clear alignments between enemies and friends, or formal arrangements of any sort, military, political, legal, or ethical – the inevitable danger lies in reproducing it endlessly.'[21]

The real tragedy of the War on Terror, then, is that it has closely paralleled al-Qaeda in invoking homogeneous, exclusionary notions of community as a way of legitimatizing massive violence against civilians. The strategies and discourses of both the Bush administration and al-Qaeda – characterized by charged, mutually reinforcing dialectics – relied on hypermasculine notions of (asymmetric) war, invocations of a theological mandate, and absolutist notions of violence, with the goal being to create a fixed, boundless, eternal social order through the ultimate extermination of the enemy. Both have also relied heavily on the use of transnational media to reiterate a rhetoric of good versus evil and a spectacle of victimhood, demonization, dehumanization, and revenge.

CITIES IN THE PINCER

Cities have always generated fear and hatred among political and religious élites. Virtually every major religious or political movement in history has expressed a profoundly ambivalent feeling, at best, about the concentration of humanity in teeming cities. The Old Testament, for example, includes instances of a wrathful God destroying an evil city. Jacques Ellul has even argued that, from a Christian perspective, 'God has cursed, has condemned the city instead of giving us a law for it.'[22]

Our rapidly urbanizing world nevertheless holds within itself a strange parallel world of anti-urban and apocalyptic fundamentalism. This fundamentalism has a strong link with ancient religious tropes surrounding the need to take revenge against sinful cities and profligate urbanites. As the Retort collective have put it, both 'Empire and Jihad [are] virulent mutations of the Right'.[23] Both are fuelled by a revulsion against the cosmopolitanism and uncontrollable disorder of life in large cities.

---

21 Joseba Zulaika, 'The Self-Fulfilling Prophecies of Counterterrorism', 198.
22 Jacques Ellul, *The Meaning of the City*, Grand Rapids, MI: Eerdmans, 1970, 16.
23 Iain Boal, T. J. Clark, Joseph Matthews, and Michael Watts, 'The New 1914 that Confronts Us: An Interview with Retort', *Afterimage* 34: 4, 20.

RADICAL ISLAMISM AND THE OCCIDENTAL CITY

On the one hand, then, radical Islamists the world over routinely express their revulsion at the cities of the West: occidental cities. The 9/11 attack against that icon of Western urbanism, the World Trade Center – a modern Tower of Babel? – evoked an ancient 'myth about the destruction of the sinful city'.[24] There is little doubt that the repulsive character ascribed to Western, capitalist, cosmopolitan urbanism was a central motivation of the attack. Indeed, the leaders of the attack were themselves qualified urbanists who abhorred Western architectural modernism.[25]

Political theorist Julian Reid has even interpreted 9/11 as part of a 'long-standing tradition of waging war on [vertical] modern architectural forms that originate in the West'.[26] Planning historians Michael Mehaffy and Nikos Salingaros have pointed out that 'the organizer of that attack, Mohammed Atta, was a professional planner educated in Germany, and a skyscraper-hating anti-modernist [who] hated the western modernist buildings he saw wiping out the traditional vitality of its cities'.[27]

Osama bin Laden has repeatedly stressed in his speeches that he sees Americans as idol-worshippers, spreaders of idolatry throughout the world – throughout the Muslim world in particular – in the form of both secularism and Christianity. Al-Qaeda's rhetoric portrays the heartlands of Western cities as unparalleled concentrations of sin, debauchery, greed, materialism and soullessness. Far from being anti-modern, however, al-Qaeda operatives are often fully immersed within consumer societies – an immersion that leads them to believe that both Western and westernising cities are 'rootless agglomeration[s] of arrogant and cold materialists'. Ruralites, by contrast, are seen to be 'firmly in tune with nature and tradition, whose blood and sweat have mixed with the soil of the land, which they plow and know as their own.'[28]

In constructing *Ummah* – a true Islamic realm, a caliphate based on Islamist principles – the depravities of Western-style cities must be violently erased. A

24 Ian Buruma and Avishai Margalit, *Occidentalism: The West in the Eyes of Its Enemies*, London: Penguin, 2004, 14.

25 Bin Laden is a trained civil engineer. Muhhammed Atta – the leading suicide bomber – graduated in architecture at Cairo and town planning in Hamburg and wrote a thesis decrying the impacts of Western, modernist architecture in Arab cities.

26 Julian Reid, 'Architecture, Al-Qaeda, and the World Trade Center', *Space and Culture* 7: 4, 2004, 396.

27 Michael Mehaffy and Nikos Salingaros, 'The End of the Modern World', *PLANetizen*, 9 January 2002, available at www.planetizen.com.

28 Robbert Woltering, 'They Hate Us because We're Free . . . ', *Review of International Social Questions*, 28 June 2004.

pure and homogeneous community, so the argument goes, must be created from the wreckage of mongrel, capitalist cosmopolitanism – a culture which finds its apogee in the ultimate enemy, Jewishness. 'Accounts of the New Caliphate that would result if al-Qa'eda, Hezbollah and related groups got their way', Trevor Boddy points out, 'are eerily similar to the "architecture of re-assurance" in [Western] theme parks'. By this he means that 'they propose cities and countries structured by imposition of a narrative – in their case, the Koran, the Hadith, and subsequent interpretations – which will encode spaces with emotions, specifically faith and its opposite, anger against those without faith'.[29]

Ian Buruma and Avishai Margalit suggest in their book *Occidentalism*[30] that al-Qaeda taps into ancient anti-urban hatreds, long mobilized by a wide spectrum of political and religious ideologies. These encompass scorn for the bourgeois merchant, who represents the very antithesis of the self-sacrificing hero; contempt for the Western mind and its celebration of reason and science; and disgust for the unbeliever, who must be crushed to make way for a world of pure faith.[31]

ENEMY TERRITORY: THE NEOCON/CHRISTIAN RIGHT AND THE US CITY

The [Christian right] homelander vision of the city starts with a story in Genesis 11:1–9. When God saw the first city of humankind and the tower its residents had built, He destroyed the tower and confused their language, 'so that one will not understand the language of his companion' and 'scattered them from there upon the face of the entire earth, and they ceased building the city'. Later in Genesis, God destroys the towns of Sodom and Gomorrah for gross immorality, interpreted as homosexuality.[32]

Perhaps surprisingly, US Christian fundamentalists and neoconservatives hold a view of the United States' core cities that is remarkably similar to that held by al-Qaeda. As theocratic, fundamentalist Christian politics have moved into the

---

29   Trevor Boddy, 'Architecture Emblematic: Hardened Sites and Softened Symbols', in Michael Sorkin, ed., *Indefensible Space: The Architecture of the National Security State*, New York: Routledge, 2007, 281.

30   Critics of Buruma and Margalit's book stress that it is guilty of reducing 'Islam' to a mere space of resistance against the West, rather than a heterogenous array of societies with their own complex agency and power. See, for example, Martin Jacques, 'Upping the Anti', *Guardian*, 4 September 2004.

31   See Mackubin Owens, 'Against the West: Islamic Radicals Hate Us for Who We Are, Not What We Do', editorial, Ashbrook Center for Public Affairs, July 2004.

32   Jeremy Adam Smith, 'Tearing Down the Towers: The Right's Vision of an America Without Cities', *Public Eye Magazine* 21: 1, 2006.

mainstream in the United States, largely by colonizing the Republican Party, so the deep-rooted anti-urbanism at the heart of US political and technological culture has turned into all-out urban demonization.[33] The Republican Party's electoral heartlands generally 'despise the liberal modernism that shaped metro culture in the twentieth century and see it as an ideology that is every bit as foreign and threatening as communism'.[34]

As David Harvey argues, deep anti-urban revulsion taps into a wider cultural trend within conservative circles, whereby discussions of the city tend to 'conjure up a dystopian nightmare in which all that is judged worst in the fatally flawed character of humanity collects together in some hell-hole of despair'.[35] All too often, then, conservatives imagine poor neighbourhoods in cities as a sort of 'Hobbesian state-of-Nature'[36] – an image that merges seamlessly with portrayals of the 'failed' or 'feral' cities of the global South, producing an encompassing fantasy of urbanism that straddles the inside and the outside of the conservatives' United States.

Such descriptions, moreover, can legitimatize neoliberal policy solutions based on the rehabilitation of an ethos of individual discipline/responsibility within pathologized communities, combined with militarized policing or outright military operations. At the same time, coherent explanations about what produces the plight of marginalized urban people and places move ever further from view. 'In the American city', says David Simon, writer of the celebrated TV drama *The Wire*, 'the why has ceased to exist' in mainstream US political discourse.[37]

At a personal level, Republican politicians are clearly often uncomfortable with the United States' metropolitan heartlands. In 2005, for example, a minor media storm was sparked by the comments of Tom DeLay, a key Republican from Houston and at the time the House of Representatives majority leader, about the forthcoming Republican convention in New York City – the first ever.

33 Gregory K. Clancey points out that the Republican party was itself crafted, as he puts it, 'by the march across the Great Plains; an act of exodus or retreat from the urban Atlantic rim', in Jordan Crandall, ed., *Under Fire 2 The Organization And Representation of Violence*, Rotterdam: Witte de Witte, 64.

34 Jeremy Adam Smith, 'Tearing Down the Towers'.

35 David Harvey, *Justice Nature and the Geography of Difference*, Oxford: Blackwell, 1996, 404.

36 Guy Baeten, 'The Uses and Deprivations of the Neoliberal City', in BAVO, ed, *Urban Politics Now: Re Imagining Democracy in the Neoliberal City*, Rotterdam: NAi Publishers, 2008; Rowland Atkinson and Gesa Helms, eds., *Securing an Urban Renaissance*, Bristol: Policy Press, 2007.

37 David Simon, 'The Escalating Breakdown of Urban Society across the US', *Guardian*, 6 September 2008.

DeLay suggested that, rather than taking hotels across the city, delegates should instead lease a 2,240-cabin luxury cruise liner, the *Norwegian Dawn*, and moor it right next to the Javits Convention Center. To DeLay, hiring the ship was 'an opportunity [for delegates] to stay in one place, in a secure fashion'.[38]

A striking reflection of the instinctive anti-urbanism of the Republican Party towards what Paul Street called the 'enemy territory' of US cities, DeLay's proposal was lambasted by New York politicians worried that the expected economic multipliers of their city's hosting of the event might be siphoned off into the ship. Street was one of many who condemned the decision to host the convention in New York as a crass exploitation of the third anniversary of the terrorist attacks of 9/11. 'No self-respecting US city-dweller', he wrote, 'should want to encourage the Republican Party to seem like anything other than what it really is: a racist, regressive, and rightist enemy of urban America. A luxurious and city-safe offshore cruise ship? It's where they belong!'[39]

THE 'SAVAGE URBAN OTHER'

The view of US core cities as being at odds with authentic, traditional, 'American' and 'Christian' values, then, has become axiomatic among both the US neoconservative and the Christian right. As Steve Macek has shown, since the 1980s mainstream US media, cinema, fiction, advertising and commentary have routinely demonized central cities and the (often heavily racialized) subjects who inhabit them. In the process, media invent and perpetuate the poor black urbanite in the form of what Macek calls 'the savage urban other'.[40] Once again, there emerges a vision of an urban-Hobbesian 'state of nature' – an urban anarchy run with complete lawlessness by ruthless street gangs and necessitating, in response, authoritarian penology and militarization. The proliferation of digital video surveillance, moreover, makes it possible for genuine acts of urban violence to fill fast-expanding cable bandwidth: ready-made, virtually free reality TV shows. This creates a vicious circle of more calls for surveillance, more imagery produced and consumed as entertainment, and more demonization of the city by sub- and ex-urban voyeurs.

Right-wing renderings of the savage city as home to the losers in a fair and

---

38   Quoted in Paul Street, 'Republicans, Cities, and Cruise Ships', *Znet,* February 2004.
39   Ibid.
40   Steve Macek, *Urban Nightmares: The Media, The Right and The Moral Panic Over the City,* Minneapolis, MN: University of Minnesota Press, 2006, 37–70.

equal, Social Darwinian struggle[41] have fed into the erection of the 'homeland security state' by the Bush administration. Murray and Herrnstein's 1994 book *The Bell Curve*, for instance, has emerged as the bible of neoconservative urban social policy and criminology. In it, they caution that the polarization of America between 'the cognitive elites' and the IQ-deficient (and highly fertile) underclass would eventually require a 'custodial state', which, they imagine, would be 'a high-tech and more lavish version of the Indian reservations for some substantial minority of the nation's population, while the rest of America goes about its business.'[42]

Pejorative, racialized representations of urban areas abound in mainstream US media. African-American neighbourhoods are usually cast as pathological places inhabited by non-white criminals, drug dealers and threatening Others. These populations are widely portrayed as shadowy and monstrous, lurking beyond the normalized, mainly white and prosperous exurban and suburban fringe. Although largely invisible in such locales, they nonetheless pose a threat, and thus create a need for a massive ratcheting-up of fortification, militarization, securitization, and access control to generate feelings of security among the white elites or middle class. In fact, the portrayal of African-American inner-city youth in mainstream US media is strikingly similar to that of the distant terrorist being targeted by US imperial wars taking place far from the ghettos of the nation's cities. In both cases, 'the raw psychosocial material that feeds off imagined threats is all too easily manipulated into phobic forms'.[43]

Within the recent culture wars, then, central cities are widely portrayed as 'chaotic, ruined, and repellent, the exact inverse of the orderly domestic idyll of the suburbs'.[44] Mass suburban culture is cast as normal and opposed to

---

41 It is striking how Christian Fundamentalists regularly espouse the pseudo-science of Social Darwinism whilst rejecting out of hand the overwhelming accumulation of hard-scientific evidence supporting Darwinian theories of Evolution. See George Monbiot, 'How these Gibbering Numbskulls Came to Dominate Washington', *Guardian*, 28 October 2008.

42 Richard Herrnstein and Charles Murray, *The Bell Curve: Intelligence and Class Structures in American Life*, New York: Free Press, 526.

43 In Autumn 2002, US suburbanites around Washington DC's Beltway, still reeling under the impacts of the 9/11 attacks, were subjected to a campaign of murderous sniping. Ten were dead within three weeks. Several died whilst filling their cars with petrol or gas at station forecourts. Reversing over half a century of racialized dispersal, suburbanites started to drive into the centre of the city to fill up their vehicles. Andrew Ross noted in the *Harvard Design Review* that, ostensibly, this was because 'they believed that the city [core] was the only safe place to get out of their cars in public'. It was a scene, he stressed, 'that spoke volumes about the geography of safety in the US now, especially if you consider how heavily racialized that geography is.' Andrew Ross, 'Duct Tape Nation', 1–3.

44 Macek, *Urban Nightmares*, 275.

the other of core-city life which emerges, instead, as a pathology.[45] Generally, Christian right discourses normalize the exurban and rural life associated with the US Midwest as authentic and mandated by God. At the same time, writes Jeff Sharlet, cities are equated with 'more fallen souls', 'more demons' and 'more temptation'; the threats of intrinsically evil urbanism have, according to such readings, 'forced Christian conservatives to flee . . . [h]ounded by the sins they see as rampant in cities (homosexuality, atheistic school teaching, ungodly imagery)'. Right-wing Christians 'imagine themselves to be outcasts in their own land'. Pastor Ted wrote in his influential 1995 book *Primary Purpose* that 'we [Christians] have lost every major city in America'.[46]

This discourse of 'lost souls' in 'lost cities' fosters an essentialized, devilish Other. At the same time, it promotes militaristic metaphors: the 'Soldiers of Christ' must mobilize to take back the evil, un-Christian race of central-city dwellers as part of a theocratically-ordained spiritual war.[47]

Some Christian fundamentalist preachers have even suggested that both the 9/11 attacks and Hurricane Katrina were actually part of God's wraths against the sins of urban life, especially homosexuality.[48] 'Although the loss of lives is deeply saddening, this act of God destroyed a wicked city', Repent America director Michael Marcavage suggested in a 2005 press release. 'From "Girls Gone Wild" to "Southern Decadence," New Orleans was a city that had its doors wide open to the public celebration of sin. From the devastation may a city full of righteousness emerge.'[49] Meanwhile, notorious gay-hater Pastor Fred Phelps of Topeka, Kansas, has repeatedly suggested that the 9/11 attacks were 'a direct act of the wrath and vengeance of God Almighty upon this evil nation.'[50]

The urban perceptions of the Christian right, however, are ridden with contradiction. It is clear, for example, that a reasonable proportion of the Christian right themselves inhabit US cities (largely for economic reasons), and so attempt to work from within to push public policy in a reactionary and anti-urban direction.

---

45   Nicholas Mirzoff, *Watching Babylon: The War in Iraq and Global Visual Culture*, New York: Routledge, 2005, 28–9.

46   Jeff Sharlet, 'Soldiers of Christ', *Harper's Magazine*, May 2005, 41–54.

47   Ibid.

48   See, for example, Ramon Johnson, 'Gays Blamed for Hurricane Katrina', 1 September 2005, available at gaylife.about.com.

49   Repent America, 'Hurricane Katrina Destroys New Orleans Days Before "Southern Decadence"', press release, 31 August 2005, available at www.repentamerica.com.

50   Dan Kapelovitz, 'Fred Phelps Hates Fags: Straight Talk With God's Favorite Homophobe', reprinted at Kapelovitz.Com, September 2003.

In addition, as rural areas urbanize and sprawling city-regions turn into massive, boundless complexes and corridors which increasingly merge into what Richard Skeates has called the 'infinite city', it is also much less obvious in today's America what a city might actually be.[51] Thus, although in statistical terms 'the US was an urban nation only between the 1920 and the 1970 censuses', the distinction between what is urban and what is rural has subsequently eroded.[52]

Finally, it is also clear that core cities are actually the dominant generators of wealth within the US economy – the places that are overwhelmingly driving all forms of innovation and financial health. At the same time, rural and exurban places often face serious demographic and economic decline. 'Urban areas are surging ahead', writes Juan Enriquez, 'skimming the talented tenth right off small towns and generating the vast majority of taxes, investments, and patents.'[53]

Such complexities do little to inhibit the streams of invective against US cities and their inhabitants. A major part of 2008 vice presidential candidate Sarah Palin's campaign, for instance, centred on the way 'big city America' and 'metropolitan elites' were supposedly ruining the lives of rural, 'pro-American' and exurban 'hockey moms' and 'Joe Six-Packs'. Rudolph Giuliani, ex-mayor of New York and a long-time resident of one of the most expensive town houses on Manhattan's Lower East Side, congratulated Palin thus for her important 3 September speech at the Republican convention: 'I'm sorry that Barack Obama feels [Sarah Palin's] home town isn't *cosmopolitan* enough', he sneered. 'I'm sorry it's not *flashy* enough. Maybe they cling to religion there.'[54] Such a discourse camouflages the way in which the Republican Party has long been dominated by a cabal of billionaires, CEOs, and corporate and military lobbyists who have successfully shaped policy to subsidize their class interests while dramatically undermining services and subsidies for America's working and lower-middle classes.

VOICES OF THE CITY (JOURNAL)

A flick through the pages of the United States' leading 'new urban right' magazine the *City Journal*, published by the Manhattan Institute, intellectual

---

51 Richard Skeates, 'The Infinite City', *City* 2: 8, 6–20.

52 Ross, 'Duct Tape Nation', 2.

53 Juan Enriquez, *The Untied States of America: Polarization, Fracturing and Our Future*, New York: Crown, 2005.

54 Stephen Collinson, 'Obama Has Never Led Anything', News24.com, 9 April 2008.

architects of both George W. Bush's neoconservatism and Giuliani's right-wing 'counter-revolution' in 1990s New York, is telling.[55] Celebrations of positive economic, cultural, political or social aspects of metropolitan mixing are absent here. Instead, there are streams of anti-urban invective highlighting the purported failures, threats, pathologies and vulnerabilities of the nation's central metropolitan areas.

Peter Huber, for example, casts central cities as sites which will bring deadly new pathogens to the US. 'Our casual willingness to tolerate a septic underclass', he writes in the Spring 2007 issue, is 'certain to hasten the rise or much more and much worse' diseases than AIDS, syphilis, even anthrax.[56] Nicole Gelinas, meanwhile, suggests in the same issue that New Orleans is a pathologically lawless, violent and welfare-dependent city – akin, boomerang-style, to a 'Baghdad on the Bayou' – which requires massive neoliberal restructuring and militarization to sustain a real-estate- and gentrification-friendly 'renaissance' after Hurricane Katrina.[57] In an earlier issue Peter Huber and Mark Mills argue that the accidental 2003 blackout in the cities of the US Northeast was nothing compared to the mayhem that terrorists could create if they targeted US electrical infrastructures.[58] And Steven Malanga points out that 'there's really no such thing as a Blue [Democrat] state – only Blue metropolitan regions' and proceeds to demonize such places as parasitic 'tax eaters' dependent on massive public expenditures.[59] This portrayal of cities as essentially parasitic on exurban America persists despite masses of evidence that tax and political subsidies actually move from the metropolitan centres

---

55   Alice O'Connor, 'The Privatized City: The Manhattan Institute, the Urban Crisis, and the Conservative Counterrevolution in New York', *Journal of Urban History* 34, 2008, 333–53; see Jamie Peck, 'Liberating the City: Between New York and New Orleans', *Urban Geography* 27: 8, 2006, 681–713.

56   Peter Huber, 'Germs and the City', *City Journal*, Spring 2007, 14–29.

57   Nicole Gelinas, 'Baghdad on the Bayou', *City Journal,* Spring 2007, 42–53. Jamie Peck criticises the way Conservative discourses effectively blamed the African American of New Orleans for their plight after the hurricane impacted in the City. 'Most egregiously', he writes, 'this is exposed in the portrayal of New Orleans residents choosing to disregard evacuation orders in anticipation of beginning-of-the-month welfare checks and post-hurricane opportunities for looting. It was therefore not a lack of resources, private transportation, or out-of-town support systems that placed some of the most-needy New Orleans residents in the storm's path; it was the long-run consequences of urban welfarism—and its racialized cast of supported characters including the workless, the feckless, the lawless, absentee fathers, inert mothers, and criminalized youths.' Peck, 'Liberating The City', 706.

58   Mark Mills and Peter Huber, 'Can Terrorists Turn Out Gotham's Lights?', *City Journal*, Autumn 2004.

59   Steven Malanga, 'The Real Blue Engine of America', *City Journal*, Winter 2006, 66–73.

of the US – which overwhelmingly drive the national economy – to rural and exurban areas.[60]

APARTHEID AS MODEL

Writers for *City Journal* readily project their highly racialized, anti-urban vitriol elsewhere in the world. A 2002 article by Theodore Dalrymple on African immigration to Paris's suburban ring of public housing projects is a telling example. Starkly titled 'The Barbarians at the Gates of Paris',[61] this piece declares that 'surrounding the city of light are threatening Cities of Darkness'. Anti-Arab Orientalist and Islamophobic cliché pervades the discussion of the domestic urban politics of another Western nation, not unlike the demonization of Arab culture in distant lands that are targeted by US imperial aggression.

Dalrymple rails against the insecurities purportedly created for bourgeois French urbanites living in historic city cores by the 'public housing projects that encircle and increasingly besiege every French city or town of any size'.[62] His message translates geopolitical Orientalism and Manichaeanism to the microgeographies of city life: in his view, the clash of civilizations has invaded the very streets of the most enlightened and iconic Western bourgeois urban spaces, with devastating consequences for security.

His suggested solutions are startling: contemporary Paris should use not only apartheid South Africa as a model but also the urban lockdowns pursued by US forces in Baghdad and by Israeli forces in the occupied territories. Dalrymple recalls the words of an Akrikaner he once met in South Africa, a man who explained to him 'the principle according to which only a single road connected black townships to the white cities: once it was sealed off by an armoured vehicle, the strategy leaves the "blacks [to] foul their own nest".'[63] As a direct imitation of such colonial techniques, Dalrymple writes, the French

---

60 In 2003, the US States who gained more than they paid in taxation terms tended to be highly rural: New Mexico, Alaska, Mississippi, West Virginia, North Dakota, Alabama, Montana and Hawaii. Those paying more than they received, conversely, were usually highly urbanised: New Jersey, New Hampshire, Connecticut, Nevada, Minnesota, Illinois, Massachusetts and California. The Bush Administration have been extremely generous to the extractive and abri-business corporations that dominate most rural economies. In the 2004 election, 75 per cent of Bush's voters came from 'taker states' whilst 76 per cent of Kerry's came from 'Giver' States. Enriquez, *The Untied States of America*, 34.

61 Theodore Dalrymple, 'The Barbarians at the Gates of Paris', *City Journal*, Autumn 2002, 63–73.

62 Ibid., 65.

63 Ibid., 67

banlieues 'could be cut off from the rest of the world by switching off the trains and by blockading with a tank or two the highways that pass through them, (usually with a concrete wall on either side) from the rest of France', or what he calls 'the better parts of Paris'.[64]

'URBAN ARCHIPELAGO'

As Figure 2.1 shows, the electoral geography which sustained the success of the Bush administration reflected the massively disproportionate political power of fifty million, largely white exurban and rural Americans in a highly – and increasingly – urbanized nation. Many commentators highlighted the resultant culture war: urban (overwhelmingly Democratic) cosmopolitanism versus (overwhelmingly Republican) suburban and exurban conservatism marked by a growing Christian fundamentalism as well as by mounting attempts at political, fiscal and geographical secession from the core metropolitan areas that drive US economic power.[65]

John Sperling has called this contrast a clash of 'retro versus metro America'.[66] An infamous article in Seattle's online newspaper *The Stranger* identified in the county-level maps of the 2004 election results a startling 'urban archipelago' under siege by the city-hating, highly religious, hypernationalist and often extremely racist Republican landscapes beyond. 'Liberals, progressives, and Democrats', they proclaimed, 'do not live in a country that stretches from the Atlantic to the Pacific, from Canada to Mexico. We live on a chain of islands. We are citizens of the Urban Archipelago, the United Cities of America. Citizens of the Urban Archipelago reject heartland "values" like xenophobia, sexism, racism, and homophobia, as well as the more intolerant strains of Christianity that have taken root in this country.'[67]

George W. Bush's policies and utterances continually reworked this essentially anti-urban and apocalyptic vision of US geography. Urban welfare, education and infrastructure programmes were constantly undermined while church-based social programmes, organized by churches that helped fund Republicans, expanded. Meanwhile, massive resources went towards the supporting tax breaks for the (overwhelmingly exurban and suburban) rich. Even burgeoning counterterrorism funding was disproportionately dispersed

---

64   Ibid.
65   See, for example, Brain Mann, *Welcome to the Homeland,* New York: Steer Forth Press, 2006. Also, Juan Enriquez, *The Untied States of America.*
66   John Sperling et al., *The Great Divide: Retro vs Metro America,* New York: Polipoint Press, 2004.
67   Editors, 'Urban Archipelago', *The Stranger,* 14: 9, 2004.

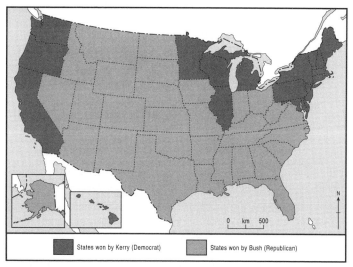

States won by Kerry (Democrat)   States won by Bush (Republican)

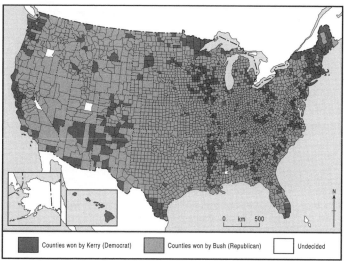

Counties won by Kerry (Democrat)   Counties won by Bush (Republican)   Undecided

2.1   The US 'urban archipelago' as revealed in the electoral geography for the 2004 election. While state-level data (above) presents a simplistic picture of South and Mid-West Republican Heartlands and Bi-Coastal democratic strongholds, the county-level data shows an archipelago of liberal, democratic cities surrounded by an uninterrupted rural, exurban Republican 'sea'.

to extremely rural heartland areas where the risks of terrorist attack are minimal or non-existent. The ratcheting-up of defense expenditures also tended to benefit the suburban, exurban and rural parts of the US – which dominate in the geography of military bases, manufacturing and recruitment – more than they benefited the central cities. Most notably, Bush virtually ignored the plight of (largely African-American) New Orleans after Hurricane Katrina. Overall, then, Bush-era policies meant that 'welfare didn't disappear – the money just shifted from cities to the homeland in the form of farm and corporate subsidies, price supports, military spending, and pork-barrel projects.'[68]

Like the anti-urban perceptions of the Christian right to which it is so closely linked, however, this polarized internal geography of the US is full of contradictions. On the one hand, what Greg Clancey calls the 'red empire' of anti-urban Republicans 'has historically been isolationist and inward-looking, and agrees to the projection of military power toward foreign places (and legislative power toward domestic urban places) when it feels itself threatened, rightly or wrongly, as it clearly does now.' On the other hand, urban – blue – Democrats, who are generally able to 'live with ambiguity and risk' tend to be against the imperial aggression that characterized Bush's wars. At the same time, they are the ones who inhabit the cities and infrastructure complexes that are most likely to be targeted by terrorists.

To Clancey, the crucial tensions in contemporary US political culture actually run between affluent, powerful suburbs and exurbs and central, core cities. 'At the end of the day', he writes, 'the grand division in American politics is not East vs. West or North vs. South. It's not even "rural" vs. "urban middle class,"' because the really powerful red [Republican] squares are suburbs and exurbs, full of more recent settler-refugees from the blue flecks themselves.' Thus the key political tension works longitudinally between the core and the exurban periphery of each metropolitan region: 'No one dislikes the blue [Democratic, urban] flecks more than those who re-settled its edges; the trekkers in that great exodus that began in the 1940s and continues strongly today.' Clancey argues further that the 2004 election demonstrated that US core cities are now doubly targeted, inasmuch as they face 'foreign religiously based organizations on the one hand, and . . . domestic religiously based ones on the other'.[69]

---

68   Smith, 'Tearing Down the Towers'.
69   Clancey, *Under Fire 2*, 64.

GLOBAL SOUTH CITY-AS-TARGET

> I know most Americans do not want to hear this, but the real battlegrounds in the global war on terrorism are still *over there*. If gated communities and rent-a-cops were enough, September 11 never would have happened.[70]

The supposed social pathologies, unconstrained sexualities and 'weak ego structures' deemed by neoconservative social critics to lie at the root of the problems in US cities are identical to the supposed traits of the essentialized 'Arab mind' conjured by neoconservatives and senior military officials during the War on Terror.[71] Thus, a wide range of comparable depictions demonize the core cities of the US and cast the growing cities of the global South as the intrinsically anarchic, threatening Other.[72] Neoconservative writers present booming cities as the central motors of the 'coming anarchy'[73] of the post–Cold War world – essentially feral places which breed lawlessness, drug abuse, crime, brutal turf wars, and security risks for the rest of the world.

The obsession with 'failed states' as the key security threats to US interests is, in fact, morphing into a concern with 'failed' cities – burgeoning urban concentrations apparently unconnected to the supposed benefits of neoliberal globalization.[74] 'Imagine a great metropolis covering hundreds of square miles', writes Richard Norton in an influential 2003 article in *Naval War College Review*. 'Once a vital component in a national economy, this sprawling urban environment is now a vast collection of blighted buildings, an immense Petri-

---

70   Thomas Barnett, 'The Pentagon's New Map', *Esquire* 139: 3, 2003, 174.

71   The racist diatribe found in Raphael Patai's 1973 book *The Arab Mind* (New York: Hatherleigh Press) was, apparently, required reading within the Bush administration during the War on Terror. See Brian Whitaker, 'Its best use is as a doorstop', *Guardian*, 24 May 2004.

72   See Luiza Bialasiewicz, et al., 'Performing Security: The Imaginative Geographies of Current US Strategy', *Political Geography* 26: 4, 2007, 405–22.

73   Robert Kaplan, *The Coming Anarchy: Shattering the Dreams of the Post-Cold War World*, New York: Random House, 2000.

74   Binary portrayals suggesting an absolute separation between 'homeland' cities and the Arab cities of the target Other are powerfully reinforced by neoconservative geopolitical ideologies. Normatively, they stress the imperative to integrate territories that threaten US interests into processes of neoliberal globalisation, if necessary through the use of 'pre-emptive' acts of US military aggression such as the 2003 invasion of Iraq. Thomas Barnett's influential book, *The Pentagon's New Map* (Putnam: New York, 2004) is one example of a range of neoliberal imaginary geopolitical renderings of the world seized upon by the Bush administration as supporting the war on terror. Barnett's global, binary schema stresses the putative 'disconnection' of the US military's target zones in the Middle East, Africa and Central America – or what he calls the 'non-integrating gap' – from the rest of the world, which is seen to be integrating benignly through the operation of neoliberal capitalism to become what Barnett calls a 'functioning core'.

dish of both ancient and new diseases, a territory where the rule of law has long been replaced by near anarchy in which the only security available is that which is attained through brute power.' Such 'feral cities', he believes, exercise 'an almost magnetic influence on terrorist organizations' and 'will be a new phenomenon and will pose security threats on a scale hitherto not encountered'.[75]

CARTOGRAPHIES OF CONQUEST

So what is the solution for the 'wild zones' of the global South's megacities and their hinterlands? For many neoconservative geopolitical thinkers, including notably Thomas Barnett, it is pre-emptive, expeditionary, permanent US imperial war.

Before the global collapse of neoliberal finance at least, Barnett argued repeatedly that such expeditionary wars would force what he calls the countries of the 'non-integrating gap' – parts of the Caribbean and northern Latin America and most of Africa, the Middle East and South-East Asia – to integrate into the benign and peaceful worlds of neoliberal globalization through the civilizing power of US capital.[76] Barnett, who sees Afghanistan and Iraq as mere demonstration projects for this forcible reordering of the world, is most notable for what Simon Dalby has called his cartographic 'blueprints for conquest'.[77] His global, Manichaean cartography is a cartography of global military targeting. Following the mind-sets of writers like Robert Kaplan, it splits the world into a zone of safety – the 'functioning core' – surrounding a zone of danger. It thus seeks to simplify 'the complex mess of human geographies into abstract human entities' in an effort to 'render people and places ready for military action'.[78]

---

75   Richard Norton, 'Feral Cities', *Naval War College Review*, Autumn 2003, 98–100. I would be the last to deny that the rapid growth of global South megacities raises great concerns, for security and otherwise. With such vast populations effectively 'delinked' from industrial growth and formal jobs, as millions move to cities because of catastrophic structural adjustment and related rural marketization and privatization programmes, the security issues are, indeed, staggering in their scale. What I question here is, first, the rendering of such cities as intrinsically 'feral', and, second, the notion that high-tech western militaries, reformed as urban counterinsurgency operations, can ever have the answer to these problems. Far better to address urban, human and ecological security from first principles in the design of global economic and political policy, so addressing the causes rather than symptoms of insecurity. See Mike Davis, 'The Urbanization of Empire: Megacities and the Laws of Chaos', *Social Text* 22: 4, 2004, 4–15.

76   Barnett, *Pentagon's New Map*.

77   Simon Dalby, 'The Pentagon's New Imperial Cartography', in Derek Gregory and Allan Pred, eds, *Violent Geographies*, New York: Routledge, 2007, 302, 306.

78   Ibid., 303.

ORIENTALISM AND TERROR

> The fact that the designation ['terrorist'] essentially strips individuals of their right to life or humane treatment means that the criteria for the designation must themselves be interrogated, tortured, and interrogated again.[79]

Relying on, and revivifying, long-standing Orientalist tropes portraying the non-Westerner as a barbaric, exotic Other, these renditions reach what Mike Davis has called the 'highest stage of Orientalism'. They conjure the burgeoning slums of the feral city to construct the besieged urban homeland.[80] As we have seen, however, the latter is always an ambivalent construct insofar as conservative, Christian right and US military cultures are all profoundly anti-urban, infused with doubt and fear of both domestic and distant cities.

Such apocalyptic discourses casting urban areas of the global South as intrinsically threatening can move seamlessly to the presentation of such cities as military targets. Especially important here is the sense that such cities undermine the vast complex of vertical surveillance capability sustaining the US military's dreams of 'full spectrum dominance' across the world. 'The vast size of a feral city', argues Richard Norton, 'with its buildings, other structures, and subterranean spaces, would offer nearly perfect protection from overhead sensors, whether satellites or unmanned aerial vehicles'.[81] Thus, any urban space beyond the penetrating electronic and vertical gaze of US power is in essence a threat.

Norton is one amongst many calling for the US military to re-organize itself into, in effect an urban counterinsurgency force, whose de facto mission, rather than peer-on-peer, high-tech warfare, would be the penetration, control and pacification of the world's feral cities. He invokes what geographers call a process of rescaling – a reorientation away from globe-spanning revolutions in high-tech warfare, and towards a dominant concern with the spaces of streets, *favelas*, *medinas* and neighbourhoods. This parallels the increasing preoccupation of military and security forces with the microgeographies of domestic cities. 'Traditionally, problems of urban decay and associated issues, such as crime', writes Norton, 'have been

---

79   Kelly Gates, 'Identifying The 9/11 'Faces Of Terror'', *Cultural Studies*, 20: 4–5, 2006, 436.

80   Dawson, 'Combat in Hell', 175; see Dag Tuastad, 'Neo-Orientalism and the New Barbarism Thesis: Aspects of Symbolic Violence in the Middle East Conflict(s)', *Third World Quarterly* 24: 4, 591–9.

81   Norton, 'Feral Cities', 99.

seen as domestic issues best dealt with by internal security or police forces. That will no longer be an option.'[82]

The Bush administration's language of moral absolutism was, in particular, deeply Orientalist. It worked by separating 'the civilized world' – the 'homeland' cities which must be 'defended' – from the 'dark forces', the 'axis of evil', and the 'terrorist nests' alleged to dwell in, to be situated in, and to define Arab cities, which allegedly sustain the 'evil-doers' who threaten the health, prosperity, and democracy of the whole 'free' world.[83] The result of such imaginative geographies has been the a-historical and essentialized projection of Arab urban civilization. This, as Edward Said remarked just before the 2003 invasion of Iraq, has been easily reworked so as to 'recycle the same unverifiable fictions and vast generalizations to stir up "America" against the foreign devil.'[84]

The Orientalist notions of differential racial worth that helped shape both the real and the imagined geographies of Western colonialism have been important foundations for the War on Terror.[85] These notions have permitted some human bodies to be 'more easily and appropriately humiliated, imprisoned, shackled, starved and destroyed than others'.[86] Discourses of 'terrorism' have been crucially important in sustaining such differential values and binaried notions of human worth.[87] Central here has been the principle of the absolute externality of the 'terrorist' – the inhumanity and monstrousness not only of those deemed to be actual or dormant 'terrorists' but also of those sympathetic to them.

Importantly, contend Jasbir Puar and Amit Rai, 'the construct of the terrorist relies on a knowledge of sexual perversity (failed heterosexuality, Western notions of the psyche, and a certain queer monstrosity)'.[88] Deep-seated racist, Orientalist, and homophobic tropes mix loosely with free-floating demonization. In the ordinary parlance of soldiers, Iraqis targeted by US

---

82   Ibid., 100.

83   Tuastad, 'Neo-Orientalism'. The depiction of cities or urban districts as terrorist 'nests' is widespread. It serves to both dehumanize urban residents and essentialise places as animalistic or barbarian. For a discussion of the Mumbai example, see Appadurai, *Fear of Small Numbers*, 87–114.

84   Said, *Orientalism*, 2003, vi.

85   Gregory, *The Colonial Present*.

86   Paul Gilroy, 'Where Ignorant Armies Clash by Night': Homogeneous Community and the Planetary Aspect', *International Journal of Cultural Studies* 6, 2003, 263.

87   John Collins and Ross Glover, eds., *Collateral Language: A user's guide to America's new war*, New York: New York University Press, 2002.

88   Jasbir Puar and Amit Rai, 'Monster, Terrorist, Fag: The War on Terrorism and the Production of Docile Patriots', *Social Text* 20: 3, 2002, 117.

military action have been called 'sand niggers'.[89] Arab men – notably bin Laden himself – have been called 'fags'. And long-standing Western assumptions about the sexual pathologies permeating Arab life – drawing on the influential quasi-academic diatribe of books such as Raphael Patai's *The Arab Mind* [90] – have recirculated in the methods of torture at Abu Ghraib and elsewhere.[91] 'The forms of power now being deployed in the War on Terrorism', Puar and Rai noted in 2002, 'draw on processes of quarantining a racialized and sexualized other, even as Western norms of the civilized subject provide the framework through which these very same others become subjects to be corrected.'

Backed by the widespread depiction of Islamic or Arab civilization as trapped in an 'innate civilizational conflict' with the West,[92] mainstream and right-wing media have found it easy, especially during the early phases of the War on Terror, to present Arab cities primarily as the recipients of US military ordnance. During that time, a voyeuristic public voraciously consumed newspaper and Web maps of such cities which rendered them as flat, cartographic surfaces made up of nothing but arrays of targets expecting ammunition. Sometimes, as with *USA Today*'s 2003 Web maps, these even had 'before and after' satellite imagery of the destruction wrought by GPS-targeted 'smart' bombs dropped by US or UK warplanes.

Such coverage combined to propagate a series of powerful and interrelated myths: that Iraqi cities existed as asocial, completely physical domains, which could be understood from the God-like perspective of remotely-sensed or cartographic imagery; that such cities were, at the same time, somehow devoid of a civilian population; and that therefore it was not inevitable that Iraqi civilians would be killed and maimed in large numbers when the cities they inhabited were subjected to large-scale aerial bombardment (which occurred even when the targeting was deemed 'precise').

As well as reducing entire cities to to the status of mere receiving points for ordnance (as is generally the case in war), the bombing of distant cities-as-targets has been widely linked to improvements in the purported 'homeland security' of urbanites. General Ricardo Sanchez, the first US commander in Iraq, stressed in early 2004 – as the insurgency raged across Iraqi cities – that 'every American needs to believe this; that if we fail here in this [Iraqi] environment, the next battlefield will be the streets of America'. Paul Bremer, the first head of American civilian command in Iraq, meanwhile reiterated

89   Mike Davis, 'The Pentagon as Global Slumlord', *Tom Dispatch*, February 2006.
90   Patai, *The Arab Mind*.
91   Derek Gregory, 'The Angel of Iraq', *Society and Space* 22: 3, 2004.
92   Qureshi and Sells, eds, *The New Crusades*, 2.

that he 'would rather be fighting [the terrorists] here [in Iraq] than in New York'.[93]

A related discursive trick early in the Iraq war was to construct certain highly symbolic Iraqi cities as dehumanized 'terror cities' – nest-like environments whose very geography was seen as undermining the high-tech omnipotence of US forces. For example, as a major battle raged in Fallujah in April 2004, when more than six hundred Iraqi civilians died, General Richard Myers, chair of the US Joint Chiefs of Staff – perhaps unwittingly following Israeli military's descriptions of Palestinian cities[94] – labelled the whole of the city a dehumanized 'rat's nest' or 'hornet's nest' of 'terrorist resistance' against US occupation that needed to be 'dealt with'.[95]

Such pronouncements were backed up by widespread popular geopolitical representations of Iraqi cities. In their pre-invasion discussions about the threat of 'urban warfare' facing invading US forces in highly urbanized Iraq, for example, mainstream media such as *Time* Magazine repeatedly depicted stylized and intrinsically devious Orientalized streets in their colorful graphics.[96] In these, every feature or element of the city seemed to be deceitful device that hid threats which needed to be addressed through the superior technological mastery of US military forces.[97]

The rhetoric of the War on Terror has become sufficiently diffuse that virtually any political opposition to the sovereign power of the US and its allies can be labelled as terrorist. 'Without defined shape, or determinate roots', writes Derek Gregory, the mantle of terrorism can now 'be cast over any form of resistance to sovereign power'.[98] Jean Baudrillard argues that 'the system takes as objectively terrorist whatever is set against it'.[99]

Those frequently labelled as terrorists by national governments or sympathetic media since 9/11 include anti-war dissenters, striking dock workers, anti-globalization protestors, campaigners against the arms trade, computer hackers, artists, critical researchers, urban sociologists, advocates for ecological sustainability and freedom of speech, and pro-independence campaigners

---

93   Cited in Jan Nederveen Pieterse, 'Neoliberal Empire', *Theory, Culture & Society* 21:3, 2004, 122.

94   Stephen Graham, 'Lessons in Urbicide', *New Left Review* 2:19, 2003, 2–3, 63–78.

95   Quoted on News24.com, 2004, see Stephen Graham, 'Remember Fallujah: Demonizing Place, Constructing Atrocity', *Environment and Planning D: Society and Space*, 23, 2005, 1–10.

96   Gregory, *The Colonial Present*, 222.

97   Ibid.

98   Gregory, *The Colonial Present*, 219.

99   Jean Baudrillard, 'This Is the Fourth World War', *International Journal of Baudrillard Studies* 1: 1, 2004.

within US allies such as Indonesia – protagonists of a wide spectrum of opposition to transnational US dominance. Indeed, almost any large group that assembles in city streets and is not preoccupied with consumption has been demonized. 'Since 9/11 the conflation of large gatherings of people in urban places with terrorism has proceeded apace', declares Ashley Dawson.[100]

Above all, groups tarred with the terrorist label become radically delegitimized. Who, after all, will speak out in favour of supposed terrorists and their sympathizers? This linguistic trick has helped sustain the juridical casting-out of whole swathes of populations caught up in the War on Terror – civilians as well as fighters – from protection under humanitarian or international law. 'The sovereign powers of the American, British and Israeli states', says Derek Gregory, 'disavowed or suspended international law so that men, women and children were made outcasts, placed beyond the pale and beyond the protections and affordances of the Modern.'[101]

Finally, the proliferation of Orientalist othering via the widespread use of the label 'terrorist' has also worked its way through domestic geographies of racialized demonization. Virginia Republicans fighting the 2008 election campaign, for example, mailed out a leaflet with Barack Obama's eyes superimposed on an image of Osama bin Laden with the strap line 'America must look evil in the eye and never flinch.' In a county in New York State, GOP leaflets with the name 'Barack Osama' were circulated.

Thus far, we have addressed the right's trite rendering of the world through Manichaean imaginative geographies based on a generalized revulsion toward the urban. We will return in detail to such 'countergeographic' challenges in the final chapter. Effective resistance and mobilization against these challenges, however, requires that we first tease out the specifics of the 'new military urbanism' as compared with previous intersections of cities and political violence. It is to these specifics that we turn in the next two chapters.

---

100   Dawson, 'Combat in Hell', 177.
101   Gregory, 'Geographies, Publics and Politics', 9.

CHAPTER THREE

The New Military Urbanism

> Above all, [the United States' new low-intensity war culture] is self-perpetuating and
> self-replicating; it normalizes and naturalizes a state of war. Peace is not the end of war
> culture. At its core, war culture seeks a postponement of peacetime 'for the duration';
> it seeks an adjustment to a state of permanent war.[1]

At the core of this book's argument is the idea that new military ideologies of
permanent and boundless war are radically intensifying the militarization of
urban life. The process is far from new: it simply adds contemporary twists to
continual transformations – political, cultural and economic – which together
serve to normalize war itself as well as the preparations for war.[2] Indeed, in
many cases, the transformations associated with the new military urbanism
merely extend and revivify the urban militarization, securitization, Manichaean
thinking, and fear-mongering that were a central feature of, notably, the Cold
War but also of earlier wars.

Military sociologists broadly categorize such processes as 'militarization'.
Michael Geyer defines it as 'the contradictory and tense social process
in which civil society organizes itself for the production of violence'.[3]
Such a process, inevitably, is complex and multidimensional, though its
components are as old as war itself. As we saw in the previous chapter,
these invariably involve the social construction of a conceptual division
between the inside and the outside of a nation or other geographic area,
and the orchestrated demonization of enemies and enemy places beyond
the boundaries of inside. Militarization also involve the normalization
of military paradigms of thought, action and policy; efforts at the
aggressive disciplining of bodies, places and identities deemed not to befit
masculinized (and interconnected) notions of nation, citizenship or body;
and the deployment of a wide range of propaganda which romanticizes
or sanitizes violence as a means of righteous revenge or the achievement
of some God-given purpose. Above all, militarization and war organizes

---

1 Deer, 'The Ends of War', 1.

2 Rachel Woodward, 'From Military Geography to Militarism's Geographies:
Disciplinary Engagements with the Geographies of Militarism and Military Activities',
Progress in Human Geography 29: 6, 2005, 718–40.

3 Michael Geyer, 'The Militarization of Europe, 1914–1945', in John Gillis, ed., *The
Militarization of the Western World*, New Brunswick, NJ: Rutgers University Press, 1989, 79.

the 'creative destruction' of inherited geographies, political economies, technologies and cultures.

So, what exactly is new about the 'new military urbanism'? How is it different from the intense militarization experienced by the cities of, say, the Cold War or total war? I shall point to seven related trends which, I argue, introduce palpably new dimensions to the contemporary militarization of urban life.

RURAL SOLDIERS, URBAN WAR

First, new relationships are emerging between nations, soldiers and citizens, which have major implications for the contemporary urbanization of warfare. Deborah Cowen has pointed out that the professionalized, high-tech militaries of the West are now often 'made up overwhelmingly of rural soldiers'.[4] Drawing on Gramsci, she argues that this 'suggests that a political–geographic rift had emerged between urbanism and cosmopolitanism on the one hand, and ruralism and nationalism on the other.'

Thus, writes Cowen, 'rural areas have become the heartland of militarism and "authentic" patriotism' in many Western nations. Grounded in the long-standing naturalization of nations which appeal to 'a kind of bucolic territorial authenticity' based on whiteness, the conservative politics of rural areas are, as we have seen, frequently based on hatred of or suspicion towards the perceived horrors or the racial, cosmopolitan and multicultural impurities and threats posed by cities. In both the US and Canada, Cowen argues, a 'powerful cultural discourse of the rural ideal identifies the rural as the authentic space of patriotic militarism'. The rural is thus widely understood by military recruiters 'to have both the economic motivations for mass enlistment coupled with small-town culture of patriotic nationalism'. Indeed, despite the US being one of the most urbanized nations on Earth, rural soldiers now dominate its military. Between 2003 and 2004, '47.6 per cent of all soldiers killed in action during Operation Enduring Freedom and 44.3 per cent of those killed in action during Operation Iraqi Freedom through February 5, 2004, were from communities with populations under 20,000.'

Yet these largely ruralized Western militaries must now deploy primarily to cities, both domestic and foreign. Given that right-wing media, especially in

---

4   Deborah Cowen, 'National Soldiers and the War on Cities', *Theory and Event* 10: 2, 2007.

the US, construct cities in general, in Steve Macek's words, as places of 'the savage urban other,'[5] and given the anti-urban character of military cultures, it seems likely that many recruits are easily socialized to see all urbanized places as intrinsically foreign, threatening and dangerous, wherever they may be. In other words, enemy places. Cowen cites many military blogs where 'positive statements about rural patriotism are interspersed with and inextricable from others that construct the city as a place of degeneration and dependency'.[6]

Given that Western militaries deploy from overwhelmingly exurban and rural bases, the widespread discourse that cities must be 'targeted' and 'pacified' through military power – whose exurban and rural heartland is the normalized space of 'authentic' nationalism – is likely to gain added force from the increasingly rural make-up of recruits. Domestic and foreign cities thus become Others, to be addressed and penetrated from afar – from the authentic spaces where military personnel are based and, increasingly, raised.

With urban deployment abroad and at home generally targeting (and often abusing) black or brown bodies, the racialization of urban targeting becomes both clear and contradictory. Even though the US military is now the largest employer of African-Americans, for instance, urban military exercises predominantly target African-American urban neighbourhoods. Following one such exercise in the housing projects of Philadelphia and Chester, Pennsylvania, in 1999, one angry resident complained that 'they wouldn't have done it if this wasn't a Black community'.[7]

TRACKING: CITIZEN–CONSUMER–SOLDIER

> Contemporary militarization runs on an economy of *desire* as well as an economy of fear.[8]

The second trend is the unprecedented extent to which the new military urbanism fuses and blurs civilian and military applications of the technologies for control, surveillance, communications, simulation and targeting. This is hardly surprising, given that control technologies originally intended for military use have become fundamental to virtually all acts of urban life and consumption in advanced industrial cities, and that

---

5   Macek: *Urban Nightmares*, Chapter 3.
6   Cowen, 'National Soldiers'.
7   Ibid.
8   Marieke de Goede, 'Beyond Risk: Premediation and the Post–9/11 Security Imagination', *Security Dialogue* 39: 2/3, 168.

commercial modifications of such technologies are, in turn, being widely reappropriated by militaries.

Their fortifications long forgotten, erased, or turned into tourist sites, contemporary cities are now, in Paul Virilio's words, 'overexposed' to a wide range of ambient, mobile and transnational security threats.[9] Among these threats are mobile pathogens, malign computer code, financial crashes, 'illegal' migration, transnational terrorism, state infrastructural warfare, and the environmental extremes triggered by climate change.

The permeability of contemporary cities to transnational circulation means that systems of (attempted) electronic control – expanded to match the transnational geographies of such circulation – become the new strategic architectures of city life. These increasingly supplant, without completely replacing, the confined architectures or 'disciplinary spaces' – prisons, schools, clinics, factories, workhouses, barracks – noted by Michel Foucault. At such sites in eighteenth and nineteenth century Western cities, panoptic social control operated through the direct supervisory gaze of humans.

By contrast, argued French philosopher Gilles Deleuze, because networked electronic control and surveillance devices are now distributed throughout society, everyday urban life is now modulated by a sense of ever-present tracking, scrutiny, and electronic calculation. Contemporary societies, he said, are 'societies of control'.[10] The surveillance devices build profiles, analyse patterns of behaviour and mobility, and increasingly – because memory is now digitized – never forget.[11] Thus, an individual's movements between different spaces and sites within cities or nations often entails a parallel movement of what sociologists call the 'data subject' or 'statistical person' – the package of electronic tracks and histories amassed as a means of judging the individual's legitimacy, rights, profitability, security or degree of threat. The attempted social control increasingly works through complex technological systems stretched across both temporal and geographical zones. These constitute a working background, a ubiquitous computerised matrix of ever more interlinked devices: ATM cards and financial databases; GPS transponders, bar codes, and chains of global satellites; radio-frequency chips and biometric identifiers; mobile computers, phones and e-commerce sites; and an extending universe of sensors built into streets, homes, cars, infrastructures and even bodies.

Increasingly, then, behind every social moment operates a vast array of computerized calculations dispersed through a global matrix of linked

9   Paul Virilio, *The Lost Dimension,* San Francisco: Semiotext(e), 1991, Chapter 1.
10 Gilles Deleuze, 'Postscript on the Societies of Control', *October* 59, 1992, 3–7.
11 Ibid.

computers and computerized devices. Databases communicate and their content is continuously mined across a diversity sources, scales and sites by advanced computer algorithms that assess a commensurate diversity of bodies, transactions, and movements. Crucially, the volume of data in this 'calculative background' is so vast that only automated algorithms can deem what or who is considered normal and thus deserving of protection, and what or who is considered abnormal and thus a malign threat to be targeted.

Such control technologies increasingly blur into the background of urban environments, urban infrastructures and urban life. Layered over and through everyday urban landscapes, bringing into being radically new styles of movement, interaction, consumption and politics, in a sense they *become* the city. Examples include new means of mobility (congestion charging, smart highways, Easyjet-style air travel), customized consumption (personalized Amazon.com pages) and 'swarming' social movements (social networking, smart and flash mobs).

Discussions about 'homeland security' and the high-tech transformation of war emphasize the need to use some of those very techniques and technologies – high-tech surveillance, data-mining, computerized algorithms – to try to continually track, identify and target threatening Others within the mass of clutter presented by our rapidly urbanizing and increasingly mobile world. The technological architectures of consumption and mobility thus merge into those used to organize and prosecute a full spectrum of political violence, from profiling to killing. And the multiple links between cities and post–Second World War military history suggest that this connection should not surprise us. As Gerfried Stocker notes, 'there is no sphere of civilian life in which the saying "war is the father of all things" has such unchallenged validity as it does in the field of digital information technology'.[12]

Moreover, the new military urbanism has been the foundry of the new control technologies. After the Second World War, a constellation of military strategies known as C3I – command, control, communications, and information – dominated the military's approach to war-fighting and strategic deterrence, and also colonized the minutiae of modernizing urban life, especially in Western nations. 'No part of the world went untouched by C3I', Ryan Bishop writes, 'And it delineates the organizational, economic, technological and spatial systems that derive from, rely on, and perpetuate military strategy'.[13]

---

12 Gerfried Stocker, 'InfoWar', in Gerfried Stocker and C. Schopf, eds, *Ars Electronica 98: Infowar*, Springer-Verlag Telos, 1998.

13 Ryan Bishop, '"The Vertical Order Has Come to an End": The Insignia of the Military C3I and Urbanism in Global Networks', in Ryan Bishop, John Phillips and Yeo Wei Wei eds, *Beyond Description: Space, History, Singapore,* London: Routledge, 2004, 61.

Since the start of the Cold War, for example, it has been common for the US to devote 80 per cent of all government expenditures on technological research and development to 'defence'.[14] Technologies such as the Internet, virtual reality, jet travel, data-mining, closed-circuit TV, rocketry, remote control, microwaves, radar, global positioning, networked computers, wireless communications, satellite surveillance, containerization and logistics – which now collectively facilitate daily urban life – were all forged in the latter half of the twentieth century as part of the elaboration of systems of military control.

Viewed thus, 'this "insignia of the military" . . . manifests itself in a myriad of ways in global urban sites . . . The global city would not be a global city, as we have come to understand the phenomenon, without being deeply embedded in these processes'.[15] Certainly the relationship between commercial and military control and information technologies has always been a complex two-way affair, but one must keep in mind that the technological architectures of contemporary life and the imperial geographies of empire converge within the new military urbanism.

In today's professional Western militaries, relatively small numbers of recruits are deployed, injured or killed in the new imperial wars. Citizens of the homelands are only rarely exposed to true acts of (terrorist) violence. In addition, only the most strategic urban sites show visible signs of militarization. As a consequence, for the vast majority of people it is the control and media technologies that constitute their main experience of military urbanism.

Take the salient example of GPS. Since the US military first deployed it in support of the 'precision' killing of the First Gulf War, GPS has been partly declassified and made available to an ever-widening universe of commercial, governmental and civilian applications. It has become the basis for civilian mobility and navigation, a ubiquitous consumer technology used in PDAs, watches, cars, and a broad range of geo-location services. It has been used to reorganize agriculture, transportation, municipal government, law enforcement, border security, computer gaming and leisure activities. Few people, however, consider how military and imperial power pervades every GPS application.

With a suite of surveillance and control technologies now organized to pre-empt and anticipate consumption as well as risk, 'the production of knowledge [is] no longer intended to secrete and clarify what can be known, but rather

---

14   Pierre Mesnard y Méndez, 'Capitalism Means/Needs War', *Socialism and Democracy* 22:2, 2002.
15   Bishop, '"The Vertical Order Has Come to an End"', 61.

to "clarify" what cannot be known'.[16] Increasingly the city is 'defined by the military goal of being able to know the enemy even before the enemy is aware of himself as such'.[17] The overarching feature of the new militarized surveillance, whether its targets are located in Manhattan or Baghdad, London or Fallujah, is the building of systems of technological vision in which computer code, along with databases of real or imaged targets, tracks, identifies and distinguishes 'abnormal' targets from the background 'normality' or clutter of a homeland or a war-zone city.

Tracking – what media theorist Jordan Crandall calls 'anticipatory seeing'[18] – is thus central to emerging modes of governance and military power. The key question now, he suggests, is 'how targets are identified and distinguished from non-targets' within 'decision making and killing'. Crandall points out that this widespread integration of computerized tracking with databases of targets represents 'a gradual colonization of the now, a now always slightly ahead of itself'. This shift is a profoundly militarized process because the social identification of people within civilian law enforcement is complemented or even replaced by the mechanistic seeing of 'targets'. 'While civilian images are embedded in processes of identification based on reflection', writes Crandall, 'militarized perspectives collapse identification processes into "Id-ing" – a one-way channel of identification in which a conduit, a database, and a body are aligned and calibrated.'[19]

In this way, for example, radio-chip public transport cards or systems for electronically tolling highways or central urban road systems morph into urban 'counterterrorist' screens protecting 'security zones'. The Internet is appropriated as a global system of financial and civil surveillance. Just-in-time logistics chains sustaining both global trade and airline travel are reorganized to allow for permanent profiling, tracking and the targeting of malign bodies and circulations. Everything from mobile phones to passports is fitted with microchip radio frequency tags that have the potential to turn their hosts into tracking devices.

Hence, technologies with military origins – refracted through the vast worlds of civilian research, development and application that help constitute high-tech economies, societies and cultures – are now being reappropriated as the bases

---

16 Anne Bottomley and Nathan Moore, 'From Walls to Membranes: Fortress Polis and the Governance of Urban Public Space in 21st Century Britain,' *Law and Critique* 18: 2, 2007, 171–206.

17 Ibid.

18 Jordan Crandall, 'Anything that Moves: Armed Vision', CTheory.net, June 1999.

19 Ibid.

for new architectures of militarized control, tracking, surveillance, targeting and killing. Mark Mills is thankful that this 'tectonic shift fortunately mirrors the threat environment' of distributed, unknowable enemies and dangerous circulations. 'While much of this capability has focused on producing iPods, cell phones, video games, gigabit data streams, and Internet server farms', he writes, 'the digital economy's underlying intellectual property and machinery is now turning to civilian and military security. All of this augurs well for the prospects of better security, and robust new opportunities for entrepreneurs, large and small.'[20]

Through such processes, 'more and more sectors of civil society are being integrated into a global infrastructure generated through the military', notes Simon Cooper.[21] And all of it occurs in the name of security – of a nameless and shapeless us against the infinite threats of a shapeless Other lurking within the 'new normal' of a state of exception, a permanent emergency. Citizens and subjects are thus mobilized for militarized control and conscripted into neoliberal consumption systems which encourage them to consume for the good of the economy – as Bush urged after the 9/11 attacks – while at the same offering up their 'data selves' for continuous, pre-emptive analysis, tracking, profiling, targeting and threat assessment.

Randy Martin has shown how the massive data and surveillance systems that are emerging at this moment of military–civil fusion reinforce the transfer of principles of speculation and pre-emption from neoliberal fiscal policy into the heart of militarized war-making by states, both within and without their territorial boundaries.[22] So-called securitization involves both military and financial dimensions, acting in parallel. Such systems, Martin argues, are geared towards protecting the people and urban enclaves that have benefited from the superabundant wealth arising from neoliberal political economies – protecting them, that is, from the risks embodied by the surrounding masses. Attempts to separate good risks from bad, however, end up creating their own financial markets, organized through the same techniques of pre-emption, profiling and targeting used by the military.

In such a context, 'legitimacy is garnered to citizens only to the extent that they are integrated into a high-tech network'.[23] Caren Kaplan argues that the

20 Mark Mills, 'Photons, Electrons and Paradigms', keynote address, USA Defense and Security Symposium, Orlando, Florida, 9–13 April 2007.

21 Simon Cooper, 'Perpetual War within the State of Exception', *Arena Journal*, 1 January 2003, 114.

22 Randy Martin, 'Derivative Wars', *Cultural Studies*, 20: 4–5, 2006, 459–476.

23 Cooper, 'Perpetual War within the State of Exception', 117.

deployment of militarized control technologies at the heart of contemporary 'information societies' necessarily leads to the formation of 'militarized consumer and citizen subjects in relation to technologies that link geography, demography, remote sensing, and contemporary identity politics'.[24] Marketing campaigns then target citizens, using the same technologies and targeting algorithms as weapons. 'The digital mingling of position and identity into target subjects', writes Kaplan, 'underscores the martial and territorial aspect of mapping throughout the modern period.'[25]

However, the new culture of digital surveillance is not simply imposed on coerced, oppressed citizens, as in some Orwellian Big Brother scenario. Very often, as with the use of webcams, mobile phone tracking, and geo-positioning systems, it is embraced and actively deployed as the means for organizing new expressions of mobility, identity, sexuality and everyday life – as well as resistance.

CAMERA-WEAPON: SPECTACLES OF URBAN VIOLENCE

> The enduring attraction of war is this: even with its destruction and carnage it can give us what we long for in life. It can give us purpose, meaning, a reason for living.[26]

Thirdly, the new military urbanism and its wars are overwhelmingly performed and consumed as visual and discursive spectacles within the spaces of electronic imagery. The vast majority of participants, at least in US or Western European cities, are unlikely to be subjected to either military deployment or violent targeting. Instead they participate via TV, the Net, video games and films. The new wars – geared towards the idea that permanent and pre-emptive mobilization is necessary to sustain public safety – increasingly 'take the form of mediatized mechanisms and are ordered as massive intrusions into visual culture, which are conflated with, and substitute for, the actual materiality and practices of the public sphere'.[27]

As the 9/11 attacks demonstrate, insurgents and terrorists are themselves careful to organize their violence with extraordinary urban media spectacles in mind – spectacles of apocalyptic urban annihilation, which bear an

---

24   Caren Kaplan, 'Precision Targets: GPS and the Militarization of US Consumer Identity', *American Quarterly* 58: 3, 2006, 696.

25   Ibid., 698.

26   Chris Hedges, *War Is a Force Which Gives Us Meaning*, New York: Public Affairs, 2002, 3.

27   Allen Feldman, 'Securocratic Wars of Public Safety', *Interventions: International Journal of Postcolonial Studies* 6: 3, 330–50

uncanny resemblance to the well-versed tropes of Hollywood disaster movies but are delivered live, in real time and in real places, to real bodies.[28] The 9/11 attacks, for example, 'were organized as epic horror cinema with meticulous attention to the *mise-en-scène*', writes Mike Davis, 'The hijacked planes were aimed precisely at the vulnerable border between fantasy and reality.' As a result, 'thousands of people who turned on their televisions on 9/11 were convinced that the cataclysm was just a broadcast, a hoax. They thought they were watching rushes from the latest Bruce Willis film'.[29] A common response to those events was that 'it was just like watching a movie!' Indeed, Hollywood dramatic tradition relies heavily on both the spectacular demise of cities and the collapse of towering buildings. The history of New York in particular – the archetypal modern metropolis – can be told through histories of its imagined, imaged demise in films, comics, video games and novels.

These visual and electronic circuits impart to warfare and the military urbanism a certain legitimacy and consent, however precarious. At the same time, the divisions between military simulation, information warfare, news and entertainment are becoming so blurred as to be less and less meaningful. Together, in the US at least, they now fuse into a fuzzy world of self-reinforcing 'militainment'.[30]

Thus, the US military employs Hollywood's finest to merge their digital simulations for training directly into mass-market video games. Closing the circle, it then uses video-game consoles to model the control stations for the unmanned drones used to patrol the streets of Baghdad or undertake extrajudicial assassinations and targeted killings. In addition, the military 'mobilizes science fiction writers and other futurologists to plan for the wars of tomorrow just as they consciously recruit video-game playing adolescents to fight the same conflict'[31] on weapons whose controls directly mimic those of PlayStations. The profusion of digital video sensors in turn provides an almost infinite range of material for reality TV shows like *Police, Camera, Action!*, which provide the citizenry with voyeuristic and eroticized experiences of urban violence. The invasion of Iraq in 2003 'was the first war to emerge in the electronic informational space as a fully coordinated "media spectacle",

28 Iain Boal, T. J. Clark, Joseph Matthews and Michael Watts, *Afflicted Powers: Capital and Spectacle in a New Age of War*, London: Verso, 2006.

29 Mike Davis, *Dead Cities*, New York: New Press, 2002, 5.

30 Jonathan Burston, 'War and the Entertainment Industries: New Research Priorities in an Era of Cyber-Patriotism', In Daya Kishan Thussu and Des Freedman, eds., *War and the Media*, London: Routledge, 2003 163–75.

31 Chris Hables Gray, *Postmodern War*, London: Routledge, 1997, 190.

complete with embedded reporters, interactive websites, and 3D models and maps all at the ready'.[32]

Shrill and bellicose, the commercial news media meanwhile appropriate their own digital simulations of the cities and spaces targeted by imperial war. They provide a 24/7 world of war and infotainment which eroticizes high-tech weaponry while making death curiously invisible. In the US especially, commercial news content in the run-up to the 2003 invasion was massively skewed towards pro-war arguments. Material was preselected and approved by Pentagon officials serving as resident consultants within each TV studio. Sets, images, maps, simulations and footage orchestrated what James Der Derian calls 'a techno-aesthetic'. 'When the war premiered', he writes, using the term deliberately, 'the television studios introduced new sets that mimicked the command and control centers of the military (Fox News actually referred to its own, without a trace of Strangelovian irony, as the "War Room").'[33]

Der Derian also notes that 'computer-generated graphics of the Iraq battlespace were created by the same defense industries (like Evans and Sutherland and Analytical Graphics) and commercial satellite firms (like Space Imaging and Digital Globe) that supply the US military." Ultimately, technophilic erotics of weaponry filled the screens. 'The networks showcased a veritable *Jane's Defense Review* of weapon-systems', Der Derian writes, 'providing "virtual views" of Iraq and military hardware that are practically indistinguishable from target acquisition displays.'[34]

More generally, corporate news media both contribute to and benefit from the discourses of fear, demonization and boundless emergency that sustain the new military urbanism. The 'media coverage and terrorism are soul mates, virtually inseparable', admits James Lukaszewiski, a US public relations consultant who advises the US military. 'They feed off each other. They together create a dance of death – the one for political or ideological motives, the other for commercial success. Terrorist activities are high profile, ratings-building events. The news media need to prolong these stories because they build viewership and readership.'[35]

These blurrings and fusions are symptoms of the broader emergence of what

32   John Jordan, 'Disciplining the Virtual Home Front: Mainstream News and the Web During the War in Iraq', *Communication and Critical/Cultural Studies* 4: 3, 2007, 276–302.

33   James Der Derian, 'Who's Embedding Whom?', *9/11 INFOinterventions*, 26 March 2003, available at www.watsoninstitute.org/infopeace/911.

34   Ibid.

35   Cited in Sheldon Rampton and John Stauber, *Weapons of Mass Deception: The Uses of Propaganda in Bush's War on Iraq,* London: Robinson, 2003, 34.

Der Derian[36] has called the 'military-industrial-media-entertainment network', a potent agent in the concoction of events and the manipulation of news. 'Battle simulations, news, and interactive games exist within an increasingly unified space', adds Jordan Crandall. 'With military-news-entertainment systems, simulations jostle with realities to become the foundation for war. They help combine media spectatorship and combat, viewing and fighting'.[37]

In the process, the domestic home – the main site of this continuous performance of electronic screening – becomes a militarized site for the potentially 24/7 enactment of both symbolic and real violence against far-away Others, which can of course exist at a variety of geographic distances from the home screen and its surrounding security architectures. A similar logic operates on the racialized downtown ghetto and the Arab city.

While mediatized urban violence provides a very different experience than does being an actual presence in its cross-hairs, the media experience of massive terrorist or state onslaughts against cities can nonetheless often be 'characterised as sublime: our minds clash with phenomena that supersede our cognitive abilities, triggering a range of powerful emotions, such as pain, fear and awe'.[38] Thus, television observers were profoundly unsettled and also awe-struck by both the aestheticized spectacle of the 9/11 attacks and the equally aestheticized 'shock and awe' bombing campaign against Baghdad that putatively constituted the US response to those attacks.

The multiple circuits of 'civilian' media have thus been inscribed into the latest variations on military doctrine as major elements of contemporary battlespace. Indeed, military theorists now commonly describe TV and the Internet as 'virtual weapons' within the crucial domains of 'information warfare'. They also bemoan how 'asymmetric' struggles such as the second Palestinian Intifada gain massive global political credibility because they lead to such images as Palestinian children confronting Israeli tanks with stones.[39]

Informational and psychological aspects of US military operations are now a central concern of military planners. Think of the 2003 shock-and-awe pyrotechnics, with ordnance devastating targets symbolic of the Hussein regime (as well as Iraqi civilians) a safe but camera-friendly distance away from the serried ranks of journalists lined up in a nearby hotel. Or think of the

36 Der Derian, *Virtuous War.*

37 Jordan Crandall, ed., *Under Fire.1*, 15.

38 Roland Bleiker and Martin Leet, 'From the Sublime to the Subliminal: Fear, Awe and Wonder in International Politics', *Millennium: Journal of International Studies* 34: 3, 2006, 713.

39 Thomas Hamms, *The Sling and the Stone: On War in the Twenty-First Century*, New York: Zenith Press, 2006.

1991 Gulf War press conferences filled with video footage taken by cameras mounted on missiles showing these weapons 'precisely' hitting their Iraqi targets. Remember, too, that the Pentagon banned the circulation of images of the US war dead being returned home, and explicitly discussed the need to launch completely fabricated news stories.[40] Finally, consider the violence used against media providers who had the temerity to show images of Baghdad's dead civilians, casualities of US force: Al Jazeera's offices in both Kabul and Baghdad were bombed by the US, killing one journalist.[41]

Clearly, US 'information operations' focus on 'visually distribut[ing] death and destruction into domains of the event and the non-event'. As a result, 'shock and awe is a carefully staged media event at the same time that the hundreds of thousands of civilian deaths and maimings through "collateral damage" is a continuous non-event which actually requires, ironically, violent obfuscation', as Allen Feldman puts it.[42]

At the same time, through increasingly direct intervention from the Pentagon, military action movies and right-wing TV stations such as Fox News have turned into extended ads for the US military or the War on Terror. In effect, 'the military [took] over the television studios'.[43] Through their public-affairs offices located within the studios,

> retired general and flag officers exercised full spectrum dominance on cable and network TV as well as on commercial and public radio. The new public affairs officers of the military-industrial-media-entertainment network included Clark and Sheppard on CNN, Nash and Hawley on ABC, Kernan and Ralston on CBS, McCaffrey and Meigs on NBC, and Olstrom and Scales on NPR. Fox News alone had enough ex-military to stage their own Veteran's Day parade.[44]

Yet the same digital circuits of imagery that have been organized so successfully to propagandize the war in Iraq have also helped instigate its undoing. The global circulation of the tourist-style digital images of the Abu Ghraib torturers, for example, provided not only a massive boost to the war's opponents but also iconic images of torture to activists and investigators who

---

40   Most notable here was the idea of the 'Office of Strategic influence, see Der Derian, 'The Rise and Fall of the Office of Strategic Influence', *INFOinterventions*, 4 March 2002, available at www.watsoninstitute.org/infopeace/911.

41   Lisa Parks, 'Insecure Airwaves: US Bombings of Al Jazeera', *Communication and Critical/Cultural Studies* 4: 2, 2007, 226–231.

42   Allen Feldman, 'Securocratic wars of public safety', 330–350.

43   Der Derian, 'Who's Embedding Whom?'

44   Ibid.

had suspected widespread brutality within the US system of incarceration without trial. Efforts by US military information-operations campaigns to buy up relevant satellite imaging during the invasions of Iraq and Afghanistan have not kept Google Earth, for instance, from being widely used by anti-war activists and Iraqi insurgents alike. And while digital video cameras have been used to sustain cheap cable TV channels offering demonized depictions of the dangers lurking in city cores, those very same technologies enabled bystanders to reveal the regular killings of Iraqi civilians by the private military corporation Blackwater.

SECURITY SURGE

A fourth new component of contemporary urbanism is that as the everyday spaces and systems of urban everyday life are colonized by militarized control technologies, and as notions of policing and war, domestic and foreign, peace and war become less distinct, there emerges a massive boom in a convergent industrial complex encompassing security, surveillance, military technology, prisons, corrections, and electronic entertainment. Within the broader apparatus of the military-industrial-media-entertainment network, these fusing industries exploit the cross-fertilization and blurring between the traditional military imperatives of war, external to the state, and those of the policing internal to it.

The proliferation of wars sustaining permanent mobilization and preemptive, ubiquitous surveillance within and beyond territorial borders means that the security imperative now 'imposes itself on the basic principle of state activity'.[45] Giorgio Agamben argues that 'what used to be one among several decisive measures of public administration until the first half of the twentieth century, now becomes the sole criterion of political legitimation'.[46]

The result is an ever-broadening landscape of 'security' blending commercial, military and security practices with increasingly fearful cultures of civilian mobility, citizenship and consumption. As William Connolly suggests:

> Airport surveillance, Internet filters, passport tracking devices, legal detention without criminal charges, security internment camps, secret trials, 'free speech zones', DNA profiles, border walls and fences, erosion of the line between internal security and external military action – these security activities resonate together, engendering a national security machine that pushes numerous issues outside the range of legitimate

45   Giorgio Agamben, 'Security and Terror', *Theory and Event* 5: 4, 2002, 1–2.
46   Ibid.

dissent and mobilizes the populace to support new security and surveillance practices against underspecified enemies.[47]

It is no accident that security-industrial complexes blossom in parallel with the diffusion of market-fundamentalist notions for organizing social, economic and political life. The hyperinequalities, the urban militarization and the securitization sustained by neoliberalization are mutually reinforcing. In a discussion of the US government's response to the Hurricane Katrina disaster, Henry Giroux points out that the normalization of market fundamentalism in US culture has made it much more 'difficult to translate private woes into social issues and collective action or to insist on a language of the public good'. He argues that 'the evisceration of all notions of sociality' in this case has led to 'a sense of total abandonment, resulting in fear, anxiety, and insecurity over one's future'.[48]

Added to this, Giroux argues, 'the presence of the racialized poor, their needs, and vulnerabilities – now visible – becomes unbearable'. Rather than address the causes of poverty or insecurity, however, political responses now invariably 'focus on shoring up a diminished sense of safety, carefully nurtured by a renewed faith in all things military'.[49] One also witnesses the looting of state budgets for post-disaster assistance and reconstruction by cabals of lobbyists with intimate links both to governments and to the burgeoning array of private military and security corporations.[50]

Given that context, it is not surprising that, amidst a global financial crash, market growth in security services and technologies remains extremely strong: 'International expenditure on homeland security now surpasses established enterprises like movie-making and the music industry in annual revenues', announces a December 2007 issue of India's *Economic Times*.[51] Homeland Security Research Corporation (HSRC) notes that 'the worldwide "total defense" outlay (military, intelligence community, and Homeland Security/Homeland Defense) is forecasted to grow by approximately 50 per cent, from $1,400 billion in 2006 to $2,054 billion by 2015.' By 2005, US defense expenditures alone had reached $420 billion a year – comparable to those of the rest of the world combined.

---

47 William Connolly, *Pluralism*, Durham, NC: Duke University Press, 2005, 54.

48 Giroux, 'Reading Hurricane Katrina', 171.

49 Ibid., 172.

50 Eric Klinenberg and Thomas Frank, 'Looting Homeland Security', *Rolling Stone,* December 2005.

51 'Spending on Internal Security to Reach $178 bn by 2015', *Economic Times*, 27 December 2007.

More than a quarter of this was devoted to purchasing services from a rapidly expanding market of private military corporations. By 2010, such mercenary groups are in line to receive a staggering $202 billion from the US federal government alone.[52]

Meanwhile, worldwide homeland-security expenditures are forecast to double, from $231 billion in 2006 to $518 billion by 2015; 'where the homeland security outlay was 12% of the world's total defence outlay in 2003, it is expected to become 25% of the total defence outlay by 2015', according to HSRC.[53] Even more meteoric growth is expected in some key sectors of the new control technologies: global markets in biometric technology, for example, are expected to increase from the small base of $1.5 billion in 2005 to $5.7 billion by 2010.[54]

Although there is little good research on the complex structures of what the OECD call the 'new security economy',[55] it is clear that global consolidation is creating an oligopoly of massive market-dominated transnational security corporations. In 2004 the top six companies took 20 per cent of the global market for security services.[56] Coalitions between governments and corporate interests are running rampant beyond democratic scrutiny. 'Growth in the industry is assured by massive government contracts and generous subsidies for homeland security research and development', write Ben Hayes and Roche Tasse.[57] A variety of institutional fusions and alliances between civilian, military and communitarian sectors, marked by complex cross-overs between the application of civilian and military control technologies, are taking place at different geographical scales of operation (Figure 3.1).

52   Fred Schreier and Marina Caparini, 'Privatising Security: Law, Practice and Governance of Private Military and Security Companies', *Occasional Paper no. 6*, Geneva Centre for the Democratic Control of Armed Forces (DCAF), Geneva, March 2005.

53   Homeland Security Research Corp, 2007, available at www.photonicsleadership. org.uk.

54   Ibid.

55   Organisation for Economic Cooperation and Development, *The Security Economy*, Paris: OECD, 2004.; see also Sven Bisley, 'Globalization, State Transformation, and Public Security', *International Political Science Review* 25: 3, 2004, 281–96.

56   Frank Seavey, 'Globalizing Labor in Response to a Globalized Security Industry', paper presented at the 'Policing Crowds' Conference, Berlin, June 2006, available at www. policing-crowds.org.

57   Ben Hayes and Roche Tasse, 'Control Freaks: "Homeland Security" and "Interoperability"', *Different Takes* 45, 2007, 2.

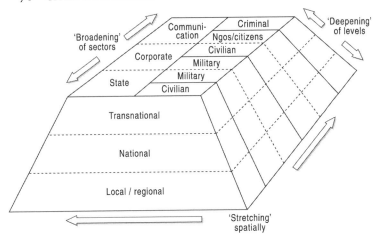

3.1   Peter Gill's conception of the convergence of state,
corporate and civilian sectors to create global 'security' industries
operating at local, national and transnational scales.

Hayes, of the organization Statewatch, argues that the EU's efforts to establish a continent-wide Security Research Programme is best described as '"Big Brother" meets market fundamentalism'.[58] The programme's large development and supply contracts are organized by a network of 'EU officials and Europe's biggest arms and IT companies'.[59] As in the US, moreover, EU security policy and research are heavily influenced by intensive lobbying by the main corporate-security companies (many of which are recently privatized state operations). Rather than the ethics of massive securitization, the prime EU concern has been how European corporation could take a bigger chunk of booming global markets for a 'myriad of local and global surveillance systems; the introduction of biometric identifiers; RFID, electronic tagging and satellite monitoring; "less-lethal weapons"; paramilitary equipment for public order and crisis management; and the militarization of border controls'.[60] Urban securization may thus become a shop-window for industrial policy within the burgeoning security marketplace.

58   Ben Hayes, *Arming Big Brother: The EU's Security Research Programme*, Washington, DC: Statewatch, 2006.
59   Ibid.
60   Ibid.

COLONIZING TRANSNATIONAL URBANISM

> The recalibration of an inside-outside problematique from the point of view of the United States is full of explosive contradictions.[61]

Our fifth component is this: in a rapidly urbanizing world marked by intensifying transnational migration, transport, capital and media flows, all attempts at constructing a mutually exclusive binary – a securitized 'inside' enclosing the urban places of the US homeland, and an urbanizing 'outside' where US military power can pre-emptively attack sources of terrorist threats – are inevitably both ambivalent and ridden with contradiction.

'National sovereignty' is now the rationale for constructing transnational systems of attempted social control. Certain people become 'national' subjects only after they become terrorist victims. And 'national' borders simultaneously permeate the spaces within and beyond the territorial limits of nations, as they become inscribed into increasingly ubiquitous systems intended for tracking and control.

Globally, the new military urbanism is being mobilized for the securing of the strung-out commodity chains, logistics networks, and corporate enclaves that constitute the neoliberal geo-economic architectures of our planet. These key nodes, enclaves, circulations and infrastructures that together sustain the architectures of transnational urbanism[62] tend to lie, cheek by jowl, with populations and urban places deemed likely to be sources of insurgent resistance, social mobilization, or infrastructural terrorism. As we shall see in Chapter 5, there are extremely lucrative attempts underway to re-engineer global finance, communication, airline and port systems to achieve a kind of ubiquitous border, a 'global homeland' which follows the infrastructural architectures of a global network of cities and economic enclaves rather than the territorial limits demarcating nation-states.

The geography of such an imagined, ubiquitous border separates and secures the valorized, strategic 'global cities' of the North as well as the economic enclaves of the South – with their security zones and high-tech surveillance – from the threatening multitudes outside the increasingly fortified urban, national or supra-national gates. Here the discourse of high-tech, 'clean' and 'humane' war surrounding the Revolution in Military Affairs merges with

---

61 Roger Keil, 'Empire and the Global City: Perspectives of Urbanism after 9/11', *Studies in Political Economy* 79, 2007, 167–92.

62 The term 'transnational urbanism' was coined by Michael Peter Smith in 1996 in his book *Transnational Urbanism: Locating Globalization*, Oxford: Blackwell, 2001.

the glossy ideologies of high-tech globalization at the core of neoliberal economic orthodoxy and market fundamentalism. As Patrick Deer writes, such ideologies claim 'to occupy a clean, smooth space in the command-and-control networks of the first-world global cities, with their frictionless, speedy flows of metropolitan labor and capital.' However, they operate in 'stark contrast to the "dirty" quotidian world of the sweatshops and *maquiladoras* or the *favelas* and refugee camps of the underdeveloped global South.'[63]

Increasingly, the city-to-city architectures of 'network-centric' or infrastructural warfare converge on the dominant city-to-city architectures of globalized urban life – airline systems, port systems, electronic finance systems, the Internet – that sustain transnational capitalism. The result is the fast-militarizing borders between North and South, the proliferating extraterritorial refugee and torture camps, and colonized urban spaces akin to mass prison camps. This is what geographer Peter Taylor has called the 'world city network'[64] – the transnational complex of strategic cities, parts of cities, and infrastructures, destined to be bordered, fenced off, and rebuilt into global homelands. And that is how neoliberal globalization, so dominant in Western culture in the 1990s, morphs into permanent war: the architectures of globalization merge seamlessly into the architectures of control and warfare.[65]

In this way, the most basic and banal processes of modern urban life are rendered as (net)war. As Deer writes, "the pervasive metaphorization of war blurs the boundaries between military and civilian, combatant and noncombatant, state and war machine, wartime and peacetime."[66] Acts of protest, civil disobedience, resistance, social mobilization, labour activism, computer crime, or even attempted survival after disasters are thus deemed acts of urban warfare, requiring a military or paramilitary response as part of low intensity conflict.

Given the critical importance of the system of 'world' cities to the global geographies of imperialism, all this should come as no surprise. Indeed, the burgeoning industrial complex within which the industries of security, technology, biotechnology, corrections, prison, torture, electronics, military, entertainment and surveillance are melding yields large chunks of the lucrative core economies of cities like London and New York.

Yet the centrality of war and imperial power to the economic dynamics of contemporary world cities is continually obscured by the suggestion that

---

63 Deer, 'The Ends of War', 2.
64 Peter Taylor, *World City Network: A Global Urban Analysis,* London: Routledge, 2004.
65 Deer, 'The Ends of War', 2.
66 Ibid., 1.

such cities, in these post-colonial times, are defined by their cosmopolitan and 'hybrid' mixing – a mixing viewed by such policy gurus as Richard Florida as a key competitive feature of the creative hubs, the 'foundries', of the 'knowledge-based economy'.[67] To define cities 'generically and one-sidedly as endogenous "engines of growth" and laboratories of cosmopolitanism', write Stefan Kipfer and Kanishka Goonewardena, 'is to ignore other formative aspects of urban history: economic and ecological parasitism, forms of socio-political exclusion (against non-city-zens as well as residents) and a dependence of commercial exchange on militarism, imperial expansion, and other forms of primitive accumulation'.[68]

COSMOPOLITANISM AND HOMELAND

Are fear and urbanism at war?[69]

The sixth and penultimate attribute of the new military urbanism is the way it is marked by intense contradictions between discourses stressing powerful disconnection and difference between US cities and those elsewhere, and those emphasizing the proliferation of connection, linkages and interdependences between these two groups of cities. Such contradictions are most evident in the world cities. In the most globalized and cosmopolitan of US cities, New York being the prime example, the notion of an ethno-nationalist homeland is utterly alien – an idea dredged up for the consumption of suburban or exurban Republicans, rather than one describing with any viability the social world of the contemporary city. And yet, as Roger Keil stresses, the United States is now a predominantly suburban nation, whose suburbs, 'although thoroughly urbanized are designed in such a way that any association with the city is avoided'.[70] For many Americans, Keil points out, 'the insight that the city is at the core of their circumferential world power was not immediately plausible before September 11, 2001.'[71] Moreover, suburban life is so powerfully idealized within US culture as being the authentic 'American way of life' that a sense of connection to the larger world is often noticeable by its absence. 'For

---

67 Richard Florida, *The Rise of the Creative Class,* New York: Basic Books, 2002.

68 Kipfer and Goonewardena, 'Colonization and the New Imperialism'.

69 Todd Swanstrom, 'Are Fear and Urbanism at War?', *Urban Affairs Review* 38, 2002, 135–40.

70 Keil, 'Empire and the Global City'.

71 Ibid.

many Americans', says Keil, 'the world, which constitutes their existence in a global economy of empire, remains outside of their experience'.[72]

The 'rebordered' discourse of 'homeland' is an attempt to construct a domesticated, singular, and spatially fixed imagined community of US nationhood.[73] Such an imaginary community – tied to some familial 'turf ' – valorizes a privileged national population of exurbanites and suburbanites, separated from racialized Others in both US cities and colonial frontiers. Despite the unavoidable, ongoing interconnections between US cities and more or less distant elsewheres, 'the rhetoric of "insides" needing protection from external threats in the form of international organizations is pervasive'.[74] Which is presumably why the relatively new US Department of Homeland Security sought to re-engineer information, transport, border and logistics systems with new control technologies so as to constantly monitor the multiple circuits linking US cities to those elsewhere.[75]

Amy Kaplan detected a 'decidedly anti-urban and anti-cosmopolitan ring' to this upsurge of nationalism after 9/11.[76] Even the very word 'homeland' itself, she suggests, invoked some 'inexorable connection to a place deeply rooted in the past'. Such language offered a 'folksy rural quality, which combined a German romantic notion of the folk with the heartland of America to resurrect the rural myth of American identity', while at the same time precluding 'an urban vision of America as multiple turfs with contested points of view and conflicting grounds upon which to stand'.[77] This kind of discourse was particularly problematic in global cities like New York, constituted as they are by massively complex constellations of diasporic social groups and tied intimately into the international (and interurban) divisions of labour that sustain capitalism today. 'In what sense', asks Kaplan, 'would New Yorkers refer to their city as the homeland? Home, yes, but homeland? Not likely.'[78]

Paul Gilroy goes further, proposing that the widespread invocation of 'homeland' by the Bush administration, following Huntington's extremely

72   Ibid.

73   Peter Andreas and Thomas Biersteker, *The Rebordering of North America.* New York: Routledge, 2003.

74   Simon Dalby 'A Critical Geopolitics of Global Governance', International Studies Association.

75   See Matt Hidek, 'Networked Security in the City: A Call to Action for Planners', *Planners Network*, 2007; Katja Franko, 'Analysing a World in Motion: Global Flows Meet "Criminology of the Other"', *Theoretical Criminology* 1: 2, 2007, 283–303

76   Amy Kaplan, 'Homeland Insecurities: Reflections on Language and Space', *Radical History Review* 85, 2003, 82–93.

77   Ibid.

78   Ibid.

influential image of a 'clash of civilizations', necessarily 'requires that cosmopolitan consciousness is ridiculed' in the pronouncements of the US state and the mainstream media.[79] In the 'Post 9/11' world he diagnosed a pervasive 'inability to conceptualize multicultural and postcolonial relations as anything other than ontological risk and ethnic jeopardy.'[80]

The 'hybrid' identities of many neighborhoods and communities in US cities, shaped by generations of transnational migration and diasporic mixing, have thus become problematized. Inevitably, such places and groups stretch across the resurgent 'them and us' and 'home and foreign' binaries. 'When "frontiers" (however reconstructed) and their surveillance become crucial aspects of a constituent passage', Lorenzo Veracini argues, 'diasporas – their composition, their sensibilities, their strategies, their politics, their histories – also become a strategic site for contestation.'[81] Domestic counterinsurgencies and internal colonial strategies invariably target the cosmopolitan urban districts in which diasporic communities and ethnic, post-colonial in-migrants concentrate. Sally Howell and Andrew Shryock call this domestic front of the War on Terror a 'cracking down on diaspora.'[82] It involves concentrated geographical profiling, increases in raids, extraordinary renditions, clamp-downs targeting undocumented workers, the mobilization of new counterterror powers to search and scrutinize everyday life, and widespread incarceration without trial. In the US, such strategies have particularly targeted Arab American neighbourhoods such as that of the city of Dearbon, Michigan, near Detroit.

City- and neighbourhood-level political concepts, of course, grate against the resurgent nationalism that is part and parcel of the new military urbanism. The events of 9/11 themselves underline conflicting ideas of how geographical territory links with political community in an urbanizing, globalizing world. At least a hundred nationalities were represented on the list of the dead that grim day, and many of those people were 'illegal' immigrants working in New York City. 'If it existed', as Jennifer Hyndman writes, 'any comfortable distinction between domestic and international, here and there, us and them, ceased to have meaning after that day.'[83]

79   Paul Gilroy, "Where Ignorant Armies Clash by Night": Homogeneous community and the planetary aspect', *International Journal of Cultural Studies* 6: 3, 2003, 266.

80   Ibid., 261.

81   Lorenzo Veracini, 'Colonialism Brought Home: On the Colonialization of the Metropolitan Space', *Borderlands* 4: 1, 2005.

82   Sally Howell and Andrew Shryock, 'Cracking Down on Diaspora: Arab Detroit and America's "War on Terror"', *Anthropological Quarterly* 76:3, 2003, 443–62.

83   Jennifer Hyndman, 'Beyond Either/Or: A Feminist Analysis of September 11th', *ACME: An International E-Journal for Critical Geographies*, February 2006.

'Global labor migration patterns . . . brought the world to lower Manhattan to service the corporate office blocks', writes Tim Watson. Those who died along with white-collar office workers that day – 'the dishwashers, messengers, coffee-cart vendors, and office cleaners' – were 'Mexican, Bangladeshi, Jamaican and Palestinian'.[84] Only in death, however, could such people gain visibility, fleeting though it was. To Watson, 'one of the tragedies of September 11, 2001, was that it took such an extraordinary event to reveal the everyday reality of life at the heart of the global city'.[85]

Posthumously, the dead of 9/11 were aggressively nationalized, re-emerging as heroic Americans whose deaths necessitated a global war orchestrated through Manichaean renderings of world geography. The transformation is ironic, to put it kindly, given that many would no doubt have been struggling as 'illegal aliens' to attain such nationalization during their lifetime. As Allen Feldman remarks, 'The World Trade Center, despite its transnational frame of reference, was [quickly] eulogized as a violated utopian space of Americanized capital, labor, and the inclusive production of wealth'.[86]

As for the devastating suicide bombings in London by so-called home-grown terrorists on 7 July 2005, the responses of Londoners were markedly different from those that of Prime Minister Tony Blair. The prime minister's immediate response to the atrocities, as Angharad Closs-Stevens suggests, 'was a characteristic affirmation of a British community-in-unity'. That affirmation 'worked very successfully [on the national level] in creating a binary logic between the "British people" [and] those people [who are trying] to cow us, to frighten us out of doing the things we want to do'.[87] Blair thereby managed to neutralize what could perhaps have been a massive political backlash against the UK's involvement in the Iraq war, an involvement that in Spain, by contrast, had resulted in the swift removal of the Aznar government after the terrorist bombings on Madrid's suburban trains on 11 March 2004.

London's then mayor, Ken Livingston, responded differently, however. Stressing the role of London as a pre-eminent cosmopolitan and diasporic hub, living within as well as beyond any simple notion of British national identity, Livingstone's message revolved around 'the idea of London as an urban,

---

84   Tim Watson, 'Introduction: Critical Infrastructures After 9/11', *Postcolonial Studies* 6, 109–11.

85   Ibid.

86   Allen Feldman, 'Securocratic Wars of Public Safety', 330–50.

87   Tony Blair, statement to the Press Association, 7 July 2005, quoted in Angharad Closs-Stephens, '7 million Londoners, 1 London': National and Urban Ideas of Community in the Aftermath of the 7th July Bombings', *Alternatives* 32: 2, 2007, 155–76.

multicultural community' and emphasized 'the principle of difference rather than unity'.[88]

Paul Gilroy has a similar criticism of the UK government's response to the London bombings, especially the instigation of a simplistic idea of Britishness and British unity. 'This wholesome alternative', he says, 'would supposedly offer immediate benefits in the form of popular national feeling akin to'[89] the civic patriotism manifested in the US. Gilroy worries that the proponents of such a tidy vision of Britishness 'turn willfully and . . . deceitfully away from the exhilarating cultural interaction common in cities like [London] which are not – not yet anyway – segregated according to the principles of the racial nomos which, as we saw in the aftermath of the New Orleans flood, is the silent, dominant partner of stubbornly colour-coded US political culture.'[90]

NEW STATE SPACES OF VIOLENCE

The fate of empires is very often sealed by the interaction of war and debt.[91]

Finally, the new military urbanism goes far beyond a concern with the technologies, doctrine, and military/security tactics needed for an attempt to control, pacificy or profit from demonized populations or spaces. It goes beyond the complex intersections of visual culture and military-control technologies, beyond the tensions between urban and national ideas of community. It uses the powers of the state to violent reconfigure or erase urban space, as a means to allay purported threats, to clear new space for the exigencies of global-city formation, neoliberal production, or the creation of an urban tabula rasa capable of generating maximally profitable bubbles of real-estate speculation. To justify such violent assaults, often against a (demonized and fictionalized) urban, racial or class enemy, it regularly resorts to invocations of exception and emergency. Such states of exception are declared not only to constitute the geographies of permanent violence that sustain the dominant economy but also to create what Achille Mbembe calls 'death worlds' – spaces such as Palestine, where vast populations are forced to exist as the living dead.[92] In this way, states of emergency support broader geographies of accumulation through

88 Close-Stephens, '7 Million Londoners, 1 London'.

89 Paul Gilroy, 'Multiculture in Times of War: An Inaugural Lecture Given at the London School of Economics', *Critical Quarterly* 48:4, 29.

90 Ibid.

91 John Gray, 'A Shattering Moment in America's Fall from Power', *Observer*, 28 October 2008.

92 Achille Mbembe, 'Necropolitics' *Public Culture* 15: 1, 2003, 11–40.

dispossession, which, while as old as colonialism, prove especially useful for neoliberal globalization.

Here we confront the complex political economies of the new military urbanism and their central integration into what Naomi Klein has diagnosed as the tendency within contemporary neoliberal capitalism to engineer and/or to profit from catastrophic 'natural' or political-economic shocks.[93] At issue is the character of what could be called the 'new state spaces' of war and violence, and their relation to political violence and contemporary geographies of dispossession.[94]

Citing the systematic Israeli bulldozing of homes and towns in Palestine, the similar erasure of Fallujah and other loci of Iraqi resistance, and the widespread erasure of informal settlements across the globe as city authorities entrepreneurially reorganize urban spaces, Kanishka Goonewardena and Stefan Kipfer point to 'an ominously normalised reality experienced by the "damned of the earth" after the "end of history"'. This, they argue, has summoned a new keyword in urban studies and allied disciplines: urbicide.[95]

Defined as political violence intentionally designed to erase or 'kill' cities, urbicide can involve the ethno-nationalist targeting of spaces of cosmopolitan mixing (as in the Balkans in the 1990s); the systematic devastation of the means of living a modern urban life (as with the de-electrification of Iraq in 1991, the siege of Gaza in 2006–8, or the attack on Lebanon in 2006)[96]; or the direct erasure of demonized people and places declared to be unmodern, barbarian, unclean, pathological, or sub-human (as with Robert Mugabe's bulldozing of hundreds of thousands of shanty dwellings on the edge of Harare in 2005).[97]

The wiping-out of people and places is an extremely common, though often overlooked, feature in urban areas of the global South, where political and economic elites seek to recast their spaces as 'global cities' – to transform them into 'the next Shanghai' and thus legitimize planning-as-erasure. Supermodern accoutrements – highways, malls, airports, office blocks, sports stadia, luxury condo complexes – are inevitably considered to be more suitable to global status than are the dilapidated, self-made, often 'illegal' shanty districts which house the urban poor. A recent survey by the United Nations found that

---

93 Naomi Klein, *The Shock Doctrine: The Rise of Disaster Capitalism*, London: Allen Lane, 2007.

94 The term 'new state spaces' comes from the pioneering book of that title by Neil Brenner, *New State Spaces: Urban Governance and the Rescaling of Statehood*, Oxford: Oxford University Press, 2004.

95 Goonewardena and Kipfer, 'Postcolonial Urbicide'.

96 See Chapter 9 and also Stephen Graham, 'Switching Cities Off: Urban Infrastructure and US Air Power', *City* 9: 2, 2005.

97 Kipfer and Goonewardena 'Colonization and the New Imperialism'.

between 2000 and 2002, a total of 6.7 million people in sixty countries were forcibly evicted from their informal settlements, compared with 4.2 million in the previous two years.[98] Frantz Fanon's words are as relevant as ever here: 'the business of obscuring language is a mask behind which stands the much bigger business of plunder'.[99]

To Goonewardena and Kipfer, the contemporary proliferation of urbicide reflects the shift to a world where the politics of the city are utterly central to the production and constitution of social relations. In a majority urban world, they write, 'the struggle for the city [now] coincides more and more with the struggle for a social order'.[100] With urbanization intensifying, this coincidence can only harden further.

As a consequence, architectural and urban theory emerge not only as a key element in efforts – whether imperial, neoliberal, corporate or military – to produce or reorganize urban space, but also in the resistances and countergeographies that arise in response to such interventions.[101] Strange appropriations take place here. Eyal Weizman, for instance, has shown how certain Israeli generals have appropriated the radical, post-structuralist writings of the French philosopher Gilles Deleuze to fashion new military doctrine for taking and controlling the labyrinthine spaces of Palestinian refugee camps.[102] Here, writes Weizman, 'contemporary urban warfare plays itself out within a constructed, real or imaginary architecture, and through the destruction, construction, reorganization, and subversion of space'.[103] By breaking through the linked walls of entire towns and thus creating paths, the Israeli military seeks to 'create operational "space as if it had no borders", neutralizing the advantages accorded by urban terrain to opponents of occupation'.[104]

Many of the new urban-warfare techniques used by state militaries – which Goonewardena and Kipfer label 'colonization without occupation' – are imitations of techniques of urban resistance used *against* state militaries in earlier centuries. 'This non-linear, poly-nucleated and anti-hierarchical strategy of combat in urban areas', they point out, 'in fact plagiarises the tactics of the defenders of the Paris Commune, Stalingrad and the Kasbahs of Algiers, Jenin and Nablus'.[105]

Techniques of urban militarism and urbicidal violence serve to discipline or

---

98   UN HABITAT, *State of the World Cities 2006/7*, Nairobi: United Nations, xi.
99   Frantz Fanon, *The Wretched of the Earth*, New York: Grove, 2004.
100 Goonewardena and Kipfer, 'Postcolonial Urbicide', 28.
101 See Chapter 11.
102 Eyal Weizman, *Hollow Land*, London: Verso, 2007.
103 Eyal Weizman, 'Lethal Theory', *LOG Magazine* April 2005, 74.
104 Goonewardena and Kipfer, 'Postcolonial Urbicide', 28.
105 Ibid., 29.

displace dissent and resistance. They erase or delegitimatize urban claims and spaces that stand in the way of increasingly predatory forms of urban planning[106] that clear the way for super-modern infrastructure, production centres, or enclaves for urban consumption and tourism.[107] Merging as it does into the authoritarian turn in criminology, penology and social policy, this new military urbanism seeks to control or incarcerate the unruly populations of the post-colonial metropolis, as in what have been termed the 'internal colonies' of the French *banlieues*.[108]

Beyond all this, though, the global processes of securitization, militarization, disinvestment and erasure provide sustenance to metropolitan economies. Cities are at the very centre of 'the military-industrial establishments of corporate capitalism, led by the US one, which produce "life-killing commodities" as the most profitable part of global trade'.[109]

Consider the assemblage of resurgent and strategic global cities through which capitalist accumulation increasingly operates. They organize and fix financial flows, shape uneven geographic development, and draw off surpluses towards dominant corporate sectors and globalized socio-economic elites which are closely integrated with national and international states. They dominate the production aspects of the military-industrial-security-surveillance complex and are fringed by 'garrison cities' whose economies are dominated by deployed militaries and private industrial corporations. With their stock markets, technopoles, arms fairs, high-tech clusters and state weapons labs, such cities are the brains sustaining the highly militarized globalization of our time.

The imperial military conflict that fuels capital accumulation through the global city system is increasingly based on new forms of 'primitive accumulation', reliant on high rates of return (especially for the petrochemical complex) which are stimulated by resource and oil wars, rather than on the use of military contracts to provide Keynesian stimulation to the economy, as was true in the late twentieth century.[110]

---

106 'Predatory planning' can be defined as 'the intended process of dispossession through aggressive, global-powered planning processes and use of multiple redevelopment tactics (building blocks), in the wake of existing trauma. The result is a traumatic stress reaction called root shock and the dismantling of our cultural commons'. Kiara Nagel, Design Studio for Social Intervention, available at ds4si.org/predatoryplanning.

107 A pivotal example here is the attempted reconstruction of New Orleans as a gentrified, tourist city whilst attempting to deny 250,000 African-Americans the rights to return to the city after Katrina.

108 Mustafa Dikeç, *Badlands of the Republic: Space, Politics and Urban Policy*, Oxford: Blackwell, 2007.

109 Méndez, 'Capitalism Means/Needs War'.

110 Shimshon Bichler and Jonathan Nitzan, 'Dominant Capital and the New Wars', *Journal of World-Systems Research* 10: 2, 2004, 255–327.

Contemporary city-building can thus be seen, argues Neil Smith, as an 'accumulation strategy in a far more intense way than at any previous moment. Militarization, massive reconstructive reinvestment and a supposed humanitarian agenda (bombs dropped alongside care packages on Kabul) all feed into this strategy of city building.'[111] In this way, military destruction and forcible appropriation can act as agents of rapid creative destruction. This in turn provides major opportunities for privatization, for gentrification, and for the appropriation of assets through global stock markets.

It follows that, in analyzing our 'colonial present', we face the challenge of simultaneously addressing the macro-political economies of what David Harvey calls 'accumulation by dispossession'[112] through economies of permanent war, and developing a sophisticated understanding of the everyday tactics and strategies of urban control and urbicide. There is thus a need to comprehensively reconsider the relationship between violence and the national/ transnational state system. Although beyond the scope of this book, such a re-theorization must address the ways in which shocks and crises are not only exploited but also manufactured for corporate exploitation. It must address the connections between the global diffusion of the US economic crisis – caused by unregulated financialization, hyper-indebtedness, and unsustainable balance-of-payments deficits – and the longer-term trajectories of the authoritarian and 'post-Fordist' geographies and political economies that nourish the new military urbanism.[113] Lastly, it must help explain the political-economic and cultural importance of hypermilitary ideologies of pre-emptive war, permanent mobilization, and anticipatory risk-management, which render everything a military problem requiring, a priori, a military solution.[114]

Ultimately, the seven interrelated elements of the new military urbanism – the disjuncture between rural soldiers and urban wars, the blurring of civilian and military control technologies, the treatment of attacks against cities as media events, the security surge, the militarization of movement, the

---

111 Neil Smith, 'The Military Planks of Capital Accumulation: An Interview with Neil Smith', Subtopia Blog, 10 July 2007.

112 David Harvey, *The New Imperialism*, Oxford: Oxford University Press, 2006.

113 For an insightful discussion, see George Steinmetz, 'The State of Emergency and the Revival of American Imperialism: Toward an Authoritarian Post-Fordism', *Public Culture* 15: 2, 2003, 323–45. Steinmetz argues that the 'emerging condition [following the global financial crisis and recession] does not mark a return to the Fordist–Keynesian welfare state but rather a transition toward and enhanced police state. Security in the disciplinary, not the social, sense in the focus of current government activity'.

114 See Jonathan Michel Feldman, 'From Warfare State to "Shadow State": Militarism, Economic Depletion, and Reconstruction', *Social Text*, 25, 2007, 143–68, and De Goede, 'Beyond Risk'.

contradictions between national and urban cultures of fear and community, and the political economies of the new state spaces of violence – are responsible for forging perhaps its greatest feature. That feature is the radical reorganization of the geography and experience of borders and boundaries. It encompasses a series of Foucauldian 'boomerang effects' which continually shift between the colonial metropole and the war-zone frontier – a process so central to the new military urbanism that it warrants a separate chapter, devoted to the emerging 'ubiquitous border'.

CHAPTER FOUR

Ubiquitous Borders[1]

National borders have ceased being continuous lines on the earth's surface and [have] become non-related sets of lines and points situated within each country.[2]

The act of targeting is an act of violence even before any shot is fired.[3]

How does one reconcile the proliferation of hard, militarized borders – not just within war-zones such as Baghdad or the West Bank, but between nations and within cities all over the world – with the sense that people and things everywhere on the planet are becoming ever more mobile? What, in other words, is the relation between the proliferation of transnational and urban circulations that surround globalization, and the parallel profusion of what Ronen Shamir calls 'closure, entrapment and containment'[4] in the contemporary world?

In this chapter I develop the argument that a major shift is underway regarding our world's borders – a shift that derives from transformations in the nature of nation-states. In our time, nation-states are moving away from their role as guarantors of a community of citizens within a territorial unit, charged with the policing of links between 'inside' and 'outside'. Instead, these states are becoming internationally organized systems geared towards trying to separate people and circulations deemed risky or malign from those deemed risk-free or worthy of protection. This process increasingly occurs both inside and outside territorial boundaries between nation-states, resulting in a blurring between international borders and urban/local borders. Indeed, the two increasingly seem to meld, to constitute a 'multiplicity of control points'[5] that become distributed along key lines of circulation and key geographies of wealth and power, crossing territorial lines between states as well as those within and beyond these boundaries.

---

1   This term was first used by Dean Wilson and Leanne Weber in their article 'Risk and Preemption on the Australian Border', *Surveillance & Society* 5: 2, 2008, 124–41.

2   Paul Andreu et. al, 'Borders and Borderers', *Architecture of the Borderlands*, London: Wiley/Architectural Design, 1997, 57–61.

3   Samuel Weber, *Targets of Opportunity: On the Militrization of Thinking*, New York: Fordham University Press, 2005, 105.

4   Ronen Shamir, 'Without Borders? Notes on Globalization as a Mobility Regime', *Sociological Theory* 23: 2, 2005, 199.

5   Karine Côté-Boucher, 'The Diffuse Border: Intelligence-Sharing, Control and Confinement along Canada's Smart Border', *Surveillance & Society* 5: 2, 2008, 153.

WESTPHALIAN BINARIES

The blurring of lines demarcating civilian law enforcement from military power, the inside from the outside of the nation, and peace from war is taking place because of a gradual unravelling of the so-called Westphalian order of the modern, liberal state. 'The promise of the traditional liberal state', write Didier Bigo and colleagues, 'was to preserve the liberal order inside, while the realm of the outside was thought to be condemned to be dominated by resolutely illiberal state practices.' With policing organized to preserve peace inside the nation, and war organized beyond it, 'what was normal within the national state borders was exceptional outside and vice versa.'[6]

Whilst each nation offers its own unique historical case, the imagined national 'we' of Western nationhood was widely naturalized and became fundamentally opposed to the imagined 'them' outside the nation's territorial limits. It became possible to construct a view of the world based on the naturalized binary of 'domestic' and 'foreign'.[7] All too easily, but not inevitably, such difference was translated into otherness. Those outside were often denigrated, while the ethnic, racial or cultural superiority of the national 'we' was asserted.

The Westphalian international order was thus based, on the one hand, on the notion that the external defence of nation-states required that military force be projected outside its borders against the figure of the enemy during times of war.[8] On the other hand, Westphalian states also followed the internal logic of policing; criminal law was mobilized internally to address culprits as well as actors considered threatening to the social order.[9]

SECUROCRATIC WAR

In practice, such efforts at separation have always been fragile, messy and contradictory. Now, however, the very notion of the inside/outside separation

---

6   Didier Bigo and Tsoukala Anastassia, 'Illiberal Practices of Liberal Regimes, the (In) Security Games', 14 November 2006, project information for the Sixth Framework Research Programme of DG Research (European Commission) on Liberty and Security, available at www.libertysecurity.org.

7   For the story of how this occurred in the US case, see David Campbell's *Writing Security: United States Foreign Policy and the Politics of Identity*, Minneapolis, MN: University of Minnesota Press, 1998. Campbell stresses that, in the case of the treatment of indigenous groups within colonial nations such as the US, 'foreignness' could also inhabit the geographical spaces within the nation.

8   Susanne Krasmann, 'The Enemy on the Border: Critique of a Programme in Favour of a Preventive State', *Punishment Society* 9, 2007, 301.

9   Ibid.

is being radically reimagined. The contemporary world is marked by 'a merging, a de-differentiation of the realm of the internal and the realm of the external', writes Bigo and Anastassia. 'The difference between the liberal and the illiberal, the norm and the exception, is no longer fixed by state borders. The limits between the internal and the external are moving.'[10] Ideas of national citizenship, rather than necessarily being merely opposed to the outside and foreign, are now increasingly being remade against others deemed to be outside or beyond citizenship, whether they lie inside or beyond the actual geographical borders of nation states. This reconfiguration in the nature of borders is being fuelled by what Allen Feldman calls 'securocratic wars'[11] – open-ended and de-territorialized wars (on drugs, crime, terror, illegal immigration, biological threats) organized around vague, all-encompassing notions of public safety rather than around territorial conquest. Their purpose is to maintain state sovereignty, not through external war combined with internal policing, but through raising the spectre of mobilities and flows deemed to contaminate societies and threaten the social order, both internally and externally. Unknown and unknowable, these dangers – terrorism, demographic infiltration, 'illegal' immigration, disease (SARS, bird flu, tuberculosis) – are understood to lurk within the interstices of urban and social life, blending invisibly with it.[12]

EVENTS AND NORMALITY

> The virtual border, whether it faces outward or inward to foreignness, is no longer a barrier structure but a shifting net, a flexible spatial pathogenesis that shifts round the globe and can move from the exteriority of the transnational frontier into the core of the securocratic state.[13]

At their root, open-ended, securocratic wars are an attempt to police both subnational and supranational dichotomies of safe and risky places, both within and beyond the territorial limits of nation-states.[14] An important component is the distinction between event and background. Thus, 'security events' emerge when 'improper or transgressive circulations'[15] seem to threaten the normalcy

---

10 Bigo and Anastassia, 'Illiberal Practices of Liberal Regimes, the (In)Security Games'.
11   Allen Feldman, 'Securocratic Wars of Public Safety', *Interventions: International Journal of Postcolonial Studies*, 6:3, 330–50.
12 Simon Jenkins, 'Oh! What a Lovely War on Terror', *Guardian*, 14 September 2007.
13 Feldman, 'Securocratic Wars of Public Safety'.
14 Ibid., 333.
15 Ibid.

of transnational capitalism. Such events range from incursions of pathogens,[16] terrorists, or migrant bodies to criminality, pirated commodities, hazardous wastes, malign financial transactions, dangerous computer code, or toxic ideology.

The figure of the terrorist looms large here because terrorists are seen to breed improper circulation of bodies, money, and drugs.[17] State discourses ensure the vague fusion of these malign presences and mobilities, and political opportunism ensures that counterterror legislation is applied to all manner of putative threats. In 2008, for example, in the thick of the global financial crisis, the UK government used recently minted counterterror legislation as the rationale for the seizure of Icelandic financial assets held in the UK.

At the same time, the global logistics, the tourism, the migration, and the continual flows of commodities and currencies that sustain neoliberal capitalism are rendered invisible, normal. These are the non-events of 'safe circulation' that link transnational archipelagos of risk-free spaces. 'The interruption of the moral economy of safe circulation is characterized as a dystopic "risk event",' suggests Feldman. 'Disruption of the imputed smooth functioning of the circulation apparatus in which nothing is meant to happen. "Normalcy" is the non-event, which in effect means the proper distribution of functions, the occupation of proper differential positions, and social profiles'.[18] Paradoxically, then, events which disrupt and destroy normal circulation – terrorist attacks, power outages, technical failures, pathogen alerts, worker strikes – serve to reveal the complex architectures of mobility, continually rendered invisible by their very normality.[19]

Securocratic wars assert the politics of the 'new normal', based on what Feldman calls the 'symbiosis of internalized fear and other-directed aggression'.[20] They recycle and update the demonization from the days of the Cold War and the long era of racialized colonization. Here, however, the 'Other ceases to be a colonial subject, a proletarian, a disenfranchised but struggling racial minority, a communist and re-appears as the drug dealer, the person living with AIDS, the illegal immigrant, the asylum seeker, and the terrorist'.[21]

---

16   See for example Harris Ali and Roger Keil, *Networked Disease,* Blackwell: Oxford, 2008.

17   Feldman, 'Securocratic Wars of Public Safety', 333.

18   Ibid.

19   See Chapter 9 and also Stephen Graham and Simon Marvin, eds., *Disrupted Cities: When Infrastructures Fail,* New York: Routledge, 2009.

20   Feldman, 'Securocratic Wars of Public Safety', 331.

21   Ibid.

Crucially, such wars invoke a linked series of vulnerable borders – of the body, the home, the neighbourhood, the city, the nation, cyberspace, the system of circulation – as being perilously transparent and facing unprecedented assault by a proliferating range of mobile incursions, threats or ruptures. This condition of vulnerability necessitates a culture of perpetual vigilance, anticipation and preparedness, as citizens are mobilized as citizen-soldiers to personally surveil their everyday landscapes, to be always on the look-out for the ever-elusive and ill-defined 'unusual'.[22] 'In an era of flexible warfare', suggest James Hay and Marc Andrejevic, 'everyone must be understood as both potential suspect and therefore, necessarily, proactive spy'.[23] Paranoia and neurosis are embedded into geography, with calls for the 'rebordering' of national limits;[24] the definition of 'illegal' immigrants as 'invaders';[25] the application of military-style command and control techniques to civilian flows; the fortification and 'hardening' of bodily, domestic, urban, infrastructural or national 'targets'.

All processes of surveillance, of course, are effective only when, as with the security event, they invoke an idea of normality against which the abnormal can occur. This is where ideas of securocratic war powerfully cross-fertilize with wider shifts in the logics of social surveillance, engendering an inclination towards the 'social-sorting' of people, places, and circulations. Databases captured in the past are continuously processed by computer algorithms to classify, profile, prioritize, exclude and anticipate the future. This is done for any number of reasons: to maximize profitability (withdrawing services from 'failed' or unprofitable consumers; profiling neighbourhoods as geo-demographic groups); to customize or personalize services (tailored amazon.com Web pages); to allow premium users to by-pass congestion (road-priced highways; differential call-centre queueing based on records of customers' profitability; the 'prioritized' switching of Internet packages); to support new means of individualized risk management.[26] Because these new trends of digitized

---

22 James Hay and Marc Andrejevic, 'Towards an Analytic of Government Experiments in these Times: Homeland Security as the New Social Security', *Cultural Studies* 20: 4–5, 2008, 341.

23 Ibid.

24 Engin Isin, ' The Neurotic Citizen', *Citizenship Studies* 8: 3, 2004, 217–35.

25 See Kathleen Arnold, 'Enemy Invaders! Mexican Immigrants and US Wars Against Them', *Borderlands* 6: 3, 2007.

26 See Stephen Graham, 'Software-Sorted Geographies', *Progress in Human Geography* 29: 5, 2005, 1–19.

consumption and tracking straddle the inside and the outside of the nation-state, they interlock with and facilitate broader shifts towards securocratic war.

AUTHORITARIAN RENEWAL

'Homeland security' is becoming the point of view through which the urban condition is framed, judged, analysed and consequently designed.[27]

As securocratic transformation proceeds, welfare states are simultaneously being re-engineered as risk-management systems, geared not towards the social welfare of communities but towards controlling the location, behaviour and future of seemingly risky 'anti-citizens'.[28] Phil Scraton terms this 'authoritarian renewal'.[29]

A priori incarcerations, bans, and a creeping mass criminalization begin to puncture already precarious legal norms of due process, habeas corpus, the right to protest, international humanitarian law and the human rights of citizenship. Increasingly, the always-fragile notions of homogenous national citizenship fray and disintegrate as different groups and ethnicities are pre-emptively profiled, screened, and treated differently. The rights of citizenship are disaggregated or 'unbundled'.[30] Law is deployed to suspend law, opening the door to more or less permanent 'states of exception' and emergency.[31] Systems of camps, militarized borders, and systems of illicit, invisible movement now straddle nations and supranational blocs. The resulting transnational archipelagos of incarceration, torture and death exhibit startling similarities to those that sustain global geographies of tourism, finance, production, logistics, military power and the lifestyles

---

27   Adrian Parr, 'One nation under surveillance', *Journal of Theoretical Humanities* 11: 1, 2006, 100.

28   Anne-Marie Singh, 'Private security and crime control', *Theoretical Criminology* 9: 2, 2005, 153–74; 2005. Jock Young, *Exclusive Society: Social Exclusion, Crime and Difference in Late Modernity*, London: Sage, 1999; see D. Meeks, 'Police Militarization in Urban Areas: The Obscure War Against the Underclass', *Black Scholar* 35: 4, 2003, 33–41

29   Phil Scraton, 'Streets of terror: Marginalisation, criminalisation and authoritarian renewal', Statewatch, 2006.

30   A good example here is the US effort to force the UK government to require British citizens of Pakistani origin to apply for visas to visit the US when this need is waived for all other UK citizens. See Jane Perlez, 'US Seeks Closing of Visa Loophole for Britons', *New York Times*, 2 May 2007. See also Seyla Benhabib, 'Disaggregation of Citizenship Rights', *Parallax* 11: 1, 2005, 10–18.

31   See Giorgio Agamben, *State of Exception*, Chicago: Chicago University Press, 2005.

of élites. The 'enemies within', the persons adjudged risky or worthless or out of place – the African-Americans of New Orleans, the troublesome inhabitants of Paris's *banlieues*, the Roma encamped in the suburbs of Naples or Rome, the *favela* dwellers on the edges of Rio's tourist hot spots, the undocumented immigrants, the beggars, the homeless, the street vendors everywhere – become increasingly disposable, assaulted, forcibly excluded.

Those who fail to sustain themselves within increasingly privatized and authoritarian systems become ever more demonized and their lives ever more precarious. 'The neoliberal climate is such that it has become an accepted urban policy not to solve the problems of the poor neighbourhoods and poor people but to annihilate those places through either sophisticated or brutal tactics', writes Guy Baeten.[32] 'Predatory planning' generates cycles of speculation, gentrification, rapid rent rises, and physical dispersal, subtle or unsubtle, all of which enable the attempted replacement of poor neighbourhoods by lucrative real estate, corporate, upscale or tourist zones.[33]

Thus the collective and mutualized risk-management strategies at the heart of the Keynesian welfare state are, in many cases, becoming undermined by the individualized culture of service allocation, pre-emptive risk assessment, and biographical tracking.[34] Utopian dreams of an inclusive welfare society metamorphose into the realities of an exclusive society based on punitive, pre-emptive control.[35] Drawing on right-wing anti-urbanism, a resurgent 'inner city Orientalism'[36] blames the pathologies of individuals or social classes within post-colonial metropoles for their own failures. Biometric and genomic technologies assist in projecting the future trajectory of individualized bodies,[37] while at the same time, prisons concern themselves less with reform and rehabilitation than with the simple warehousing or wholesale removal of entire subclasses of the risky.

---

32 Baeten, 'The Uses and Deprivations of the Neoliberal City', 48.

33 See Kiara Nagel, 'Predatory Planning', Design Studio for Social Intervention, available at ds4si.org/predatoryplanning.

34 See Rowland Atkinson and Gesa Helms, eds, *Securing an Urban Renaissance*, Bristol: Policy Press.2007.

35 Young, *Exclusive Society*.

36 Baeten, 'The Uses and Deprivations of the Neoliberal City', 49.

37 Nikolas Rose, 'The Biology of Culpability: Pathological Identity and Crime Control in a Biological Culture', *Theoretical Criminology* 4, 2000, 5–34.

MILITARY-POLICE

> While disciplinary power isolates and closes off territories, measures of security lead to an opening and globalization; while the law wants to prevent and prescribe, security wants to intervene in ongoing processes to direct them.[38]

As security politics centre on anticipation and profiling as means of separating risky from risk-free people and circulations inside and outside the territorial limits of nations, a complementary process is underway. Policing, civil law enforcement, and security services are melding into a loosely, and internationally, organized set of (para)militarized 'security forces'. A 'policization of the military' proceeds in parallel with the 'militarization of the police' (Figure 4.1).[39] Militaries increasingly deploy within domestic urban spaces, just as major urban police departments, such as New York's, construct global chains of offices in the major cities of other sovereign nations to address the transnational circulations.[40] 'High intensity policing' and 'low intensity warfare' threaten to merge, challenging historic legal constraints on the deployment of military force within Western nations.[41]

In the process, both the police and the state militaries increasingly gear up for the targeting of purported enemies and risks both within and without national territorial limits. In the absence of a uniform-wearing enemy, urban publics themselves become the prime enemy. The 'generalized figure of the enemy' thus 'effectively turns the outside inside', notes Susanne Krasmann.[42] Militarized policing and politicized military operations manage the boundaries surrounding complex archipelagos of privilege and power – where those who are risk free and in need of protection live, work and play – as well as enforcing the rules in emerging archipelagos of human disposal, warehousing and incarceration. A burgeoning array of private security and military organizations, geared largely to the perceived security needs of the powerful and wealthy groups – provide an added layer of securitized protection (Figure 4.2).

---

38   Agamben, 'Security and Terror', *Theory*, 1–2.

39   Feldman, 'Securocratic wars of public safety', 334.

40   Deborah Natsios, 'Watchlisting the Diaspora', paper presented at the Targeted Publics Conference, Centre for Contemporary Culture, Barcelona, 2–33 October 2008.

41   See Gilberto Rosas, 'The Thickening Borderlands: Diffused Exceptionality and "Immigrant" Social Struggles during the "War on Terror"', *Cultural Dynamics* 18: 3, 2006, 335–349.

42   Krasmann, 'The Enemy on the Border', 304.

4.1   Militarized police, 'policized' military: A Special Weapons and Tactics
(SWAT) training complex at Redwood City, California, and a US army 'non-
lethal' riot-control exercise at the Muscatatuck Urban Training Center, Indiana.

Country	Number of companies	Turnover (million €/y)	Private security employees	Police staff (1997)
Denmark	413	n/a	5,000	12,230
France	3,000	1,356	107,000	227,000
Germany	3,000	4,000	145,000	263,000
Greece	400	n/a	5,000	39,,350
Italy	800	1,100	45,000	279,000
Poland	6,000	n/a	200,000	102,000
Spain	990	2,367	90,000	180,000
Turkey	4,000	1,300	82,000	175,000
U.K.	2,000	1,300	220,000	185,000

Year	1970	1980	1990	1997	1998	2002	2005
Companies	325	542	835	2,065	2,100	3,000	3,000
Employees	47,400	61,700	105,000	121,329	138,000	145,000	200,000
Turnover, billion €	0.3	0.51	1.2	2.0	5.1	4.0	6.0

4.2   The burgeoning worlds of private security across Europe
(above) and a detailed picture from Germany (below).

As these developments proceed, deployment of the military within nations becomes much more common. Local, urban and international security agencies converge. Law enforcement practices become more militarized, with simulations of domestic 'urban warfare' and 'low intensity conflict', deployment of unmanned drones, SWAT teams, 'non-lethal weapons', and military satellite reconnaissance used to manage domestic cities. In Australia, for example, a 2006 policy review established 'domestic security' as the new 'core business' of the Australian armed forces. Special missions for the Australian army therefore now include 'special event security' (conventions, summits, sporting events) and responding to 'whole-city terrorism'.[43] In the US, meanwhile, municipal

---

43   Michael Head, 'Militarisation by Stealth', *Overland* 188, 2007, 68–70.

police have been asked by federal authorities to take increased responsibility for the enforcement of international immigration controls.[44]

At the same time, techniques of expeditionary warfare increasingly address policing-style challenges. Criminological theories are absorbed as armies employ anthropologists to explicate the cultural terrain of occupied cities. Finally, the militarized colonial presence must now pre-emptively distinguish the insurgent, the terrorist and the merely risky from the millions of non-risky or less risky people, when in fact the people are, to all intents and purposes, identical and indistinguishable.

CONTROL ARCHITECTURES

> As the policing function of the border is undermined or interrupted, a more general policing of the population must take place.[45]

Sustaining this complex blurring are a complex parallel set of architectures and controls that centre on check-points, walls and security zones, integrated with systems of computerized tracking and surveillance (biometrics, closed-circuit TV, data-mining, radio frequency chips, GPS). Thus, write Louise Amoore and colleagues, 'in addition to its traditional geophysical characteristics, the border has taken on virtual, de-territorialized attributes as well. Castles, walled cities, and extensive border battlements have been replaced by gated communities, expansive border zones, and management by "remote control".[46]

The point here is simple: if contemporary power in the cities of both 'homeland' and 'war zone' is about attempting to separate the spaces, zones, privileges and mobility of the risk-free (who need protection) from risky surrounding populations and infiltrations, then the only possible way to do this is pre-emptively, digitally and with a high degree of technological automation. As a result, militarized targeting becomes crucial, and the software algorithms that continually police the 'data-sphere' of machine-readable information, searching for potentially hazardous behaviours, circulations, people, or presences, assume political and sovereign power.

---

44 See Jennifer Ridgley, 'Cities of Refuge: Immigration Enforcement, Police, and the Insurgent Genealogies of Citizenship in US Sanctuary Cities', *Urban Geography* 29: 1, 2008, 53–77.

45 Elia Zureik and Mark Salter, 'Global Surveillance and Policing: Borders, Security, Identity', in Elia Zureik and Mark Salter, eds, *Global Surveillance and Policing: Borders, Security, Identity*, Cullompton, Devon: Willan Publishing, 2005, 4.

46 Louise Amoore, Stephen Marmura and Mark Salter, 'Editorial: Smart Borders and Mobilities: Spaces, Zones, Enclosures', *Surveillance & Society* 5: 2, 2008, 96.

This process 'reinscribe[s] the imaginative geography of the deviant, atypical, abnormal "other" *inside* the spaces of daily life', writes Amoore.[47] Here, in an intensification of the logic of militarized control, imagined enmity enters the code which drives computerized simulations of normality, threat, and securocratic war. Electronic systems blend sensors, databases and communications networks; they promise to be capable of being 'switched on and off to distinguish between friend and enemy'.[48] They cover the full gamut, from the automatic identification of 'risky' bodily movements on a subway platform, through unusual electronic transactions or patterns of Internet usage, to automated targeting systems in unmanned drones. In this way, security technologies introduced for a specific group, problem or purpose threaten to evolve into generalized, interoperable, multi-purpose systems.

JITTERY ENCLAVES

> The fortress . . . exists in two zones: a zone of physical actuality (walls and ramparts), as well as a zone of virtuality (concerned with the movements or flows of information and intelligence.[49]

Securocratic war involves the reconfiguration of sprawling cities, as increasing numbers of spaces within them are turned into camp-like environments supported by private security forces; hardened, impermeable or militarized boundaries; high-tech security systems and customized infrastructural connections to elsewhere. Urban geographies become increasingly polarized, and cities experience palpable militarization as secessionary elites strive to sequester themselves within fortified capsules.

Geographer Stephen Flusty has noted that urban enclaves, as he puts it, are becoming more 'jittery' and 'prickly'.[50] More inward-looking as well, they militarize the effort to draw and police their boundaries with the urban outside. It is made very clear to intruders judged as illegitimate that they must leave or face serious consequences.

---

47   Louise Amoore, 'Algorithmic War: Everyday Geographies of the War on Terror', *Antipode* (forthcoming).

48   Anne Bottomley and Nathan Moore, 'From Walls to Membranes', 178.

49   Ibid.

50   Steven Flusty, 'Building Paranoia', in Nan Ellin, ed., *Architecture of Fear*, Princeton: Princeton University Press, 1997, 47–59; Steven Flusty, *Building Paranoia: The Proliferation of Interdirectory Space and the Erosion of the Spatial Justice*, Los Angeles: Ram Distribution, 1994.

4.3   A Cruise ship anchored off the 'garrison tourism' resort of Labadee, Haiti, 2008.

Hard-edged urban enclaves, notable among the 'spatial products' of transnational neoliberalism, are difficult to miss nowadays. Foreign-trade and export-processing zones, established to entice corporations to use cheap, disciplined local labour for their manufacturing and logistics functions, increasingly operate as quasi-autonomous realms, bordered off from their host cities and nations.[51] Offshore financial enclaves, as well as the hypergentrified cores of key global cities such as London, present themselves as utopias for the super-rich. Enclaves of 'garrison tourism' emerge, surrounded by the razor-wire fences more typical of military bases, especially when located in developing nations dominated by mass immiseration, such as Haiti.[52] Projected giant cruise ships, such as the 'Freedom Ship', are marketed as veritable sea-borne cities. Replete with its own deck-top runways, shopping arcades, and even ice rinks, the Freedom Ship promises to provide the world's über-wealthy with the comforts of permanent yet mobile territorial secession (Figure 4.3).

---

51   See Keller Easterling, *Enduring Innocence*, Cambridge, MA: MIT Press, 2005.
52   Rory Carroll, 'Paradise and Razor Wire: Luxury Resort Helps Haiti Cling On to Tourist Trade' *Guardian,* 7 August 2008.

Even some open city cores are now being reorganized as patchworks of private business improvement districts (BIDs),[53] beholden to the agenda of local businesses and often equipped with their own security organizations. Geared towards improving the quality of life of more affluent consumers, these security enterprises are charged with the exclusion of persons who do not 'belong'. Taking the logic of 'malls without walls' still further, certain districts in city centres, such as Liverpool's Paradise St area, have now been completely privatized. Within the privatized urban streets, corporate owners may now stipulate rights of access and styles of security management more typical of purely commercial environments.

In the UK, for instance, the widespread equation of privatization with 'urban renaissance' or 'regeneration' in de-industrialized cities has led to the wholesale transfer of city streets and districts to corporations. In a survey of the trend, the *Guardian*'s Paul Kingsnorth finds that 'from parks to pedestrian streets, squares to market places, public spaces are being bought up and closed down, often with little consultation or publicity. Widening corporate ownership of public space means that legal norms now legitimize consumption whilst proscribing begging, homelessness, busking, skateboarding, cycling, and political activity.'[54]

Such trends are closely linked to the growth of 'zero-tolerance' urban policing. Security regimes centre on achieving 'controlled urbanity', which involves the removal, demonization or incarceration of failed consumers; the installation of new means of controlling access to space; and the establishment of key facilities for entrepreneurial urban leisure, tourism, and sports mega-events. Policing focus increasingly addresses 'quality of life' crimes – the behaviours and bodies seen to be out of place and transgressive within the polarizing geographies of highly unequal cities.

More than this, though, social policy, urban design, and policing contribute to what Jock Young has called a 'sociology of vindictiveness': an array of instruments designed to humiliate and demean through the stereotyping and scapegoating of failed bodies, failed communities, and transgressive social worlds.[55]

Thus, street furniture is redesigned as a means of inhibiting comfort for the homeless. Welfare supports are reduced to punish groups considered to be irresponsible, disrespectful, slothful, or unsightly. The punitive treatment of

---

53   See, for example, Kevin Ward '"Creating a Personality for Downtown": Business Improvement Districts In Milwaukee', *Urban Geography* 28:8, 2007, 781–808.

54   Paul Kingsnorth, 'Cities for Sale', *Guardian,* 29 March 2008.

55   Jock Young, *The Vertigo of Late Modernity*, Chapter 3.

'illegals' is justified by portraying them not as essential to successful Western economies but as invasive, criminal contagions that threaten a narrowly defined nationhood. In the process, juridical policing increasingly 'becomes a variation of counterinsurgency as crime is increasingly administered and contoured as a mode of clandestine economic circulation'.[56]

Such transformations lead the philosopher Gijs van Oenen to propose that the current period is marked by a shift away from the modern urban ideal of interactive citizenship towards what he calls an 'interpassive security-scape'. This, he suggests, is marked by an urban culture where 'the primary quest is not for encounter or confrontation, but for security'.[57] Van Oenen argues that this shift helps explain the proliferation of urban security guards, as citizens outsource 'the concern for civilized behaviour'.[58] The passivity should not be overstated, however: many state security initiatives, for example, now actively recruit the eyes of citizens to police the everyday spaces of cities for signs of the unusual.

Strategic financial commercial centres, meanwhile, are increasingly ringed with medieval-style city walls as well as security zones forged out of smart CCTV cameras, check-points, and roadblocks. As well as being reorganized through the installation of check-points, strategic city cores, such as Washington, DC and New York, have had their street furniture and landscape architecture redesigned as stealthy means of counterterror 'target hardening'[59] (Figure 4.4). Many embassy districts are being similarly redesigned. In actions reminiscent of the Cold War, the US government has also encouraged some of its key central-city office complexes to bunker down in remote 'edge cities'. In such places, Deborah Natsios worries, 'civil space is becoming coincident with state security space – a *threatscape*', which is to say a key domain of the multilayered informational battlespace of military control technologies and 'network-centric warfare'. The 'security accoutrements of bollards, barbed wire, blast-resistant and tinted glazing, closed-circuit cameras and confrontational signage' in exurban militarized complexes, she writes, are merely 'external clues of more covert technologies being deployed to manage the civilian milieu'.[60]

56 Feldman, 'Securocratic Wars of Public Safety', 335.
57 Gijs van Oenen, 'Languishing in Securityscape', *Open* 6, 2004, 7.
58 Ibid.
59 See Leonard Hopper and Martha Droge, *Security and Site Design*, New York: Wiley, 2005.
60 Deborah Natsios, 'Towards a New Blast Zone: Washington DC's Next Generation Hunting Forest', in *Architectures of Fear*, Barcelona: Centre de Cultura Contemporània de Barcelona, 2007.

a

b

c

4.4   Jeremy Nemeth's research on green zones and passage-point urbanism,
Manhattan-style. Images (a) and (b) show the situation in New York; map (c)
shows public spaces that have been limited or completely closed in and around the
burgeoning 'security zones' in the civil government district centring on City Hall
(pictured 4.4b) and the financial district centring on Wall Street (pictured 4.4a).

4.5   The entire base section of 7 World Trade Center – one of the skyscrapers constructed on the site of the destroyed World Trade Center – is made of a blast-proof concrete, which was later hidden by a colourfully lit screen.

Urban design thus becomes imbued with what Trevor Boddy has called 'an architecture of disassurance' as set-backs are increased, roads are closed, barriers and bollards are inserted around perimeters, and fountains and landscape features are designed to act as collapsable 'tiger traps' to intercept truck bombers.[61] In some highly visible cases, most notably the prolonged redevelopment of 'Ground Zero' in Lower Manhattan, entire lower portions of building designs are being rendered as massive concrete bunkers designed to accommodate blasts rather than people (Figure 4.5). 'For security reasons the design [of the 'Freedom Tower'] has been turned into nothing other than a bunker: a structure two hundred feet in height consisting of titanium and stainless steel', observes Angelaki Parr.[62]

61   Boddy use this phrase to highlight the contrast with the 'architecture of reassurance' long used in the planning of theme parks and themed urban spaces. See Martin Boddy, 'Architecture Emblematic: Hardened Sites and Softened Symbols', in Michael Sorkin, ed., *Indefensible Space: The Architecture of the National Security State*, New York: Routledge, 2007, 277–304.

62   Adrian Parr, 'One Nation Under Surveillance', *Journal of Theoretical Humanities*, 99–107.

4.6   A new gated community on England's South Coast

PASSAGE-POINT URBANISM

> The new bunker is a passage from one point to another.[63]

The hardening of urban enclaves, of course, did not commence on 12 September 2001. Such processes are long-established, have deep genealogies, and predate the War on Terror. As Barbara Hooper suggests, the sense of vertigo created by the economic, cultural and political restructuring of global cities has long 'produced a heightened concern over borders; a situation of struggle over spaces and meanings; a milieu of fear that manifests itself as nefarious racism and xenophobia' and in which certain bodies are marked as 'dangerous carriers of the disorder, incubators and contagions in the global epidemic of shrinking western power'.[64]

Such places are ripe for the proliferation of social architectures of urban

---

63   Paul Virilio and Sylvere Lotringer, *Pure War*, 2nd ed., Los Angeles: Semiotex(e), 2008, 210.

64   Barbara Hooper, 'Bodies, Cities, Texts: The Case of Citizen Rodney King', in Edward W. Soja, ed., *Postmetropolis: Critical Studies of Cities and Regions*, Oxford: Blackwell, 2000, 368.

secession. The past few decades have seen the spread of horizontally and vertically gated communities, in particular; their growth has been especially rapid in cities marked by hyperinequality and by middle- and upper-income anxieties about open streets. In the US, for example, more than half of the new housing within parts of the South and West is now built within gated, master-planned communities.[65] In cities such as São Paulo, Manila, Bogotá and Jakarta, elites have long clustered within heavily militarized enclaves, linked by armadas of bullet-proof cars and, in the case of São Paulo, by the ultimate form of urban secession: more than seventy thousand helicopter flights a year within the central city.[66] Gated communities are also proliferating in the UK (Figure 4.6). In post-apartheid South Africa, meanwhile, as crime and the fear of crime have grown, the architectures of street closures and neighbourhood gating have emerged from within the dismantled large-scale systems of apartheid segregation[67] (Figure 4.7).

Such architectures operate 'in the false hope of creating rigidity and secure difference'[68] within the volatilities and polarizations of contemporary city life. They are the materialization of othering: As ever more capsular and lavish domestic spaces, with their mythic allure of certainty, homogeneity, order and control, are constructed, they are being surrounded by configurations of attempted withdrawal from the risky, racialized, and often poverty-stricken open city. Gated communities thus embody ideas of securocratic war just as powerfully as does the militarization of international boundaries. But they operate at a different, and complementary, scale. Both architectures of exclusion, in Vincenzo Ruggiero's words, 'associate elsewhere with that which is contaminated, filthy, offensive to morality and olfaction'.[69]

Indeed, the withdrawal into increasingly defended homes, gated enclaves and interiorized lives seems closely linked to the marshalling of explicitly militarized means of managing the wider public realms of the city. Rowland Atkinson and Sarah Blandy point to the mounting 'agoraphobia of the contemporary urban subject and the need to find shells to inhabit in order that security, the life of the household and the project of self are more fully assured'.[70] They also suggest

65 See Setha M. Low, *Behind the Gates: Life, Security, and the Pursuit of Happiness*, New York: Routledge, 2003.

66 Tom Phillips, 'High above São Paulo's Choked Streets, the Rich Cruise a New Highway', *Guardian*, 20 June 2008.

67 Claire Bénit-Gbaffou, 'Unbundled Security Services and Urban Fragmentation in Post-Apartheid Johannesburg', *Geoforum* 39: 6, 2008.

68 Jock Young, *The Vertigo of Late Modernity*, 5.

69 Vincenzo Ruggiero, *Crime and Markets: Essays in Anti-Criminology*, Oxford: Oxford University Press, 2000, 1.

70 Rowland Atkinson and Blandy, 'The City, Public Space and Home: The Nesting of Scales of Security and Strategies of Defensive Social Engagement', unpublished paper.

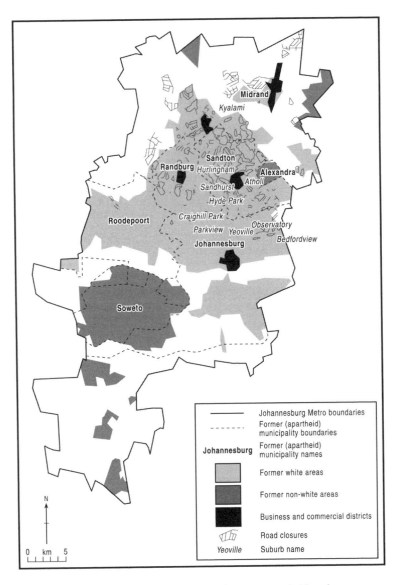

Midrand

Kyalami

Sandton

Randburg   Hurlingham   Atholl   Alexandra

Sandhurst

Hyde Park

Roodepoort   Craighill Park

Parkview   Yeoville   Observatory

Johannesburg   Bedfordview

Soweto

N

0   km   5

	Johannesburg Metro boundaries
	Former (apartheid) municipality boundaries
Johannesburg	Former (apartheid) municipality names
	Former white areas
	Former non-white areas
	Business and commercial districts
	Road closures
Yeoville	Suburb name

4.7   Claire Bénit-Gbaffou's research on post-apartheid road
closures organized by middle and upper classes in post-apartheid
Johannesburg as a response to the spiralling fear of crime.

that residents of gated enclaves within hyper-unequal societies routinely use extralegal force against people seen as transgressing their boundaries. The result is a kind of social, civil war to control domestic space, which becomes integrated into the social routines of households.[71]

FLOATING COLONIES, GLOBAL GULAGS

> Abu Ghraib, Guantánamo and other US military prisons mark the kind of penal expansion that takes place in the context of wars with no end: wars on drugs, crime and terror.[72]

Not to be forgotten, above and beyond the proliferation of fortressed or jittery urban enclaves, are the archipelagoes of incarceration – surrounded by the ultimate in urban boundaries – that are also growing at a remarkable rate worldwide. This proliferation of prisons is taking place as increasingly punitive and authoritarian policing and legal systems not only criminalize but altogether remove larger segments of undesirable groups. As post-colonial diasporas have brought the colonial 'exterior' to the metropolitan 'interior', zones of intensifying urban poverty have often failed to sustain normal markets in services, housing and labour, permitting places like the French *banlieues* to, in Alain Joxe's words, 'become purely military marches again.'[73]

Militarized control, of course, also encompasses penal incarceration. In many nations, heavy prison sentences are now imposed for petty crimes, quality-of-life incursions, protests and simple poverty. Whole swathes of the urban population are being criminalized and incarcerated to protect the rest of the public from their predicted future behaviour.[74] Indeed, as Zygmunt Bauman argues, rather than being organized for social rehabilitation, confinement now increasingly serves as '*an alternative to employment*; a way to dispose of, or to neutralize a considerable chunk of the population who are not needed as producers'.[75]

The most neoliberalized and hyperunequal societies are now reaching a stage which Jonathan Simon labels 'hyper-incarceration'.[76] In the United States

---

71 Rowland Atkinson and Sarah Blandy, *Domestic Fortress*, forthcoming.

72 Michelle Brown, '"Setting the Conditions" for Abu Ghraib: The Prison Nation Abroad', *American Quarterly* 57: 3, 2005, 990.

73 Alaine Joxe, *Empire of Disorder*, Los Angeles: Semiotext(e), 2002, 197.

74 David Rose, 'Locked Up to Make Us Feel Better', *New Statesman*, 19 March 2007.

75 Zygmunt Bauman, *Globalization: The Human Consequences*, Cambridge: Polity, 1998, 111–2 (italics in original).

76 Jonathan Simon, 'The "Society of Captives" in the Era of Hyper-Incarceration', *Theoretical Criminology* 4: 3, 2000, 285–308.

– perhaps the most extreme example – more than 2.3 million overwhelmingly poor people were incarcerated within a burgeoning gulag of corrections facilities by 2008, sustaining a booming privatized prison industrial complex (Figure 4.8).[77] This represents a near 1,000 per cent growth since 1950. With 5 per cent of the world's population, in 2004–5 the US had fully 24 per cent of its prisoners. More than a million of these inmates were black.[78] Whilst more than 1 in 100 US adults were behind bars in 2008, fully one in nine US black men between 20 and 34 were incarcerated.[79]

In many ways, the trend towards hyperincarceration in the US can best be understood as a process of state warfare *within* the US homeland. This war targets entire racial and social classes and their urban districts; meanwhile, the nation becomes an unsurpassed 'penal democracy'.[80]

Here we have another powerful example of a Foucauldian boomerang effect. For the explosion of incarceration within the US is paralleled by the construction of a global system of extraordinary rendition, incarceration and torture of Others, with both systems using similar techniques,[81] private security corporations, means of abuse,[82] and legal suspensions. This 'American archipelago', Brady Thomas Heiner suggests, works as both matrix and circuit. 'It is a circuit insofar as its carceral techniques and modes of governance are generated, normalized, and refined', he writes, and it is organized 'within a colonial feedback-loop that circulates among the US's colonial "black sites" both domestic and foreign'.[83]

Increasingly, then, US colonial interiors and exteriors are mutually organized. In a neglected dynamic of globalization, they blur into a transnational archipelago of subjugation which combines what Heiner calls the 'macro-geographical' and 'micro-architectural' aspects of military urbanism. 'Having been deployed for the purpose of colonizing the US's racialized interior and refined by the prison

77   N.C. Aizenman, 'New High in US Prison Numbers: Growth Attributed to More Stringent Sentencing Laws,' *Washington Post*, 29 February 2008.

78   Brady Thomas Heiner, 'The American Archipelago: The Global Circuit Of Carcerality And Torture', in Gary Backhaus and John Murungi, eds, *Colonial and Global Interfacings: Imperial Hegemonies and Democratizing Resistances*, Newcastle: Cambridge Scholars Publishing, 2007, 99.

79   Aizenman, 'New High In US Prison Numbers'.

80   Joy James, ed., *Warfare in the American Homeland: Policing and Prison in a Penal Democracy*, Durham, NC: Duke University Press, 2007.

81   Michelle Brown, for example, argues that 'the institutional similarities between Abu Ghraib and the rise of the 'supermax' prison in the United States marks a particularly dangerous pattern in the exportation of punishment'. Brown, '"Setting the Conditions" for Abu Ghraib', 997.

82   See Hazel Trice Edney, 'Experts Say US Prisoners Are Subjected to Iraqi-Style Abuse', *The Wilmington Journal*, 8 June 2004.

83   Heiner, 'The American Archipelago', 84.

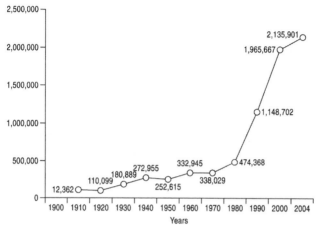

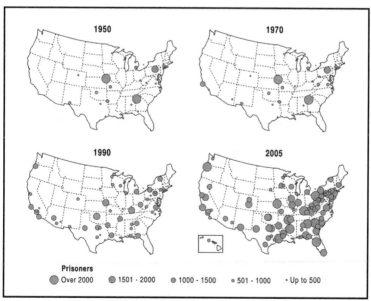

Prisoners
● Over 2000 ● 1501 - 2000 ● 1000 - 1500 ● 501 - 1000 • Up to 500

4.8   Population incarcerated in US federal jails, 1910–2004 (top) and the geographic proliferation of such prisons between 1950 and 2005 (bottom).

industrial complex', he writes, 'the techniques of carcerality and torture are now being systematically redeployed abroad by the US military and outsourced mercenary regime to colonize its racialized populations overseas'.[84]

Judith Butler calls this complex the new war prison.[85] The first four years of the War on Terror saw more than eighty thousand people around the world detained without trial by the US.[86] By March 2007, the numbers of civilians detained without trial in Iraq by US forces stood at more than seventeen thousand.[87] By September of that year, following the US military's Baghdad 'surge', the figure had grown to 23,508. A further 21,327 Iraqis were incarcerated by Iraqi security forces. Even these totals were expected to grow significantly.[88]

Brady Thomas Heiner argues that the construction of such a transnational US war prison has the effect of clearing the path for American capital investment abroad and neutralizing the resistance waged in other lands against evolving US colonial governance.[89] Indeed, Amy Kaplan, in response to the revelations of systematic torture at Abu Ghraib and Guantánamo Bay, foresees a future dominated by a normalized 'floating colony' where homeland security 'will increasingly depend on proliferating these mobile, ambiguous spaces between the domestic and the foreign'.[90]

Meanwhile, in the expanding cities of the global South, securocratic warfare is often being launched against informal settlements, which are commonly demolished, erased, or surrounded by militarized borders because of the threat they seem to pose to the body politic, or to public health, or to achieving the city's goal of being regarded as global, high-tech, modern or attractive to the wider world.[91] As Loïc Wacquant points out, regarding state violence against the *favelas* of Rio or São Paulo, many states are resorting to a strategy of 'punitive containment' towards informal cities – 'the management of dispossessed and dishonored populations in the polarizing city in the age of triumphant neoliberalism'.[92]

---

84   Ibid.

85   Judith Butler, *Precarious Life*, London: Verso, 2004, 53.

86   Suzanne Goldenberg, 'More than 80,000 Held by US since 9/11 Attacks in Washington', *Guardian*, 18 November 2005.

87   Walter Pincus, 'US Expects Iraq Prison Growth Crackdown Likely to Mean More Inmates at 2 Detention Centers', *Washington Post*, 14 March 2007.

88   Gregory, 'The Rush to the Intimate', 2008.

89   Heiner, 'The American Archipelago', 85.

90   Amy Kaplan, 'Violent Belongings and the Question of Empire Today: Presidential Address to the American Studies Association, Hartford, Connecticut, October 17, 2003', *American Quarterly* 56: 1, 2004, 14.

91   Stephen Graham, 'Postmortem City: Towards a New Urban Geopolitics', *City* 8: 2, 2004.

92   Loïc Wacquant, 'The Militarization of Urban Marginality', 56.

To Wacquant, Brazilian cities, especially, serve as a 'historical revelator of the full consequences of the penal disposal of the human detritus of a society swamped by social and physical insecurity.' He argues that as 'proving grounds' for the neoliberal state, moreover, Brazil's favelas, African-American ghettos, the French banlieues, and other sites for the disposal or warehousing of capitalism's surplus humanity are the places where exemplars for securocratic warfare are 'concretely being assembled, tried, and tested.'[93] Naomi Klein has argued that Israel's experiments in incarcerating the entire population of Gaza and the West Bank serve a similar role.[94] In the Indian city of Chandigarh as well, residents of the slums must now 'furnish details of their fingerprints, photographs, face recognition, voice recognition, signature, shape of the hand' for a biometric ID system which will not cover the rest of the city's population.[95]

In extreme cases, paramilitary forces mobilized for internal securocratic wars attempt to impose new internal biopolitical borders based on denying racialized minorities the rights of citizenship or international humanitarian law.[96] The resulting intraterritorial states of exception are exemplified by a lengthening list of examples, of which the systematic ignoring of New Orleans' poor, disposable African-Americans in 2005 is perhaps the most startling.[97] The crack-down on residents of Paris's banlieues entering central Paris since the major 2005 riots is another telling example, marked by a widespread discourse of 'barbarians' now being within the gates, not just of the city, but of the iconic city of Western modernity.[98] A third relevant example is the use of Israeli-style shoot-to-kill tactics to enforce the new internal border politics, which resulted in the killing of Jean Charles de Menezes in a London tube station on 22 July 2005.[99] Finally, within Italy, the mobilization, registration, and attempted erasure of Gypsy and Romany individuals and their camps by the post-2008 Berlusconi government reveal the risk of neo-fascist takeovers in liberal democracies in the early twenty-first century.[100]

---

93   Ibid.

94   Klein, *Shock Doctrine*.

95   'Biometric Test: Residents Stage Demonstration', *Times* (India) 30 March 2006.

96   See Georgio Agamben, *Homo Sacer: Sovereign Power and Bare Life*, Stanford: Stanford University Press, 1998.

97   Giroux, 'Reading Hurricane Katrina', *College Literature* 33: 3, 2006, 172.

98   Jason Burke, 'Bustling Gateway to Paris Becomes the Brutal Frontline in a Turf War', *Observer*, 20 April 2008.

99   Nick Vaughan-Williams, 'The Shooting of Jean Charles de Menezes: New Border Politics?', *Alternatives* 32, 2007, 177–195.

100   See Seumas Milne, 'This Persecution of Gypsies Is Now the Shame of Europe', *Guardian*, 10 July 2008.

FACES OF TERROR

In practices that mimic the techniques of urban counterinsurgency on the streets of Baghdad, entire city districts and infrastructure systems are now subject to remote, visual electronic scrutiny. As the exemplar of the new 'surveillance society', the UK has been pushing the limits, most notoriously through the spread of advanced CCTV systems. Whilst public CCTV systems are rapidly being installed across the world's cities, they cover UK cities more intensively than those of any other nation. To function, the four and a half million CCTV cameras currently installed in the UK rely overwhelmingly on the discretion of human operators. Substantial evidence of their ineffectiveness, combined with their extraordinary cost,[101] has not kept such systems from being marketed as friendly 'eyes in the sky', warding off the myriad threats of British urban life. Despite the fact that these cameras were obviously powerless to stop suicide bombers from committing the atrocities on London's transport systems on 7 July 2005, this projection of ostensibly benign (and almost divine) scrutiny beneath a myriad of electronic eyes has actually intensified during the War on Terror (Figure 4.9).

Following early experiments with face-recognition software in Newham, Birmingham, Tameside, Manchester, and elsewhere, a shift to digital CCTV, which uses computer algorithms to do automated searches for stipulated people or behaviours, has been gaining momentum. This shift again exemplifies the boomerang effect, as it parallels experiments with face recognition and smart CCTV to pacify urban insurgencies in Iraq (see the discussion of 'Combat Zones That See' initiative in Chapter 6, p. 164).[102]

---

101   See, for example, Stephanie Leman-Langlois, 'The Myopic Panopticon: The Social Consequences of Policing Through the Lens, *Policing and Society* 13:1, 2002, 43–58, and *The Nacro Report On CCTV Effectiveness*, 1999, available at www.crimereduction.homeoffice.gov. uk/cctv, and Kate Painter and Nick Tilley, eds., *Surveillance of Public Space: CCTV, Street Lighting and Crime Prevention,* Crime Prevention Studies vol. 10., New York: Criminal Justice Press, 1999.

102   The Pentagon's Next Generation Face Recognition (NGFR) programmes are also attempting to develop systems which would work on open city streets or 'unstructured environments' using advances in what the Defense Advanced Research Projects Agency (DARPA) labels 'three-dimensional imagery and processing techniques, expression analysis, and face recognition from infrared and multi-spectral imagery.' The aim here is to produce face recognition systems that are robust to time differences between facial imagery (aging) and variations in pose, illumination, and expression. Both US special forces and DARPA, for example, are developing three-dimensional face recognition CCTV systems, designed for application in open city streets rather than the 'passage points' in airports. Potential Foucauldian boomerangs, these might ultimately be employed 'by the military, law enforcement and the commercial market sector.' All quotes from SITIS Archive, '3-D Facial Imaging System', available at www.dodsbir.net.

4.9 'Secure Beneath Watchful Eyes': London Transport's 2006 ad campaign.

Although major technical obstacles still prevent face-recognition CCTV systems from operating effectively outdoors on city streets, considerable research and development is being done to address the problems – part of a much broader exploration, often funded with support from the US/UK War on Terror, of the use of 'smart' CCTV systems to track millions of people in both time and space. In industry parlance, this is called 'multi-scale spatiotemporal tracking' based on 'intelligent video analytics'.[103]

This advanced tracking depends on linking 'islands' of first-generation CCTV into extensive, integrated systems and employing computer algorithms to search 24/7 for behaviours, movements, objects and people categorized as risky or deviant. Computers, not camera operators, do the actual watching. When such a system recognizes a human figure in a given location, for instance, it can build up an assessment over time of the 'normal' activities of people at that location. A behaviour or event that is 'unusual' or 'abnormal' at that location, such as the arrival of a cyclist in an automobile dominated parking space, would then be automatically identified and targeted as a potential threat.

Since September 2001, industry groups and lobbyists have widely claimed that 'if our [face-recognition] technology had been deployed [in US airports on 9/11], the likelihood is [the terrorists] would have been recognized'.[104] As a consequence, facial recognition CCTV has quickly colonized easily surveilled passage-points, especially airport passport and security controls and high-profile sporting events. This technology, the lobbyists promise, will 'truthfully' track malign individuals, remotely and in real time, overcoming their efforts at disguise. One report by Visionics, a leading manufacturer, promised that its face-recognition technologies would do no less than 'Protect . . . Civilization from the Faces of Terror'.[105] Seduced by such hyperbole, Interpol announced in October 2008 that it was seeking to develop an international face-recognition CCTV system to integrate screening across main borders.[106]

The dramatically intensified investment and research in face-recognition CCTV after 9/11 has exploited perfectly the notion of what Kelly Gates calls an 'amorphous, racialized, and fetishized enemy Other that had penetrated

103 See Arun Hampapur, Lisa Brown, Jonathan Connell, Ahmet Ekin, Norman Haas, Max Lu, Hans Merkl, Sharath Pankanti, Andrew Senior, Chiao-Fe Shu, and Ying Li Tian], 'Smart Video Surveillance', *IEEE Signal Processing Magazine*, March 2005, 38–51.

104 Tom Colasti, chief executive of Visage Technology cited in Kelly Gates, 'Identifying the 9/11 "Faces Of Terror"', *Cultural Studies* 20: 4, 424.

105 Ibid. 426

106 Owen Bowcott, 'Interpol Wants Facial Recognition Database to Catch Suspects', *Guardian*, 20 October 2008.

both the national territory and the national imagination'.[107] The race is on to develop systems appropriate to the 'nation's new "unidentifiable" Other' – people of 'Middle Eastern appearance'.[108] The technophilic search for an extended, distributed system for tracking the biometrically scanned faces of suspect individuals thus parallels the idea, propagated through the moral panic flooding the national media, 'that certain faces could be inherently "faces of terror" – that individuals embody terror or evil in their faces'. This, Gates argues, could 'not help but invoke a paranoid discourse of racialized otherness'.[109]

The prospect of 'smart' CCTV continually searching for 'abnormal' or 'threatening' elements across entire cities and nations may ultimately prefigure the collapse of the age-old notion of urban anonymity. If the many technical difficulties that currently limit the use of such technologies are successfully addressed, security and law enforcement personnel may soon be able, remotely and covertly, to identify individuals via databases and continuously track them no matter where they go. To Phil Agre, a shift to widescale social tracking using face-recognition CCTV would usher in a 'tremendous change in our society's conception of the human person': people, he suggests, 'would find strangers addressing them by name'[110] during previously anonymous encounters in city streets and commercial spaces.

Predictably, authoritarian regimes such as China's are rapidly exploiting these new technologies. The Chinese state's Golden Shield plan envisages centralized facial-image databases of the nation's 1.5 billion people linked to integrated CCTV tracking systems that cover all the major cities. Shenzen alone, with its approximately ten million people, is likely to have two million cameras.[111] The UK government, too, is straining at the leash. Already a UK Home Office report has called for research to 'establish the police requirement and business case for a facial images national database'[112] that would link with equivalent databases of iris, DNA and fingerprint information and would build on the existing database of biometric passport images. With DNA testing already mobilized in cases of minor misdemeanours in the UK (Figure 4.10), the clear concern is that a comprehensive, national biometric database can become a medium through which both securocratic war and authoritarian renewal will operate.

---

107 Gates, 'Identifying the 9/11 "Faces Of Terror"', 424, 434.

108 Ibid., 424, 436.

109 Ibid., 424.

110 Phil Agre, 'Your Face Is Not a Bar Code: Arguments Against Automatic Face Recognition in Public Places', *Whole Earth* 106, 2001, 74–77.

111 Naomi Klein, 'Police State 2.0', *Guardian*, 3 June 2008.

112 Cited in Ian Brown, *Privacy & Law Enforcement*, report for the UK Information Commissioner Study Project, 2007.

4.10   Notice announcing the use of DNA testing to deter anti-social behaviour on public transport in Sheffield, UK.

URBAN 'POLITICAL EQUATORS'

The trend towards the biometric bordering of cities tends to be most advanced where international borders between rich and poor countries cut through and constitute urban complexes. These present paradigmatic instances of securocratic war, because the dense interdependencies of city life are continually in tension with racialized othering and the hardening of boundaries between privilege and poverty.

The mutually dependent urban complex of San Diego–Tijuana, for example, is bisected by the rapidly militarizing US–Mexico border. This follows what Teddy Cruz calls the 'political equator' (Figure 4.11, top) separating global North and global South. Here, however, it acts as an architectural feature of a fast-growing metropolis rather than as a geopolitical abstraction (Figure 4.11, bottom). This urban-national-global border is currently being wired with a '"virtual fence" consisting of an array of sensors, motion detectors, infrared cameras, watchtowers and drone planes' supplied by Boeing and the Israeli defence company Elvit.[113]

The urbanizing edges of 'fortress Europe' display similar architectures of attempted control. The Red Cross estimated in 2007 that between two thousand and three thousand Africans drown each year trying to cross from Africa to mainland Spain and the Canary Islands.[114] Given such figures, it is hardly surprising that critics label the militarizing frontiers along the world's North-South political equator 'invisible walls of death'.[115] As Ben Hayes and Roche Tasse write, 'The EU is now "defended" from those fleeing poverty and destruction by a formidable apparatus that includes landmines placed along the Greek-Turkish border, gunboats and military aircraft patrolling the Mediterranean and the coast of West Africa, and trigger-happy border guards and barbed wire fences around the Spanish enclaves of Ceuta and Melilla in Morocco.'[116] Added to this, unmanned drones are now being deployed through a consortium led by Dassault Aviation, Europe's largest manufacturer of combat aircraft, to target the bodies of 'illegal immigrants'.[117]

113   Ben Hayes and Roche Tasse, 'Control Freaks: "Homeland Security" and "Interoperability"', *Different Takes* 45, 2007, 2.

114   Graham Keeley, 'Grim Toll of African Refugees Mounts on Spanish Beaches', *Observer*, 13 July 2008.

115   Sebastian Cobarrubias, et al., 'Delete the Border! New Mapping Projects, Activist Art Movements, and the Reworking of the Euro-Border', paper given at the Association of American Geographers' Congress, Chicago, 2006.

116   Hayes and Tasse, 'Control Freaks'.

117   Ibid.

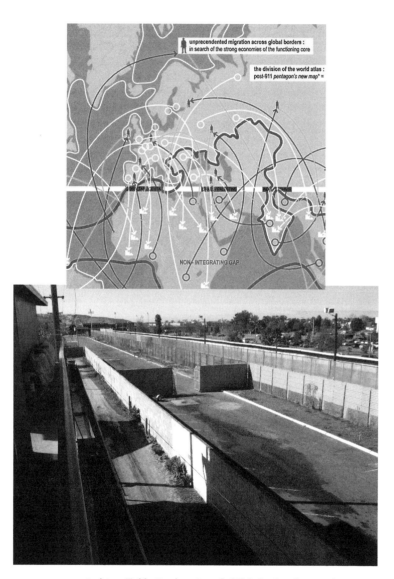

4.11   Architect Teddy Cruz's notion of a 'Global political equator'
(top), and its architectural manifestation on the rapidly militarizing
San Diego–Tijuana border (bottom, the San Ysidro checkpoint).

'POP UP ARMIES,' MOBILE GREEN ZONES

Walling, cordoning and pre-emptive incarceration reach further extremes during the 'states of emergency' that now hold sway when political summits, global sports events, and high-profile spectacles take place. Here, mimicking the 'rings of steel' around financial cores like the City of London, security strategies turn open city districts into temporary, mobile 'security islands' replete with paramilitary forces, militarized cordons, and even surface-to-air missiles[118] – reminiscent of Baghdad's militarized 'Green Zone', carved out to help protect occupying forces and Western journalists from the spiraling violence outside.

Iconic examples of these mobile green zones include the 'Battle of Seattle' in 1999, the Genoa confrontations in 2001, and the uprisings at the World Economic Forum in Cancún in 2003 (Figure 4.12). Such cases demonstrate the use of militarized tactics of command and control to organize the tightly defined geographies of what Steve Herbert has called the 'protest zoning state',[119] where 'the expression of dissent at major events is controlled with a territorial strategy: it is banned from some areas and confined to others'. Special zones are established – zones of 'restricted access' and 'no protest' (Figure 4.13). Militarized police cordons, often supplemented with pre-emptive detentions and bans on the right to protest, try – often violently – to confine protestors for long periods in spaces where they have little exposure to the media and few opportunities to communicate their political message.[120] What urbanist Robert Warren has termed 'pop up armies'[121] are a feature of the quasi-medieval urban battles that now surround major summits of the G8, the IMF and the World Bank. In Genoa these forces, influenced by fascist ideologies and perhaps individuals, killed one protestor and dispensed bloody injuries to many others as collective punishment.[122]

---

118   Wood and Coaffee, 'Security Is Coming Home', 503–517.

119   Steve Herbert, 'The "Battle of Seattle" Revisited: Or, Seven Views of a Protest-Zoning State', *Political Geography* 26, 2007, 601–19.

120   Don Mitchell and Lynn Mitchell Staeheli, 'Permitting Protest: Parsing the Fine Geography of Dissent in America', *International Journal of Urban and Regional Research* 29, 2005, 796–813.

121   Robert Warren, 'City Streets – the War Zones of Globalization: Democracy and Military Operations on Urban Terrain in the Early 21st Century', in Graham, ed., *Cities, War and terrorism*, 2004, 214–230.

122   Nick Davies, 'The Bloody Battle of Genoa', *Guardian,* 17 July 2008.

4.12   Anti-globalization protests at the 2003 World
Economic Forum in Cancun, Mexico.

4.13   The 'Protest Zoning State': The reorganization of central Sydney
into a series of passage-points as part of the security operations for the
Asia–Pacific Economic Cooperation summit, September 2007.

Gan Golan argues that such militarization of the police, backed up by manipulative media reports misrepresenting protestors simply as hordes of violent anarchists or terrorists, threatens to de-link the historic relationship between democracy and cities. As his data in Figure 4.14 shows, the policing of major urban demonstrations in the US now routinely invokes pre-emptive states of emergency as the basis for the withdrawal of constitutional rights, the arrest of protestors in advance of any crime being committed, and the detention of journalists suspected of being sympathetic to protestors.[123] Demonstration policing now routinely employs a whole gamut of pre-emptive spatial techniques as well as carefully orchestrated techniques of intimidation.

		WTO 1999 Seattle	IMF 2000 Washington DC	RNC 2000 Philadelphia	DNC 2000 Los Angeles	Inaug 2001 Washington DC	WEF 2002 New York City	Anti-war 2003 Portland, Oregon	IMF 2002 Washington DC	Anti-war 2003 New York City	FTAA 2003 Miami	G8 2004 Sea Island, Georgia	DNC 2004 Boston	RNC 2004 New York City	Inaug 2005 Washington DC
Legal Tactics	Ordinances, "State of Emergency" Used to restrict assembly										X	X	X		
	Delayed issuance of permits										X		X	X	
	Improper termination of event				X						X				
	False / mass / pre-emptive arrests	X		X	X		X		X		X			X	
	Arrest of journalists / legal obs / medics	X	X		X		X	X	X		X			X	
	Prolonged detention	X		X			X		X	X	X	X		X	
	Exorbitant bails	X		X	X										
	Random detention or searches and seizure				X						X	X			
Spatial Tactics	'Free speech' Zones / 'No-protest Zones	X			X		X			X	X		X		
	Restrict protester access to protest site	X			X	X	X			X	X	X		X	X
	Maximum security perimeter / fencing					X	X			X	X	X	X		
	Mobile netting barriers to corral									X				X	
	Shut down business areas of city	X			X						X	X			X
Intimidation Tactics	Public training drills						X					X	X	X	
	Media showcase of weapons, tactics				X		X					X	X	X	
	Massive presentation of force on streets				X		X					X	X		X
	US armed forces delpoyed on streets	X						X				X	X		
	Helicopters or Armoured Personnel Carriers	X			X		X					X	X		X
	Activists' homes surveilled		X				X					X	X	X	
	Activist meeting spaces raided		X	X	X							X			

WTO = World Trade Organisation; IMF = International Monetary Fund; RNC = Republican National Convention; DNC = Democratic National Convention; Inaug = Presidential Inaugration; WEF = World Economic Forum Summit; FTAA = Free Trade Area of the Americas Summit; G8 = G8 Summit

4.14   Legal, spatial and intimidation tactics used by US police in dealing with major urban protests, 1999–2005.

123   Golan, 'Closing the Gateways of Democracy'.

4.15   Security ring and roadblock around stadium for
the 2008 European Soccer Championship.

In many ways, these operations are similar to those which now fortify huge sporting events like the Olympics or the World Cup (Figure 4.15).[124] 'Mass citizen political mobilizations and mega-sports and entertainment events now automatically produce martial law conditions', notes Robert Warren.[125] Yet the erection of cordons, walls and enclosures, often for whole cities or systems of cities within which the spectacles are staged, is as much about managing global branding and TV imagery as it is about keeping risks at bay (Figure 4.16).[126]

COLONIZING THE FUTURE

The military commander must be able to live in the future.[127]

Now that both urban warfare and urban securitization are becoming organized around the permanent targeting of future behaviours and risks through the analyses of past surveillance tracks, political power is focusing increasingly on the computer algorithms needed to wade through masses of data. Besides further blurring military-civil and inside-outside distinctions, the development of such algorithms 'has brought the logic of pre-emption into the most mundane and prosaic spaces'.[128] The integration of radio-frequency tags into public transport 'smart cards', customer loyalty cards, consumer goods, and passports, for example, now yields detailed tracks of personal movements – a boon to data mining for security purposes. In many cases, the formation of urban enclaves is accelerated and hardened through such technologies.

Computer algorithms that continuously mine streams of data 'make it possible for the imagination of an open global economy of mobile people,

124   See Kimberly Schimmel, 'Deep Play: Sports Mega-Events and Urban Social Conditions in the US', *The Sociological Review* 54: 2, 2006, 160–74. Beyond the enormous securitization efforts, Olympic events are associated with war-like levels of eviction and erasure. For example, in the build-up to the 2008 Beijing games, it was appromixed that 'over 1.25 million people [were] forced to move because of Olympic construction; it was estimated that the figure would reach 1.5 million by the end of 2007'. Bryan Finoki, 'An Olympic Distraction', 17 July 2008, available at subtopia.blogspot.com.

125   Robert Warren, 'The Military Siege of Urban Space as the Site of Local and Global Democratic Practice', paper presented at the Policing Crowds Conference, Berlin, 2006.

126   Francisco Klauser, 'FIFA Land™: Alliances Between Security Politics and Business interests for Germany's City Network', in *Architectures of Fear*.

127   Paul Phister and Igor Plonisch, 'Joint Synthetic Battlespace: Cornerstone for Predictive Battlespace Awareness', unpublished paper, Rome, NY: Air Force Research Laboratory/Information Directorate, 1.

128   Amoore, 'Algorithmic War', *Antipode* (forthcoming).

objects and monies, to be reconciled with the post 9/11 rendering of a securitized nation-state', writes Louise Amoore.[129] Such techniques work by identifying 'hidden' associations among people, groups, transactions and behaviours. They produce, as Amoore points out, a 'form of "guilt by association" within which risky bodies, transactions and circulations are designated and identified'. Their very real results include the freezing of financial assets; the targeting of financial remittances from migrants; no-fly lists; and incarceration or extraordinary rendition at borders.[130]

A crucial element here is the adaptation of commercial practices of data-mining and predictive analytics. As in 'smart' CCTV, algorithms search the masses of captured data for patterns that signal the unusual or abnormal, and then search for 'target' people, transactions or flows deemed to have such characteristics[131] (Figure 4.16).

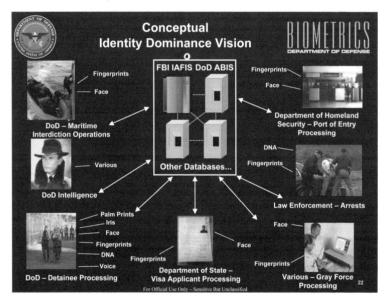

4.16   THE US Department of Defense's vision of 'Identity dominance' through the continuous 'fusion' of biometric databases continuously updated with inputs from international sites of incarceration, interdiction, travel, and law enforcement.

---

129   Ibid.
130   Ibid.
131   Colleen McCue, 'Data mining and predictive analytics: Battlespace awareness for the war on terror', *Defense Intelligence Journal* 13: 1–2, 47–63.

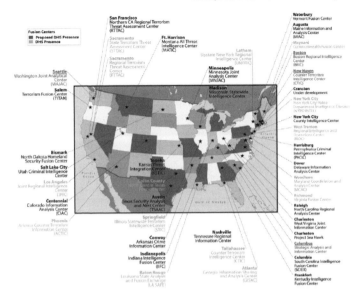

Fusion Centers
■ Proposed DHS Presence
▨ DHS Presence

San Francisco
Northern CA Regional Terrorism
Threat Assessment Center
(RTTAC)

Sacramento
State Terrorism Threat
Assessment Center
(STTAC)

Sacramento
Regional Terrorism
Threat Assessment
Center
(RTTAC)

Seattle
Washington Joint Analytical
Center
(WAJAC)

Salem
Terrorism Fusion Center
(TITAN)

Bismark
North Dakota Homeland
Security Fusion Center

Salt Lake City
Utah Criminal Intelligence
Center

Los Angeles
Joint Regional Intelligence
Center
(JRIC)

Centennial
Colorado Information
Analysis Center
(CIAC)

Phoenix
Arizona Counter Terrorism
Information Center
(ACTIC)

Ft. Harrison
Montana All Threat
Intelligence Center
(MATIC)

Latham
Upstate New York Regional
Intelligence Center
(UNYRIC)

Minneapolis
Minnesota Joint
Analysis Center
(MNJAC)

Madison
Wisconsin Statewide
Intelligence Center

Topeka
Kansas Threat
Integration Center
(KTIC)

Union County
Intelligence Center

Austin
Texas Security Analysis
and Alert Center
(TSAAC)

Springfield
Illinois Statewide Terrorism
Intelligence Center
(STIC)

Conway
Arkansas Crime
Information Center

Indianapolis
Indiana Intelligence
Fusion Center
(IIFC)

Baton Rouge
Louisiana State Analysis
and Fusion Exchange
(LA SAFE)

Nashville
Tennessee Regional
Information Center

Tallahassee
Counter Terrorism
Intelligence Center
(CTIC)

Atlanta
Georgia Information Sharing
and Analysis Center
(GISAC)

Waterbury
Vermont Fusion Center

Augusta
Maine Information and
Analysis Center
(MIAC)

Boston
Commonwealth Fusion Center

Boston
Boston Regional Intelligence
Center
(BRIC)

New Haven
Counter Terrorism
Intelligence Center
(CTIC)

Cranston
Under development

New York City
New York City Police
Department Intelligence Division
(NYPD INTEL)

New York City
County Intelligence Center

West Trenton
Regional Intelligence and
Operations Center

Harrisburg
Pennsylvania Criminal
Intelligence Center
(PACIC)

Dover
Delaware Information
Analysis Center

Woodlawn
Maryland Coordination and
Analysis Center
(MCAC)

Richmond
Virginia Fusion Center

Raleigh
North Carolina Regional
Analysis Center

Charleston
West Virginia Joint
Information Center

Charleston
Project Sea Hawk

Columbia
Strategic Analysis and
Information Center

Columbia
South Carolina Intelligence
Fusion Center
(SCIEX)

Frankfort
Kentucky Intelligence
Fusion Center

4.17   Current and planned data-mining 'fusion' centres in the US.

Such visions fuel highly controversial moves towards what the US military calls 'predictive battlespace awareness'.[132] An infamous case of this was the 2003 proposal, by then US national security advisor Admiral John Poindexter, to establish an office of Total Information Awareness (TIA). This proposal was 'designed to fight terrorism through data mining and link analysis, and by exploiting such technologies as "biometric signatures of humans" and "human network analysis"'. In practical terms, this meant that TIA would 'attempt to identify terrorists by linking databases, then scanning for suspicious activity the financial, medical, travel, and government records of millions of Americans'.[133]

The TIA proposal was rejected by the US Congress in 2003 because of the enormous controversy it generated. Nevertheless, its constituent programmes

132   Ibid.
133   Richard Pruett and Michael Longarzo, 'Identification, Friend Or Foe? The Strategic Uses and Future Implications of the Revolutionary New ID Technologies', unpublished paper, US Army War College, Strategy Research Project, Pennsylvania: US Army War College Carlisle Barracks, 2006.

are still underway; they have simply been dispersed among other, lower-profile offices. One of these programmes, a comprehensive series of local and regional 'fusion centres', within which the continual mining of diverse and unimaginably vast sets of data will be attempted, is already being established (Figure 4.18).[134]

It has also become clear that geographical data mining underpins pre-emptive surveillance at home and abroad. Such a system – the Rigel geographical profiling system, developed by Environmental Criminology Research Inc. (ECRI) of Vancouver – was used to search for snipers in Washington, DC, in 2002. In 2004 ECRI was awarded a contract under the US government's National Technology Alliance (NTA) programme to extend the Rigel system to support the War on Terror. In late 2007 the Los Angeles Police Department caused a major stir when it announced a large programme to map geographical clusters of Muslims in LA as a means to undertake systematic risk analyses.

BIOMETRIC BORDERS

> If the body becomes password, does it cease to be the body?[135]

Besides all the foregoing security technologies that blur the inside/outside and civil/military divides, there are the biometric technologies of iris, voice, gait, finger and hand recognition. As with face-recognition CCTV, the goal here is to overcome the clutter, camouflage and anonymity of the city through technologies that objectively fix identity through the physical scanning of the supposedly unique features of each human body. This, however, is political obfuscation and myth. 'Biometric technology, in its current form', writes Heather Murray, 'serves to categorize bodies with a dangerous discriminatory logic that cannot be touted as "true" or "objective"'.[136]

In 2004, US forces in Iraq began to use Israeli-style tactics such as walling, cordoning-off, bulldozing of 'free fire' zones around newly walled urban districts, and punishing the families of alleged fighters by threatening to demolish their houses. The occupation forces also installed check-points and ID card systems within towns and cities. In December 2004 an NBC reporter

---

134   Todd Masse, Siobhan O'Neil, and John Rollins, 'CRS Report For Congress Fusion Centers: Issues and Options for Congress', 6 July 2007, Order Code RL34070.

135   John Measor and Benjamin Muller, 'Securitizing the Global Norm of Identity: Biometric Technologies in Domestic and Foreign Policy', Dahrjamailiraq.com, 17 September 2005.

136   Heather Murray, 'Monstrous Play in Negative Spaces: Illegible Bodies and the Cultural Construction of Biometric Technology', *Communication Review* 10: 4, 359.

named Richard Engel observed that the entire population of Fallujah[137] – that is, those who had survived the almost complete devastation of the city by the two US attacks that year – was to be 'fingerprinted, given a retina scan and then an ID card, which will allow them to travel around their homes or to nearby aid centers, which are now being built'. He also noted, almost in passing, that 'the Marines will be authorized to use deadly force against those breaking the rules'.[138]

As part of the radical 'creative destruction' brought about by the war in Iraq, new model cities were meant to emerge from the ruins. They would be 'replete with a high-tech security infrastructure centered on biometric identification strategies to manage returning citizens',[139] collectively dubbed by the US military the 'biometric automated toolkit' (BAT). Since 2004, BATs have been used 'throughout the theatre of operations [in Iraq and Afghanistan] in order to keep a database of terrorists, insurgents, local workers, and detainees'.[140] According to a US Marine Corps report, utilizing BATs means that in 'a matter of seconds, a Marine working at a gate or check point can collect biometric data from an individual, search the database in the computer, and look for a match with the many other records already in the database'.[141]

Since April 2007, biometric technologies have been rolled out in parallel with the attempted reconstruction of Baghdad as an archipelago encompassing ten Palestine-style blast-walled enclaves organized around ethnic or sectarian lines and accessible only through biometrically or militarily controlled passage-points (Figure 4.19).[142] US military spokespersons have cynically labelled these enclaves 'gated communities' and invoked parallels with the master-planned enclaves for the well-to-do that dominate suburbia and exurbia in the US.[143] 'They've been doing it in Florida, and the old people seem to like it', quipped one platoon leader, Sgt. Charles Schmitt, as his men put the finishing touches to a new gated wall.

---

137   In attempting to, in Measor and Muller's words, 'put in order that which lies "outside" the norm', American war planners identified Fallujah as a state of exception requiring extreme 'solutions'. 'Fallujah, with its long history of resisting central control only magnified by its experience with the American occupation, had doubtlessly rebuked American attempts to control the city. These attempts saw US military forces increasingly identify it as unique and exceptional in its role in the insurgency'. Measor and Muller, 'Securitizing the Global Norm of Identity'.

138   Cited in Measor and Muller, 'Securitizing the Global Norm of Identity'.

139   Ibid.

140   Ibid.

141   Corporal Chris Prickett, II Marine Expeditionary Force, 'Coming to Your Town Soon? Tracking Locals with the BAT of an Eye', *Marine Corps News*, 28 March 2005.

142   Mitchell M. Zais, 'Iraq: The Way Ahead', *Military Review*, January–February 2008, 112.

143   Spencer Ackerman, 'Tear Down this Wall', *Guardian*, 24 April 2007.

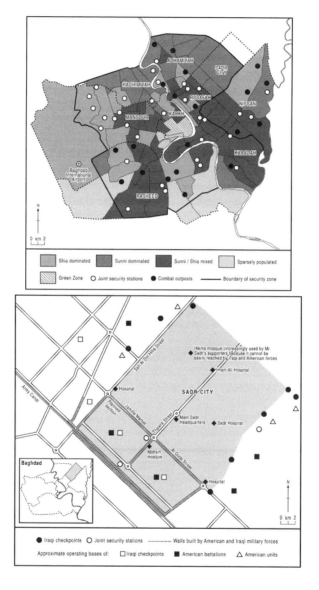

4.18   Map of Baghdad restructuring in 2008 (top), sectarian enclaves separated by walls and checkpoints; and (bottom) a detailed map of the system in Sadr City.

However, the effectiveness of biometric techniques, even in military terms, is highly questionable. Ironically, the war has so physically brutalized Iraqis that 'the very body parts necessary to prove identity may now be damaged too severely to offer an accurate read'.[144] Moreover, as Andrew Hom has reflected in *Military Review*, US biometric systems in Iraq have been drastically counter-productive, as they have generalized humiliation and imposed singular identities through technological rationalism, rather than engaging meaningfully with 'social history and semantic meaning'. He wonders whether these systems simply represent a form of 'ontological and epistemological imperialism'.[145]

John Measor and Benjamin Muller stress that 'the gratuitous destruction of one's enemy is a thinly veiled norm of modernity, not to mention the subsequent reordering and repopulation of these ruined spaces/places'.[146] The capturing of 'pure' biometric traces of the occupied bodies thus means that the age-old colonial problematics of biopower are rendered more manageable. The biometric check point thus 'precludes the need to come face-to-face with the Other'; instead, the Other 'is simply rearticulated through biometric applications into the suspect identity'.[147]

GLOBAL HOMELANDS

Power itself goes nomadic.[148]

With global wars of public safety, classifying and surveilling pathogenic space has expanded as a geopolitical strategy.[149]

The final striking aspect of the use of control technologies to try to achieve ubiquitous borders is the effort by the US state to extend homeland securitization to the global scale. Just as ideas of international security are 'coming home' to reorganize domestic urban life, so efforts to classify risky versus risk-free populations, activities, and circulations are 'moving out' to colonize the infrastructures, systems and circulations which sustain transnational capitalism.

Mobility is thus increasingly being policed in what James Sheptycki calls

---

144 Russell B. Farkouh, 'Incorporating Biometric Security into an Everyday Military Work Environment', *SANS GIAC GSEC Practical Version 1.4b, Option 1*, 2004.

145 Andrew R. Hom 'The New Legs Race: Critical Perspectives on Biometrics in Iraq', *Military Review*, Jan–Feb 2008, 88.

146 Cited in Measor and Benjamin Muller, 'Securitizing the Global Norm of Identity'.

147 Ibid.

148 See Bülent Diken and Carsten Bagge Laustsen, *The Culture Of Exception: Sociology Facing The Camp,* London: Routledge, 2005, 64.

149 Feldman, 'Securocratic Wars of Public Safety', 330–50.

'informated space',¹⁵⁰ a dynamic that of course parallels the Bushian logic of pre-emptive, colonial, securocratic war to shore up domestic safety by anticipating and exterminating threats as they build globally.¹⁵¹ Many elements of the security apparatus of nations now challenge long-standing Westphalian separations of 'internal' and 'external' security established along traditional geopolitical and civil/military lines. 'The discourses that the United States and its closest allies have put forth asserting the necessity to globalize security have taken on an unprecedented intensity and reach', writes Didier Bigo. 'This globalization is supposed to make national borders effectively obsolete, and to oblige other actors in the international arena to collaborate'.¹⁵²

Ultimately there is a point at which borders cease to be geographical lines and filters between states (always an over-simplified idea) and emerge instead as increasingly interoperable assemblages of control technologies strung out across the world's infrastructures, circulations, cities, and bodies. Rather than being the simple blockading of territorial borders, the imperative is the permanent anticipation, channeling and monitoring of flows so that proper ones can be distinguished from improper ones. In the process, borders become transformed 'from a two-dimensional line across an absolute space that divides inside and outside, to a transitional zone, defined by exceptional forms of government that blur established categories, jurisdictions and spaces'.¹⁵³

Inescapably, the attempt to securitize the sustenance of transnational capitalism is simultaneously urban and global, a response to the fact that a network of global cities orchestrates capitalism's strategic processes across transnational space, that the city's reach 'now stretches outward to a global scale'.¹⁵⁴ It is possible to see world cities as 'fluid machines' – 'fixes' in space and time constructed to organize a vast and usually hidden universe of connection, process and flow.¹⁵⁵ At the same time, as we have seen, such cities, as the

---

150   James Sheptycki, 'The Global Cops Cometh: Reflections on Transationalization, Knowledge Work and Policing Subculture', *British Journal of Sociology* 49: 1, 1998, 70.

151   Marieke de Goede, 'Beyond Risk: Pre-Mediation and the Post-9/11 security Imagination', *Security Dialogue* July 2007.

152   Didier Bigo, 'Globalized-in-security: The Field and the Ban-opticon', in John Solomon, eds., *Translation, Philosophy and Colonial Difference*, Naoki Sakai, Hong Kong, 2005, 1.

153   Deborah Cowen, 'Securing Systems: Struggles over Supply Chains and the Social', unpublished paper, 2006, 3.

154   Edward Soja, 'Borders Unbound: Globalization, Regionalism and the postmetropolitan Transition', in Henk van Houtum, Olivier Framsch and Wolfgang Zierhofer, eds., *B/Ordering Space*, ed. London: Ashgate, 2005, 40.

155   Laurent Gutierrez and Valérie Portefaix, *Mapping HK*, Hong Kong: Map Books, 2000.

dominant centres of corporate and financial power for the world's military-security-industrial complex, are the 'brains' of the global war machine itself.

Peter Taylor and colleagues at Lougborough University have mapped the transnational networks of 'global cities' (Figure 4.19), earmarking dominant hubs ('alpha' world cities), secondary centres ('beta' world cities) and peripheral cities which act as gateways between regions and the world economy ('gamma' world cities). It is the flows between these cities that lie at the heart of the drive towards securitization.

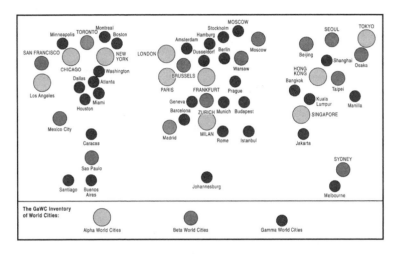

4.19   The 'World City Network' as envisaged by Loughborough
University's Globalization and World Cities research centre.

Similarly, advocates of transnational border security argue that traditional efforts at drawing and enforcing territorial borders are a problem rather than a solution.[156] One reason is the delays and costs they cause by interrupting the legitimate and necessary flows that enable global capitalism. Another is the failure to allow flows and people to be profiled, located and tracked *before* they reach vulnerable and strategic targets in and around the North's global cities. Thus, instead of merely policing flows across territorial borders, as in the Westphalian idea, the emerging architectures of control and securocratic war seek to colonize what security analysts call the various 'seams' between war and crime, between policing, intelligence and military activity, and between the outside and inside of national territories. By trying to establish anticipatory surveillance systems which parallel the key architectures of

---

156   Cowen, 'Securing systems', 2.

circulation – electronic finance, Internet communications, airline travel, seaports and trade – they oscillate continually between the scale of the human body, the city, the nation, and transnational capitalism.

Of great importance here are new ideas of US national security, expressed in the notions of 'defending forward' and 'global defense in depth'.[157] The new security doctrine is based on the argument that no matter how much money, technology or militarized fencing is thrown at the problem of filtering the boundaries which separate the US nation from the rest of the world, such geopolitical ideas of security are rendered less and less useful in a world where the flows continually work *through* US cities and regions via a myriad of infrastructural connections and systems.[158]

Homeland security is thus increasingly seen as an 'away game'. As US Navy admiral Timothy Keating says, 'We don't want [identified security threats] to get in our airspace, on our land or close to our shoreline in the maritime domain.'[159] Instead, he claims, the US national security state is 'working very hard with the other regional combatant commanders so as to roll up the bad guys, capture or kill them and interrupt their attacks' long before they reach the continental margins of North America.[160]

Such an approach helps address the problem that the 'the imperatives of national security and global trade are in many ways conflicting projects'[161] if homeland security focuses merely on the erection of barriers – which translate into costs and delays – to interrupt the circulations connecting the US and the rest of the world. 'US prosperity – and much of its power – relies on its ready access to North American and global networks of transport, energy, information, finance and labor', argues Stephen Flynn. 'It is self defeating for the United States to embrace security measures that isolate it from those networks.'[162]

Advocates of the new doctrine also stress that terrorist threats are already 'within the wire'[163] of the transnational circulations that tie US cities so

---

157   Antulio Echevarria and Bert Tussing, *From 'Defending Forward' to a 'Global Defense-In-Depth': Globalization and Homeland Security,* Strategic Studies Institute, 2003, available at *www.strategicstudiesinstitute.army.mil.*

158   Deborah Cowen and Neil Smith, 'After Geopolitics? 'From the Geopolitical Social to Geoeconomics', Antipode, 41: 1, 2009, 22–48.

159   Donna Miles, 'With Ongoing Terror Fight Overseas, NORTHCOM Focuses on Homeland', *SecurityInnovator.com*, 17 November 2006.

160   Ibid.

161   Deborah Cowen and Neil Smith, 'After Geopolitics?'.

162   Stephen Flynn, 'The False Conundrum: Continental Integration versus Homeland Security', in *The Rebordering of North America*, Peter Andreas and Thomas Biersteker, eds, New York: Routledge, 2003, 11.

163   Echevarria and Tussing, *From 'Defending Forward' to a 'Global Defense-In-Depth'.*

intimately to the rest of the world. Terrorists themselves already inhabit US and other Western cities, where the tools they use to launch their attacks are close at hand, and their targets are the myriad structures and persons that constitute the cities themselves. Even when terrorists are located in colonial peripheries rather than the in US itself, access to the transnational circuits of the Internet, containerized shipping, logistics and air travel enables them to project attacks towards US cities at any instant.

CONTAINING INSECURITY[164]

Attempts to extend US homeland-security initiatives through worldwide systems continue apace. One focus is the series of enclaves which jointly orchestrate global divisions of labour and the resulting trade flows.[165] The Container Security Initiative (CSI), for example, covers major seaports and the flows that link them.[166] The CSI's goal is 'to push [America's] borders out and pre-screen containers in specially created security zones before they are loaded in foreign ports'.[167] It is a key component of the overall effort to 'secure the entire maritime supply chain, from the factory gate in a foreign country to the final destination of the product in the United States'.[168]

The driving concept here is that the US Department of Homeland Security must control, police, and track movements within what it terms a 'global security envelope'.[169] By 2003, fifteen of twenty-five major containers ports had agreed, under considerable pressure from the US, to establish a control system which theoretically would allow containers to be continually tracked, reduce the potential for tampering with them in transit, and enable ports to keep delays for inspections to a minimum. This securitization campaign blends seamlessly into the 'forting up' of US port spaces and provides justification for the suspension of normal labour and privacy rights in the name of national security.[170] The recasting of US and Canadian ports and urban waterfronts as key national security spaces means they are being physically securitized as

---

164 This term draws on Deborah Cowen's idea of 'containing insecurity' published in her contribution to a book I edited, *Disrupted Cities: When Infrastructures Fail*, New York: Routledge, 2009.

165 See Keller Easterling, *Enduring Innocence*, Cambridge MA: MIT Press, 2006.

166 This system organizes 90 per cent of global trade through global supply chains and advanced logistics and delivers 95 per cent of the overseas trade entering the US.

167 'When trade and security clash', *The Economist*, 4 April 2002.

168 Jon Haveman and Howard Shatz, *Protecting the Nation's Seaports: Balancing Security and Cost*, San Francisco: Public Policy Institute of California, 2006.

169 IBM, *Expanded Borders, Integrated Controls*, marketing brochure.

170 Cowen and Smith 'After Geopolitics?'.

spaces of legal exception, enrolled into national systems of government power, and re-regulated in ways that dramatically undermine the labour rights of port workers. Thus, 'national security, at least in the ports, is conceptualized as almost interchangeable with the security of international trade flows'.[171]

GLOBAL BIOMETRIC REGIME

> The globe shrinks for those who own it; for the displaced or the dispossessed, the migrant or refugee, no distance is more awesome than the few feet across borders or frontiers.[172]

In the airline and airport sectors, US homeland security efforts are meant to ensure that the 'border guard [is] the last line of defense, not the first, in identifying potential threats'.[173] The dream system features interoperable 'smart' borders, globalized border control, and pre-emptive risk management.[174] To this end, the US has developed the US-VISIT programme – US Visitor and Immigrant Status Indicator Technology – for air travel, another application of biometric attempts to 'objectively' fix bodies and identities while coercing key US partner nations to adjust their passport systems to biometric standards defined by the US.[175]

In the Enhanced Border Security and Visa Act of 2002, for example, the US Congress imposed a requirement that the twenty-seven countries within the US Visa Waiver Program (VWP) begin using machine-readable passports that incorporate both biometric and radio-frequency tag (RFID) technology. Nations or blocs that fail to undertake these radical shifts are threatened with losing their coveted status within the VWP. 'Our leveraging of America's visa aiver partners, in order to promote the use of the new ID technologies for purposes of national security', Richard Pruett and Michael Longarzo of the US Army War College write, 'may prove to be a paradigm for the coming age'.[176]

---

171   Cowen, 'Securing Systems', 7.

172   Homi Bhabha, 'The Third Space: Interview with Homi Bhabha', in J. Rutherford, ed., *Identity: Community, Culture, Difference*, London: Routledge, 1990, 208–24.

173   Accenture Digital Forum, 'US DHS to develop and implement US VISIT program', 2004, available at www.digitalforum.accenture.com, 4.

174   Hayes and Tasse, 'Control Freaks, 2'.

175   Mark Salter, 'The Global Visa Regime and the Political Technologies of the International Self: Borders, Bodies, Biopolitics', *Alternatives* 31, 2006, 167–89.

176   Richard Pruett and Michael Longarzo, 'Identification Friend or Foe? The Strategic Uses and Future Implications of the Revolutionary New ID Technologies', unpublished paper, US Army War College, Strategy Research Project, Pennsylvania: US Army War College Carlisle Barracks, 2006, available at www.strategicstudiesinstitute.army.mil.

The passage-point architectures of overseas airports thus now display symbols of both US and domestic sovereignty (Figure 4.20).

4.20   The 'global homeland' orchestrated through the extension of US sovereignty as part of the US visit initiative: Frankfurt airport, Germany.

A shift to biometrically organized international borders, structured according to US stipulations, centres on the separation of 'mobile bodies . . . into kinetic élites and kinetic underclasses'.[177] Re the latter, a process of 'punitive pre-emption' profiles individuals already deemed risky and seeks to immobilize them before they can travel to the US; it 'incorporates a range of disciplinary, punitive and militaristic technologies aimed at pre-empting [their] arrival at the physical border'.[178] Border-crossers who do not go through the screening systems and passage-points are criminalized. By contrast, kinetic élites can increasingly by-pass immigration controls altogether by opting into biometrically controlled schemes such as Amsterdam Airport's Privium system or the SmartGate system in Australia, which pre-emptively clear their bodies as safe and legitimate.

177   Dean Wilson and Leanne Weber, 'Risk and Pre-emption on the Australian Border', 125.

178   Ibid.

1	Full name	28	Details of passengers on booking with a different itinery
2	Gender	29	E-mail address
3	Date of birth	30	Ticket number and date of issue
4	Nationality	31	Any other information the ticket agent consider of interest
5	Type of travel document	32	Number on ticket
6	Travel document number	33	Reserved seat number
7	Issuing country of travel document	34	Date ticket issued
8	Expiry date	35	No show history
9	Registration of any vehicle used to travel	36	Bag tag numbers
10	Place of birth	37	Details of whether travel arrangements are 'flexible'
11	Issue date of travel	38	Names of any infants or staff in travelling party
12	UK visa or entry clearance expity date	39	Is traveller an unaccompanied minor?
13	Booking reference number	40	Details of who made the booking
14	Date of reservation	41	All historical changes to travel arrangements
15	Date(s) of intended travel	42	Number of travellers in party
16	Passenger name (if different to full name)	43	Seat information, including whether first class
17	Other passengers on same booking	44	Is the ticket one-way only?
18	Passenger's address	45	Any other biographical information
19	Form of payment, including any credit card number	46	Cost of fare
20	Billing address	47	Check-in time
21	Contract numbers, including hotel or relative being visited	48	Actual seat number
22	Travel itinery and route	49	How much luggage checked-in
23	Frequent flyer information (miles flown and addresses)	50	Check-in agents initials
24	Travel agency	51	Out-bound travel indicator
25	Person at travel agent who made booking	52	Where did journey begin, if not first leg of trip
26	Reference number of any shared booking	53	Group indicator of whether a party is a family or friends etc.
27	Status of booking e.g. confirmed, wait-listed		

4.21   The fifty-three pieces of information required, at point of reservation, from 2007 for anyone entering or leaving the UK as part of the UK's 2007 e-Borders strategy.

The key principle here is automated risk profiling, starting when would-be passengers initially book, so that those deemed malign or improper can be intercepted even before embarkation to the US.[179] In the UK's smart-border initiative, for instance, fifty-three variables (Figure 4.21) are automatically scanned

---

179   Karine Côté-Boucher notes that such 'remote control border' strategies, that is the pushing of border functions into foreign countries, have a long history. They were 'already in use in the US management of Chinese immigration as early as the beginning of the 20th century'. Karine Côté-Boucher, 'The Diffuse Border: Intelligence-Sharing, Control and Confinement along Canada's Smart Border', *Surveillance & Society* 5: 2, 2008, 142.

for signals of 'risky' or 'abnormal',[180] under a programme developed mainly by the US defence corporation Raytheon, maker of Tomahawk cruise missiles. 'The screened appearance of a security threat', writes Louise Amoore, 'is always already calculated by the algorithmic performance of association rules'. These rules highlight data that imply possible risk – Was the ticket paid in cash? What is the past pattern of travel? Is the individual a frequent flyer? Which in-flight meal was ordered? – and in turn shape the treatment of the passenger as he or she attempts to board the plane.

4.22   E-Z Pass nation: Automated tollbooth, Buffalo, New
York, which allows pre-registered drivers to enter premium
'fast lanes' to the Canadian border without stopping.

The US–Canada border is a strong case study of multiple circuits being constructed to process kinetic élites and kinetic underclasses in quite different ways. Here, the well-established E-ZPass 'fast lane' on the urban highway (Figure

180 Amoore, 'Algorithmic War'. Among the 34 items of passenger data required under the EU–US passenger name record (PNR) or Advance passenger information system (APIS) agreement, legally challenged by the European Court of Justice in 2006, are credit card details, criminal records and in-flight meal choices. The data is extradited to the US within 15 minutes of flight departures from Europe.

4.22) is being translated into the architectures of what we might call the E-ZPass nation – but for a privileged minority only. The experimental NEXUS programme, for example, permits regular business travellers between Canada and the US to undergo profiling and pre-clearing, gain a special wireless biometric ID card, and so go through a priority lane, thus by-passing the usual congestion and delays at the border. Cameras take iris scans to verify the connection between driver and card. For such privileged and ostensibly risk-free travellers, even the crossing of more and more militarized borders becomes 'a mere technical formality'.[181]

Whilst business-class or frequent-flyer travellers lucky enough to be enrolled into what Matthew Sparke has called a kind of 'transnational para-citizenship' smoothly cross transnational space, the kinetic underclasses who cannot so enrol in the same way or are deemed risky face harassment, targeting, incarceration and diminished legal and human rights. Such a status thus has 'altogether more oppressive and more unpredictable outcomes', including the ultimate threat and immobility of incarceration or torture. 'It should be noted', Sparke writes, 'that as well as representing ever more appalling exclusions from the privileges of citizenship and civil rights, those surviving on this bleak underside of . . . privilege also sometimes ironically experience very rapid movement too: rapid movement into detention centers, rapid movement between detention centers, and, ultimately, rapid transnational movement out of America, sometimes into incarceration elsewhere'.[182]

The mobilization of biometrics as a measure of 'true' identity in urban war zones as well as in the broader rearticulations of nation, citizenship and circulation acts as a powerful Foucauldian boomerang. In these overlapping domains, politics narrows as all subjects are rendered suspects, targets, who can be 'legitimately subjected to such disciplinary technologies'[183] as actually or potentially criminalized Others. This convergence between war zone and home zone exemplifies what John Measor and Benjamin Muller call an 'evolving global norm of securitized identity', which further destabilizes conventional separations between domestic and foreign policy.

CYBER PASSAGE-POINT

Our final 'global homeland' of concern centres on US efforts to surveil global Internet traffic, even when that traffic neither originates nor terminates within

---

181   Karine Côté-Boucher, 'The Diffuse Border', 157.
182   Matthew Sparke, 'A neoliberal nexus: Economy, security and the biopolitics of citizenship on the border', *Political Geography* 25: 2, 2006, 167–170.
183   Measor and Muller, 'Securitizing the Global Norm of Identity'.

the US itself. Of great relevance here is the fact that a large proportion of the world's Internet traffic is routed through the US (Figure 4.23). This arrangement is a legacy of the system's history: because of the invention of the Internet in the US and because of cheaper international telephone tariffs, Internet traffic now overwhelmingly works through 'a handful of key telephone switches and perhaps a dozen [Internet exchange points] in coastal cities near undersea fiber-optic cable landings, particularly Miami, Los Angeles, New York and the San Francisco Bay area'.[184] This means that 'the NSA [National Security Agency] could scoop up an astounding amount of telephone calls by simply choosing the right facilities'.[185]

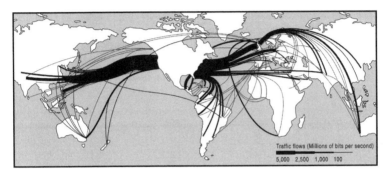

Traffic flows (Millions of bits per second)
5,000   2,500   1,000   100

4.23   Much of the globe's international traffic flows through a few key 'telecom hotel' buildings in he United States, dramatically simplifying the NSA's attempts at global Internet surveillance.

More incredibly still, these facilities amount to just a few buildings, known as 'telecom hotels', which house the key Internet and telephone switching centres of the entire planet. 'There are about three or four buildings you need to tap', reveals Stephen Becker of TeleGeography, a research consultancy. 'In LA there is 1 Wilshire; in New York, 60 Hudson, and in Miami, the NAP of the Americas'.[186] Obviously, this situation provides the US with a huge opportunity for data-mining, data fusion and other surveillance efforts, and US security institutions have not been slow to exploit its potential: the RESTORE[187] Act

184   Ryan Singel, 'NSA's Lucky Break: How the US Became Switchboard to the World', *Wired*, 10 October 2007.

185   Stephan Beckert, research director at Telegeography, cited in Singel, 'NSA's Lucky Break'.

186   Singel, 'NSA's Lucky Break'.

187   'RESTORE' stands for 'Responsible Electronic Surveillance That is Overseen Reviewed and Effective'.

of 2007 states that the NSA is free to tap this traffic at will, even when both its origin and its destination lie outside US borders.[188]

Spurred on by fears that the Internet will be used to co-ordinate and finance terrorist actions and be appropriated as a weapon of 'cyberterror' to destroy or disrupt the electronic systems that sustain advanced capitalist nations,[189] the NSA has launched globe-spanning efforts to surveil every packet of Internet traffic. Other initiatives are directed towards the monitoring of global financial transactions to (again) pre-emptively identify 'unusual' or 'threatening' patterns of activity.[190]

DIGITAL MEDIEVAL

> [We] seem to be reverting to the neo-feudal times ... where the boundaries of civilization, dignity and hope no longer coincide with the boundaries of the nation.[191]

In 2007 the influential US security analyst John Robb published *Brave New War,* one of numerous popular books about 'security' that have peppered US bestseller lists since 2001. In it, he predicts that the coming decade will likely be dominated by a string of major, unpredictable, 9/11-style 'Black Swan' terror attacks in US cities, combined with the periodic use of cyberterror techniques by insurgents dotted around the world, whose aim is to bring down large swaths of US energy, communications, transport, finance and health infrastructure. US urban citizens would thus be regularly plunged into a pre-modern existence of dark disconnection. Robb ends with a scenario of US urban life in 2016.

What Robb anticipates is that, combined with a radical shift away from the centralized, bureaucratic security structures of national and local states, such trends would usher in a 'withering of the [national] security apparatus'.[192] This will be combined, he predicts, with the 'development of an entirely new, decentralized security system' involving government, private firms and individuals. Such trends would mean that 'security will become a function of where you live and whom you work for' – rather like US health care. As nation-state security provision is replaced by uneven and highly localized security markets, organized through booming military corporations, 'healthy

188   Singel, 'NSA's Lucky Break'.
189   See Chapter 9.
190   See Amoore and Goede, 'Transactions after 9/11' 173–185.
191   Ghassan Hage, *Against Paranoid Nationalism: Searching for Hope in a Shrinking Society,* Sydney: Pluto Press, 2003, 18.
192   John Robb, *Brave New War: The Next Stage of Terrorism and the End of Globalization,* New York: Wiley, 185.

individuals and multinational corporations will be the first to hire private military companies ... to protect their homes and establish a protective perimeter around daily life', Robb suggests. 'Parallel transportation networks – evolving out of time-share aircraft . . . will cater for this group, leapfrogging its members from one secure, well-appointed lily pad to the next'. Members of the middle class, he imagines, 'will follow, taking matters into their own hands by forming suburban collectives to share the costs of security . . . These "armored suburbs" will deploy and maintain back-up generators and communications links; they will be patrolled by civil police auxiliaries that have received corporate training and boast their own state-of-the-art emergency response systems'.[193]

And everyone else? 'They will have to make do with the remains of the national system', Robb predicts. 'They will gravitate to the cities, where they will be subject to ubiquitous surveillance and marginal or nonexistent services. For the poor, there will be no refuge.'[194]

As with most good pulp-political, post-9/11 nonfiction in the US, Robb's book weaves a deceptively simple, apocalyptic tale which dramatically exaggerates selected contemporary events. And yet contemporary evidence does suggest the emergence of internationally organized security assemblages intended to remove the risk-free from the risky, raising major questions about the future political geography of our world. Surely Robb's vision cannot be entirely dismissed. Are the three-dimensional archipelagos of apartheid-style splintering, connection, fortification, and militarization, so palpable in Gaza and the West Bank, a grim exemplar of the future? Will the blurring of internal and external archipelagos of exception fatally 'unbundle' the role of nation-states as the key economic and fiscal building blocks of global capitalism? Will affluent cities and sectors of cities gradually secede and de-link from the residualized territories and people surrounding them – in a generalized version of the exploitative, tightly controlled relationship of, say, Singapore and its hinterlands in Malaysia and Indonesia? Will transnational structures of policing, surveillance and law enforcement continue to strengthen, to the extent that they eclipse or swallow the legacies of national security states? How will the splintering,[195] fragmentation and polarization enforced by the new military urbanism be reflected in, and sustained by, the politics, civil societies and landscapes of the world's burgeoning cities? Whither ideas of national citizenship in such a context?

---

193 Ibid.
194 Ibid., 186.
195 Graham and Marvin, *Splintering Urbanism*.

It is especially important to consider whether the current trends towards ubiquitous bordering mean that our planet faces, as Nezar Alsayyad and Ananya Roy have argued, a kind of (computerized) 'medieval modernity' that is fostering 'the emergence of forms of citizenship [which are] fundamentally about protection [and are] located in urban enclaves'.[196] Such developments challenge the established idea of modern citizenship as 'constituted through a set of abstract individual rights embedded in the concept of the nation-state'.[197] Similarly, Allen Feldman wonders whether the architectural and spatial production of American identity, now so often organized through what he calls 'armored sacralized fortresses of secure commodification, be these malls, gated communities, or corporate keeps', helps to 'determine citizenship by whom they [endow] with security passes'.

Rather than using the term 'medieval' to mean a simple reversal of Enlightenment notions of progress and a return to societal 'backwardness', as right-wing commentators like John Robb currently contend,[198] Alsayyad and Roy suggest something altogether more subtle – and more convincing. Within the transnational urban geographies of capitalism, they see coexisting modalities of 'modern nationalism, medieval enclaves and imperial brutality'.[199]

Thus, nation-states don't simply wither away in some completely globalized future. Rather, camp-like enclosures and privatized circulations erupt within, through and between what are conventionally understood as cities and nations. Such a complexity of enclaves, assemblages, and passage-points radically 'complicates the whole issue of progress and backwardness, the modern and pre-modern'.[200] It also forces us to be wary of deploying the usual teleologies, which declare that the barbarian, Orientalized Others living in their urban sites within the present world in fact inhabit the 'savage past'.

Processes of urban securitization and fragmentation existed long before 9/11. As these processes accelerate, the politics of geography and security becomes almost fractally layered, filled with superimposed and often contradictory or antagonistic assemblages. Rather than amounting to a shift from a society of discipline based on enclosure (Foucault's panoptic society) to one of decentralized systems of surveillance (Deleuze's control society), what is emerging is a society organized through assemblages of urban and

196   Nezar Alsayyad and Ananya Roy, 'Medieval Modernity: On Citizenship and Urbanism in a Global Era', *Space and Polity*, 10: 1, 2006, 1–20.

197   Ibid.

198   See, for example, Stephen Kobrin, 'Back to the Future: Neomedievalism and the Postmodern Digital World Economy', *Journal of International Affairs* 51, 1998.

199   Alsayyad and Roy, 'Medieval Modernity', 17.

200   Ibid.

infrastructural passage-points. These assemblages utilize both architectures and electronic technologies, working in parallel; their purpose is to stipulate legitimacy – whether of presence or of circulation – in advance of movement. Thus, both cities and citizenship become progressively reorganized based on notions of provisional – rather than absolute – mobility, rights and access.

To back up their arguments, Alsayyad and Roy deploy a wide range of examples: affluent gated communities, regulated squatter settlements, a proliferating range of incarceration facilities and torture-camp cities where 'violence is constantly deployed in the name of peace and order'.[201] They also mention the insurgent urban governance which is emerging in places like Hezbollah-controlled towns in Lebanon, Hamas-controlled Gaza, and other 'neighbourhood-level Islamic republics being declared by religious fundamentalist groups'.[202] To this list one could add the proliferation of camp-like security architectures which sustain global financial cores, export-processing zones, tourist enclaves, offshore finance enclosures, logistics hubs, ports, airport cities, research complexes and 'technopoles', as well as the temporary urban militarizations imposed for mega sports events and political summits.

All their examples, argue Alsayyad and Roy, involve 'private systems of governance that operate as medieval fiefdoms, imposing truths and norms that are often contrary to national law'.[203] As in medieval times, the result is the emergence of the modern city as what Holston and Appadurai have called a 'honeycomb of jurisdictions', a 'medieval body [of] overlapping, heterogeneous, non-uniform, and increasingly private memberships'.[204] Permeating all of this are the biometric technologies, mobilized to track, to identify and to control access.

DIFFERENCE AND ILLUSIONS OF CONTROL

> Why has the entire world become a frontier to be simultaneously pushed back, opened up to American colonization, and at the same time sealed off, guarded against foreign incursion?[205]

It is tempting to finish this chapter on an apocalyptic note. But such a temptation must be avoided, for borders and bordering strategies inevitably

---

201   Ibid., 13.
202   Ibid.
203   Ibid.
204   James Holston and Arjun Appadurai, eds., *Cities and Citizenship*, Durham, NC: Duke University Press, 1999, 13.
205   Robby Herbst, 'Hinting at Ways to Work in Current Contexts; an Interview with Brian Holmes', Journal Of Aesthetics and Protest.org.

remain permeable and contradictory – especially in large cities. Technophilic dreams of perfect ordering and perfect power will inevitably fail to bring the longed-for levels of geographical and social control. Fortressed enclaves are often surrounded and overwhelmed by the sheer mass and pulse of urban mixing in large, fast-growing cities. The density and unpredictability of city life often swamps simple strategies of boundary enforcement. Moreover, the notions of 'security' which surround the shift to ubiquitous borders are often tenuous at best, even for those who organize or benefit from the drive towards securitization.

Despite the military-security complex's fondness for throwing money at R&D for technological 'silver bullets' – such as the technology needed to enable the diverse bordering strategies explored in this chapter – in practice, the bullets often fall far from their target. They fail to function, continually break down, do not deliver the anticipated results, and do nothing to address the root causes of feelings of insecurity. Without huge and continuing inputs of work and resources, ubiquitous bordering cannot be even remotely effective. The complex assemblages through which it operates are in fact highly precarious. Often, they merely pander to symptoms, rather than causes, of the spiraling insecurities faced by the world's burgeoning urban poor, living as they do within societies driven to ever greater extremes of hyperinequality by the faltering systems of neoliberalization.

It is crucial, then, to stress that imaginations and fantasies of perfect control and absolute separation between the risky and the risk-free, of the security 'event' and 'normality', remain just that: imaginations and fantasies. Like the ideas of robotic warfare discussed in the next chapter, such discourses are shot through with technological fetishism and day-dreams of omniscience and all-powerful control. But efforts to employ new control technologies inevitably involve a myriad of messy improvisations, strung out across diverse geographies and always necessitating control-at-a-distance. Even increased efforts to integrate groups of previously separate surveillance systems have not produced an all-seeing Big Brother or a single 'global panopticon'. Rather, we have a multitude of Little Brothers – an 'omnopticon' encompassing multiple surveillance systems of diverse scope, scale, effectiveness and reach, which sometimes interact but very often – despite the hype – do not.

Moreover, the new technological borders are prone to technological breakdown, ineffectiveness, errors and unintended effects. Paul Edwards stresses that the actual experience of military information technology often amounts to 'the world of impossibly irritating, frequently crashing, klugedtogether software that nonetheless works pretty well most of the time'.[206] Rather than a system that is all-seeing and all-knowing, what takes place within the proliferating control rooms is marked by narrow, contingent, unwieldy practices. In many cases, the techno-dreams fail simply because the technology breaks down or fails to mesh with a myriad of other technologies or because operators are unable to deal with the system's complexity. Thus 'the geometry of control is never complete', as Michael Shapiro puts it.[207] And as Hille Koskela suggests, it follows that 'urban space will always remain less knowable and, thus, less controllable than the restricted panoptic space'.[208]

It must also be remembered that all fortressed enclaves are not nearly as solipsistic as they appear. They must be sustained by (often hidden) connections elsewhere; they require multiple mobilities and migrations in order to function. Feldman points out, for example, that many 'gated edifices . . . depend on small armies of undocumented migrant labor'.[209] When overzealous crack-downs on 'illegal immigrants' occur, as happened around Long Island's gated communities in 2008, the super-rich residents of such enclaves soon find their houses uncleaned, their parks untended, their children lacking day care and, ironically, their borders unpoliced. Paradoxically, then, the collapse of such services reveals how 'illegal immigration' works across complex, transnational labour geographies and militarizing borders – invisibly sustaining economies, cities and social norms. Yet such migrants live extremely perilous lives. 'As long as they stay behind the scenes, their brawn and skills are highly appreciated',[210] write Carlos Decena and Margaret Gray, but when they become visible, especially in suburbs, it frequently sparks controversy, demonization, violence and removal.

Often, too, the deployment of borders and new security technologies are symbolic, at odds with the radical openness of many places to connections elsewhere. Processes which render spaces 'secure' are always laden with theatre; the symbolism and performance mixes reassurance with the seeding of anxiety. David Murakami Wood and Jonathan Coafee[211] stress that some practices of temporary securitization – around major summits or sporting events, for

---

206   Paul Edwards, in Jordan Crandall, ed., *Under Fire. 2*: 58.

207   Michael Shapiro, 'Every Move you Make: Bodies, Surveillance, and Media', *Social Text* 23: 2, 2005, 29.

208   Hille Koskela, '"Cam Era" – the Contemporary Urban Panopticon', *Surveillance and Society* 1, 2003, 292–313.

209   Feldman, 'Securocratic Wars of Public Safety', 330–350.

210   Carlos Decena and Margaret Gray, ' The Border Next Door: *New York Migraciones'*, *Social Text* 88: 24, 2007, 3.

211   Murakami Wood and Coaffee, 'Security Is Coming Home', 503–517.

instance – are in a sense theatrical, in that their purpose is as much to stage performances of highly visible military and security power as it is as to prevent protest, terrorism or unrest. Anthropologist Cindi Katz also emphasizes the symbolism of camouflaged soldiers lingering, bored, on the streets of New York after 9/11. 'That, of course, is their point', she writes. 'Banal terrorism is sutured to – and secured in – the performance of security in the everyday environment'.[212]

Nor are such performances of security merely about the policing of purported risks. Francisco Klauser points out that the massive systems of temporary fortification that surround events like the Olympics or the World Cup are also efforts to construct new, highly saleable exemplars of state-of-the-art 'security solutions' and snare global media exposure for particular brand cultures.[213]

Finally, all borders and borderings are always in tension with everyday attempts at transgression and resistance. The order and experience of a particular city is 'determined, at least partially, by the unintended, and cumulative, consequence of all border controls'.[214] As demonstrated in the movie *Minority Report,* which depicts a dystopian future dominated by pre-emptive surveillance, there are always complex 'tension[s] between the machines of capture and the micro-politics of escape'.[215] Indeed, writes John Kaliski, noting the curiousness of the pattern, 'many of the social transactions that are shaping the tenor of culture occur in the very places most subject to the scan of globalism. Shopping mall culture, gated enclaves (whether suburbs or rock houses), omnipresent recording, and surveillance of every aspect of daily life do not seem to limit ever new and evolving cultural expressions and mutations born of unexpected gatherings'.[216]

---

212   Cindi Katz, 'Banal terrorism', in Derek Gregory and Allan Pred, eds.,*Violent Geographies,* New York: Routledge, 349–362.

213   Francisco Klauser, 'FIFA Land TM: Alliances Between Security Politics and Business Interests for Germany's city network'.

214   Mats Franze, 'Urban Order and the Preventive Restructuring of Space: the Operation of Border Controls in Micro-Space', *The Sociological Review* 49: 2, 2001, 202–18.

215   M. J. Shapiro, 'Every Move You Make: Bodies, Surveillance, and Media', *Social Text* 23: 2, 2005, 29.

216   John Kaliski, 'Liberation and the naming of paranoid space', in Stephen Flusty, ed., *Building Paranoia: The Proliferation of Interdictory Space and the Erosion of Spatial Justice*, Los Angeles: Los Angeles Forum for Architecture and Urban Design, 1994.

CONSEQUENCES

Such important caveats do not offer an excuse for complacency, however. Rather, they make the costs, impacts and politics of ubiquitous bordering easier to disentangle. Thus a panoply of questions emerge:

At what point, asks Adrian Parr, 'does an urban environment stop working as one?'[217] Do ubiquitous borders threaten to extinguish the political and cultural potential of what Adrian Parr calls the 'cacophony of civic life'? Will the allure of security technologies and camp-like architectures, ask Bülent Diken and Carsten Bagge Laustsen, help create 'islands of order' amid an urban 'sea' of violence, desperation and horror?[218]

Are cities, then, becoming little more than a series of interconnected 'camps' organized through militarized and surveilled passage-points, where all presences and circulations are pre-screened and pre-approved through continuous electronic calculations? What becomes of the 'right to the city'[219] and the politics of urban citizenship in a world of ubiquitous borderings that threaten to render urban life increasingly passive, consumerized, surveilled, and algorithmically marshalled? Will these trends fatally undermine the roles of cities as the main centres of political, cultural, social and economic innovation? Does the pervasive security surge 'infantilize the social body' of the city, as Angelaki Parr argues, by imposing a paternalistic-authoritarian power which claims 'the privileged status of being the only one who can and knows how to say "no" to terrorism'?[220] And does the trend towards securocratic war, and therefore ubiquitous borders, inexorably point to a generally fascist transnational polity, as Naomi Wolf has argued?[221]

How are geographies of democratic dissent affected by the overall 'chilling' of the political culture and the assertion of executive power over democratic scrutiny that are so closely associated with the trends discussed above? How are different traditions of urban political culture and diverse traditions of military and police power contributing to the shaping of specific trajectories within the broader trends towards attempted ubiquitous bordering? Finally, are the processes of ubiquitous bordering as much the result of industrial policy as they are a response to real threats – which is

---

217 Parr, 'One Nation Under Surveillance', 99.
218 Diken and Laustsen, *The Culture Of Exception*, 73.
219 Don Mitchell, *The Right to the City: Social Justice and the Fight for Public Space*, New York: Guildford, 2003.
220 Parr, 'One Nation Under Surveillance', 105.
221 Naomi Wolf, 'Fascist America, in 10 Easy Steps', *Guardian*, 24 April 2007.

to say, are states and supranational blocks (such as the EU) launching their own securitization drives as industrial stepping-stones, a way of assisting their own corporate players to compete effectively within booming global security markets?

This second tier of questions raises concerns about the relation between the rush towards ubiquitous bordering, the construction of difference, and the process of othering. Here we confront the argument that constructions of zoning and borders represent sovereign attempts to *create* illusions of difference rather than to *respond* to difference and its putative risks. In this regard, Seri Guillermina argues that the 'the concrete features of what is captured under the protection of sovereign power and what is excluded matter little. What is crucial is that the distinction is made'.[222]

Ubiquitous borderings, Guillermina contends, 'are about creating the *illusion* of differences, although in actuality there may be none', and she suggests that such 'virtual' productions of difference and antagonistic conflict are now 'crucial to the definition of safe and lawless zones'. Practices of securocratic war and ubiquitous bordering thus become self-fulfilling, so that constructing zones of security and insecurity, organized within and through ubiquitous borders, actually involves 'the critical task of recreating dangers and threats'. To Guillermina, this allows the channelling of 'peoples' and investors' moves in a world scenario in which state territories increasingly resemble its own borders, the social landscape of borders reemerges in metropolitan inner cities, and the exception stains irregularly but progressively the world map'. In this way, securocratic war produces the very 'tools of sovereign power'.

COSMOPOLITAN SECURITY?

A final question arises here, which lays a path to considerations raised at the close of this book. Above and beyond all the concerns, caveats, and crises, we must consider how a successful counterpolitics of security might be mobilized – a counterpolitics which resists and recasts the violent shift towards a biopolitics of pre-emption, exception and extreme polarization. Such a counterpolitics must not only challenge the mythologies sustaining securocratic war and ubiquitous bordering; it must also confront the transnational complexes that feed off the all-pervasive mantra of militarized 'security' that increasingly permeates every crevice of urban life.

---

222 Seri Guillermina, 'On Borders and Zoning: The Vilification of the "Triple Frontier"' paper prepared for delivery at the meeting of the Latin American Studies Association, Dallas, TX, March 27–19 2003.

In the current context, it is profoundly subversive to ask the following simple question: What might be the lineaments of a politics of security that genuinely addresses the real risks and threats facing humankind in a rapidly urbanizing world prone to exhaustion of resources, spiraling food and water insecurity, biodiversity collapse, hyper-automobilization, financial crises, and global warming – and that addresses these threats from a cosmopolitan, rather than a xenophobic and militaristic, starting-point? What might be the characteristics of a politics of security in which the human, urban and ecological aspects of security are foregrounded, rather than the tawdry machinations and imagineerings that surround constellations of states and transnational corporations integrated through dubious or corrupt relationships into an overarching and burgeoning security-industrial-military-media complex?

Conceiving such a counterpolitics must clearly begin by contesting the increasingly widespread mobilization of 'hard' – i.e., profitable – borders and security strategies, by questioning whether these do anything but exacerbate a vicious circle of fear and isolation, and a quest for the holy grail of certainty through technological omniscience combined with the architectures of withdrawal. 'The growth of enclave societies', writes Bryan Turner, 'makes the search for cosmopolitan values and institutions a pressing need, but the current trend towards the erection of walls against the dispossessed and the underclass appears to be inexorable.'[223]

Cosmopolitan notions of security must be open to, indeed forged through, difference. They must work against the habitual translation of difference into objectification, otherness and violence. They must assert the reinstatement of rights within states of *re*-ception as a means of overcoming the murderous sovereignties exercised by the states of *ex*-ception that increasingly characterize neoliberal capitalism.[224] Finally, our counterpolitics must reject the ubiquitous bordering of mobility, circulation and social life both within and without the territorial limits of 'homeland' states. It must, in short, reject securocratic war.

A useful starting-point is provided by the work of philosopher Adrian Parr, who urges that a politics counter to that of the ubiquitous border begin by opening up the 'parameters of this debate in a way that no longer understands

223 Bryan Turner, 'The Enclave Society: Towards a Sociology of Immobility', *European Journal of Social Theory* 10, 2007, 301.

224 Stephen Legg, 'Beyond the European Province: Foucault and Postcolonialism', in Jeremy W. Crampton and Stuart Elden, eds, *Space, Knowledge and Power: Foucault and Geography,* Aldershot: Ashgate, 2007, 265–89.

the outside as terrifying and a source of contamination, against which the inside defensively freezes itself in an effort to contain and ward-off encroachment'.[225] In the final chapter we shall return at considerable length to the challenges of building a viable counterpolitics.

225 Parr, 'One Nation Under Surveillance', 106.

CHAPTER FIVE

Robowar Dreams

People say to me that the Iraqis are not the Vietnamese. You have no jungles or swamps to hide in. I reply: 'let our cities be our swamps and our buildings our jungles.'[1]

The widening adoption of urban-warfare doctrine among Western militaries follows centuries during which its planners observed Sun Tzu's 3,500-year-old dictum that the 'worst policy is to attack cities'.[2] It also follows the Cold War, during which Western military discourse emphasized complete urban extermination through the nuclear targeting of enemies, alongside massive, superpower-led 'air–land' engagements that took place not within cities but on the Northern European plain, within and above the spaces between the by-passed urban regions. Whilst Western forces fought numerous battles in developing world cities during the Cold War as part of wider struggles against independence movements or of 'hot' proxy wars, such conflicts were regarded by Western military theorists as atypical side-shows to the superpowers' projected nuclear and air-land engagements.

Consequently, the already marginal doctrine of urban warfare received little attention during the Cold War and became extremely peripheral within Western military rhetoric. On the rare occasions when Cold War military doctrine explicitly addressed urban warfare, US forces tended (note the characteristically euphemistic language) to 'approach the urban area by rubbling or isolating the city',[3] using tactics unchanged since the Second World War. That is, the US either ignored or sought to systematically annihilate targeted cities.

Today, by contrast, the institutional battles now being waged within the US military and its associated research institutions over how best to respond to counterinsurgency operations within large urban areas are amongst the most important within US military politics.[4] Dominant conceptions of US military engagement, which ignore the urbanization of conflict, are now widely

---

1 Then Iraqi Foreign Minister Tariq Aziz quoted in Chris Bellamy, 'The Iraq Conflict: If the Cities Do Not Fall to the Allies, there May Be No Alternative to Siege Warfare', *Independent*, 28 March 2003.

2 Sun Tzu, *The Art of War*, London: Filiquarian Publishing, 2006.

3 Lee Grubbs, 'In Search of a Joint Urban Operational Concept', Fort Leavenworth, KA:, School of Advanced Military Studies, 2003, viii.

4 Alice Hills, *Future Wars in Cities*, London: Frank Cass, 2004.

contested, and the perceived perils of engaging in 'military operations on urban terrain' (MOUT) are being widely debated and addressed.

US military research on the challenges involved in such transformations dwarfs that of all other nations combined. The repercussions of bloody Iraqi urban insurgencies loom large in these debates. A substantive review of US urban warfare doctrine, prepared by Major Lee Grubbs in 2003, stated baldly that 'as the Iraq plan evolves, it is clear that the enemies of the United States' military have learned a method to mitigate the Joint [US] Forces' dominance in long range surveillance and engagement. The enemy will seek the city and the advantages of mixing with non-combatants.'[5]

One especially important feature of US military discourse on urbanization dominates the debates: how the three-dimensional complexity and the scale of cities in the global South can undermine the US's expensively assembled and hegemonic advantages in surveillance, targeting and killing at-a-distance through 'precision' air- and space-based weapons systems. The present chapter analyses US military theorists' view that the world's rapid urbanization is significantly undermining US military and technoscientific dominance. It then reviews what I call the 'urban turn' in high-tech warfare: the emergence within the US military of technophilic dreams of perfect power, specifically of the adaptation of high-tech warfare to the task of controlling the microgeography of the cities of the global South.

DREAMS FRUSTRATED

> Having seen occupied Iraq up close and on the ground throughout 2003 and 2004, I can report this: Rumsfeld's dreamy RMA [Revolution in Military Affairs] starship has crash-landed in the desert.[6]

Military strategies to project, sustain and deepen US geopolitical power in the post–Cold War period have rested on the 'transformation' of US military power through the so-called Revolution in Military Affairs. Centring on technologies of 'stealth', 'precision' targeting, networked computing, and satellite geo-positioning, the RMA has been widely hailed by US military planners as the path to sustaining US dominance (see Figure 5.1).

---

5   Grubbs, 'In Search of a Joint Urban Operational Concept', 56.
6   Christian Parenti, 'Planet America: The Revolution in Military Affairs as Fantasy and Fetish', in Ashley Dawson and Malini Johar Schueller, eds., *Exceptional State: Contemporary US Culture and the New Imperialism*, Durham, NC: Duke University Press 2007, 101.

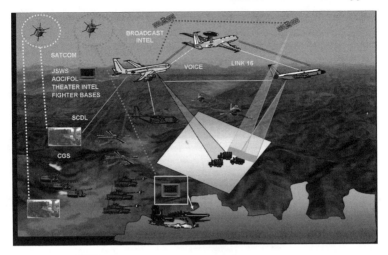

5.1   The US Military's 'Revolution in Military Affairs', conducted
through uninterrupted surveillance and networking.

Interlinkage is central to the RMA. The use of networked sensing and computing to establish a 'system of systems' of US military technologies means that a truly 'network-centric' form of warfare should now be possible, enabling US forces to continually dominate adversaries through surveillance and 'situational awareness' that approach omnipotence, through devastating and precisely targeted aerial firepower, and through the suppression and degradation of the communications and fighting ability of any and all opposing forces.[7] RMA theorists imagine US military operations to be a giant, integrated 'network enterprise' – a 'just-in-time' system of cyborg warriors which utilizes many of the principles of logistics-chain management and technology-based tracking that so dominate contemporary business models.[8]

A crucial argument in support of the RMA is that it reduces the risk of undertaking military operations – the risk for US forces, that is. Hence, such interventions become more common, more aggressive, and more pre-emptive. They become a basis for US strategy. Such perceptions were central to the

7   See John Arquilla and David Ronfeldt, eds., *Networks and Netwars*, Santa Monica, CA: RAND, 2001.

8   Chris Hable Gray, 'Posthuman Soldiers and Postmodern War', *Body and Society* 9: 4, 2003, 215–26.

Bush administration's launching of 'pre-emptive war' as part of an ongoing, unbounded War on Terror post-9/11, and to earlier, influential pronouncements by the neoconservative Project for a New American Century that US forces must be redesigned for the post–Cold War era so that they could 'fight and decisively win multiple, simultaneous major theatre wars'.

'It is now possible to use America's military might', wrote US military theorist Raymond O'Mara in 2003, 'with a greatly reduced chance of suffering friendly casualties or equipment loss'. By reducing US casualties to negligible levels, he argued, military deployment was becoming politically much less problematic. As a result, the US military had to 'adapt to its new role as a tool of choice, rather than a tool of last resort'.[9]

Technophilic language may depict the RMA as ushering in a reduced-risk, 'clean' and seemingly painless strategy of US military dominance, but this picture assumes that the vast, integrated networks of sensors and weapons would work uninterruptedly. In addition, global scales of flow and connection dominate the discourse: technological mastery, omnipotent surveillance, real-time situational awareness, and speed-of-light digital interactions have been widely portrayed as processes intrinsically capable of endowing the US military with 'full spectrum dominance' on a planetary scale, irrespective of the geographical terrain to be dominated.

RMA discourses have, in this sense, been signally a-geographical. Little account has been taken of the specificities of the spaces and geographical terrains inhabited by US adversaries in the post–Cold War period, or of the changes wrought through urbanization. A key axiom of RMA rhetoric has been the new US capability to prosecute global strategies for geopolitical dominance through a 'radical non-territoriality'.[10]

In response to the RMA's neglect of global urbanization, and spurred by the catastrophic and continuing urban insurgencies within Iraq since the 2003 invasion, an increasingly powerful range of counterdiscourses have emerged within the US military. These have focused on the collapse of the original RMA fantasies of planetary control when confronted with the microgeographies of Iraq's cities and the nation's complex insurgencies. 'Somewhere on the way to frictionless global military dominance', writes Christian Parenti, 'the United States found itself stuck in a radically asymmetric urban guerrilla war'. All of

---

9   Raymond O'Mara, 'Stealth, Precision, and the Making of American Foreign Policy', *Air and Space Power Chronicles*, June 2003, available at www.airpower.maxwell.af.mil/airchronicles.

10   Mark Duffield, 'War as a Network Enterprise: The New Security Terrain and Its Implications', *Cultural Values* 6, 2002, 153–65.

a sudden, 'America's military fantasy had morphed into its military nightmare: a cumbersome high-tech army of soft American kids bogged down in Iraqi cities fighting a low-tech and determined insurgency'.[11] Nevertheless, far from retreating from technophilic fantasies, most of the military's counterdiscourses have merely suggested that high-tech US militarism be redirected to the task of addressing the complex geographies of cities rather than the domains of aerial and space power. The pronouncements of advocates of an 'urban turn' for the RMA have had two main features.

SIGNAL FAILURES

In simple terms, walls tend to get in the way of today's battlefield communications and sensor technologies.[12]

First, proponents of the urban turn strongly suggest that the urban terrain in the poor countries of the global South is a great leveller between high-tech US forces and their low-tech, usually informally organized and poorly equipped adversaries. The complex, congested terrain that lies below, within, and above cities is seen as a set of physical battlespaces which limit the effectiveness of GPS-targeted bombs, air and space-based surveillance systems, and automated, 'network-centric' and 'precision' weapons.

A major US Marine Corps strategy document, for example, argued in 1997 that 'the urban environment negates the abilities of present US military communications equipment'.[13]

In fact, the principles and technologies of network-centric warfare break down drastically in cities. Dense concrete environments reduce the advantages of a high-tech over a lower-tech force. 'Buildings mask targets and create urban canyons, which diminish the capabilities of the air force', caution Phillip Misselwitz and Eyal Weizman. As a result, 'it is hard to see into the urban battlespace; it is very difficult to communicate in it, because radio waves are often disturbed' and therefore 'it is hard to use precision weapons because it is difficult to obtain accurate GPS satellite locations'.[14] All in all, argues British academic Aidan Harris, 'the technologies

---

11 Parenti, 'Planet America', 89.

12 Mark Hewish, and Rupert Pengelley. 'Facing Urban Inevitabilities: Military Operations in Urban Terrain', *Jane's International Defence Review*, August 2001, 13–18.

13 Defense Intelligence Reference Document (DIRC), 'The Urban Century: Developing World Urban Trends and Possible Factors Affecting Military Operations', Quantico, VA: Marine Corps Intelligence Agency, 1997.

14 Phillip Misselwitz and Eyal Weizman, 'Military Operations as Urban Planning', in Anselme Franke, ed., *Territories*, Berlin: KW Institute for Contemporary Art, 2003, 272–5.

5.2   Interrupting dreams of vertical mastery: US
military satellite image of a part of Baghdad.

traditionally ascribed to the current Revolution in Military Affairs phenomenon
will have negligible impact on Military Operations in Urban Terrain.'[15]

Many US commentators on urban warfare contend that the urbanization
of battlespace reduces the ability of US forces to achieve vertical omniscience
(Figure 5.2) and to fight and kill at a distance (always the preferred way,
because of the dread of casualties combined with the desire for technological
supremacy). Cities present escalated risks for US forces fighting pre-emptive,
expeditionary wars: 'From refugee flows to dense urban geography, cities

15   Aidan Harris, 'Can New Technologies Transform Military Operations in Urban
Terrain?', research paper, Lancaster University, March 2003.

create environments that increase uncertainty exponentially', states the Marines' 1997 study.[16] Military operations in cities are therefore seen as treacherous events, akin to a Trojan horse, that might allow weak, poorly equipped insurgents to score victories over the world's remaining military superpower.

 The Clutter of Concealment

July 6, 2006   Transparent Urban Structures - Industry Day   30

5.3   The Office of Navy Research argued that cities provide a 'clutter of concealment' inhibiting the United States' military's high-tech systems of tracking and targeting.

THE URBANIZATION OF INSURGENCY

> Opposition forces will camouflage themselves in the background noise of the urban environment. Within the urban environment, it is not the weapon itself but rather the city which maximises or mutes an arm's effectiveness. In claustrophobic alleys and urban canyons, civilians are impossible to control or characterise as friendly or not. Weapons hidden beneath a cloak, in a child's carriage, or rolled in a carpet, can get past security personnel undetected.[17]

The second main feature of the urban-turn discourse shifts the focus from the

---

16   Defense Intelligence Reference Document (DIRC), 'The Urban Century: Developing World Urban Trends and Possible Factors Affecting Military Operations'.
17   DIRC, 'The Urban Century'.

national scale – the challenges presented by 'failed states' – to the urban scale, the military and political challenges of well-armed insurgent groups hiding within, and controlling, fast-growing urban areas. An important element is US military commentator Richard J. Norton's influential concept of 'feral cities' – highly disorderly urban areas in the global South which are controlled by violent non-state militias of various sorts.[18]

Some protagonists in this debate argue that the breakdown of high-tech sensors and weapons, caused by the 'clutter of concealment' provided by cities, is leading directly to an increased tendency among US political adversaries to take refuge within cities (Figure 5.3). 'The long-term trend in open-area combat', writes the leading US urban-warfare commentator, Ralph Peters, 'is toward overhead dominance by US forces'. Peters predicts that 'battlefield awareness [for US forces] may prove so complete, and 'precision' weapons so widely available and effective, that enemy ground-based combat systems will not be able to survive in the deserts, plains, and fields that have seen so many of history's main battles'.[19] As a result, he argues, US 'enemies will be forced into cities and other complex terrain, such as industrial developments and inter-city sprawl'.[20]

Encouraging what RAND theorists Jennifer Taw and Bruce Hoffman have termed the 'urbanization of insurgency'[21] is a key incentive: the notion that insurgents who exploit the material geographies of global South cities can force US military personnel into close physical proximity to insurgents and so expose them to much higher casualty rates than those portrayed in RMA doctrine. 'The weapons [such insurgents] use may be 30 to 40 years old or built from hardware supplies', says the Marines' 1997 report. 'But at close range many of their inefficiencies are negated. The most effective weapon only needs to exploit the vulnerabilities that the urban environment creates'.[22]

Finally, military commentators regard the enormous and exploding scale of global South megacities as completely at odds with the diminishing scale of professional Western militaries (Figure 5.4). Given the inescapably soldier-intensive nature of urban operations, traditional attempts to occupy such cities become increasingly untenable – absent radical increases in the use of high-tech solutions to replace manpower.

---

18 Norton, 'Feral Cities'.
19 Ralph Peters, 'The Future of Armored Warfare', *Parameters* 27: 3, 1997, 50–60.
20 Ibid.
21 Jennifer Taw and Bruce Hoffman, *The Urbanization of Insurgency: The Potential Challenge to US Army Operations*.
22 DIRC, 'The Urban Century'.

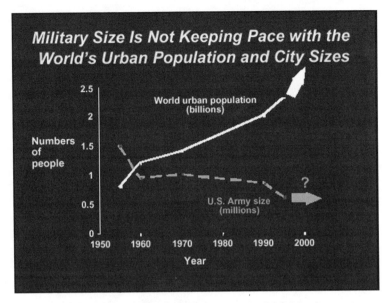

5.4 Perceived mismatch between the scale of global South urbanization and the diminishing size of the US military.

DREAMS RECLAIMED

It is time to tell Sun Tzu to sit down . . . Instead of fearing it, we must own the city.[23]

Clearly, then, there is a widespread perception that the intensifying urbanization of areas in the global South that the US military envisages as its dominant areas of operation is radically undermining broader US efforts at technoscientific transformation. Thus, almost predictably, a wide range of new technoscientific initiatives is emerging, aimed at tailoring the RMA to the geographies of just those sorts of urban areas. With the urban insurgency in Iraq as a fulcrum, a shift is taking place – from celebrating the death of geography because of new technologies, to developing surveillance, communications and targeting systems specifically tailored to the fine-grained physical and human geographies of global South cities. A classic Foucauldian boomerang effect, this transformation overlaps with, and resonates through,

---

23 Robert Leonhard, 'Sun Tzu's Bad Advice: Urban Warfare in the Information Age', *Army Magazine* 53: 4, 2003.

the wider effort (discussed in the previous chapter) to build ubiquitous borders across the world's urban sites.

One should read these emerging US high-tech urban warfare and counterinsurgency programmes as symptoms of desire – technophilic dreams and fetishistic urges for mastery and control, adjusted to the new imperatives of urban counterinsurgency warfare and declining US political and economic power. These programmes and imaginings also reflect deep-seated, long-standing tendencies within US military culture to seek all-conquering superweapons that can annihilate all enemies – if possible, from a distance.[24] Superior technology is thus the key to all locks, the silver bullet.

But as the Iraq debacle demonstrates, silver-bullet weaponry cannot address the morass of political problems generated by ideologies of pre-emptive colonial urban warfare, or by the resistance to them. Populations that fought fiercely to throw off the shackles of Western colonialism are unlikely to be rendered supine by US colonial occupation, however high-tech it may be. Indeed, the very design and deployment of new high-tech weaponry for purposes of dominating occupied cities are likely to inflame, rather than intimidate, insurgencies and resistances against occupation. In many ways, America's new 'asymmetric' wars address what Jonathan Schell has called 'unconquerable worlds'[25] – social, political and urban formations in which notions of technological and military domination are merely examples of what Parenti, thinking along somewhat the same lines, calls 'delusional techno-fetishism'.[26] Thus, write the Report collective and colleagues, the military planners behind the invasion of Iraq were clearly 'so dazzled by the Revolution in Military Affairs that it never dawned on them that no Revolution in Occupation Affairs had accompanied it'.[27]

A NEW MANHATTAN PROJECT?

Fetishism? Perhaps. But such is the nexus between a vast, sprawling military-technological-industrial complex feeding at the trough of US defense budgets and a vast, deep-seated US techno-culture doting on future weapons fantasies and science fictions that hopes for high-tech show remarkable obduracy, persistence, and adaptability. The current trend is adaptation: the adjustment of ideas of global

---

24   H. Bruce Franklin, *War Stars: The Superweapon and the American Imagination,* Boston: University of Massachusetts Press, 1990.

25   See Jonathan Schell, *The Unconquerable World: Power, Nonviolence, and the Will of the People,* Penguin: London, 2005.

26   Parenti, 'Planet America', 88–104.

27   Boal, Clark., Matthews and Watts, *Afflicted Powers,* 187.

dominance through high-tech military transformation to the microgeographical realities of protracted and asymmetric urban counterinsurgency warfare.

An excellent example can be found in a major report published by the Pentagon's Defense Science Board (DSB) in December 2004.[28] One of many early attempts to draw military lessons from the urban insurgency in Iraq, this report called for a 'new Manhattan Project', invoking the code-name famously used in the 1940s to describe the massive programme which developed the atomic bombs used to devastate Hiroshima and Nagasaki. The DSB's report urged a similar concentration of military resources on what it regarded as the key strategic priority for the twenty-first century: the technological unveiling of cities and urban life in a rapidly urbanizing world. Specifically, the report raised the possibility of exploiting ubiquitous computing technologies to develop a massive, integrated, world-spanning system of surveillance that would be tailored to penetrating the increasing complexity and mobility of urban life. Such a system, it argued, would again render the US military's targets trackable and destroyable. The purpose of the new Manhattan Project, then, would be to 'locate, identify, and track, people, things and activities – in an environment of one in a million – to give the United States the same advantages in asymmetric warfare [as] it has today in conventional warfare'.[29] In 2005 the ideas in the DSB report were (temporarily) cemented as one of eight principal areas of development areas described in the Pentagon's strategy for a 'Long War', a revamping of the military's language related to the fight against terrorism.

The United State's hegemonic capabilities for surveilling Earth from the distant, vertical domains of air and space were deemed by the DSB to show 'poor capability for finding, identifying and tracking' what it called 'unconventional war targets', such as 'individuals and insurgent or terrorists groups that operate by blending in with the larger society'.[30] What was needed, argued the DSB report, were intimate and persistent military surveillance systems which penetrated the details of everyday urban life, both at home and abroad. Little less than a comprehensive rescaling of military surveillance would be necessary; 'more intimate, terrestrial, 21st century ISR [Intelligence, Surveillance and Reconnaissance] were required'.[31]

The gaze of hegemonic military power, the report contended, must not only colonize the planetary scales of surveillance; it must penetrate the fine-grained local geographies of urban and infrastructural battlespaces. Such a transformation

---

28 Defense Science Board (DSB), *Transition To and From Hostilities*, Washington, DC: Office of the Undersecretary of Defense, 2004, 163.

29 Ibid., 163.

30 Ibid., 153.

31 Ibid., 2.

would be temporal as well as geographical. 'The surveillance of people, things and activities required to populated the databases needed for identification, location and tracking,' the DSB report stated, 'will require a persistence beyond that typical of many of today's' military and security surveillance systems.

These new systems, local and global at the same time, must thus be 'always on' – enabling them, through 'evidence-correlating and backtracking algorithms,'[32] to call upon memories, via databases which record the history of movements and associations of things, activities and people, as well as to anticipate, so that threatening and 'abnormal' behaviours and events can be detected and addressed prior to an attack.

The new 'close-in, terrestrial means' of surveillance, intelligence and targeting focus on those data-mining and tracking techniques discussed in the previous chapter. Through the use of finger or palm prints, iris scans, DNA, face recognition, voice recognition, even odour and gait recognition, biometric sensors will verify and code the identity of persons as they cross borders.[33]

COMBAT ZONES THAT SEE

The new visions of close-in surveillance involve pervasive, interlinked arrays of 'loitering' and 'embedded' sensors, overcoming all the limits and interruptions that megacity environments place in the way of successful network-centric warfare. Robert Ackerman suggests, for instance, that such sensor suites will be designed to observe 'change' rather than 'scenery' – to automatically track dynamic situations rather than to constantly soak up data from unchanging environments. In other words, algorithms will be designed to function only when definable changes occur, as against a background of normality. 'Abnormal' behaviours and patterns would then be assessed as targets.[34]

One major example of this development is the tellingly titled Combat Zones That See (CTS) project, led by the US Defense Advanced Research Projects Agency (DARPA). Launched at the start of the Iraq insurgency in 2003, CTS 'explores concepts, develops algorithms, and delivers systems for utilizing large numbers (1000s) of algorithmic video cameras to provide the close-in sensing demanded

---

32 Ibid., 159.

33 The DSB report favours combinations of iris and fingerprint scans, combined with face recognition, as 'offering a reasonably effective compromise among speed, accuracy, ease of implementation and cost', 159.

34 Robert Ackerman, 'Persistent Surveillance Comes into View', *Signal Magazine,* May 2002.

for military operations in urban terrain.[35] By installing computerized CCTV across entire occupied cities, the project organizers envisage that, when deployed, CTS will sustain 'motion-pattern analysis across whole city scales' via the tracking of massive numbers of cars and people through intelligent computer algorithms linked to the recognition of number-plates and scanned photos of human faces.

5.5   DARPA's VisiBuilding Programme: An attempt to build and deploy sensors that render the city fabric transparent (ISR: Intelligence, Surveillance and Reconnaissance).

CTS is a direct response to the interruptive effects of city environments on older notions of air- and space-based network-centric warfare. Its planners envisage that, once developed, it 'will generate, for the first time, the reconnaissance, surveillance and targeting information needed to provide close-in, continuous, always-on support for military operations in urban terrain.'[36] A key factor will be the generation of electronic ideas of 'normality' in the day-to-day routines of city life; lacking a concept of the normal, of course, the abnormal cannot be identified or targeted. As with data-mining, past histories of movement and association will

35   Defense Advanced Research Projects Agency, *Combat Zones That See Program: Proper Information*. 2003, 6, Available at www.darpa.mil.
36   Ibid.

be used to continually imagine the near future and thus, in DARPA's words, allow 'operators to provide real-time capabilities to assess potential force threats'.[37]

Following a stream of protests from US civil liberties groups, DARPA stressed that, whilst the initial testing of mass urban tracking was to take place at an army base within the US (Fort Belvoir, Virginia), the deployment of CTS would only occur in 'foreign urban battlefields'.[38] However, the sorts of smart video surveillance technologies being mobilized for the CTS programme are effectively identical to those being used to support the construction of security zones in cities like London and New York.[39]

DARPA has other programmes as well, of course. One of them, VisiBuilding, is dedicated to the development of sensors through which ground forces and unmanned aerial vehicles can remotely sense the people and objects within buildings (Figure 5.5). The Navy's equivalent programme, Transparent Urban Structures, seeks to use 'geotypical' stereotypes about the internal structures and activities within Iraqi (or other) households – stereotypes that are generated by virtual simulations of the country[40] – against which possible threats and risks would be automatically highlighted. Again, this targeting works via automated scanning for the 'abnormal' against a state of normality derived from military anthropologists' stereotypical portrayals and imaginings of Iraqi urban norms and culture.

Other arms of the US defence research establishment are developing new aerial radars built into giant airships designed to loiter permanently above occupied cities, doing comprehensive data-mining. This dream of omniscience involves linking suites of databases of past movements and histories in the city with surveillance of present activities so as to anticipate future attacks and to respond to those that have been carried out. One airship under development by DARPA is driven by the idea of 'rewinding history' following an attack by a car bomb or improvised explosive device (IED), thereby revealing the perpetrators. This airship would be tethered above a city for a year or more. Its very structure is a giant radio-frequency radar apparatus designed to penetrate urban structures and record histories of movement (Figure 5.6). Sensors fuse information from cell phones, TVs and radios, as well as smart CCTV, biometric scanners and a myriad of radio-frequency tags 'sown' into the battlespace as 'smart dust.' This, suggests the rhetoric, will enable the US military to undertake 'advanced target acquisition' within the dominated city.[41]

37   Ibid., 11.
38   *Defense Watch* magazine, 'Combat Zones that 'See' Everything', 2004, available at www.argee.net/DefenseWatch.
39   See Chapter 9.
40   See Chapter 6.
41   Edward Baranoski, 'Urban Operations, The New Frontier for Radar', Defense Advanced Research and Projects Agency, Washington, DC, 2005.

TOWARDS AUTONOMOUS KILLER ROBOTS

> Military leaders are developing a vision of the tactical operations future where adversaries will have to decide if they should send flesh and blood troops to fight nuts, bolts, circuits and sensors.[42]

It is but a short step from imagining and designing systems to automatically 'acquire targets' within a city, to developing robotized weapons systems designed to kill or destroy those targets under ever-diminishing human supervision. The second main element of the urban turn in high-tech warfare, then, focuses on the development of robotic air and ground weapons which, when linked to the sorts of persistent surveillance and target identification just discussed, will be deployed to continually, automatically destroy purported targets in potentially endless streams of automated killing.

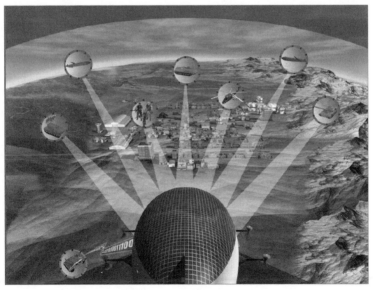

5.6 Data-mining an adversary city for 'advanced target acquisition': DARPA's 'Integrated Sensor Is System' (ISIS), a radar built into an airship that loiters for a year or more over a targeted city.

---

42 Maryann Lawlor, 'Robotic Concepts Take Shape', *Signal Magazine*, November 2003.

These ideas within the RMA's urban turn are a key feature of the US military's latest fantasies of omnipotence and omniscience. Here the fixation is with using robots to underpin 'sentient' surveillance, tailored to the detailed microgeographies of global South cities. Reams of fantasies of godlike 'situational awareness' are emerging, all suggesting that the urban turn will finally help oversee and placate the intrinsically unruly megacities of the enemy.

The RMA's urban turn also emphasizes the dovetailing of new surveillance infrastructures with automated killing machines. What is envisioned is 'a perpetual global war waged not by human beings who die, rebel, or come home wounded and crazy, but a war waged by labor that is already dead, crystallized into machinery'.[43] A telling example of this comes from the discussion of a model near-future US urban operation described by *Defense Watch* magazine during a discussion of DARPA's Combat Zones That See programme. Soon, the author gushes, 'our guys are in for a mind-boggling treat at the expense of the bad guys'.[44]

In this scenario, swarms of microscale and nanoscale networked sensors are blown into the target city, pervading it and thus providing continuous streams of information to arrays of automated weaponry. Jointly, these systems produce continuous killing and target destruction: a kind of robotized counterinsurgency operation with US commanders and soldiers doing little except overseeing the automated killing systems from a safe distance – safe for themselves, that is.

'Several large fans are stationed outside the city limits of an urban target that our guys need to take', the *Defense Watch* description begins. 'Upon appropriate signal, what appears like a dust cloud emanates from each fan. The cloud is blown into town where it quickly dissipates.' Then a swarm of unmanned vehicles colonizes the city. 'The little drones dive into selected areas determined by the initial analysis of data transmitted by the fan-propelled swarm'. Quickly the swarms of mobile sensors produce 'a detailed visual and audio picture of every street and building in the entire city'. As well as the physical city, 'every hostile [person] has been identified and located. From this point on, nobody in the city moves without the full and complete knowledge of the mobile tactical center'.[45]

Automated surveillance then merges seamlessly into automated killing. 'Unmanned air and ground vehicles can now be vectored directly to selected

43 Parenti, 'Planet America', 89.
44 *Defense Watch* magazine, 'Combat Zones that 'See' Everything'.
45 Ibid.

targets to take them out, one by one. Those enemy combatants clever enough to evade actually being taken out by the unmanned units can then be captured or killed by human elements who are guided directly to their locations, with full and complete knowledge of their individual fortifications and defenses.'[46]

Such dreams of continuous, automated, robotized urban targeting and killing are hardly limited to the realm of futuristic speculation. Rather, as with the CTS programme, they feed contemporary weapons research aimed at the development of ground and aerial vehicles which not only navigate and move robotically but which, on the basis of algorithmically driven 'decisions', select and destroy targets. Human decision-makers are left out of the loop.

As part of the broader shift towards robotic vehicles that fuels major competitions such as Urban Challenge (discussed in Chapter 10), the US Army envisages that one third of all US military ground vehicles will be entirely robotic by 2015. In a 2004 article, defence journalist Maryanne Lawlor[47] discusses the development of 'autonomous mechanized combatant' air and ground vehicles, as well as what she calls 'tactical autonomous combatants' under development for the US Air Force. These are being designed, she notes, to use pattern-recognition software for 'time-critical targeting'. This involves rapidly linking sensors to automated weapons so that targets that are automatically sensed and 'recognized' by databases can be quickly, continually, and automatically destroyed. In US military parlance, such doctrine is widely termed 'compressing the kill chain' or 'sensor to shooter warfare'.[48]

According to Lawlor, the 'swarming of unmanned systems' project team at US Joint Forces Command's Joint Concept Development & Experimentation Directorate, based in Norfolk, Virginia, has made so much progress that 'autonomous, networked and integrated robots may be the norm rather than the exception by 2025'.[49] By that date, she predicts, 'technologies could be developed . . . that would allow machines to sense a report of gunfire in an urban environment to within one meter, triangulating the position of the shooter and return fire within a fraction of a second', and she argues that such robo-war systems will 'help save lives by taking humans out of harm's way'.[50] Apparently, only US military personnel fall within the category 'human'.

The US Army's Project Alpha is already developing an armed robot that automatically fires back when it detects enemy gunfire within an occupied

---

46 Ibid.
47 Lawlor, 'Robotic Concepts Take Shape'.
48 Adam Hebert, 'Compressing the Kill Chain', *Air Force Magazine* 86: 3, 2003, 34–42.
49 Lawlor, 'Robotic Concepts Take Shape'.
50 Ibid.

city. The aim of this robot-soldier is that 'if it can get within one meter, it's killed the person who's firing', reports Gordon Johnson, team leader for the Unmanned Effects component of the project. 'So, essentially, what we're saying is that anyone who would shoot at our forces would die. Before he can drop that weapon and run, he's probably already dead'. Are future urban insurgents 'going to give up blood and guts to kill machines?' Johnson wonders. 'I'm guessing not'.[51]

KILLER ROBOTS IN IRAQ, AFGHANISTAN AND PALESTINE

By 2007, these sorts of fantasies were heading into the early stages of implementation. The zones of experimentation were provided by the streets of Iraqi and Palestinian cities.[52] In June 2006, for example, the first armed and remotely controlled ground robots in the history of warfare – so-called SWORDS,[53] armed with machine guns – were deployed in Baghdad.[54] Soldiers could remotely fire the system's guns from up to a kilometre away. It is estimated that by 2008, the US military had deployed four thousand SWORDS and other armed robots to Iraq and Afghanistan.[55]

'Many people are fearful that armed robots will run amok on the battlefield', admits a press release from the US Armament Research, Development and Engineering Center, describing trials of the SWORDS system.[56] In an attempt at reassurance, the release stresses that the robots still 'employ a "man in the loop" where they are always under director control of a soldier [who] issues commands to the robot and weapons through an operator control unit. Commands to rocket and grenade launchers are communicated through a newly developed remote-firing and control system'.[57]

Col. Terry Griffin, head of the joint US Army and Marine Corps robot programme – tasked with deploying the next armed machine, known as Gladiator – argues that the machine's first job will be to disband groups of 'undesirables'. He describes three stages of escalation during that process: first,

---

51   Cited in Lawlor, 'Robotic Concepts Take Shape'.

52   Steve Featherstone, 'The Coming Robot Army: Introducing America's Future Fighting Machines', *Harper's Magazine*, February 2007, 43–52.

53   'SWORDS' stands for 'Special Weapons Observation Reconnaissance Detection System'.

54   Jörg Blech, 'Attack of the Killer Robots', *Der Spiegel* online, August 2007.

55   Charlie Carpenter, 'Autonomous Weapons and Asymmetric Conflict', Complex Terrain Laboratory, available at www.terraplexic.org.

56   Armament Research, Development and Engineering Center, 'ARDEC Provides Glimpse of Possible Future Warfare', press release, 2007, available at www.pica.army.mil/.

57   Ibid.

'the robot issues warnings through a loudspeaker. It fires rubber bullets. Finally, the robot starts firing its machine gun'.[58]

Such programmes are not the exclusive province of US researchers. In 2007 the Israeli army announced that 'the border between Israel and Gaza will be the first "automated border" in the world, with robotic snipers able to fire at intruders, thanks to pictures relayed to a control room'.[59] Meanwhile, the Israeli military already relies on a robotic and remote-controlled machine-gun turret, as part of the See-Shoot system developed by the state-owned entity Rafael, to deploy lethal force along the thirty-seven-mile border with the Gaza Strip. 'Combined with a Rafael-developed acoustic sensor detection and direction-finding device, [it] essentially becomes a robotic anti-sniper weapon for wheeled or tracked vehicles', according to the Tel Aviv correspondent for *Defense News*. 'Each machine-gun-mounted station serves as a type of robotic sniper, capable of enforcing a nearly 1,500-meter-deep no-go zone'.[60] The guns and their long sensors are 'tied in by optic fibre to a command network which will also be able to draw information from existing ground sensors, manned aircraft, and overhead drones'.[61]

Although the Israeli military envisions a longer-term shift towards true automation of firing, initially Israeli soldiers will be required to approve See-Shoot's decisions to fire. 'At least in the initial phases of deployment, we're going to have to keep the man in the loop', an unnamed IDF commander remarked. 'We don't want to risk making tragic and politically costly mistakes with such a lethal system'.[62]

This fails, however, to reassure human rights groups, who are extremely concerned by the incipient robotization of lethal border weaponry. Sarit Michaeli, who works for the Israeli Information Center for Human Rights in the Occupied Territories, reports that between Israel's withdrawal from Gaza in 1995 and June 2007, fourteen unarmed Palestinians were killed by Israeli security forces at ranges between one hundred and eight hundred metres from the border fence. Moreover, she claims, 'there have been many cases in which people with no hostile or terrorist intentions were shot approaching the perimeter fence. Some attempted to enter Israel to find work, others suffered from disabilities, and still others were children who may have wandered into

---

58   Jörg Blech, 'Attack of the Killer Robots'.
59   Arieh Egozi, 'Automated Border', *Israel News*, 6 October 2007.
60   Barbara Opall-Rome, 'Israeli Arms, Gear aid US Troops', *Defense News*, 29 March 2007.
61   Defense Update.com, 'Elbit Expands Range of Autonomous Ground Vehicles', 2007.
62   Opall-Rome, 'Israeli Arms, Gear Aid US Troops'.

the forbidden areas.' Michaeli argues that 'from a human rights perspective, the technology here is not as important as the need to evaluate each potential threat on a case by case basis'.[63] Such complex ethics of discretion, however, are unlikely to fall within the capabilities of fully automated robotic border killers.

KILL-CHAIN SOLUTIONS

As with armed ground robots, the shift away from piloted armed drones towards fully autonomous aerial weapons systems, without what the military call a 'human in the loop', is already underway. The US Air Force's emerging Low Cost Autonomous Attack System (LOCAAS), for example – one output of the massive Future Combat Systems programme – is a jet-powered 'stand off' bomb designed to 'autonomously search for, detect, identify, attack and destroy theatre missile defence, surface to air missile systems, and interdiction/armour targets of military interest'.[64] It will be equipped with a laser radar system as well as an autonomous target-recognition capability that will allow it to search for and identify targets within an eighty-five-square-kilometer area.[65]

Such munitions will depend on computer algorithms designed to automatically separate 'targets' from 'non-targets'. The ultimate goal, according to an unmanned combat air vehicle (UCAV) engineer at Raytheon, is what he calls a 'kill chain solution' based on each vehicle continuously seeking out and destroying targets on its own.[66] In 2002 John Tirpak, executive editor of *Air Force Magazine*, envisioned that humans would be required to make the decisions to launch weapons at targets only 'until UCAVs establish a track record of reliability in finding the right targets and employing weapons properly'. Then the 'machines will be trusted to do even that'.[67]

In the domains of both air and ground, then, much effort is already going into establishing the technologies and ethical protocols that would allow armed robots, equipped with artificial intelligence, to autonomously 'decide' to launch their weapons at targets. These efforts focus on unpiloted armed drones which automatically fire at targets; armed ground robots which operate independently; and missiles, bombs and munitions which are designed to hover over a district or city for days at a time, 'seeing' and seeking out targets to attack.[68]

---

63   Barbara Opall-Rome, 'Robots to Guard Israeli Border Kill Zone', *Defense News*, 2007.

64   Robert Sparrow, 'Killer Robots', *Journal of Applied Philosophy* 24: 1, 2007, 63.

65   Ibid.

66   Chuck Pinney, *UAV Weaponization*, Washington DC: Raytheon, 2003, 16.

67   John Tirpak, 'Heavyweight Contender', *Air Force Magazine* 85: 7, 2002.

68   See Sparrow, 'Killer Robots', 63.

Consider the US Army's vision for automonous killer robots as clearly described in a 2007 call for development proposals. 'Armed UMS [Unmanned Systems] are beginning to be fielded in the current battlespace, and will be extremely common in the Future Force Battlespace', it states. 'This will lead directly to the need for the systems to be able to operate autonomously for extended periods, and also to be able to collaboratively engage hostile targets within specified rules of engagement'. For the moment, the 'final decision on target engagement [is] being left to the human operator [but] fully autonomous engagement without human intervention should also be considered, under user-defined conditions'.[69]

A whole universe of 'automated target recognition' software is presently evolving, intended to enable robots' computers to continuously compare the electronic signatures of 'targets' with those stored on electronic databases. Before the SWORDS robot fires its bullets in Iraq, writes Jörg Blech in *Der Spiegel*, 'it needs the permission of two human operators . . . However, it is only logical that decisions over life and death will increasingly be transferred to the machine – just as soon as engineers have figured out how to overcome the problem of distinguishing between friends and foes'.[70]

ARMED ENTOMOLOGY

Even more chillingly, the notion of swarms of minuscule aerial vehicles or even armed, robotic insects is now being widely explored in blue-sky military thinking and research. Already, robotic insects such as the Black Widow, Wasp and Hornet, which weigh about forty grams and are a few centimetres across, are being developed to mimic the flight mechanisms of biological insects. These systems are intended for use by 'ground units fighting military operations in urban terrain' and 'can fly over buildings, into rooms, see who is there, what weapons they do or do not have'.[71]

Looking to the future, USAF Lieutenant Colonel Daryl Hauck speculates that within twenty years, the combination of nanotechnology and genetic technology will bring about a new era of biological warfare, operating at micro or microscopic scales. Such a technological convergence, he argues, would allow swarms of flying micro-robots to target an individual's DNA

---

69   US Army SBIR Solicitation 07.2, Topic A07-032, 'Multi-Agent Based Small Unit Effects Planning and Collaborative Engagement with Unmanned Systems', 2007, 57–68.

70   Blech, 'Attack of the Killer Robots'.

71   Tim Blackmore, 'Dead Slow: Unmanned Aerial Vehicles Loitering in Battlespace', *Bulletin of Science, Technology and Society* 25, 2005, 199.

(determined via DNA databases) by injecting biological or genetic 'weapons' into the subject's bloodstream. 'Single microteeth-like devices', he writes, 'could fit well within a [human] blood vessel to carry and insert genetic material into cells'.[72] Such commentary seems to come straight off the script of a dystopian sci-fi movie. Yet the launch of the Hybrid Insect programme by DARPA in 2006 means that, as Nick Turse puts it, 'researchers are already growing insects with electronics inside them. They're creating cyborg moths and flying beetles that can be remotely controlled'.[73] According to DARPA, this programme is 'aimed at developing tightly-coupled machine-insect interfaces by placing micro-mechanical systems inside the insects during the early stages of metamorphosis'.

In brief, sci-fi is now reality. Placing micro-electronics within the pupa produces a cyborg insect which can be remotely controlled after it leaves its cocoon. As well as carrying microsurveillance systems able to permeate, and permanently inhabit, any adversary city, it is envisaged that such swarming systems might eventually deploy the kinds of micro-scale weaponry imagined by Lieutenant Colonel Hauck. In such a context, Nick Turse asks his readers to 'imagine a world in which any insect fluttering past your window may be a remote-controlled spy, packed with surveillance equipment'. Even more disturbing, he writes, 'is the prospect that such creatures could be weaponized, and the possibility, according to one scientist intimately familiar with the project, that these cyborg insects might be armed with "bio weapons"'.[74]

ROBOT IMPERIUM / TECHNOPHILIA AND DESIRE

> The ultimate expression of sovereignty resides . . . in the power and capacity to dictate who may live and who must die.[75]

The discourses, imaginations and representations surrounding the RMA's 'urban turn' point overwhelmingly towards the rendering of whole cities as mere physical battlespaces to be controlled and dominated through technology. They revivify the seductive hope of removing US military personnel from the bloody, face-to-

---

72   Daryl Hauck, 'Pandora's Box Opened Wide: Micro Unmanned Air Vehicles Carrying Genetic Weapons', research paper, Air War College, Air University, Maxwell Air Base, 2004, 21.

73   Nick Turse, 'Weaponizing the Pentagon's Cyborg' Insects A Futuristic Nightmare That Just Might Come True,' *Tom Dispatch*, 30 March 2008.

74   Nick Turse, 'Weaponizing the Pentagon's Cyborg Insects'.

75   Mbembe, 'Necropolitics', 11.

face, and asymmetric struggles seen in Iraq's cities. They render urban civilians, and urban citizenship, invisible – or, rather, urban civilians are re-constructed as 'bare life',[76] inhabiting urban landscapes re-constituted as collections of physical and military targets. Finally, these discourses are replete with racist fantasies of colonial omnipotence, featuring the long-standing military dream of automated, cyborganized warfare[77] in which distantiated systems of surveillance, targeting and killing gain total mastery over the complex three-dimensional landscapes of future megacities of the global South. The effect of these discourses is to 'abstract the link between acts and their consequences'.[78]

Dreams of omnipotence and robotized killing must be examined with caution and care, however. I raise two caveats.

The first is that the US military and its associated complex of R&D outfits have long cherished fantasies of superweapons which would deterministically realize their dreams of mastery and, indeed, of omnipotence. These technophilic dreams have usually evolved in tandem with the wider discourses of speculative fiction, popular geopolitics, and mass entertainment. The 'technological fanaticism' of both has deep roots within US political, popular and military culture.[79]

As Jeremy Black suggests, we must therefore be careful to interpret the RMA, along with its 'urban turn', not as some quasi-rational response by US military and political élites to changing geopolitical conditions, but rather as 'symptomatic of a set of cultural and political assumptions that tell us more about modern western society than they do about any objective assessment of military options'. Moreover, it is possible to identify the ingredients of the complex cocktail created from these 'cultural and political assumptions'. Two of them, as Michael Sherry has noted, are the casualty aversion and technological fanaticism that so dominate recent US military tradition.[80] These blend with newer ideologies suggesting that contemporary warfare is becoming unbound in time and space, and that technological capital, rather than manpower, is the only way the US can 'win' today's wars.[81] Underpinning all this is the even

76   Agamben, *State of Exception*.

77   Charles Gannon, *Rumors of War and Infernal Machines: Technomilitary Agenda-Setting in American and British Speculative Fiction*, Liverpool: Liverpool University Press, 2003.

78   Simon Cooper, 'Perpetual War Within the State of Exception', *Arena Journal* 21, 2003, 109.

79   Michael Sherry, *The Rise of American Air Power: The Creation of Armageddon*, New Haven, CT: Yale University Press, 1987.

80   Sherry, *The Rise of American Air Power*.

81   Jeremy Black, *War*, London: Continuum. 2007, 97.

broader 'machine fetish endemic to the capitalist mode of production'[82] – with its notions of the 'just-in-time' production of 'kill chains', perfect 'situational awareness', and the omnipotent control of geographical space.

Add to these ingredients the widespread fascination among the US military with the future-warfare dystopias of cyber-punk and other science fiction – a fascination widely exploited by the baroque surveillance-corrections-commercial-military-entertainment complex, which in turn profit from the propagation and consumption of a huge supply of military technophilic fantasies, novels, films, video games and weapons programmes.[83]

Spiking this lethal cocktail are the West's deeply rooted Orientalist tropes. Through Western media, military and political élites alike deem the far-off urban spaces of Asia, Africa and the Middle East to be sites of great intrinsic deviousness, requiring the mobilization of the latest Western technoscience in acts of purification, unveiling, and (attempted) control.

The second caveat is this: we must remember that the 'US military' is far from being some single, unitary actor. All of the discourses, projects and programmes analysed in this chapter remain extremely contested. Within the vast institutional complex that comprises the US military and its associated security and military industries and lobby groups, there are major political battles continually underway. Fuelled by the ongoing nightmare in Iraq as well as, for instance, Israel's failures against Hezbollah in Lebanon in 2006, these battles rage over whether, even in military terms, these dreams of omnipotence, achieved through some urbanized version of RMA or network-centric warfare, are to any significant degree realistic. On top of all this, such battles are complicated by long-standing inter-service rivalries.

Many in the US Army and Marine Corps, in particular, are deeply skeptical that the horrors and the 'fog of war' in bloody urban operations like the Iraqi insurgency can ever be technologized, mediated, and saturated with sentient surveillance and targeting systems to a degree even approaching that found in the discursive imaginings driving the programmes discussed above.[84] Many military theorists worry, especially given the Iraq debacle, that the US military displays hugely naive blind faith in new military technology and that its 'technological superiority may prove less resilient than [it] imagine[s]'.[85] US defense policy critic John Gentry

---

82 Parenti, 'Planet America', 93.

83 Der Derian, *Virtuous War*.

84 See Frank Hoffman, 'Transforming for the Chaordic Age', *Marines Corps Gazette* 86, 2002, 47.

85 John Gentry, 'Doomed to Fail: America's Blind Faith in Military Technology', *Parameters*, Winter 2002. Hoffman, 'Transforming for the Chaordic Age', 47.

suggests, for example, that the Pentagon's technological fetishism produces systems which are 'expensive, limited in capabilities, subject to chronic technical and operator-induced failures, and vulnerable to attack'.[86]

Military-technological fetishism and triumphalism are also often used to mask a startling level of political and cultural ignorance amongst military and political élites about the distant places and people against which the US throws itself into war. As a 2001 editorial in *Foreign Policy* declares, 'The Global Positioning System, unmanned drones, unrivaled databases, and handheld computers – much has been made of the technological resources available to the US military and diplomatic establishments. But what do you do if you're trying to wage war in or against a country where you don't know the locals, can't speak the language, and can't find any reliable maps?' It goes on to welcome readers 'to the front lines of the war against terrorism, likely to be waged primarily in "swamp states" about which the United States knows little.'[87]

Notwithstanding such cautions and qualifiers, these dreams of clinically identifying and surgically killing only the 'fighters' within cities, through the use of 'autonomous' computer algorithms and 'brain scans' and automated weapons systems, remain both dangerously deluded and deeply disturbing. Here we confront yet another profoundly troubling development: that software agency can serve as the ultimate 'intelligence', automatically stipulating who should die and who should live, while at the same time US military personnel are to be removed as far as possible from risk of death or injury.

Four key objections may be made to these developments.

MYTHS OF PRECISION

For critics of the US drive towards the deployment of armed robots, the above caveats provide no room for complacency. True, the urban turn in the Revolution in Military Affairs is being driven by often wild and fantastical discourses, but its effects are likely to be quite material and profound. As we have shown, massive technoscientific efforts to enable the US military to saturate the cities of the global South with real-time surveillance, targeting and killing systems are already underway on, in, and above the urban streets of Iraq, the West Bank, and Gaza. The sovereign power to kill is already being delegated to computer code.

Whether such systems will ever function as imagined is, then, beside

---

86 Gentry, 'Doomed to Fail'.
87 Foreign Policy, 'It's All Pashto to Them', *Foreign Policy* 127, 2001, 18.

the point. The very existence of quasi-imperial projects to launch armies of autonomous killer air and ground vehicles into crowded cities – projects organized through the world's dominant military power and its close ally, Israel – will, if implemented, lead to widespread civilian casualties. The likelihood of this scenario increases with the emergence of new algorithmic systems which become the actual agents of continuous, autonomous killing; it increases yet further as 'kill chains' are 'compressed', 'sensors' are linked automatically to 'shooters', and dreams of 'persistent area dominance' achieve full expression through the Long War against lurking urban enemies.

Remotely controlled killer robots have been involved in a litany of war crimes. Raids have been launched robotically against adversary spaces even when these spaces notionally fall within nation-states that are US allies, such as the continuous raids by armed drones sent into Pakistan's territorial space without the permission of the Pakistani state. On 13 January 2006, for example, an armed Predator drone, piloted from an air base at the edge of Las Vegas, was sent to assassinate a senior al-Qaeda leader, Ayman al-Zawahri, in the Pashtun area of Pakistan. The attack killed fourteen villagers, including five children, and prompted mass demonstrations across Pakistan's main cities.[88] In June 2008 a Predator attack in Afghanistan killed eleven Pakistani soldiers, prompting more outrage. By October 2009, the newamerica.net project estimated that well over 1,000 Pakistanis had been killed by US drone attacks.[89]

In addition to such 'accidental' killings, there is increasing evidence that US and Israeli forces administer massive collective punishment against those who try to target their military apparatus of vertical domination. In Beirut's Shiyyah district in 2006, for instance, as the *Independent*'s celebrated journalist Robert Fisk picked through the rubble of an apartment block bombed minutes earlier by Israeli warplanes, killing at least seventeen civilians, he wondered why that particular building had been destroyed. It turned out, Fisk discovered, that prior to the missiles exploding, an Israeli drone had flown over the district. 'Without warning, someone . . . fired into the sky with a rifle [and] not long afterwards, the two missiles came streaking down on the homes of the innocent'. The moral lesson? 'Don't shoot at drones'.[90]

---

88   James Rupert, 'CIA Takes Calculated Risk in Pakistan', *Newsday*, 23 January 2006.
89   Declan Walsh, 'US Bomb Kills 11 Pakistani troops', *Guardian*, 12 June 2008.
90   Robert Fisk, 'What Do You Say to a Man Whose Family Is Buried under the Rubble', *Independent*, 9 August 2006.

POLITICAL TEMPTATIONS OF ROBOTIZED WAR

Can the empire run on intimidation and [the] dead labor [embodied in robots] alone? Or does it require dead workers, that is, soldiers sent from the metropole to control the wild zones and perhaps come home in body bags?[91]

The second objection to the technophilia of the US military is this: discourses urging that US soldiers be withdrawn from the streets of urban war-zones introduce the risk of justifying the deployment of automated killing systems, thereby pushing urban civilians in the global South into the cross-hairs of an aggressive hegemon already dizzy with fantasies of high-tech war. At least one US Air Force lieutenant colonel has admitted in print that armed robots are 'a very appealing option for the politicians faced with use-of-force decisions due to reduced forward basing requirements and the possibility of zero friendly . . . casualties'.[92] As Tim Blackmore puts it, in the case of unmanned aerial vehicles, there remains a risk that 'the machine may be lost'. But that wouldn't be too crushing a loss, because the vehicle's actual crew will be somewhere else: 'on the ground, hidden by walls, hardened bunkers, or distance (the controllers may operate the craft from another continent)'. Above all, 'there will be no widow-making, no embarrassing prisoners of war'.[93] And with the dramatic slide of US economic and financial power trigged by the onset of the global financial crisis, fantasies of automated counterinsurgencies in the global 'badlands' may have even more allure now than before.

A good strategy for achieving broad approval of automated war is to reduce global South cities, with all their complexity and humanity, to mere physical spaces whose very geographies present a threat to the vertical dominance of the US military. Such a discourse leads directly to the dehumanization of the cities' residents and citizens, and renders their lives, deaths, and citizenship of no account.

It seems inevitable that the shift towards autonomous killer robots will 'reduce even further the costs, both fiscal and human, of the choice to wage war'.[94] Thus, the development and deployment of armed robots may considerably increase the propensity of states armed with them actually to undertake wars.

---

91   Parenti, 'Planet America', 97.
92   James Dawkins, 'Unmanned Combat Aerial Vehicles: Examining The Political, Moral, and Social Implications'.
93   Blackmore, 'Dead Slow', 199.
94   Featherstone, 'The Coming Robot Army', 50.

'Robots do not have to be recruited, trained, fed or paid extra for combat duty', writes Steve Featherstone. 'When they are destroyed, there are no death benefits to disburse. Shipping them off to hostile lands doesn't require the expenditure of political capital, either'.[95] Within two decades, he predicts, 'robots will give us the ability to wage war without committing ourselves to the human cost of actually fighting a war'.[96]

The possibility of deploying swarms of armed and unarmed robots to 'loiter' persistently across regions of the world deemed 'trouble spots' is clearly a good fit with the Pentagon's latest thinking surrounding the Long War. The danger here is relinquishing the state's sovereign power to kill and delegating it to assemblages of silicon, titanium and software code – to perform acts of killing which not only are unbound from the defined times and spaces of traditional wars but also fall conveniently distant from the capricious gaze of mainstream media.

FANTASIES OF HUMANE WAR

> To suggest that robots can be programmed to be 'precision weapons' that can avoid collateral damage is self-delusion of the worst sort. There will be unintended consequences and, most assuredly, a great many funerals.[97]

Third, the political temptations of deploying robotized armies are deepened by the argument that the conscientious and ethically equipped 'robotic warriors' of the future might somehow be more 'humane' than human warriors. Ronald Arkin of the Georgia Institute of Technology is developing a set of ethical rules for US killer robots. He argues that, equipped with a 'software conscience', combat robots would not be tempted to commit atrocities against civilians. Thus, 'robots could behave more humanely than human beings', because they could select the ethical framework most suitable to a given mission and would then disobey commands that contradicted it.[98]

Such arguments miss a key point, however. It is only through the use of pre-defined databases of 'targets' that armed robots will ever be able to fire autonomously. The political act of targeting and killing will thus be strongly shaped by the electronic signatures of supposed enemies and enmity –

---

95   Ibid., 43–52.
96   Ibid.
97   Daniel Davis, 'Who Decides: Man or Machine?', *Armed Forces Journal*, November 2007.
98   Cited in Blech, 'Attack of the Killer Robots'.

signatures that have been identified, standardized, and translated into software code by human programmers.

Given that 'targets' now blend inseparably into mass urban civilian life at home and abroad, the predictive definition of persons suitable for targeting by autonomous killer robots will inevitably lead to errors and the widespread death and maiming of people who happen either to be in the way of those who have been targeted or to be, as far as the robot's sensors are concerned, essentially identical to them. 'In practice, unless insurgents carry recognizable weapons', writes Edward Luttwak, 'it is simply impossible to differentiate between them and innocent people going about their peaceful business.'[99]

The dangers are as clear as day. Automated sensing and killing systems are likely to construe everyone and everything as real or potential targets within an all-compassing battlespace. They will act accordingly if they are ever given autonomy from human supervision. John Armitage suggests that automated high-tech killing systems will be prone to widespread, and sometimes fatal, errors as they go about their work, inevitably destroying the wrong 'targets' from time to time. He cites the 1988 example of the shooting-down of Iran Air Flight 655 by the highly automated Aegis air-defence system aboard the USS *Vincennes*, with the resulting death of all civilians on the aircraft.[100]

ARMED ROBOTS AND THE LAWS OF WAR

As we advance across the field of possibilities from advanced weapons to semi-autonomous weapons to completely autonomous weapons, we need to understand the ethical implications involved in building robots that can make independent decisions.[101]

We arrive at the final, and ultimate, objection – that it will, as the philosopher Robert Sparrow worries, become increasingly impossible to attribute war crimes to humans at all. 'It is a necessary condition for fighting a just war under the principle of *jus in bellum* [the laws of just war governing military actions]', he writes, 'that someone can be justly held responsible for deaths that occur in the course of the war'.[102]

Sparrow raises the very real prospect of autonomous robots committing the atrocity of killing unarmed civilians. 'Who should we try for a war crime in

---

99   Edward Luttwak, 'Dead-end: Counterinsurgency Warfare as Military Malpractice', *Harper's Magazine*, February 2007, 33–42.

100   John Armitage in Crandall, ed., *Under Fire. 2*, 89.

101   David Bigelow, 'Fast forward to the Robot Dlemma', *Armed Forces Journal*, November 2007.

102   Sparrow, 'Killer Robots', 63.

such a case?' he asks. 'The robot itself? The person(s) who programmed it? The officer who ordered its use? No one at all?' His conclusion is clear: 'as this condition [of just war] cannot be met in relation to deaths caused by an autonomous weapon system, it would therefore be unethical to deploy such systems in warfare'.[103]

US Army Major David Bigelow offers a robot-war scenario for the year 2025. He posits a continuous low-intensity war in which armed, independent robots fight at the intersection of a developed world – fanatically devoted to the preservation and extension of human life, and seduced by dreams of immortality – and a heavily overpopulated, conflict-ridden developing world where life is cheaper than ever. In this sort of global war, characterized by the 'expanded use of military robots by the developed nations, . . . forces in the underdeveloped world willingly sacrifice dozens of their own soldiers in exchange for a single enemy soldier's life'.[104]

Anticipating the global media controversy that would be caused if an armed robot worked with Australian forces in Mogadishu, Somalia, killing unarmed civilians, Bigelow concludes that the solution is not to prevent autonomous killer robots from emerging in the first place. Rather, echoing current work on the development of ethical software for robotic weapons, he urges that future robots be 'designed to screen [their] decisions through a sound moral framework'.[105] Such a 'screening' process seems dubious, however, and would do nothing to address Robert Sparrow's concerns. His position is certainly clear: it is urgent that truly autonomous weapons systems be judged unethical and made illegal under international law.

---

103   Ibid.
104   Bigelow, 'Fast Forward to the Robot Dilemma'.
105   Ibid.

CHAPTER SIX

Theme Park Archipelago

A hidden archipelago of between eighty and a hundred mini cities is rapidly being constructed across the world – far from the planet's main metropolitan corridors. Situated at obscure edges of cities and in rural areas, these constructions are set deep within military bases and training grounds. The vast majority are located in the United States, and present a jarring contrast with the surrounding strip-mall suburbia. Others are rising out of the deserts of Kuwait and Israel, the downs of southern England, the plains of Germany, and the islands surrounding Singapore.

Some such cities are replete with lines of drying laundry, wandering donkeys, Arabic graffiti, tape loops endlessly playing the call to prayer, even ersatz minarets and mosques. Others boast 'slum' or 'favela' districts and underground sewers with built-in olfactory machines capable of producing on demand the simulated smell of rotting corpses or untreated sewage. Still others are populated occasionally by itinerant groups of Arab-Americans, bussed in to wander about in Arab dress and role-play.

Besides these temporary inhabitants, few people other than military personnel ever see or enter these new urban complexes. Unnoticed by urban design, architecture and planning communities, and invisible on maps, these sites constitute a kind of shadow global system of military urban simulations, lurking in the interstices between the planet's rapidly growing real metropolitan areas.

PRACTISED DESTRUCTION

Rather than monuments to dynamism and growth, these 'cities' are theme parks for practicing urban destruction, erasure, and colonial violence. Constructed by US military specialists with the help of military corporations, theme-park designers, video game companies, Hollywood set designers and special-effects experts,, they are training grounds for the targeting of real, far-off cities. These sites are small capsules of space designed to simulate in some way what US military theorist Richard Norton pejoratively labels the 'feral' cities of the burgeoning Arab and Third World – the de facto zones of current and future warfare for Western forces, the strategic environments dominating contemporary geopolitics.[1]

---

1   Norton, 'Feral Cities', 97–106.

Eyal Weizman[2] emphasizes that Israeli and Western military doctrine now stresses the need not just to enter, and not just attempt to control, large urban areas, but also to physically reorganize colonized city spaces so that high-tech weapons and surveillance systems can work to the occupiers' advantage. Weizman calls this 'design by destruction'. As he puts it, 'contemporary urban warfare plays itself out within a constructed, real or imaginary architecture, and through the destruction, construction, reorganisation, and subversion of space'.[3]

In keeping with the post–Cold War mutation of Western military doctrine into the planned remodelling of cities by force, the purpose of these simulated urban warfare 'training cities' is to allow US, Western and Israeli forces to hone their skills in designed urban destruction. Following extensive training at these sites, units deploy to the real cities of Iraq, Palestine, Lebanon, and elsewhere to undertake so-called Military Operations on Urban Terrain – MOUT for short.

Like the rest of the world, then, military training sites are rapidly being urbanized. Colonel Thomas Hammes, writing in the US Marine Corps Gazette in 1999, was one of many defence planners then asserting the need to build new mock cities because US military training sites were out of phase with 'the urban sprawl that dominates critical areas of the world today. Continuing in that vein, he wrote, 'We know we will fight mostly in urban areas. Yet, we conduct the vast majority of our training in rural areas – the hills of Camp Pendleton, the deserts of Twenty Nine Palms, the woods of Camp Lejeune, the jungles of Okinawa, Japan'.[4]

The US military's response has been dramatic. The US Army alone has plans to build sixty-one urban-warfare training cities across the world between 2005 and 2010. While some are little more than sets of portable containers, designed to provide basic urban warfare training when deployed around the world, others are complex spaces mimicking whole city districts or groups of villages, as well as surrounding countryside, infrastructure, even airports. Leading examples of the more complex sites include Fort Carson, Colorado (which by 2006 included three different mock Iraqi villages); the national Joint Readiness Training Center at Fort Polk, Louisiana; Fort Benning, Georgia; the Marine Corps' main site at Twentynine Palms, California; and Fort Richardson, Alaska.

Along with a wide range of simulated Western cities developed as sites

---

2   Misselwitz and Weizman, 'Military Operations as Urban Planning', 272–5.
3   Eyal Weizman, 'Lethal Theory', LOG Magazine, April 2005, 74.
4   Thomas Hammes, 'Time to Get Serious about Urban Warfare Training', Marine Corps Gazette, April 1999.

within which to practise police and military responses to terror attacks, civil unrest or infrastructural collapse, these mock Third World sites provide a shadow archipelago of 'cities' which mimic the urbanization of real wars and conflicts around the world. These sites 'tackle calamity in an amusement park of unrest, insurgency and its abatement', writes Bryan Finoki. 'Architectures both elaborate and artful, [they are] designed solely for the purposes of being conquered and reconquered'.[5]

Urban warfare training cities starkly embody both imagined and real urban geographies that lie at the heart of the War on Terror. Powerful materializations of what Derek Gregory has called our colonial present,[6] they must be understood as part of a much wider effort at the physical and electronic simulation of Arab or global South cities for the tightly linked reasons of war, profit and entertainment. Indeed, these training complexes take their place within a broad constellation of simulated Arab cities and urban landscapes which, drawing on Orientalist tropes and traditions, are also emerging in video games, virtual reality military simulations, films, newspaper graphics and novels. Together, they present a single massive discursive trick: the construction of Arab and Third World cities as stylized, purely physical, labyrinthine worlds which are, somehow, both intrinsically terroristic and largely devoid of the civil society that characterizes normal urban life.[7] As a result, Arab cities emerge as little more than receiving points for US military ordnance and colonial military incursions, real or fantastical.

Moreover, where the cultures and sociologies of Arab cities are factored into these simulations of urban warfare, Orientalist cliché and high-tech dehumanization are still the norm.[8] Some simulated Arab cities, for example, have been 'populated' by locally recruited bit players, dressed in keffiyehs and told to mutter stereotypic phrases. Meanwhile, the populating of electronically simulated cities is simply generated by computer software, which creates 'crowds' to be attacked. Either way, these constellations of urban simulacra do the important geopolitical work of continually reducing the complex social and cultural worlds of global South urbanism to mere targets, mere battlespaces, existing for the sole purpose of being assaulted in urban campaigns against 'terror' or for 'freedom'.

For militaries to construct physical simulations of places to be targeted and destroyed is nothing new, of course. Nor is the close relation between play, toys,

5 Personal communication.
6 Gregory, *The Colonial Present*.
7 Ibid., 201–3.
8 Ibid., 229–30.

and war, or the mobilization of Hollywood special effects for a war effort. In the Cold War, for example, atomic and thermonuclear bombs were regularly exploded near simulated suburban homes, complete with white picket fences and nuclear families of mannequins placed around the table having a mock meal.

Even earlier, during the Second World War, the Dugway Proving Grounds in Utah was the site for the construction of a village of extremely accurate Berlin tenements as well as a cluster of Japanese houses built of wood and rice paper.[9] The former were designed by modernist luminary Eric Mendelsohn, freshly exiled from Germany. The latter were created by Antonin Raymond, a Czech-American architect with Japanese experience, who scoured the US for authentic Russian spruce board. These buildings were repeatedly burned by the US Chemical Warfare Corps, which was then able to tailor the composition and design of incendiary bombs to best suit the task of razing Japanese and German cities. To ensure accuracy, real German furniture was placed within the tenements, and the buildings were watered to mimic the temperate climate of Berlin.

BAGHDAD IS EVERYWHERE

Twenty-first century urban-warfare training cities have a different relationship to political violence than do the atom-bombed suburban homes or fire-bombed tenements and rice-paper structures of the twentieth century. No longer is the simulation designed to explore outright urban annihilation through total war. Now the purpose is to hone skills of occupation, counterinsurgency warfare, and urban remodelling via expeditionary, colonial war.

A bizarre, reverse urban beauty contest emerges here – a mirror image to the more familiar marketing campaigns through which real cities parade themselves through gentrification, cultural planning, and boosterism. For the new training cities, the marks of success are decay, collapse, and squalor. A US squadron commander named Colonel James Cashwell reported recently, after an exercise in one such city within George Air Force base in California, that 'the advantage of the base is that it is ugly, torn up, all the windows are broken [and trees] have fallen down in the street. It's perfect for the replication of a war-torn city'.[10] Ted Leza, who runs the US Baumholder training site in Germany, reflects that soldiers using his site have repeatedly asked that it be populated by

---

9   Davis, *Dead Cities*, 65–84.
10   Cited by J. R. Wilson, 'Army Expands Home-Based MOUT Training', Military Training Technology.com, March 2003.

various dead and living animals to help simulate life in Iraqi cities. So, along with realistic Baghdad-style orange-and-white taxis, a simulated taxi stand, and a market, Baumholder's operators are 'trying to get that for them. I don't know if we'll get a camel. Maybe a donkey, goats . . . stuff like that'.[11] Urban-warfare training sites also integrate multi-sensory systems for projecting warlike special effects into the ersatz buildings, streets and structures. 'We have a wide variety of special effects smells we can do', says Manuel Chaves, who runs the special-effects suite built into the site at Fort Wainwright, Alaska. 'For instance: coffee, apple pie, dead bodies, burning rubber, diesel fumes. I can do nine different buildings, nine different smells. Generally, if it's a burning building, we put something really nasty in there like burning bodies'.[12]

A rather different complex, built (with unintended irony) from some twenty-three thousand cluster-bomb containers discarded during the Vietnam War, is emerging at Yodaville, in the Arizona desert (Figure 6.1) This site, which opened in 1998, is the first simulated global South city created specifically for live urban bombing and close support training.[13] The complex is said to have 178 'buildings', 131 personnel targets, thirty-one vehicle targets, and streetlights. According to a RAND report, from the ground it looks 'like stacks of shot-up shipping containers'; from the viewpoint of the fighter pilots who continually target it with cluster and precision munitions, however, it is 'convincingly urban'.[14] Mark Shaffer, a reporter with the *Arizona Republic*, notes that the site has a 'decidedly Third World' feel: 'A mock soccer field is painted green on the edge of town. Streets are narrow. There's a large shantytown. And talk about ambience. The searingly hot desert teems with sidewinders and an occasional scrub creosote bush or cactus'.[15]

Apparently, local right-wing militia groups – never slow to jump to conspiratorial conclusions – are convinced that the Yodaville complex is being used to train US and UN forces at the behest of what they often call the New World Order. As the site is seven miles from the Arizona–Mexico border, bombing runs are stopped at least twice weekly so that newly arrived

11   Cited in Terry Boyd, 'Training Site Replicates Iraqi Village', *Stars and Stripes*, 26 July 2006, available at www.stripes.com.

12   Associated Press, 'Urban Combat Training Center Will Be Army's Largest', 24 December 2002.

13   Mark Shaffer, 'Yodaville Exists for Bombing Runs – Arizona's Newest Town Inviting Target', *Arizona Republic*, 23 August 1999.

14   Russell Glenn et. al, 'Preparing for the Proven Inevitable: An Urban Operations Training Strategy for America's Joint Force', report for the US Secretary of Defense, Santa Monica, CA: RAND National Defense Research Institute, 2006.

15   Shaffer, 'Yodaville Exists for Bombing Runs'.

6.1 The Yodaville Target Complex in Arizona: A mock Arab town used in aerial bombing practice, constructed from containers used to ship cluster bombs to Vietnam in the 1960s.

immigrants can be removed before the ordnance once again rains down,[16] though the removals may not always be thorough. A man named Madzukes – presumably a US Marine – asks during a Marine video on YouTube if 'any border jumpers ran out of Yodaville after a rocket shoot this time'.[17]

'HOLLYWOOD HAS NOTHING ON US!'

One of the most important urban-warfare training cities for US ground forces is at Fort Knox, Kentucky, where a thirty-acre, $13 million MOUT facility named Zussman Village has been constructed.[18] The site can accommodate hundreds of role-playing 'insurgents', who wear keffiyehs on their heads and are armed with AK-47s and rocket propelled grenades, as well as fifteen hundred US military personnel, along with their tanks, personnel carriers and helicopters. It includes mock junkyards, mosques, cemeteries, petrol stations, sewers, electrical substations, train tracks and bridges. It is even equipped with radio and TV stations which can broadcast in Hebrew, Arabic or Russian. An ostensible Third World slum is being constructed near the railroad.

To simulate a war-torn environment, the Zussman site is deliberately smothered in dirt and mud. The grass grows tall and the un-maintained sewer system is filled with live possums and rats, as well as rubber snakes bought from local toy shops. Simulated odours can be produced on demand. In five of the buildings, built-in pyrotechnic systems, modelled on those used for Hollywood film sets, can send vapourized propane into aerial fireballs, thus 'burning' the buildings on command. Ware Corporation, which set up the pyrotechnics, declares that when you enter the site, 'deafening explosions rattle your body. Gun-toting guerrillas, the odor of raw sewage, the chaos and confusion of civilians on the street, and burning buildings with large, fiery explosions await those soldiers who train at Zussman Village'.[19] Daniel Hawkins, the engineer for Zussman's special effects, boasts, 'Hollywood has nothing on us. Whatever scenario you can imagine, you can create here. We've paid attention to the smallest detail – everything from our sewer "smell-o'vision" to fully furnished hotel rooms. We also have several rigged "surprises", like blowing up the bridge, knocking down a utility pole, or

---

16 Ibid.

17 YouTube video since removed.

18 Roxana Tiron, 'Army Training Site Brings to Life the Horrors of War', *National Defense Magazine*, July 2001.

19 Ware Corporation, project summary, 'Zussman Village, Fort Knox, Kentucky', undated, available at www.wareinc.com.

springing a dummy from behind furniture in a building.[20] Andy Andrews, Zussman's site manager, recalls planning the site:

> We wanted it to be dirty and nasty – the way real war really is. Natural gas was out because the flame looks blue and [the planners] wanted a realistic yellow/orange wood-burning fire. Liquid propane was considered because it produced the right color and it sticks and lingers. However, it was simply not a safe option, and, at that time, there was a new [health and safety] code being implemented for fire effects performed in front of an audience . . . Ultimately, vaporised propane fitted the bill. It was easier to control, and since propane holds to the ground, it was easier and safer to create the mushroom or fireball effect. The propane would shoot up into the air and would bellow back down to the ground, creating a spectacular effect.[21]

The largest US urban warfare complex of all is emerging at the Joint Readiness Training Center at Fort Polk, Louisiana. It parallels a similar facility being built at Fort Irwin, California (Figure 6.2), whose commander is quoted as saying that 'the reality that we've created at the Joint Readiness Training Center is like one big reality TV show'.[22] At Fort Polk, eighteen mock Iraqi villages are being constructed in what *Wired* Magazine has dubbed 'the World's most violent theme park'.[23] This complex, which covers a hundred thousand acres, is detailed down to the kebab stands and the simulated mass graves, the latter created by burying piles of rotting bones and meat from local butchers shops. During the exercises – which in 2005 alone were attended by forty-four thousand soldiers bound for Iraq – the facility is 'inhabited' by twelve hundred role players, dressed in Arab-style clothing and impersonating Iraqi tribesmen, police and civilians.[24] Two hundred of them are Arab-Americans, mostly from Iraq itself. Screen writers are on hand to do 'character sheets' for each participant, based on whether they are programmed to be 'friendly', 'neutral' or 'hostile' towards US forces.

'Before, the role players were all local guys with Southern accents who would say "you ran over my goat"', says Brigadier General Mike Babero, the base commander. 'Now you go into a "Kurdish" village, and the "mayor" is from northern Iraq'.[25] Some role players now do the $220-a-day job full-time. During

---

20 Ibid.

21 Ibid.

22 Quoted in *Full Battle Rattle*, online streaming video, directed by Tony Gerber and Jesse Moss, 2009, available at www.fullbattlerattlemovie.com.

23 Vince Beiser, 'Baghdad, USA', *Wired Magazine* 14:6, 2006.

24 Ann Scott Tyson, 'US Tests New Tactics in Urban Wargame', *Christian Science Monitor*, 9 November 2004.

25 Ibid.

6.2 Exercises within the mock Iraqi villages at the National Joint Readiness Training Center at Fort Irwin, California, including a mock riot using local role players.

exercises, *Wired* reporter Vince Beiser found that 'a goofy Renaissance Faire atmosphere reigns' at the site. 'People crack each other up talking in snippets of Arabic and Aladdin-esque gibberish: "Yaahabla blanabla!" One greets another. "Mohammed Jihad!" comes the reply'.[26]

'THIS IS OUR PLAYGROUND'

> It is here, in this parallel world, that the occupation of the Palestinian territories is played out by generations of Israeli soldiers, over and over again.[27]

By far the most ambitious and controversial mock Arab city so far constructed, however, is not a US facility at all. Ostensibly, it is Israeli: the Baladia facility at Israel's Tze'elim base in the Ne'gev desert (Figure 6.3). Given

---

26 Beiser, 'Baghdad, USA'.
27 Adam Broomberg and Oliver Chanarin, *Chicago*, London: SteidlMack, 2006.

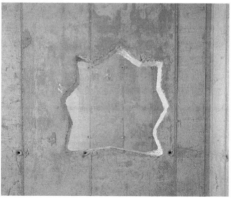

6.3   The Baladia mock Palestinian city in the Ne'gev desert, built for the
Israelis by the US Army. Top: Overview of the scale of the 'facility'. Centre:
Simulated Palestinian street. Bottom: A 'worm hole' allowing Israeli forces to
practise moving through the walls of Palestinian cities and refugee camps.

that the site has been paid for by US military aid, was built between 2005 and 2006 by the US Army Corps of Engineers, and is used by US Marines, perhaps 'US–Israeli' would be a more accurate description.

Costing $40 million and covering 7.4 square miles, Baladia has 472 complete concrete structures and four miles of roads. It is one of the first urban-warfare mock cities which approach the scale of a real urban area. Baladia has been explicitly built to generalize the military 'lessons learned' from Israel's regular incursions into Palestinian cities and refugee camps since 2002, and to make them available to the entirety of Israel's armed forces as well as to the forces of friendly nations. The complex simulates a complete Palestinian town,[28] split into four 'quarters' and wired up with surveillance equipment to monitor 'combat'.

Baladia is impressively equipped. It has simulated apartment buildings, a market place, mosque and a concrete 'casbah.' Its cemetery 'doubles as a soccer field, depending on the operational scenario'; its 'nature reserve' hides Hezzbollah-style rocket launchers. The streets are littered with burned cars, burned tires, and mock booby-traps.[29] Besides the complex surveillance system, there is an elaborate audio system that replicates the noise of helicopters, mortar rounds, calls to prayer, and twenty or so other distinctive sounds. One notable touch is the array of mechanical cut-outs, such as the bearded caricatures of Arab men which are programmed to pop up in windows and street corners during live-fire exercises. Baladia even has ready-made 'worm holes': openings routinely blasted in the walls of buildings by Israeli soldiers so as to make their way through Palestinian cities and refugee camps while avoiding the vulnerability of being out in the street. As in US complexes, 'hundreds of soldiers, most of them 19- and 20-year-old women, graduates of Arabic language and cultural programs, [operate as] play-acting civilians and enemy fighters'.[30]

The scale of the complex allows for flexible re-arrangement, making it possible to set up a simulation of a specific city against which the Israel Defence Forces (IDF) or other forces are planning to launch operations. Baladia can thus be easily reconfigured into 'Gaza', 'Lebanon', the 'West Bank' or 'Syria'. 'This is our playground to practice for anything we need', declared Lt Col Arik Moreh, the base's second in command. During 2007, for example, Lebanon and Syria were Israel's main preoccupations. Thus, writes Barbara Opall-Rome, 'creative

---

28 Arieh O'Sullivan, 'Army Inaugurates Warfare Village', *Jerusalem Post*, 13 January 2005.

29 Barbara Opall-Rome, 'Marines to Train at New Israeli Combat Center.' *Marines Corps Times*, 25 June 2007.

30 Ibid.

engineering [was] required to transform the area into what IDF officers here call Hezbollahland. During a late-May visit [in 2007], IDF planners were busy transforming large portions of Baladia City into Bint Jbeil, a Hezbollah stronghold from which extremist Shiite forces extracted a heavy price on IDF ground troops in last summer's Lebanon War'.[31]

In 2006, Adam Broomberg and Oliver Chanarin, two Israeli photographers, succeeded in making a detailed study of Baladia (whose other name is, strangely, 'Chicago'). Their research led them to conclude that it 'was not based on a specific town but is a generic "Arab" place, designed by the soldiers themselves, building on their intimate experience of the minutiae of Arab cities'. Great attention has been paid to detail, the photographers report. 'Graffiti has been applied to the walls in Arabic: "I love you Ruby" and "Red ash, hot as blood"'.[32]

Baladia exhibits strange contortions of simulation and denial. As Broomberg and Chanarin suggest, 'This convention of using the name "Arab", rather than Palestinian, effectively obscures identity, and in this sense Chicago as a ghost-town evidences the thread of denial that runs through much of Israeli discourse about relations with Palestine, towns like Ramallah and Nablus'. Following their final visit to the complex, the photographers spoke about its deeply unnerving qualities. 'It is difficult to pinpoint what it is about the place that is so disturbing', they said. 'Perhaps it's the combination of the vicariousness and the violence. It's as if the soldiers have entered the enemy's private domain while he's sleeping or out for lunch . . . It's a menacing intrusion into the intimate.[33]

By December 2006 the complex was also receiving regular visits from US military commanders. 'This is a world-class site that the Israelis have built,' Lieutenant General H. Steven Blum, chief of the National Guard Bureau, enthused during a December visit. 'We probably should have a facility like that of our own; in the interim, we should explore the opportunities to train here . . . It couldn't be more realistic unless you let people actually live there'. To Lt Gen. Blum, Baladia provides a much closer approximation of Arab urban geographies than did the mock cities he encountered in the United States. 'It is the most realistic, extensive replication of the sort of urban area typical of this region of the world that I've ever seen', he gushed. 'It is just such a superb training facility for all the nuances and the situational awareness and the battlefield conditions that soldiers face in this part of the world'.[34]

---

31   Ibid.
32   Broomberg and Chanarin, *Chicago*, London, 23.
33   Ibid.
34   Ibid.

By mid-2007, as the complex was being routinely used by Israeli forces, regular use by US forces was already being explored. Israel Moskovic, commander both of the complex and of the IDF's Gaza Division, reported that Baladia would soon host US Army and Marine Corps units for training before they headed off to Iraq. 'This is something developed by us in cooperation with the U.S. Army; we intend for it to become a valuable center of knowledge that will also benefit our American allies and other friends'.[35] Early on, Israel had offered the Chicago facility for hire to Western forces that required training in urban warfare, yet despite the IDF's close co-operation with such forces on training and equipment, beginning with the 2002 invasion of West Bank cities, those offers were rejected. Nevertheless, the operators of 'Chicago' remained confident that Western militaries would eventually train there, and by 2007 it was clear that US Marines would be using Baladia, despite initial fears that this would generate negative publicity.

WAR GHOST TOWNS

Despite the recent proliferation of urban warfare training sites, senior Pentagon officials are convinced that these sites are completely inadequate to the task of training US forces to counter future urban insurgencies in fast-growing megacities. As a result, the US Congress commissioned the RAND Corporation, the nation's long-time military think-tank, to explore other options. The resulting four-hundred-page report was published in 2006.[36]

The report starts off with the premise that 'US armed forces have thus far been unable to adequately reproduce the challenges their soldiers, sailors, marines and airmen meet in the towns and cities of Iraq and Afghanistan'.[37] First the RAND researchers evaluate the existing urban-warfare training sites in terms of whether they offer the most challenging architectural and infrastructural features encountered when military operations are undertaken within large cities of the global South. Those that scored highest, such as the Marines' Twentynine Palms facility in California or the Army's billion-dollar mock Iraqi city at Fort Irwin, have 'clutter/debris/filth', 'slums/shanty towns/walled compounds', 'subterranean complexes' and simulated 'government, hospital/prison/asylum structures'.[38]

To address the need for more realistic physical simulations of whole cities

---

35 Opall-Rome, 'Marines to Train at New Israeli Combat Center'.
36 Glenn, et al., 'Preparing for the Proven Inevitable'.
37 Ibid., xv.
38 Ibid., 243.

and city districts, the RAND team recommends the construction of four new urban-warfare cities that would each include more than three hundred structures, one to be located in the Kentucky/North Carolina/Georgia region, another somewhere in the US Southwest, another at Fort Polk in Louisiana, and the fourth at Fort Hood in Texas.

RAND also explored the possibility of appropriating entire ghost towns within the continental US – towns that have been de-industrialized and largely abandoned; the report states that 'the use of abandoned towns [for urban warfare training] has moved beyond the concept phase into what might be considered the early test and development phase'.[39] One such place is the virtually abandoned copper-mining town of Playas, in the southwestern corner of New Mexico (Figure 6.4), which has already been used for the training of anti-suicide bomb squads for the US Department of Homeland Security. 'Over the course of time, towns and cities eventually die', writes Steve Rowell of the Center for Land Use Interpretation in Culver City, California. 'Despite this and despite the receding US economy, the industries of defense and disaster preparedness are flourishing, reversing this trend in some of the most remote areas of the nation. The war on terror is redefining the American pastoral in an unexpected way'. In the case of Playas, its new role is to play a 'generic American suburb under simulated attack' and, in future, a simulated Arab city within which military personnel can hone their skills of expeditionary war.[40]

The entire town of Playas is rented from the New Mexico Institute of Mining and Technology, who bought it explicitly for use as an urban warfare training site. Live-fire exercises will probably not be possible in Playas, however, 'since the owners of the town would consider the structural repair costs prohibitive', according to the RAND report.[41] The investigators suggest that Playas would be improved as a training site if its structures were rebuilt along Arab lines – that, for instance, the town's architecture be 'modified to include walled compounds of the type that US troops in Iraq and Afghanistan must at times isolate and clear'.[42]

Despite Playas being labelled a 'ghost town', a few remaining residents cling on there. As their down-at-heel town makes its living being repeatedly assaulted and targeted by military power, its inhabitants, apparently grateful for this new

39   Ibid., 63.
40   Steve Rowell, 'Playas, New Mexico: A Modern Ghost Town Braces for the Future', *The Lay of the Land* 28, 2005, Centre for Land Use Interpretation, available at www.clui.org.
41   Glenn, et. al. 'Preparing for the Proven Inevitable', 63.
42   Ibid.

6.4 Playas, New Mexico, a ghost town converted into an
urban warfare and counter-terrorist training facility.

economic niche, largely make their living as extras in urban war and terrorist exercises. 'We're glad things are going on down here', Linda McCarty, a Playas resident, remarked to *USA Today*. 'Until New Mexico Tech took over' – which is when the town was re-assigned to urban warfare training – 'it was really sad'.[43] Currently the population of Playas is some twenty-five families, and most of the adults work for the training programme as role players.[44]

Nor has the potential for real US metropolitan areas to serve as urban-warfare training grounds been ignored by RAND. It recommends a new range of urban-warfare exercises, modelled on the Urban Warrior and Project Metropolis exercises, in which Marines 'invaded' Little Rock, Arkansas; Chicago, Illinois; Oakland, California; and Charleston, South Carolina, between 1999 and 2002.[45] In 1999, in a precursor to the treatment of Fallujah five years later, the Urban Warrior exercise in Oakland even involved the biometric scanning of 'resistance fighters'.[46]

Such exercises will be even more necessary in the future, RAND argues, because 'no purpose-built urban training site and no simulation for many years to come will be able to present the heterogeneity and complexity of a modern megalopolis'.[47] Such exercises centre on learning to disable the electrical, communications, transport and water infrastructures of a real city. The Oakland experience in March 1999, for example, involved major amphibious and airborne landings, staged to generate recruitment interest as well as to conduct exercises in abandoned hospitals and sewer networks.

To RAND, all these proposals, though recreating some of the challenges US forces face in occupying global South cities, will nonetheless fall far short of approaching those cities in scale. To address this problem, RAND's most ambitious proposal, therefore, is for the construction of a 'mega-MOUT' complex – covering four hundred square kilometres and incorporating a complete town of nine hundred buildings – at the Marine base at Twentynine Palms, California.[48] Slated to cost $330 million by 2011, such a complex will, RAND imagines, allow an entire brigade to simulate, with unprecedented levels of realism, the taking of a large-size Iraqi or Arab town. For the first time, Air

---

43   Mimi Hall, 'War on Terror Takes Over a Thankful Town', *USA Today*, 13 March 2005.

44   Richard Stolley, 'Postcard: Playas', *Time Magazine*, 3 April 2008.

45   Elizabeth Book, 'Project Metropolis Brings Urban Wards to US Cities', *National Defense Magazine*, April 2002.

46   John Lettice, 'Marine Corps Deploys Fallujah Biometric ID Scheme', *The Register*, 12 September 2004.

47   Glenn, et. al, 'Preparing for the Proven Inevitable', 83.

48   Ibid., 152.

Force elements will be completely integrated with ground forces; there will be port and industrial facilities as well. In addition, live ground and even artillery fire will now be possible.

DESTRUCTION DIORAMA

Whilst physical simulations for urban warfare training draw heavily on the expertise of Hollywood and theme park designers (Figure 6.5), a widening range of electronic simulations have close links with the booming video-game and electronics industries. Increasingly, physical and electronic simulations of Arab cities are being packaged together. The theory here, according to Scott Malo and Christopher Stapleton of the Media Convergence Laboratory at the University of Central Florida, is that 'the theme park technology of today adds the thrilling nature of full body stimulation and activity. So what if theme parks and video game combined their strengths?'[49]

6.5   A simulated Third World urban environment for the training of infantry.

One such project, a one-house space called the Urban Terrain Module, has been set up at Fort Sill, Oklahoma. It merges the latest electronic

49   Scott Malo and Christopher Stapleton, 'Going Beyond Reality: Creating Extreme Multimodal Mixed Reality for Training Simulation', paper presented at the Interservice/Industry Training, Simulation and Education Conference (I/ITSEC), 2004.

simulation technologies with physical dioramas of devastated 'Arab' urban environments. This module, situated in a large media studio, is 'decorated in a decidedly Middle-Eastern manner. A picture hangs on the wall, the smashed remnants of a small vase lie on a small circular table near the kitchen area. Like a Broadway show, walls and other set pieces can be swapped out as the training merits'.[50]

Built with the help of Hollywood stagecraft professionals, this site can conjure up electronically simulated 'virtual humans' – seemingly lifelike 'Arabs', with suitably swarthy features, who are programmed to 'populate' the electronic screen spaces within the physical, ruined diorama and to serve as targets for the US military personnel 'embedded' within the module for their training sessions. Also part of the mix is the familiar stage-set paraphernalia of simulated explosions, smoke, and a computerized desert landscape. The project's designers contend that Fort Sill's electronic simulations are so convincing that the borders between the virtualized and the physical elements are increasingly indistinguishable to the soldiers being trained there.[51] One promotional brochure distributed at a major military-simulation conference stated that this sort of artificial-intelligence package 'allows trainers to manipulate character responses on the fly, changing crowds into violent mobs with a keystroke'.[52] For extra realism, the tricks of Hollywood's 'war-wound artists' are used along with the digitized human targets. At a similar facility, embedded within San Diego's only TV and movie studio, amputee Marines returning from Iraq 'would go out on patrol with their squad' through the hybrid physical and virtual spaces of the simulated Iraqi city, reports Stu Segall, owner of the studio. 'A bomb would explode, and we'd pretend they lost a leg'.[53]

Fort Sill's operators imagine that simulations will soon be modified to project real satellite and digital mapping data from Iraq or other urban warfare locations, so that, as project director Colonel Gary Kinne puts it, 'individuals could train on the actual terrain that they would occupy someday – maybe in a future theatre of war'.[54] Simulated smells like those used in physical facilities are also envisaged.

---

50   Associated Press, 'Army Unveils New, Ultra-Real Simulation', 20 December 2004.

51   Heidi Loredo, 'Hollywood Magic Prepares Marines for Combat', Marines.Com, July 2004, available at www.marforres.usmc.mil.

52   Ibid.

53   Ibid.

54   Ibid.

JAKARTA, 2015

Much larger, and purely electronic, simulations of developing world megacities are becoming major sites for the war-games through which US forces now imagine full-scale, future counterinsurgency warfare. In the most important electronically simulated urban war-game – Urban Resolve 2015 – a huge swath of about twenty square kilometres of Jakarta, the capital of Indonesia, has been accurately digitized and 'geo-specifically' simulated in three dimensions, including the interiors of 1.6 million of the city's buildings, 109,000 mobile 'vehicles' and 'civilians', and the subterranean infrastructures. A virtual Baghdad has been similarly rendered. Both cities have been conjured up within arrays of supercomputers as future 'toxic environments for extremist ideologies', necessitating massive US military response.[55] The vital security-defence complex in Suffolk, Virginia, meanwhile, has been simulated as a site for a major counterterrorist and homeland security mobilization.

6.6   Players in the Urban Resolve exercise.

---

55   James Winnefeled, director of the Joint Forces Command's Joint Experimentation Directorate, cited in Dawson, 'Combat in Hell', 170.

Between 2003 and 2008, Urban Resolve served as the basis for a series of massive military simulations across nineteen separate military bases, involving more than fifteen hundred participants and using some of the US military's most sophisticated supercomputers (Figure 6.6). The simulations projected sites of massive urban wars involving US forces in 2015, complete with a range of imagined new US sensors, surveillance systems, and weapons geared specifically towards the kind of warfare that could unveil the 'fog of war' in a megacity. Opposition forces, programmed to fight autonomously within the virtualized megacity, were equipped with technologies projected to be available on the open market in 2015 – including their own robotic vehicles.

As part of its mandate to 'replicate real-world geography, structures and culturally relevant population behaviors',[56] Urban Resolve even simulated the daily rhythms of the virtualized Jakarta and Baghdad: At night the roads were quiet; during the weekday rush hours, traffic clogged the roads. At the times of daily prayers, the presence of traffic and people increased around the mosques. The virtualized inhabitants went to work, stopped for lunch breaks, visited restaurants, banks and churches – apparently unaware that they inhabited a major war-zone.[57]

Players in Urban Resolve 2015 projected their conceptions of future war into a completely virtualized rendition of Jakarta or Baghdad. The city became pure battlespace, a reception area for future ordnance. Reporting as he watched the players in one exercise in October 2006, Bryan Axtell, a military PR spokesman, noted how 'targeting crosshairs float across alleys and rooftops while one hand delicately nudges the ergonomic control sporting weapons toggles, and the other dances across the top of a box full of backlit red buttons and more joystick controls'.[58]

Urban Resolve 2015 provided a major experimental context for the development of future US high-tech weapons geared towards urban insurgencies. It amounted, in effect, to a trial run for the technophilic fantasies of robotic domination discussed in Chapter 6. As part of the exercise in October 2006, for example, armed drones 'flying' above Jakarta were equipped with imaginary versions of the 'directed-energy', or laser, weapons actually being developed by military R&D. Apparently, the findings of Urban Resolve

56 Bryan Axtell, 'Urban Warfare Experiment Draws Many Players', USJFCOM Public Affairs, 24 October 2006, available at www.jfcom.mil.
57 Peter Wielhouwer, 'Preparing for Future Joint Urban Operations: The Role of simulation and the *Urban Resolve* Experiment', *Small Wars Journal*, July 2005.
58 Ibid.

were of such significance that they 'led to overhauling the entire US Defense Department master plan' for future urban warfare.[59]

Notwithstanding all the state-of-the-art high-tech, Urban Resolve still seems to have had 'a curiously hermetic feel to it'.[60] Ashley Dawson, who visited one of the simulations, noted that 'balding white men with handlebar moustaches' dominated the ranks of participants – 'the same blend of superannuated spooks and worn-out Special Forces hot-shots who have been running the real occupation of Iraq to such disastrous effect since 2003'.[61] Behind all this, in Urban Resolve as elsewhere, Dawson diagnosed a 'blinkered disavowal of the fact that it is the US occupation itself that is creating a toxic environment in Baghdad'.[62]

AN ARMY OF GAMERS 1

Today's troops received their basic training as children.[63]

The simulation of Arab cities as little but receiving spaces for US military fire-power goes well beyond the confines of the military. As the military cross-fertilizes with the electronic entertainment industry,[64] so the electronic simulations of Arab cities are used both for US military training and for successful commercial video games. By 2008, the US military had formally adopted twenty-three video games for internal training purposes. Notably, *America's Army* (Figure 6.7) and the US Marine Corps equivalent, *Full Spectrum Warrior*,[65] have been developed by their respective forces in partnership with entertainment companies, based in part on urban training simulations.

Both *America's Army* and *Full Spectrum Warrior* – amongst the world's most popular video game franchises in 2008 – 'propel the player into the world of the gaming industry's latest fetish: modern urban warfare'.[66] Both focus around the military challenges presumed to be involved in the occupation and pacification of stylized, Orientalized Arab cities. Players must undertake basic training in

59   Maryann Lawlor, 'Military Changes Tactical Thinking', *Signal Magazine*, October 2007.

60   Dawson, 'Combat in Hell', 170.

61   Ibid.

62   Ibid.

63   William Hamilton, 'Toymakers Study Troops, And Vice Versa', *New York Times*, 30 March 2003.

64   Derian, *Virtuous War*.

65   See the Games' websites at www.americasarmy.com and www.fullspectrumwarrior. com respectively.

66   Steffan DelPiano, 'Review of Full Spectrum Warrior', GamesFirst.com, 2004.

6.7   Orientalized cityscapes of *America's Army*.

an electronic simulation of Mount McKenna, one of the US military's largest physical urban-warfare training sites. Andrew Deck argues that the proliferation of urban warfare games based on actual, ongoing US military interventions in Arab cities 'call[s] forth a cult of ultra-patriotic xenophobes whose greatest joy is to destroy, regardless of how racist, imperialistic, and flimsy the rationale' for the simulated battle.[67]

America's Army, in particular, has been called 'a monumental step into twenty-first-century military-consumer culture.'[68] By 2008, the game – marketed under the strap line 'Citizens. Countries. Video Games. The US Army keeps them all free' – had been downloaded more than thirty-eight million times, more than eight million of which were by registered users.[69] The 'mission' of the game, writes Steve O'Hagan, 'is to slaughter evildoers, with something about "liberty" . . . going on in the background . . . These games may be ultra-realistic down to the caliber of the weapons, but when bullets hit flesh people just crumple serenely into a heap. No blood. No exit wounds. No screams.'[70] Roger Stahl notes that 'sometimes a mist of blood escapes an invisible wound, but the victims neither flail nor cry. Bodies tend to disappear as if raptured up to heaven.'[71]

Games like *America's Army* and *Full Spectrum Warrior* construct the US soldier as a hypermasculine agent of (just and honorable) violence, while they construct the stylized Arab Other as a loose and unspecified existential threat to vague ideas of 'freedom' and 'America'. These two constructions, of course, are complementary, inseparable: 'in articulating the Other the Army concomitantly constitutes itself', writes Abhinava Kumar.[72] Depictions of this vague, threatening, patently evil, and racialized Other reinforce imaginary geographies equating Arab cities with 'terrorism' and the need for 'pacification' or 'cleansing' through US military invasion and occupation. Further blurring the already fuzzy boundaries that separate war from entertainment, these games demonstrate that the US entertainment industry 'has assumed a posture of co-operation towards a culture of permanent war'.[73]

67   Andy Deck, 'Demilitarizing the Playground', *No Quarter*, 2004, available at www.artcontext.net/crit/essays/noQuarter.

68   Roger Stahl, 'Have You Played the War on Terror?', *Critical Studies in Media Communication* 23: 2, 2006, 122.

69   Susan Land, 'Best Practices for Software Engineering: Using IEEE Software and System Engineering Standards to Support America's Army: Special Forces', presentation, 2007, available at www.dau.mil.

70   Steve Hagan, 'Recruitment hard drive', *Guardian Guide.* 19–25 June 2004, 12–13.

71   Stahl, 'Have You Played the War on Terror?', 130.

72   Abhinava Kumar, 'America's Army Game and the Production of War', YCISS working paper 27, March 2004, 8.

73   Deck, 'Demilitarizing the Playground'.

Within urban-warfare video games, Arab cities are, strikingly, represented merely as 'collections of objects not congeries of people'.[74] And when people are represented, almost without exception they are rendered not only as Arab but as shadowy, subhuman, radicalized, absolutely external terrorists – figures to be repeatedly annihilated in sanitized 'action', either as entertainment or as military training or as a blurry version of both. *America's Army*, for example, simulates counterterror warfare in densely packed Arab cities in the fictional country of Zekistan. Almost every building is dark, shadowy, burning, and designed in a stylized version of Islamic architecture.

Once again, Arab cities serve only as environments for military engagement. The militarization of the everyday sites, artefacts, and spaces of the simulated city is total: 'Cars are used as bombs, bystanders become victims [although they die without spilling blood], houses become headquarters, apartments become lookout points, and anything to be strewn in the street becomes suitable cover'.[75] To some extent, the actual physical geographies of Arab cities are being digitized to provide the three-dimensional battlespaces for these video games. One games developer, Forterra Systems, which also develops training games for the US military, boasts, 'We've [digitally] built a portion of the downtown area of a large Middle Eastern capital city where we have a significant presence today'.[76]

The main purpose of such games, however, is public relations: they are a powerful and extremely cost-effective means of recruitment. 'Because the Pentagon spends around $15,000 on average wooing each recruit, the game needs only to result in 300 enlistments per year to recoup costs', asserts Stahl.[77] Indeed, 40 per cent of those who join the Army have previously played *America's Army*.[78] The video game also provides the basis for a sophisticated surveillance system through which Army recruitment efforts are directed. In the marketing-speak of its military developers, *America's Army* is designed to reach the substantial overlap in 'population between the gaming population and the Army's target recruiting segments', to address 'tech-savvy audiences and affor[d] the army a unique, strategic communication advantage' (Figure 6.8).

74 Gregory, *The Colonial Present*, 201.
75 DelPiano, 'Review of Full Spectrum Warrior'.
76 Deck, 'Demilitarizing the Playground'.
77 Stahl, 'Have You Played the War on Terror?', 123.
78 Ibid.

The Game Addresses Tech-Savvy Audiences and Affords the Army a Unique, Strategic Communication Advantage

High Potential Accessions are Gamers:

- *77% of the Males in the West Point Class of 2007 Played Games Like America's Army.*

- *18% of the Males in the West Point Class of 2007 Played America's Army*

Games Can Show the Army of Today, Tomorrow – Through the Objective Force

- *Unlike Other Media, America's Army Can Present the Dynamic Future of Soldiering*

Source: Col. Casey Wardynski

Veteran "First Person" Gamers Exhibit Higher Performance in Certain Military Skills Requiring High Visual Attention

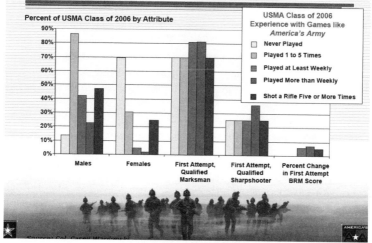

6.8 The reasoning behind the US military's development of urban warfare video games.

Most startling of all, *America's Army* is carefully designed as a recruitment device to exploit the fact that 'veteran [video] gamers exhibit higher performance in certain military skills requiring high visual attention'. In other words, the US military considers the playing of video games to be an effective form of preparatory military training.[79] There is, moreover, no attempt to disguise this fact. An article in *Defense Horizons* magazine, for example, argues that 'video games made better soldiers and sailors faster, safer and cheaper'.[80]

The lobby group Empowered Muslim Youth argues that the targeting of children and young people through these games amounts to a form of cultural brainwashing. 'These visual games are a perfect opportunity to psychologically prepare and even mentally train children to fight in battle', the group contends. 'There is no doubt that this [is a] well-thought tactic, issued by high-ranking government officials'.[81] Former US Army psychologist Lt Col David Grossman appears to concur. He has spoken about how the use of video games and similar electronic training simulations helps indoctrinate soldiers to kill more readily in real combat. The absence of 'blood, gore and emotions' from such games, he writes, helps in the 'teaching [of] children to associate pleasure with human death and suffering. We are rewarding them for killing people. And we are teaching them to like it'.[82]

DISAPPEARING DEATH

The force of virtual realities has been growing by the day. In parallel with major commercial video game and electronic entertainment corporations seeking to build physical versions of their products in the form of theme parks and shopping malls, the US military has sought to cash in on the massive popularity of its own video games to extend its recruitment push. One result is the Virtual Army Experience – a massive, twenty-thousand-square-foot touring road show which pitches up at rodeos, car races, car shows, air shows, and 'patriotic' events and allows potential recruits to experience a propagandized, twenty-

79   Cited in Tim Lenoir, 'Taming a Disruptive Technology: America's Army, and the Military-Entertainment Complex', presentation at the Symposium on the Coevolution of Technology-Business Innovations, 24–25 September 2003, Boulder, CO.

80   J.C. Herz and Michael R. Macedonia, 'Computer Games and the Military: Two Views', *Defense Horizons,* April 2002, available at www.ndu.edu.

81   David Axe, 'America's Army Game = Brainwashing?', *Danger Room* (Wired Blog Network), 29 January 2008, available at blog.wired.com/defense.

82   Cited in David Leonard, 'Unsettling the Military Entertainment Complex: Video Games and a Pedagogy of Peace', *Studies in Media & Information Literacy Education* 4: 4, 2004.

minute version of Army life.[83] 'Only Soldiers know how it feels to fight in a combat zone, but civilians now have an opportunity to get a virtual taste of the action', announced the *Army News Service* on the road show's launch in February 2007.[84]

'Guests' are given fake Army dog tags, extensively interviewed, and then briefed on their 'mission', which is to drive a convoy of six heavily armed Humvees into an 'Arab' city and extract a terrorist leader (Figure 6.9).[85] Surrounding the six vehicles are virtual renditions of a town, drawn from the *America's Army* game. Guests use the weapons provided. As in a shoot-'em-up game, the targets 'die' when hit: 'when the bad guys die, they fall bloodlessly and disappear. They keep coming – standing atop silos, pouring from buildings'.[86] One potential recruit at the 2007 DigitalLife Expo recalled it this way:

> The action started out a bit slow with a civilian or two running by to go hide inside their home before being blasted with a stray bullet. As our Humvees began to roll forward, we were presented with varying degrees of enemies that would either pop out around corners, run out into the street, or rest atop a placement on top of a building. The actual shooting experience was fairly solid. There was a small amount of kickback with the weapon and because it was the real thing, the weight of the gun took its toll over the course of our time inside the truck.[87]

But even US military veterans themselves have expressed revulsion at this latest virtualization of military killing. A group that calls itself Democracy for Missouri, which has picketed the display, presents a picture of the experience that is quite different from the one described above: 'This obscene display has folks lining up to play virtual war complete with surround video and realistic explosion sounds. The screams of women and children were not a part of the "Experience"'.[88]

83   *America's Army*, 'Virtual Army Experience Fact Sheet', available at vae.americasarmy. com.

84   Hannah Hayner, 'Virtual Experience Lets Civilians Act as Soldiers', *US Army News*, 27 February 2007.

85   Ibid.

86   John Kessler, 'At Six Flags, War is a Virtual Reality Experience', *Atlanta Journal-Constitution*, 4 December 2008.

87   Wire.ggl.com, 'DigitalLife 2007: The Virtual Army Experience', 29 September 2007.

88   Democracy for Missouri.org, 'Democracy for Missouri confronts the "Virtual Army Experience" at Recruitment . . . er . . . Memorial . . . Day', undated.

6.9   Participants at an '*America's Army* Experience' roadshow, 2007.

VIRTUAL STRESS

The US military has tried hard indeed to focus on virtualized renditions of Arab cities rather than confront the social realities of the real ones. This effort even extends to the use of virtual-reality war games to treat US veterans of Iraq who suffer from post-traumatic stress disorder (PTSD).

The Institute for Creative Technologies at the University of Southern California, a key player in the cross-over between war and entertainment, has adapted *Full Spectrum Warrior*'s immersive simulations of stylized Arab cities as the basis for treating traumatized soldiers. Patients undergo simulations of the very events that have most traumatized them: being inside mined or bombed vehicles and helicopters; experiencing mortar attacks within compounds; patrolling and being attacked on Iraqi streets. In short, they are placed within virtual-reality 'scenarios that resemble the setting in which the traumatic events initially occurred'. Thus, the war-zone experience is replayed in what is called 'Virtual Iraq exposure therapy', an approach which is being deployed in treatment centres across the US. Given the programme's similarities to video games, its designers expect it to 'resonate well with the current generation of war fighters'. [89]

Here, then, the use of Orientalized urban immersions for US military deployment comes full circle. In addition to dominating recruitment, training, entertainment and combat, the de-realized, pixelated worlds of simulated urban warfare are now called upon to help soldiers try to cope with the realities they actually experienced while physically fighting on the streets of Iraq's cities. Perhaps the task is to enable the soldiers to push the real horrors of the war once again into the substanceless background of the endless simulations of violence and otherness that increasingly pervade Western culture. James Spira, a Navy psychologist who has experience with the institute's approach, has stressed that clinicians using the system must make certain that it is 'not too realistic, to create more trauma'. [90]

THE ULTIMATE GATED COMMUNITIES

> Bases are the state incarnate. [91]

Just as mock, stylized Arab cities dot the heartlands of the United States, so do mock, stylized US cities, in a rarely discussed parallel, now dot the fringes

---

89 Rick Rogers, 'Military to Try Virtual Combat Stress Remedy', SignOnSanDiego. Com, 17 March 2005.

90 Ibid.

91 Boal, Clark, Matthews and Watts, *Afflicted Powers*, 189.

of Empire. As Mark Gillem has shown,[92] the seven hundred or so foreign US military bases (located in about 140 of the world's 195 countries[93]) which anchor the nation's imperial and geographic power increasingly resemble carefully designed capsules of prototypical US suburbia that have been implanted into foreign nations. 'The US government has dispersed its soldiers across the globe to protect the flow of empire,' writes Gillem. And the bases inhabited by those soldiers are replete with golf courses, strip malls, drive-through fast-food franchises, manicured lawns, and perfect simulations of US schools, fire stations, split-level ranch houses, hotels, bars, parking lots and cinemas – all set within the sprawl of extremely low-density US-style suburbs surrounded not merely by razor-wire fences but by the apparatus of war (Figure 6.10).

The architecture and planning of US bases reflect the strict application of US norms of urban design. This allows America's service personnel, wherever they are posted around the world, to 'arrive in the same familiar vision of "home"'. As Major Leslie Triano said about his life at the Kunsan Air Base, 'Sometimes it's nice to go back to the United States when you're in the middle of Korea'.[94]

Enabling US military personnel and their families to inhabit a complete simulacrum of US suburbia whilst absorbing vast tranches of foreign land, US bases thus permit members of the armed forces to almost completely disengage from the world beyond the gate. Gillem argues that the new imperial land-use model sustaining the global proliferation of US bases is one of 'avoidance[95] – relocating military bases to isolated but well-appointed compounds designed to prevent contact with the residents'.[96] US service personnel, writes Gillem,

> are living a diaspora experience and are trying to define themselves with reference to their distant homeland, a common feature of diaspora communities. They have multiple homes, but they are trying to reconcile difference through design. Wherever these soldiers go, they are homeward bound – bound to the same sprawling subdivisions, franchised restaurants, and vacuous shopping malls.[97]

---

92   See Mark Gillem, *America Town: Building the Outposts of Empire,* Minneapolis, MN: University of Minnesota Press, 2007.

93   As of March 2008.

94   Gillem, *America Town,* 73.

95   Ibid., 263.

96   The author's website, markgillem.com provided a description of the book.

97   Gillem, *America Town,* 74.

6.10   Playground at Kadena Air Base, Okinawa, Japan (top);
Patriot missile battery at overseas US base (bottom).

Gillem's work suggests that the vast archipelago of US military camps and bases can perhaps be regarded as the ultimate transnational array of Ballardian gated communities. Certainly, such a perception is already common among US military personnel.

The community web page for Joint Task Force Guantanamo, for instance – where seven thousand military personnel organize a base which contains the War on Terror's most notorious torture camp – actually promotes the complex by declaring that 'sun, sand and a close knit community make the naval station one of the finest "gated communities" in the Caribbean'.[98] Meanwhile, Lt Col Goyette of Holloman Air Force Base in New Mexico admitted that her relatives, who had recently visited the base, had remarked that 'there [are] people who pay good money to live in a gated community as nice as this one'. On considering their arguments, she was convinced: 'You have a free fitness center with an amazing amount of fitness opportunities, reduced cost medical and dental care, good schools within walking distance from your house, movies for a dollar, reduced golf fees, reduced grocery costs and you get to watch really cool planes all day long'.[99]

Continuing that line of thinking, Lt Col Goyette asked, 'Isn't that an interesting way to look at how we live? My husband and I really appreciate the feeling of security we get living on base. While I still watch my kids when they play in the front yard, I know I don't have to worry about drive-by shootings or drug sales on the sidewalk. I don't have to worry about gang bangers living next to me, bringing dangerous traffic to the neighborhood'.[100]

TOYS OF WAR

Military simulations also now take their place within the proliferating spectacles and fantasy landscapes that now dominate urban consumption and tourism in the US (and elsewhere), their themed visons peppered with digital screens and digitally augmented architecture. In 2006 at Fort Belvoir, Virginia, for example, the US Army entertained a proposal from a private developer to complement the site's major new military museum with a 125-acre, $300 million military theme park and simulation centre along with a massive hotel complex. According to the *Washington Post*, the proposal promised that visitors would

---

98   See 'Community', available at www.jtfgtmo.southcom.mil.
99   Carmen Goyette, 'Perspective: Holloman Air Force Base or Gated Community?', *Holloman US Air Force Base News*, 22 March 2007.
100   Ibid.

be able to 'command the latest M-1 tank [or] feel the rush of a paratrooper's free-fall, fly a Cobra gunship'.[101]

The developer, Orlando-based Universal City Property Management, argued that the complex would put visitors 'in an interactive world where [they would] feel firsthand what it's like to defend American freedom'. Visitors would be able to 'live the greatest battles of all time in a multi-sensory 4-D presentation'. However, the proposal generated widespread criticism that it would 'make a mockery of the Army experience' and was quickly withdrawn. Since then, the Army has been seeking another 'visitor destination concept' to go with the museum.[102]

Because the experiences within such simulators are becoming ever more indistinguishable from those of the 'pilots' of the armed drones used in the CIA's frequent assassination raids in the Middle East and Pakistan, however, a further troubling blurring between metropolitan heartland and colonial frontier is now emerging. For these pilots are actually located in virtual reality 'caves', set up inside anonymous trailer housing at Nellis and Creech Air Force Bases on the edge of that icon of simulation: Las Vegas.

Here the ubiquity of games and virtual simulations blends into the game–style reality of very real weaponry and killing. A writer for *Wired* Magazine, writing about a Predator pilot named Private Joe Clark, points out that Clark has, in a sense, 'been prepping for the job since he was a kid: He plays videogames. A lot of videogames. Back in the barracks he spends downtime with an Xbox and a PlayStation'. After training, continues the writer, 'when he first slid behind the controls of a Shadow UAV [Unmanned Aerial Vehicle], the point and click operation turned out to work much the same way. "You watch the screen. You tell it to roll left, it rolls left. It's pretty simple," Clark says'.[103]

Such cross-overs have been intensifying. The newest Predator control systems from the arms maker Raytheon (Figure 6.11) deliberately use the 'same HOTAS [hands on stick and throttle] system' as a video game uses. Raytheon's UAV designer argues that there is 'no point in re-inventing the wheel. The current generation of pilots was raised on the [Sony] PlayStation, so we created an interface that they will immediately understand'.[104] Added to this is the fact that many of the latest video games depict the very same armed UAVs as those used by US forces in assassination raids. That the

101 Matthew Barakat, 'Army Shoots Down Proposal for Military Theme Park in VA', *USA Today*, 8 August 2006.

102 Ibid.

103 Noah Shachtman, 'Attack of the Drones', *Wired* 13:6, 2005.

104 Paul Richfield, ' New 'Cockpit' for Predator?', *C4Isr Journal*, 31 October 2006.

training simulators for armed drones 'are said to be so realistic that it would be difficult to distinguish, without previous knowledge, between them and the actual ground stations' adds still further to the blurring of simulation and reality.[105] These simulators, 'running 1 terabyte of memory', notes a piece on Technology.com, 'replicat[e] actual terrain and actual locations of the world, such as Afghanistan and Iraq'.[106]

6.11   An air force 'Pilot' controlling an armed Predator drone, operating from inside a 'virtual reality cave' at Nellis Air Force Base on the edge of Las Vegas.

Another UAV controller, interviewed by Robert Kaplan in 2006, pointed out the extreme geographical juxtapositions involved in 'piloting' armed drones on the other side of the planet from a metal box on the edge of Las Vegas. 'Inside that trailer is Iraq; inside the other, Afghanistan', he explained, saying that 'if you want to pull the trigger and take out bad guys, you fly a Predator'.[107] As another Predator operator-pilot admitted, in perhaps the ultimate juxtaposition of domestic suburbia and the distant

105   'Learning to Fly . . . UAVs', Technology.Com, undated.
106   Ibid.
107   Robert Kaplan, 'Hunting the Taliban in Las Vegas', *Atlantic Montly*, 4 August 2006.

projection of colonial violence, 'at the end of the work day, you walk back into the rest of life in America'.[108]

In this context, the main issue confronting military personnel is the extreme contrast between the job of hyperreal killing-at-a-distance within the trailers, and the familiar world of urban America that lies outside the door.[109] 'Inside the trailers, crews don't get even the sensation of flying that one gets in a flight simulator', writes Kaplan. 'The real tension for these pilots comes from the clash with everything outside the trailers. Beyond Nellis is the banal world of spouses, kids, homework, and soccer games, not to mention the absurdity of a city where even the gas stations have slot machines. Simply entering or leaving one of the trailers is tremendously disorienting'.[110]

But the blurring of weapons and toys – which have, of course, always been closely associated – is accelerating yet further. As well as shaping the output of toys, films and video games that encourage children to become potential recruits, the US military's weapons now reciprocate by imitating toys and video games. Some US military equipment, as we have seen with the Predator, now have control consoles which mimic that of PlayStation 2s.

The Dragon Runner urban surveillance robot, now deployed by the Marine Corps, is another example.[111] Its six-button controller also mimics that of Sony's PlayStation 2. Major Greg Heines, of the Marine's Warfighting Laboratory, stresses that the design was chosen because 'that's what these 18-, 19-year-old Marines have been playing with pretty much all of their lives, [so they] will pick up [how to drive the Dragon Runner] in a few minutes'.[112] In March 2000 the emergence of PlayStations as weapon controls actually had an unforeseen effect: they were classified by the government of Japan as '"general purpose product related to conventional weapons", a change which considerably reduced export levels [that] led to a global shortage of the consoles'.[113]

---

108   Quoted in Richard Newman, 'The Joystick War', *U.S. News*, 19 May 2003.

109   In another twist in the conflation of war-zone and domestic urban borderlands, after considerable resistance from Federal aviation safety authorities, piloted drones have now been given safety clearance to patrol the US–Mexico border. Experiments to see if large drones might defend US airports against shoulder-fired missiles are also underway. As yet, through, domestic drones remain unarmed.

110   Kaplan, 'Hunting the Taliban in Las Vegas'.

111   Nick Turse, 'Bringing the War Home: The New Military-Industrial-Entertainment Complex at War and Play', *Tom Dispatch*, 17 October 2003.

112   Ibid.

113   Stahl, 'Have You Played the War on Terror?', 112.

SIM CITIES

Along with the boom in so-called homeland security since 9/11, urban-warfare planning now puts equal emphasis on simulating Los Angeles and simulating Baghdad. It imagines the projection of forces to 'take back' US cities from civil uprisings or social protests, as much as the challenges of occupying Arab cities. The Los Angeles riots of 1992 appear as often on US military PowerPoints about 'lessons learned' as do Mogadishu, Baghdad, Jenin or Grozny.

Meanwhile, within the US, dozens of physical simulations of US city districts are joining the simulations of Arab cities. These are the places where law-enforcement and National Guard personnel practise operations against civil unrest, terrorist attack and natural disaster. 'Another architecture is rising in the expanding landscape of preparedness', notes the Center for Land Use Interpretation. 'Condensed simulacra of our existing urban environments are forming within our communities, where the first responders to emergencies, on a small or large scale, practice their craft of dealing with disaster [and where] the police contend with civil decay, robberies, hostage situations, looting, riots, and snipers'.[114]

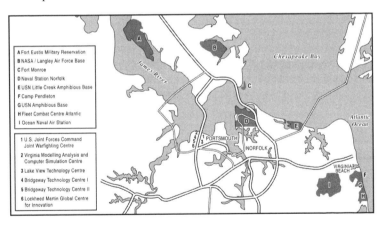

6.12   Sim City: The concentration of military, academic, simulation and security complexes, bases and research parks in Suffolk, Virginia.

---

114 Center for Land Use Interpretation, 'Exhibition Review: *Emergency State: First Responders and Emergency Training Architecture*', 2004, available at www.clui.org.

Military simulations are also helping to produce US cities in another, more direct, way: generating them now takes up large swaths of the US economy, especially in high-tech metropolitan areas. Many of the much-vaunted high-tech suburban hot spots that house what Richard Florida has called the 'creative class'[115] of the US – places such as Washington, DC's 'Beltway', North Carolina's 'Research Triangle', Florida's 'High Tech Corridor', or San Diego's 'clean tech cluster' – are in fact heavily sustained by the production of symbolic violence against both US central and Arab cities.   Being not only the foundries of the security state but also the sites of the most militarized and corporatized research universities, these locations are where the vastly profitable and rapidly growing convergence between electronic games and military simulation is being forged. Orlando's hundred large military-simulator firms, for example, generate about seventeen thousand jobs and are starting to overshadow even Disney as local economic drivers. Behind the blank façades and manicured lawns, thousands of software engineers and games professionals project their Orientalized electronic imaginaries onto the world through the increasingly seamless complex of military, entertainment, media and academic industries.

The importance of military simulation industries is not lost on those tasked with the development of local urban economies. The municipality of Suffolk, Virginia, for instance, now proudly claims that a 'world-class cluster of "Modeling and Simulation" enterprises has taken root around the US Joint Forces Command and an Old Dominion University research center' (Figure 6.12)[116] To support further growth in these sectors, partnerships beween local governments and economic developers are springing up to determine 'how the state of Virginia could better support JFCOM [Joint Forces Command] and its mission'. This economic convergence gains strength from the Virginia Modeling and Simulation Initiative (VIMSIM), which will be geared to 'stimulate development of a unique high-tech industry with multi-billion dollar revenue potential.' Already, Lockheed Martin has opened a major simulation complex in the area. 'As a growing high technology hub with proximity to major defense, homeland security and other important customer installations', Lockheed Martin's CEO, Vance Coffman, pointed out in 2003, 'Suffolk is the ideal location for our new center.'[117]

115   Richard Florida, *The Rise of the Creative Class*, New York: Basic Books, 2003.
116   'SimCity will be huge', *Suffolk News Herald*, 10 May 2005.
117   Ibid.

SELF-FULFILLING WORLDS

> All efforts to render politics aesthetic culminate in one thing – war.[118]

The complex constellation of simulations of Arab and global South cities discussed here work powerfully as a collective. The various physical, electronic and blended physical–electronic manifestations operate together, as do all simulacra, by collapsing reality with artifice, so that any simple boundary between the two effectively disappears.[119]

In keeping with what Jean Baudrillard famously stressed, it is best to consider the above simulations, not as 'copies' of the 'real' world, but as hyperreal constructions – simulations of things that don't exist – through which war and violence are constructed, legitimized, and performed. 'Simulation is no longer that of a territory, a referential being, or a substance', Baudrillard writes, 'It is the generation by models of a real without origins or reality: a hyperreal'.[120] The point, then, is not that these simulations are less 'real' than the things they purportedly represent. Rather, they provide spaces through which the violence of the 'War on Terror' can be generated and performed, and which acquire their power from their radical disassociation from any meaningful connection with the real places (or, less commonly, real people) they are said to represent.

In the process, these simulacra 'participate in the construction of a discourse of security which is self-fulfilling'.[121] Multiple layers and circuits of simulation work collectively to evacuate the possibility of authenticating what might actually be 'real'. 'Since 9/11', writes James Der Derian, 'simulations (war games, training exercises, scenario planning, and modeling) and dissimulations (propaganda, disinformation, infowar, deceit, and lies) [have produced] a hall of mirrors, reducing the "truth" about the "Global War on Terror" to an infinite regression of representations that [defy] authentication'.[122]

---

118   Walter Benjamin, 'The Work of Art in the Age of Mechanical Reproduction', in Hannah Arendt *Illuminations*, ed., trans. Harry Zohn, New York: Schocken, 1968, 241. Thanks to Marcus Power for this reference.

119   Jean Baudrillard, *The Gulf War Did Not Take Place*, Bloomington, IN: Indiana University Press, 1991.

120   Jean Baudrillard, *Simulacra and Simulation*, Ann Arbor, MI: University of Michigan Press, 1994.

121   Abhinava Kumar, 'America's Army Game and the Production of War', YCISS working paper 27, March 2004, 8.

122   James Der Derian, conference brief for Dis/Simulations of War and Peace Symposium, 6–7 June, 2004.

Because the worlds of threat and risk are projected through this simulacral collective, the perpetration of state violence and colonial war emerge from the same collective as necessary, just and honourable. More simulations are rendered necessary in turn to improve the effectiveness of such violence, to tempt and train more recruits, to deal with their psychological devastation once they return home, and so on. It follows that the very notion of 'security', at least as constructed through the military simulacral collective, becomes possible only through permanent war. 'War makes security possible by creating that which is to be protected', writes Abhinava Kumar, 'and what makes war possible [is the] mechanization of soldiers, the obscuring of the enemy and the sanitisation of violence.'[123]

The mediatization of contemporary war is such that the 'fighting' of actual wars takes place as much in TV lounges, at multiplexes, and on YouTube or PlayStation screens as in the real streets and alleys of combat-zone cities. As already-vague distinctions between civil and military media and technology dissolve, the military simulacral collective comes to permeate a host of media simultaneously. Previously considered to be largely distinct, multiple media domains are thus in the process of fusing and interpenetrating within and through the military simulacral collective – a process at once confusing, disturbing and extremely fast moving. 'We see that various genres once thought to be discrete are forging new and strange alliances', writes Roger Stahl. As a result, 'wartime news looks like a video game; video games restage the news. Official military training simulators cross over into the commercial entertainment markets; commercial video games are made useful for military training exercises. Advertisements sell video games with patriotic rhetorics; video games are mobilized to advertise patriotism. The business of play works closely with the military to replicate the tools of state violence; the business of state violence in turn capitalizes on playtime for institutional ends.'[124]

AN ARMY OF GAMERS 2

As we have seen, video game technologies are progressively merging with weapons technologies. Experiences associated with the control and use of

---

123   Kumar, 'America's Army Game and the Production of War', 8.
124   Roger Stahl , 'Have You Played the War on Terror?', 123.

real weapons are beginning to blend so thoroughly with those associated with the military simulators of such weapons, as well as with the video games that offer still other simulations of experience in the use of such weapons, that users may struggle to define which realm they inhabit at any given moment.

Projecting current trends, Bryan Finoki, author of the superb Subtopia blog, speculates about a near future in which 'video games become the ultimate interface for conducting real life warfare', as virtual reality simulators used in video gaming converge completely with those used in military training exercises. Finoki takes the video game–like existence of the Las Vegas Predator 'pilots', with their PlayStation-style controls, as his starting-point. He speculates, only half ironically, whether future video gamers could 'become decorated war heroes by virtue of their eye-and-hand coordination skills, which would eventually dominate the triggers of network-centric remote controlled warfare'.[125]

In perhaps the ultimate Foucauldian boomerang, such a trend would finally collapse any remaining distinctions between domestic spectatorship and virtual killing on the colonial frontier. 'Casual assemblages of home bodies on couches strewn across America', as Finoki phrases it, would thus 'become the new command posts for an intercontinental sprawl of robotic warfare. Good old American homes could "adopt a war bot" abroad, while little Johnny controls it with his new joystick that he's gotten for Christmas.'[126]

WAR RE-ENCHANTED: THE END OF DEATH

The military simulacral collective is the main product of what Der Derian has called the 'military-industrial-media-entertainment network',[127] dedicated to 'the disappearance of the body, the aestheticization of violence, the sanitization of war'.[128] This removal of harm from war operates across the whole spectrum of simulations – from those used for actual killing, through those used for training, to those used for sheer entertainment. All of them are variations on the axiom of what Der Derian calls 'Virtuous War', which involves 'the technical capability and the ethical imperative to threaten, and if needed, actualize violence

---

125   Bryan Finoki, 'War Room', Subtopia blog, 20 May 2006.
126   Ibid.
127   James Der Derian, Virtuous War..
128   Cited in Derek Gregory, 'The Rush to the Intimate'.

from a distance, with no or minimal casualties' (to the 'home side', that is).[129]

As a result, paradoxically, an 'enterprise expressly devoted to killing magically proceeds without death',[130] and thus the complex of simulations discussed here play a massive, perhaps a dominant, role in what has been termed the contemporary 're-enchantment' with war.[131] The military simulacral collective is especially seductive inasmuch as it manages to 'reintroduc[e] corporeality to war – cyber-cities are re-peopled, Virtual Humans made to breathe' while also managing to 'snuff out' all hints of true mortality.[132]

Denial of death moves even further beyond the marshalling of physical, electronic and blended simulations in a plethora of training sites, video games, films,[133] and recruitment fairs. Through what are euphemistically called 'perception management operations', it extends, too, to the official banning of images of dead service-members' coffins and to the careful construction of Hollywoodesque news propaganda, intended for use by the often supine mainstream media. It is now clear, for instance, that the Pentagon relies on simulation techniques to help fake material for its orchestrated news 'splashes'. Such a tactic is seen as merely one element in the apparently infinite spectrum of 'information operations' or 'psychological operations' necessary to sustain US 'full spectrum dominance' or 'information dominance' in a highly mediatized and globalized world.[134] In early 2002, for example, the Bush administration considered establishing an Office for Strategic Influence that would deliberately 'plant news items with media organizations through outside concerns that might not have obvious ties to the Pentagon'.[135] A notorious

129 Der Derian, *Virtuous War.*

130 Gregory, 'The Rush to the Intimate'.

131 Christopher Coker, *The Future of War: The Re-Enchantment of War in the Twenty-First Century*, Oxford: Blackwell, 2004.

132 Gregory 'The Rush to the Intimate'.

133 As David Robb argues, 'In many ways, Hollywood is embedded with the military', and the military 'know that when positive images are portrayed in movies and television shows, they see huge spikes in recruitment. The military is really pressing to get into these pictures . . . These films (that receive Pentagon assistance) should have a disclaimer: "This film has been shaped and censored by the military to meet recruiting goals."' Quoted in César Soriano and Ann Oldenburg, 'With America at war, Hollywood follows', *USA Today,* 2 August 2005.

134 Derik Crotts and Jonathan Metcalfe, 'Operational Implications of Public Affairs – Factors, Functions, and Challenges of the Information Battlefield', *Iosphere,* Winter 2006.

135 James Dao and Eric Schmitt, 'Pentagon Readies Efforts to Sway Sentiment Abroad', *New York Times,* 19 February 2002.

instance of this sort of deception is, of course, the stage-managed 'rescue' of Jessica Lynch.[136]

These media simulations – and suppressions – are occasionally combined with the violent targeting of media channels which do present images of the war dead to the world, such as the April 2003 bombing of Al Jazeera's Baghdad office by US aircraft, five months after the destruction of the network's Kabul office with a missile. The April action resulted in the death of a journalist. One outraged blogger writes, 'With high technology involving satellite and lap-top "cross-hair" accuracy and awareness of Al Jazeera's location for over two years, we were meant to believe that the TV station, lying in a residential neighbourhood with three satellite dishes on its roof – was an accident'.[137] Yet even that wasn't the end of the campaign against Al Jazeera: subsequently, Tony Blair and George Bush seriously considered bombing the network's headquarters in Qatar.[138]

'VIRTUAL CITIZEN-SOLDIERS'

In addition to its production of endless fields of repetitive, symbolic, sanitized and preparatory violence, the military simulacral collective forces its guests and participants to conform to the rituals of urban combat by narrowing down the range of possible actions to one and only one kind: hypermasculine military assault. Soldiers consume the assorted simulacra as well as using them as a basis

136   On 23 March 2003, Private Jessica Lynch and nine colleagues from her 507th Maintenance Company were rescued from an Iraqi hospital by US special forces. The Pentagon reported that Lynch had been 'captured after firing at Iraqis until her ammunition ran out, had been hit by a bullet, stabbed, tied up and taken to a hospital in Nasiriyah.' There she was rescued by a daring US special forces raid a week later. Later, Lynch received a Bronze Star, and her actions were widely lauded as 'the most heroic moment – perhaps the only heroic moment – in the war in Iraq.' The story seemed almost too perfect, too Hollywoodesque. It was. Lynch, under caring supervision in an Iraqi hospital, was actually 'rescued' by special forces who had as much media and film equipment as weaponry. There were no Iraqi soldiers present. Iraqi doctors gave Jessica Lynch good medical care. And Jessica Lynch was neither shot nor stabbed, but had been injured when her vehicle overturned. Dr Anmar Uday, who witnessed the event, told the BBC's John Kampfner, 'It was like in a Hollywood film. They cried "go, go, go", with guns and blanks without bullets, blanks and the sound of explosions. They made a show for the American attack on the hospital – action movies like Sylvester Stallone or Jackie Chan.' The raw footage of the rescue, moreover, was edited into the final news release by a former assistant to Ridley Scott who had worked on the Hollywood movie depicting the 1991 military operations in Mogadishu, *Black Hawk Down*. By May 2003, Robert Scheer reported in the *LA Times* that the 'fabrication has already been celebrated by an A&E special and will soon be an NBC movie.' See www.bbc.co.uk and Sam Winer, *Between the Lies*, London: Southern Universities Press, 180–1.

137   Jonathan Metcalfe, 'The Hype Dimension "Defenders Of Freedom"', personal blog, undated, available at www.cassiopaea.org.

138   Tom Regan, 'British Paper: Bush Wanted To Bomb Al Jazeera', *Christian Science Monitor*, 23 November 2005.

for their actual treatment of the spaces and inhabitants of the global South cities that they actually patrol, assault and occupy. They inhabit the stylized worlds of US military video games while passing their leisure time in the encampments of Baghdad. They even confront their post-war psychological traumas by re-immersing themselves within yet more electronic urban simulacra as the all-too-real streets of Iraq's cities recede into profoundly troubling memory.

A major concern here is that a lifetime of having been conditioned to wage war against virtual enemies in pixelated Arab cities will starkly influence soldiers' ethical behaviour once they are recruited and deployed. Soldiers brought up and trained on urban warfare computer games and simulations, with their 2-D people who repeatedly die sanitized, bloodless deaths, might thus behave in real war as they do in simulated games – with lethal results. 'When I hear a news report quoting a 22-year-old as saying it didn't really bother him too much that he had to "drop the chick" (kill a civilian woman),' Cheryl Seal writes, 'buzzers and bells are sounding big time. If this does not scream disconnect loud and clear, what could?'[139]

Citizens, meanwhile, become what Roger Stahl calls 'virtual citizen-soldiers,'[140] caught up in a boundless, networked culture of permanent war where everything transmogrifies into battlespace. Childhood experience of militarized play increasingly blends into adult acts of war as toys and weaponry fuse. The process of militarization deepens, marked by the 'recoding of the social field with military values and ideals.'[141]

What finally emerges, in line with the wider themes addressed in this book, is the 're-map[ping of] traditional lines between battlefield and home front.[142] The most disturbing part of this process is the way it forecloses the very possibility of democratic engagement. 'The conditions for this deliberation', writes Stahl, 'depend on a clear demarcation between the political role of the citizen and the apolitical role of the soldier. While the citizen's role is to deliberate, the soldier's role is to take orders'. If citizen-soldiers habituate to personal participation in a culture of permanent war against a virtualized, Orientalised Other, questions as to the necessity of this violence will recede further and further from the cultural landscape. In the end, cautions Stahl, 'the virtual citizen-soldier's integration into a sanitized fantasy of war is a seduction whose pleasures are felt at the expense of the capacity for critical engagement in matters of military might.'[143]

---

139   Cherly Seal, 'Was the Excessive Violence of US Troops in Iraq Fuelled by Military-Funded Computer Games?', Baltimore Indymedia.org, 2003.

140   Stahl, 'Have You Played the War on Terror?', 123.

141   Ibid.

142   Ibid., 130.

143   Ibid., 125.

CHAPTER SEVEN

Lessons in Urbicide[1]

In America, Palestine and Israel are regarded as local, not foreign policy, matters.[2]

Totalitarian regimes and terrorist groups commonly use violence as a means of large-scale political engineering; it is more remarkable when democratic countries such as Israel and America do so, usually in flagrant disregard of the lessons of contemporary history.[3]

In April 2002, in a dramatic shift in strategy, the Israel Defence Force – the IDF – bulldozed a forty-thousand-square-metre area in the centre of the Jenin refugee camp in the northern West Bank. A UN report estimated that fifty-two Palestinians were killed in the attack, half of whom were civilians. Operation Defensive Shield (in Hebrew, Homat Magen) involved major military operations against all major Palestinian cities. Some 140 multi-family housing blocks were completely destroyed; some fifteen hundred were damaged; some four thousand residents, in a population of fourteen thousand, were left homeless. Besides the destruction in Jenin, other major demolitions were carried out during the operation in Nablus, Hebron and Ramallah. Destruction of material infrastructure as well as cultural and administrative facilities was also widespread.

All this undermined official Israeli claims that Operation Defensive Shield was designed purely to dismantle the 'terrorist infrastructure' behind Palestinian suicide attacks, which had left scores of civilians dead on the streets of Israel's cities in the previous two years. The evidence suggests, rather, that the invasion's real purpose was to take advantage of the favourable context of America's War on Terror to attack the urban foundations of a proto-Palestinian state. Learning from setbacks in Lebanon in the 1980s, the Israelis seem to have targeted, as IDF analyst Dov Tamari put it, 'the social infrastructure, the welfare infrastructure, out of which combatants

---

1 This chapter's title draws from my article, 'Lessons in Urbicide', *New Left Review* 2: 19, 63–77. The content here, though, is a radical extension of that piece, which focused only on the aftermath of Israeli military operations in Jenin that formed part of Operations Defensive Shield in 2002.

2 Edward Said, 'Dreams and Delusions: The Imperial Bluster of Tom Delay', *CounterPunch,* 20 August 2003.

3 Pankaj Mishra, 'In Search of Monsters to Destroy', *Guardian,* 4 October 2008.

have grown and on which their families rely'. The appropriate term for this strategy was coined, more or less simultaneously in the early nineties, by both Marshall Berman and a group of Bosnian architects: 'urbicide', the deliberate wrecking or killing of a city.

Operation Defensive Shield was only the first in a long succession of initiatives, operations, training schemes and new weapons deployments through which the Israeli state has been redesigning its military so that their de facto function, rather than crushing the military forces of neighbouring Arab states, is to persistently control and placate civilians and non-state insurgents in densely packed Palestinian and Arab cities. This shift from state versus state to state versus urban civilian has been fuelled by suggestions, coming from strategic Israeli thinkers, that the spontaneous urbanization in Gaza and the Occupied Territories that has accompanied the recent rapid demographic growth of Palestinian populations risks jeopardizing long-standing aims of Zionism, by threatening to overwhelm Israel's efforts to promote in-migration of Jews into both Israel itself and the settlements.

In these debates, Palestinian cities, rather than being understood as the key spaces of civil society and of hopes for a better life for Palestinians, are cast as mere geopolitical 'weapons' undermining the fragile territorial power of the Zionist state. 'The process of urbanization around Israel's borders will result in a large Arab population, suffering from poverty and hunger, surrounding the Jewish state', writes Arnon Soffer, a leading right-wing Israeli geographer who has undertaken many analyses for the IDF. 'These areas are likely to become fertile ground for the evolvement of radical Islamic movements'.[4]

LEARNING FROM JENIN

Only a few weeks before the launch of Operation Defensive Shield, I attended a conference on 'urban warfare' organized by Soffer at Haifa University in Israel, in partnership with the influential RAND Corporation, a major think tank in the United States originally established to undertake military research.[5] Populated by senior US Marine Corps, IDF, and British Army commanders and specialists in urban warfare, along with representatives from RAND, the conference was part of an ongoing series which offered the opportunity to exchange practical tips on fighting wars and counterinsurgency operations in cities.

---

4 Arnon Soffer, *Israel, Demography 2000–2020: Dangers and Opportunities,* Haifa: University of Haifa, 2000, 2, 92.

5 See RAND.org, 'RAND Arroyo Urban Operations Team Hosts Conference in Israel' April 2002.

Catapulted into a dark corner of urban research that I – an urbanist with more than a decade of research experience – had no idea existed, I was struck at the time that US, Israeli and British experts in this emerging field of urban warfare were such close friends that they seemed to constitute a transnational social body. Through this it was clear that there had long been intense exchanges of technology, experience, training and doctrine among the three nations (and, indeed, beyond). What was striking then, and what has become ever more startling since, is that Israel's military and security technology, doctrine, and expertise have rapidly been mobilized and generalized as part of the US global War on Terror.

Operation Defensive Shield has revealed itself to be a particularly influential exemplar of a new kind of war, pitting high-tech state militaries against insurgents within densely built-up terrain.[6] Complementing the negative lessons presented by the US defeat in Mogadishu and by Russia's humiliation during its attempts to annihilate the Chechen capital of Grozny in the mid-1990s, the lessons of Israel's 'successes' have been widely interpreted as based on combining high-tech surveillance and targeting with Second World War urban-warfare techniques for erasing space and penetrating the core of resistant cities. 'In operations in Jenin in April 2002', writes Australian military theorist Michael Evans, 'the Israelis mixed information-age battlespace preparation by state of the art reconnaissance drones and UAVs with industrial-age techniques of mouseholing through walls to avoid enfiladed streets.' In addition, he continues, 'Caterpillar D9 armoured bulldozers complete with "mine plows" were employed to clear away fortified buildings, IEDs [Improvised Explosive Devices] and booby trap nests, thus allowing tank-infantry squads to manoeuvre through streets more easily'.[7]

By learning directly from these new urban wars, the US military has worked hard to improve its ability to pacify and control the cities deemed the main foci of its adversaries. Drawing on conferences like the one in Haifa, Evans notes that 'significant theoretical analyses were completed by RAND Corporation scholars focusing on the technical and tactical peculiarities involved in conducting military operations inside cities'.[8]

The US effort to exemplify, and imitate, Israeli experience during Defensive Shield was already underway as the bulldozers clawed through the the Jenin

---

6   Michael Evans, *City Without Joy: Urban Military Operations into the 21st Century*, Australian Defence College: Occasional Series No. 2, Canberra, 2007, available at www.strategicstudiesinstitute.army.mil.

7   Evans, *City Without Joy*.

8   Ibid.

camp. US military 'observers' were in fact already on-site, getting a first-hand perspective on Israeli doctrine in action. The input would prove useful during detailed planning for the invasion of Iraq's cities the following April. Eyal Weizman writes that 'an Israeli paratrooper who participated in the battle of Jenin told me that there were US officers (dressed in IDF uniform) present as spectators within the rubble of the refugee camp as the last stages of the "battle" unfolded'.[9]

On 17 June 2002, the *US Army Times* reported that 'while Israeli forces were engaged in what many termed a brutal – some even say criminal – campaign to crush Palestinian militants and terrorist cells in West Bank towns, US military officials were in Israel seeing what they could learn from that urban fight'. Lt Col Dave Booth – who oversaw US Marine–IDF exchanges on urban warfare at the time – reported in another article, this time in the *Marine Corps Times*, that the Marines wanted 'to learn from the Israeli experience in urban warfare and the recent massive search-and-destroy operations for Palestinian insurgents in the West Bank'.

The US Marine's Warfighting Lab in Quantico, Virginia, quickly took advantage of these detailed exchanges, which culminated in a Joint Chiefs of Staff delegation to Israel 17–23 May 2002, to 'make changes to the Corps' urban war-fighting doctrine to reflect what worked for the Israelis'. In early June, a major consultation took place between Israeli and Pentagon specialists on urban warfare at a Defense Policy Advisory Group meeting in Washington.

Just a few months later, in September 2002, the US Joint Chiefs of Staff laid out a new doctrine for urban operations, taking account of lessons learned from Jenin and elsewhere, with a view to an impending attack on Iraq. Seymour Hersh observed in a December 2003 issue of the *New Yorker* that 'according to American and Israeli military and intelligence officials, Israeli commandos and intelligence units have been working closely with their American counterparts at the Special Forces training base at Fort Bragg, North Carolina, and in Israel to help them prepare for operations in Iraq'.[10] By December 2003 Julian Borger, too, was reporting in the *Guardian* that 'according to two sources, Israeli military "consultants" have also visited Iraq'.[11]

General Vane, then deputy chief of staff for doctrine, concepts and strategy

9   Eyal Weizman, in Jordan Crandall, ed., *Under Fire.1: The Organization And Representation Of Violence*, Rotterdam: Witte de Witte, 2004, 83–4.
10   Seymour Hersh, 'Moving Targets: Will the Counter-Insurgency Plan in Iraq Repeat the Mistakes of Vietnam?', *New Yorker,* 15 December 2003.
11   Julian Borger, 'Israel Trains US Assassination Squads in Iraq', *Guardian*, 9 December 2003.

at the US Army Training and Doctrine Command, admitted in July 2003 that Israeli experience was pivotal as US forces tried to confront the proliferating urban insurgencies on the streets of Iraq's cities that followed the easy military defeat of Iraq's state military forces in 2002. '[Israeli] experience continues to teach us many lessons', he wrote. 'And we continue to evaluate and address those lessons, embedding and incorporating them appropriately into our concepts, doctrine and training'.[12]

Thus emerged a complex interdependence – based on imitation, partnership, trade, and bipartisan rhetoric – between Israel's policies of urban securitization and military urbanism and the global US War on Terror. Crucial here was the Bush administration's perception that the central geopolitical conflicts in the world now emanated from, and operated through, the Middle East – a 'new strategic environment [that was] characterized, first and foremost, by the asymmetrical threats stemming from rogue states and terrorist networks, driven by nihilistic ideologies bent on massive destruction at all costs'.[13]

Through such circuits of exemplification and imitation, the Israeli experience – issuing from the ultimate security state, organized through the permanent lockdown of entire colonized cities – is rapidly being exported around the world. As well as mimicking Israeli discourse about the need to suspend international law because of the unique challenges of a 'new war', the US military has also widely imitated the experience and doctrine of Israeli forces in revamping itself to address the challenges of urban colonial and counterinsurgency warfare.

All of these intimate circuits of exchange and mutual support are, of course, bolstered by a time-tested strategic context: US imperialism in the Middle East in turn providing huge financial and political support to the Israeli Zionist colonial project. This relationship also provides the US with a strategic asset within a region that provides the bulk of its foreign oil supplies – and will presumably provide much of it in the future (Figure 7.1).[14] As a consequence, 'the dynamic of American Empire/Israeli colonialism is circular', Bashir Abu Manneh argues. 'US support bolsters Israeli colonialism and occupation, which bolsters Israeli militarisation of state and society, generates new ideological and political justifications, and breeds new religious fanaticisms, leading to further Palestinian resistance and to more US interventions in the region'.[15]

---

12   Cited in Dexter Filkins, 'A Region Inflamed: Tough New Tactics by US Tighten Grip on Iraq Towns', *New York Times*, 7 December 2003.

13   Chuck Freilich, '"The Pentagon's Revenge" or Strategic Transformation: The Bush Administration's New Security Strategy', strategic assessment, Jaffee Center for Strategic Studies, Tel Aviv University, 9: 1, April 2006.

14   Bashor Abu-Manneh, 'Israel in US Empire', *New Formations* 59, 2006, 34–55.

15   Ibid., 48.

Year	Total	Military grant	Economic grant
1949-1996	68,030.9	29,014.9	23,122.4
1997	3,132.1	1,800.0	1,200.0
1998	3,080.0	1,800.0	1,200.0
1999	3,010.0	1,860.0	1,080.0
2000	4,131.8	3,121.0	949.1
2001	2,876.1	1,975.6	838.2
2002	2,850.6	2,040.0	720.0
2003	3,745.1	3,086.4	596.1
2004	2,687.3	2,147.3	477.2
2005 est.	2,612.2	2,202.2	357.0
2006 est.	2,563.5	2,280.0	240.0
Total	98,719.6	51,326.4	30,780.0

7.1   Total military and economic aid to Israel from the
US, 1949–2006 (in millions of dollars).

Given the context – even highly conservative estimates of US military and economic aid to Israel peg it at a total of $108 billion by 2006, and the funding is supplied under extremely favourable terms – it is difficult to disagree with Abu Manneh in concluding that 'Israel is a unique case in the Middle East; it is financed by imperialism without being economically exploited by it'.[16]

16 Ibid., 37.

MUTUAL MILITARISM: ISRAEL AND THE WAR ON TERROR

Following the attacks of 9/11, Ariel Sharon, then prime minister of Israel, quickly reiterated the Bush administration's worldview and sought to turn it directly to Israel's advantage. After the attacks, he announced a day of mourning and declared that 'the fight against terror is an international struggle of the free world against the forces of darkness who seek to destroy our liberty and way of life. Together we can defeat these forces of evil.'[17] In order to extract maximum political advantage from the attacks, Sharon suggested that, finally, Americans knew what it was like to experience urban terror. 'We face a common and implacable enemy, [the Israeli government] lectured us', wrote James Brooks in December 2002, 'leaving unspoken the message that we Americans had better develop some backbone and put our shoulder to the anti-terror wheel.'[18] Indeed, Sharon and other Israeli leaders hankered for a series of US-led wars to topple not only Saddam Hussein in Iraq but also regimes in Iran, Syria, and Libya.[19]

Israel then played a full, though largely covert, role in the specious propaganda campaign surrounding Iraq's non-existent 'weapons of mass destruction', the famous WMDs – a crucial premise for the invasion. One retired Israeli general later admitted that 'Israeli intelligence was a full partner to the picture presented by American and British intelligence regarding Iraq's non-conventional capabilities.'[20] It is also clear that the alleged threats posed by such weapons were not in fact threatening to the US or the UK at all. Philip Zelikow, a member of the George Bush's Foreign Intelligence Advisory Board between 2001 and 2003, revealed in 2004 that the then 'real threat' posed by Iraq was aimed not at the United States but rather 'against Israel.'[21]

The seamless rhetorical fusion of al-Qaeda, Saddam Hussein and the Palestinians that occurred during these geopolitical gymnastics meant repeated denials that Palestinian resistance and violence, targeted against a long-standing colonial aggressor, might be more legitimate than the targeting of US cities by an al-Qaeda fuelled by Islamist ideology. Just after the New York attacks, Edward Said argued that Israel was 'cynically exploiting the American

17   Joel Beinin, 'The Israelization of American Middle East Policy Discourse', *Social Text* 21: 2, 2003, 125.

18   James Brooks, 'Israelization of America', Antiwar.Com, 7 December 2002.

19   Patrick Buchanan, 'Whose War?' *The American Conservative,* 24 March 2003.

20   Shlomo Brom, 'An Intelligence Failure', strategic assessment, Jaffee Center for Strategic Studies, Tel Aviv University, 6: 3, November 2003, 9.

21   Emad Mekay, 'Iraq: War Launched to Protect Israel - Bush Adviser', ipsnews.net, 29 March 2004.

catastrophe by intensifying its military occupation and oppression of the Palestinians' and was, moreover, representing 'the connection between the World Trade Center and Pentagon bombings and Palestinian [suicide bomber] attacks on Israel [as] an absolute conjunction of "world terrorism" in which bin Laden and [then Palestinian leader Yasser] Arafat are interchangeable entities'.[22] Sharon, in particular, repeatedly equated Osama bin Laden and al-Qaeda with the Palestinian Authority, Hamas, and Lebanon's Hezbollah.

Bush quickly returned Sharon's favour by seeking to integrate Israel's intensifying colonial oppression into the War on Terror whilst portraying radical Islam as a common, civilizational enemy of both states.[23] US politicians 'quickly employed several rhetorical devices that, before 9/11, were most often found in Israel's political toolbox (domestic and foreign)', James Brooks suggests. 'Suddenly, all kinds of international and domestic issues were redefined as being part of the "war on terror", requiring new and drastic solutions that were, of course, necessary for "security", and often highly profitable for favored corporate interests'.[24]

It was in this context that Sharon launched Operation Defensive Shield, radically ratcheting up the broader strategies of repression against the fast-growing cities in the West Bank and Gaza. Besides targeting the civilizational enemy of US–Israel, this created a sort of Petri dish for developing the new military urbanism. 'From tactics and training to critical infrastructure protection', Ilan Berman wrote in 2004, 'for US politicians and military leaders: Israel has the ability to provide a major contribution to the evolving American strategic agenda by assisting the United States to adapt to new military realities'.[25]

This cycle of mutual militarism is not altogether surprising: the initial idea of the 'global war on terror' came from Israel. One of its key architects was the Israeli prime minister, Benjamin Netanyahu. Back in 1996, he – along with key neoconservative ideologue, radical Zionist, and key Bush advisor Richard Perle, among others – drafted an influential report titled *A Clean Break: A New Strategy for Securing the Realm*. The report argued that the 1993 Oslo accords, which were the legacy of ex–Prime Minister Yitzak Rabin, who was assassinated in 1995, should be comprehensively ditched. In their place, Israel and the US should forge an aggressive partnership.

---

22 Edward Said, 'Collective Passion', *Al-Ahram*, September 2003, 20–6, cited in Derek Gregory, 'Defiled cities', *Singapore Journal of Tropical Geography* 24: 3, 2003, 307–26.

23 Joel Beinin, 'The Israelization of American Middle East Policy Discourse', 125.

24 James Brooks, 'Israelization of America'.

25 Ilan Berman, 'New Horizons for the American–Israeli Partnership', *Journal of International Security Affairs*, Summer 2004, 78.

The envisaged scenario was to use aggressive military intervention to forcibly reorganize Middle Eastern geopolitics, removing the governments in Saudi Arabia, Syria, Lebanon, Iraq and Iran and substituting client régimes in the process – all under the 'principle of preemption'.[26] Such a strategy, the report argued, would bring about both a geographically expanded 'Greater Israel' and US control of the vast bulk of Middle Eastern oil reserves. Jonathan Cook argues that this 'willful pursuit of catastrophic goals', using US-Israeli pre-emptive wars to instigate 'social breakdown, a series of civil wars and the partition of Arab states', did much to shape the neocons' Washington agenda and Bush's later War on Terror.[27]

A pre-emptive war to remove Saddam Hussein from power in Iraq was in fact a central proposal of the report. 'Israel can shape its strategic environment, in cooperation with Turkey and Jordan by weakening, containing, and even rolling back Syria', the report contended. It further suggested that 'this effort can focus on removing Saddam Hussein from power in Iraq – an important Israeli strategic objective in its own right – as a means of foiling Syria's regional ambitions'.[28]

COUPLED ORIENTALISMS

> War might be said to begin when a country becomes a patriotic fiction for its population.[29]

Israeli and US targeting of their respective Arab Others has, above all, been fuelled by the most powerful urban warfare weapon of all: the imaginative rendering of geography and enmity in support of violence and militarization. Such imaginations of geography are acts of what anthropologists call 'symbolic violence'. Far from being a side-show to the 'real' work of war and security, they are, as we saw in Chapter 3, the means through which geographies of security and violence are continually performed and legitimized.[30]

The demonization of Palestinians as the barbaric, intrinsically terrorist Other

---

26 See Jonathan Cook, *Israel and the Clash of Civilisations*, London: Pluto, 2008, Chapter 3.

27 Ibid.

28 Study Group on a New Israeli Strategy Toward 2000, 'A Clean Break: A New Strategy for Securing the Realm', report prepared by the Institute for Advanced Strategic and Political Studies, 1996, available at www.israeleconomy.org.

29 Donald Pease, 'Between the Homeland and Abu Ghraib: Dwelling in Bush's Biopolitical Settlement', in Ashley Dawson and Malini Johar Schueller, eds, *Exceptional State: Contemporary US Culture and the New Imperialism,* Durham, NC: Duke University Press, 2007, 62, 65.

30 Luiza Bialasiewicz et al., 'Performing Security: The Imaginative Geographies of Current US Strategy', *Political Geography* 26, 405–22, 2007.

in Israeli political and cultural discourse resonates with similarly Manichaean demonizations of Arabs and Muslims in the US. Both tap into, and replicate, well-established Orientalist tropes constructing Arabs – and their places – as primitive, evil, uncivilized, irrational, lazy, pathological, exotic, devious and anti-modern (compared, of course, to Americans or Israelis and *their* places, which are deemed to be the precise opposite). The joint US-Israeli challenge, then, is to employ military and geopolitical strategies that can protect and police the frontier between modernity, freedom and the 'new barbarism'. Operating outside 'civilization', this devious barbarism relies on 'asymmetrical warfare' to target and terrorize at every opportunity.[31]

A central element of this viewpoint is a universal 'Arab mind' or 'Arab culture' – a simple, homogeneous entity obsessed with violence, honour, pride, shame, martyrdom or revenge. Raphael Patai's 1973 book *The Arab Mind* rests on such depictions. During George W. Bush's tenure, it was a bible for neoconservative commentators and politicians[32]; it has also been widely read within the US military and helped inspire the techniques of sexual torture and humiliation practiced at Abu Ghraib and elsewhere.[33]

A related idea prevalent within the mainstreams of 'terrorism studies' is that Arabs or Muslims who are sufficiently motivated to undertake terrorist acts against the US or Israel are pathological individuals who suffered traumatic childhoods – rather than the much more convincing argument that they are people radicalized by the long-term experience of US or Israeli colonial oppression, humiliation, and violence.

The wholesale dehumanization of Arabs within both US and Israeli culture adds to this explosive mix. At its most extreme, within the right-wing ultranationalist political culture that sustains both the Republicans and Likud, this dehumanization helps cast Arabs and Muslims *en masse* as what Giorgio Agamben calls 'bare life' – mere zoological existence, unprotected by philosophical or legal bastions of citizenship or humanity.[34] Where rights are accorded, it is usually within a frame of reference that positions people of Arab background as less than fully human – the widespread perception that Palestinians are what Omar Barghouti calls 'relative humans', that is, subjects unworthy of full political, legal, religious, economic or cultural rights.[35]

---

31 Dag Tuastad, 'Neo-Orientalism and the New Barbarism Thesis', 591–99.

32 Patai, *The Arab Mind*.

33 Mishra, 'In Search of Monsters to Destroy'.

34 Agamben, *Homo Sacer*.

35 Omar Barghouti, 'Relative Humanity – The Fundamental Obstacle to a One State Solution', *ZNet*, 16 December 2003.

Broad demonization is, of course, central to the recruitment and indoctrination of soldiery. Authors such as Patai, who essentialize an entire transnational 'race', are popular within the military cultures of both Israel and the United States. One US company commander, Captain Todd Brown, told the *New York Times* in December 2003 that his actions were motivated by the basically Pataian view that 'you have to understand the Arab mind. The only thing they understand is force – force, pride, and saving face'.[36]

To confront such ideas is part of the challenge faced by both US and Israeli soldiers who object to their countries' new urban wars. Assaf Oron, one of the Israeli reservists who refused orders to take part in Operation Defensive Shield in 2002, for example, talks of his anger at being repeatedly told by Israeli military and political élites and by the media that Israel-Palestine is characterized by 'a tribe of human beings, of pure good – the Israelis – and a tribe of sub-human beings, of pure evil'. By putting Palestinians 'under our rule', Oron argues, 'we've allowed ourselves to trample them like dirt, like dogs'. He feels that Israeli society has 'created an entirely hallucinatory reality, in which the true humans, members of the Nation of Masters, could move and settle freely and safely, while the sub-humans, the Nation of Slaves, were shoved into the corners, and kept invisible and controlled under our IDF boots'. It says a great deal that he believes it both necessary and radical to emphasize his belief that 'Palestinians are human beings like us. What a concept, eh? And before everything else, before *everything* else, we must treat them like human beings without demanding anything in return'.[37]

Of course, formal political discourses in both the US and Israel have long been bolstered and normalized by the standard depictions of Arabs in Western popular culture, especially films and video games, incessantly reiterating the suggestion that all Western or Israeli sovereign acts of power and force are by definition noble, legitimate and humane whilst all acts of the non-state Arab Other are by definition shadowy, demonic, barbaric, terroristic, and monstrous.[38] Hollywood films depicting US or Israeli encounters with Arab terrorists often stress an epic struggle between Western, modern, democratic 'civilization' and primitive Muslim 'barbarism'. Thus emerges what Carl Boggs and Tom Pollard

---

36 Dexter Filkins, 'A Region Inflamed: Tough New Tactics by US Tighten Grip on Iraq Towns', *New York Times*, 7 December 2003.

37 Assaf Oron, 'An Open Letter to Jewish Americans', Seruv.Org, March 2002.

38 Jasbir Puar and Amit Rai, 'Monster, Terrorist, Fag: The War'.

diagnose as a 'self-serving, hypocritical grand narrative that frames political violence as a monopoly of cultural/national Others whose modus operandi, mostly local attacks, contrasts with the "legitimate" military actions of powerful governments launching high-tech missile strikes and bombing raids'.[39]

Such a message, finally, penetrates into the very language of colonial war and repression: 'they "abduct" us', Alastair Crooke points out, whereas 'we "arrest" them'.[40] It also permeates visual presentations of war news: Arab cities are rendered as abstract, God's-eye maps with diagrammatic and satellite-imaged 'targets'. By contrast, a mass of personal, ground-level detail is shown when US or Israeli cities are targeted; the viewer experiences empathetic engagement with the victims, whose mangled and suffering bodies are the centre of attention.[41]

RECIPROCAL STATES OF EXCEPTION

> The security challenges of Israel are the security concerns of the United States writ small.[42]

A central component of the high-tech renaissance of Israel – what Naomi Klein has called the 'standing disaster Apartheid state'[43] – has been the gradual convergence between US military doctrine in post-invasion Iraq and the established Israeli techniques of repression, incarceration and the forcible fragmentation of geography in the Occupied Territories. In regard to the War on Terror, the Bush administration's early justifications of extra-judicial and pre-emptive assassination were clearly influenced by Israel's similar justifications. Central here was the assertion, as the international legal scholar Lisa Hajjar observes, that 'this war was "unprecedented" and thus constituted a legal *terra nulla*'. [44] She notes that such a claim has a direct Israeli precedent,

---

39 Carl Boggs and Tom Pollard, 'Hollywood and the Spectacle of Terrorism', *New Political Science* 9: 6, 2006.

40 Alastair Crooke, 'New Orientalism's "Barbarians" and "Outlaws", *The Daily Star* (Beirut), 5 September 2006.

41 Derek Gregory, 'Who's Responsible?', Zmag.org, 3 May 2004.

42 Thomas Henriksen , *The Israeli Approach to Irregular Warfare and Implications for the United States*, Joint Special Operations University Report 07-3, Hurlburt Field, FL: The Joint Special Operations University Press, 2007, available at jsoupublic.socom.mil.

43 Klein, *Shock Doctrine*.

44 Lisa Hajjar, 'International Humanitarian Law and "Wars On Terror": A Comparative Analysis Of Israeli and American Doctrines and Policies', *Journal of Palestine Studies* 36: 1, 2006, 32.

dating to Israel's use of that characterization at the start of the second Palestinian intifada.[45]

The strategic ideas of 'pre-emption' and 'preventive war' are key here. In launching its global War on Terror, the Bush administration directly used the second Intifada 'as a salient – and in some ways explicit – model for the United States' "new paradigm"' for the waging of war. This was based on the observation that both involve 'asymmetric' conflict, pitting high-tech and powerful state militaries against stateless and non-state individuals and groups which operate within dense concentrations of urban civilians.[46]

The Bush administration's obsession with pre-emption was especially influenced by Operation Defensive Shield. Azmi Bishara has suggested that the whole idea of the 'war against terror', especially the pre-emptive invasion of Iraq, represented what he terms 'globalized Israeli security doctrines', which include the understanding of terrorism as the 'main enemy'.[47] Dividing the world into the two hermetically separate groups of 'terrorists' and 'non-terrorists', the Bush White House followed a long-standing Israeli strategy: to allow coalitions of convenience, with all manner of dubious allies, to entrench their sovereign power against a generalized, demonized enemy whose geopolitical claims are radically delegitimized and whose subhuman status means that political negotiations will never be necessary.

Within the War on Terror, the construction of legal and geographical grey zones as a means of justifying the suspension of norms of international law also finds direct precedence in Israeli practice in the Occupied Territories. Here, as Darryl Li puts it, 'Israel has assiduously waged a campaign to deny the applicability of international law to the territories, especially insofar as the law interferes with processes of demographic engineering'.[48] Hajjar provides a particularly nuanced discussion of the similarities of US and Israeli practice here. 'Comparing the Israeli and American alternative legalities', she writes, 'one finds some clear commonalities' in the detailed legal justification for the state of exception and the irrelevance of international humanitarian law (IHL). Hajjar stresses that the Israeli state's description of the status of the West Bank and Gaza as *sui generis*, in order to assert that IHL does not actually apply, is legally indistinguishable from US claims that such law was inapplicable to the invasion of Afghanistan because it was a 'failed state'.[49] She also underlines that

---

45   Ibid.

46   Ibid., 22.

47   Azmi Bishara, 'On the Intifada, Sharon's Aims, '48 Palestinians and NDA/ Tajamu Stratagem', interview with Azmi Bishara, undated, available at *www.azmibishara.info*.

48   Darryl Li, 'The Gaza Strip as Laboratory: Notes in the Wake of Disengagement', *Journal of Palestine Studies* 35: 2, 2006, 48–9.

49   Hajjar, 'International Humanitarian Law and "Wars On Terror"', 32.

both the US and Israeli states have often argued that the statelessness of their enemies automatically means they have no rights whatsoever under IHL. In both cases, it is a legal trick that has been used to legitimize mass incarceration without trial. Moreover, both states have used national laws to authorize legal practices that contravene the norms and rules of IHL, a form of 'domesticating' international law for questionable purposes.[50]

ISRAEL AND THE 'PALESTINIANIZATION' OF IRAQ

In late 2003, as the US military's task in Iraq quickly morphed from the relatively simple challenge of destroying an infinitely inferior state military to the challenge of pacifying complex urban insurgencies, Israel's direct involvement in shaping the doctrine, weaponry and military thinking of US occupying forces grew dramatically – with corresponding pay-offs for the Israeli economy. As Hajjar writes, 'What had initially been termed a "conventional armed conflict" had become a "counter-insurgency conflict" that came to bear striking resemblances to Israeli operations in the second Intifada.'[51] Makram Khoury-Machool describes this process as the Palestinianization of Iraq.[52]

Thomas Henriksen, a Hoover Institution Fellow, in a detailed analysis of the lessons of Israeli practice for US special forces, is unequivocal about the direct imitation of Israeli policy in developing US strategy, doctrine and weaponry for the War on Terror. 'The Israeli Defense Forces' military actions', he writes, 'have been – and are – a crucible for methods, procedures, tactics, and techniques for the United States, which now faces a similarly fanatical foe across the world in the Global War on Terror'. Israeli experiences, he argues, 'offer an historical record and a laboratory for tactics and techniques in waging counter- insurgencies or counterterrorist operations in America's post-9/11 circumstances'.[53]

By August 2004, as complex insurgencies raged across Iraq's cities, Toufic Haddad was able to observe that 'US techniques in Iraq' were already 'unmistakably similar to Israeli techniques in the 1967 Occupied Territories'.[54]

---

50 Ibid., 37.

51 Ibid., 34–5.

52 Makram Khoury-Machool, 'Losing the Battle for Arab Hearts and Minds', Open Democracy.net, 2 May 2003. Importantly, such a process has been two-way: it has also involved the various Iraqi insurgencies and militias directly imitating the tactics of Hamas or Hezbollah as well as the US military directly imitating the IDF.

53 Henriksen, *The Israeli Approach to Irregular Warfare.*

54 Toufic Haddad, 'Iraq, Palestine, and US Imperialism', *International Socialist Review* 36, 2004, available at www.isreview.org.

This, he noted, was 'because of the active cooperation between Israeli military advisers and the Americans on the ground'. His diagnosis of similarities was indeed striking, and warrants repetition in full here:

> the use of aggressive techniques of urban warfare with an emphasis on special units, house-to-house searches, wide-scale arrest campaigns (almost 14,000 Iraqis are now in prison), and torture; the erecting of an elaborate system of watchtowers, military bases, check-points, barbed wire, and trenches to monitor, control, and restrict transportation and movement; the clearing of wide swaths of land next to roads; the use of armored bulldozers to destroy the houses of suspected militants; the razing of entire fields from which militants might seek refuge; the heightened relevance of snipers and unmanned drones; and the attempted erection of collaborator networks to extract information from the local population about resistance activities – both military and political.[55]

On the back of the widespread argument that the urban insurgencies in Iraq meant that US forces were effectively facing a scaled-up version of the second Intifada, the US Army War College undertook a major workshop titled 'Shifting Fire' in 2006. This was explicitly designed to examine Israeli experience in the Occupied Territories so as to draw US lessons on the challenges of managing propaganda and other 'information operations' within counterinsurgency warfare. The Israeli-Palestinian conflict was even used as a 'proxy' for the US invasion of Iraq, because it 'allowed for a freer debate of key issues, and avoided putting participants in the position of having to discuss specific US-led operations or the more political aspects of current US policy in Iraq and Afghanistan'.[56]

DIVIDE AND RULE

US imitation of Israeli practice relates closely to the status of the post-withdrawal Gaza Strip as a kind of laboratory for new techniques of urban control, pacification and counterinsurgency warfare – without occupation – by the Israeli military. Gaza has become a 'space where Israel tests and refines various techniques of management, continuously experimenting in search of an optimal balance between maximum control over the territory and minimum

---

55   Ibid.
56   Deirdre Collings and Rafal Rohozinski, 'Shifting Fire: Information Effects in Counterinsurgency and Stability Operations', workshop report, USAWC 10, Carlisle, PA: US Army War College, 2006, available at www.carlisle.army.mil.

responsibility for its non-Jewish population', writes Darryl Li.[57] Gaza is especially interesting to US forces because Israel's strategy there is based on the idea of 'control at a distance' through militarized boundaries, continuous raids, assassination strikes and aerial surveillance, rather than control through the continuous presence of occupying armies. 'Closure in the Gaza Strip', writes Li, 'is enforced with less military manpower and less "friction" (i.e. direct contact) with the civilian population, entailing less exposure to attack and less potential for negative publicity'.[58] Following the building of the separation barrier in the West Bank, there is evidence that Israel is trying to instigate a Gaza-style régime of control there, with each Palestinian enclave turned into a 'mini Gaza' under a much more hermetic approach to 'closure'.

There is little doubt that US attempts in early 2007 to forcibly reconstruct the urban geographies of Baghdad and other troublesome Iraqi cities, so as to reduce opportunities for insurgents to move around and launch their attacks, were directly modelled on Israeli experience in the Occupied Territories (Figure 7.2). Certain towns were completely sealed off with razor wire or walls. Biometric identity cards were enforced for all adults. Eventually, massive urban wall complexes, with associated 'security buffer zones', were enforced across thirty of Baghdad's eighty-nine official districts as a prelude to ethnic cleansing in each district.[59]

The Hoover Institution's Thomas Henriksen admits that Israeli experience with check-points was directly imitated by US forces in Iraq.[60] These, he remarked, 'have proven effective as well as road patrols in limiting terrorism. Thus a near-saturation of territory seems effective'. He also admits, however, that there were problems in 'upscaling' Israeli doctrine, developed over small and tightly packed cities within Gaza, to the much larger and more complex urban geographies in Iraq.[61]

In Iraq's newly cordoned-off towns and urban districts, civilians quickly found themselves inhabiting what Robert Fisk called 'a "controlled population" prison'. As in the Occupied Territories, these notions of security, he wrote, 'require putting [the presumably threatening population] behind a wall'. This, in turn, demands its own geography of cleared 'security buffer zones' through

---

57   Darryl Li, 'The Gaza Strip as Laboratory: Notes in the Wake of Disengagement', *Journal of Palestine Studies*, 35: 2, 2006, 38.

58   Ibid., 43.

59   Robert Fisk, 'Divide and Rule – America's Plan for Baghdad', *Independent*, 11 April 2007.

60   Henriksen, *The Israeli Approach to Irregular Warfare*.

61   Ibid.

7.2 Captive societies: the West Bank (top) and Baghdad (bottom).

which artificial separations can be imposed on complex urban geographies. The best way to secure a barrier, notes Li, 'is through a vacant "buffer zone," whose emptiness allows a handful of soldiers to monitor relatively large areas and to respond quickly, decisively, and overwhelmingly to any perceived infiltrators, all while ensconced in fortified positions'. Once 'security' or 'buffer zones' are 'cleared', Li writes, 'they become effective "free-fire" areas'. In the Occupied Territories, 'Palestinians enter [these areas] at their own risk and dozens if not hundreds have died doing so'.[62]

Such partitioning of Iraqi cities and urban districts by US forces inevitably echo the erection of massive concrete barriers in the West Bank and the increasingly militarized borders and 'shoot to kill' zones in and around Gaza. Check-points, buffer zones, enforced identity cards, collective punishments, mass incarcerations without trial, imprisonment of suspects' relatives, and associated bulldozings of landscapes and buildings deemed to be sheltering enemies – all smack of direct imitation of Israeli policy (whilst also echoing earlier counterinsurgency wars in Algeria, Vietnam, and elsewhere).

Such similarities have not been lost on Iraq's urban residents as they encounter these familiar but shocking new 'security' geographies. 'I see no difference between us and the Palestinians', a man named Tariq screamed at Dexter Filkins, a *New York Times* reporter, in December 2003. 'We didn't expect anything like this after Saddam fell'.[63] Reidar Visser was especially critical of the way that the archipelago of fenced-off enclaves established in 2007 reaffirmed sectarian violence and identity rather than working against them. 'When will Westerners realize', he asked, 'that most Iraqis – with the exception of many Kurds and a few noisy parliamentarians from other communities – view sectarianism as a perversion and not as a legitimate basis for organising the country politically and administratively?'[64]

Rather bizarrely, US justification of the post-2007 counterinsurgency policies of walling and cordoning-off entire urban districts and towns reflects a long-standing geographical trope, a Foucauldian boomerang: colonizers' use of terminology drawn from the geographies of their home cities to justify military planning in the cities they colonize. In a September 2006 article in *Army Magazine*, for example, Dennis Steele wrote about the encirclement of the Iraqi town of Taramiyah by a razor wire fence. Discussing the requirement of

---

62 Li, 'The Gaza Strip as Laboratory', 45.
63 Filkins, 'A Region Inflamed'.
64 Reidar Visser, 'Baghdad Zoo: Why "Gated Communities" Will Face Opposition in the Iraqi Capital', Historiae.org, 23 April 2007.

residents to use biometric cards to pass through the town's only check-point, he fails to mention similarities with the West Bank or Gaza. Rather, he suggested, the town had now become a 'gated community' which, like countless affluent suburbs on the edge of US cities, was now benefiting from a highly desirable characteristic: security. 'It is', he wrote, 'the Iraq version of a gated community – no luxury estates, no backyard pools, no country club – but the purposes are the same: keep out the bad elements and give the community a sense of security'.[65]

'NON-LETHAL' LETHALITIES

Given that the new military urbanism tends to pit high-tech militaries against large and dense bodies of civilians, US–Israeli co-operation also extends to the burgeoning field of so-called non-lethal weapons. Ostensibly, these systems – which are rapidly being adopted by militaries, police forces, and hybrid military-police forces alike – are designed to facilitate control of mass urban populations, and to disrupt protests, without inducing civilian deaths. The purported 'function of such weaponry is to deter, confine, remove from activity, paralyze, confuse, stop, neutralize, distract, disperse, isolate, remove from focus or deprive entry of people or vehicles [in a given area]', as Ro'i Ben-Horin puts it.[66]

US and Israeli forces are already collaborating intensively in the development of a wide range of such 'non-lethal weapons'. In a reversal of the US adoption of Israeli urban warfare technologies, Israeli forces are increasingly keen on benefiting from major US research programmes being led by the Pentagon's Joint Non-Lethal Weapons Directorate (JNLWD). Israeli forces are deemed to require what the Jaffe Center for Strategic Studies call 'a "basket" of non-lethal means'. Presumably not of the wicker variety, this basket includes irritants, malodorous substances, noise, infra-red and ultrasound, vomiting agents, strobe lights, 'stun' bombs and 'non-penetrating projectiles' (Figure 7.3).[67]

65   Dennis Steele, 'The Gated Community: Giving an Iraqi Town a Second Chance', *Army Magazine*, September 2007, 26–9.

66   Ro'i Ben-Horin, 'Non-Lethal Weapons: Theory, Practice, and What Lies Between', *Strategic Assesment* 3: 4, 2001.

67   Ibid.

Possible applications of NLW technologies

Counter Personnel

Crowd Control
Incapacitation of Personnel
Area Denial to Personnel (AD-P)
Clearing Facilities of Personnel (CFAC)

Means

Infra / ultra sound	Sonic generator that projects an acoustic pressure wave to cause discomfort to personne
Noise	Acoustic generator that produces sufficient sound to disorientate or incapacitate personnel
Malodorous sustances	Family of inorganic substances with pungent odours that cause discomfort to personnel
Irritants	Substances that cause eye and respiratory irritation / discomfort
Vomiting agents	Chemicals that cause nausea / vomiting
Optical munitions	System that radiates a microwave burst, disabling electronics
Strobe lights	Family of materials that can be deposited on optical sensors of viewing ports to obscure vision
Aqueous foams	Explosive / electric flash device to stun, dazzle or temporarily blind optical sensors
Water cannon	Family of agents that disables or destroys engines
Deception	Family of agents that cause fuel to solidify
Non-penetrating projectiles	Family of projectiles that stuns personnel without penetrating
Super-adhesives, binding coatings	Family of adhesives that prevent movement of personnel
Anti-traction	Family of substances that cause lack of traction for personnel
Entanglers, containment devices	Family of nets, meshes and the like to ensnare
Enclosure fillers	Substances or devices that rapidly fill an enclosed space, leaving occupants alive but incapable of movement (e.g. airbags)
Stun weapons	Family of weapons that subdue or immobillise personnel
Combustible dispersals	Family of substances that ignite when subject to pressure from personnel passing over
Obscurants	Family of smoke-like agents to obscure observation and disorientate
Markers	Family of substances that can be used to covertly mark personnel for later identification. Marking may be overt if desired
Voice synthesis morphing	Family of methods to destroy the tye / wheels of vehicles
3-D holograms	Family of smoke-like agents to obscure visual or electronic observation

7.3   Possible Applications of NLW Technologies: the Perspective
of Israel's Jaffe Center for Strategic Studies, 2001.

In addition to their co-operation in the development of such 'non-lethals', both the US and Israel now routinely deploy very similar weapons within their urban or 'low-intensity' warfare operations. Both, for example, now use so-called sonic weapons, which broadcast beams of sounds that are so loud as to make continued presence in a targeted area unbearably dizzying and nauseating. Such weapons 'can cause irreversible damage to the hearing apparatus'.[68] The Israeli system – fittingly called 'The Scream' – has been widely used against people who protest the construction of the separation wall in the West Bank.[69] The US equivalent – the long range acoustic device – has been deployed widely in Iraq as well as in California and post-Katrina New Orleans. Hammering home how these new weapons are being used across the full spectrum of 'urban operations' at home and abroad, it was reported in June 2008 that British police were using a similar device in the small Cornish village of Polzeath to inhibit groups of vacationing teenagers from congregating. This system – the 'Mosquito' – deliberately uses a frequency that can be heard only by young people.[70]

BULLDOZER WARS

US forces have also gone far beyond the imitation of Israeli doctrine in redesigning their forces so that urban combat against insurgents becomes the de facto mode of operation. As we saw in Chapter 6, Israeli and US forces are collaborating on many joint urban-warfare training programmes. These have culminated in the construction by US Army engineers of an entire mock Palestinian city – Baladia – in the Negev, through which both militaries can hone their skills.

In addition, a continually widening range of Israeli equipment – designed to support the Israeli doctrine of deep raids into Palestinian cities, combined with aerial dominance through armed drones and surveillance systems – can be found on the shopping lists of US and other Western militaries. Barbara Opall-Rome, a *Defense News* correspondent, reported from a conference in Tel Aviv in March 2004 that such purchases, though usually hidden under a cloud of secrecy, were wide and extensive. 'From tennis ball-sized sensors that can be thrown or shot from snipers' rifles into terrorist lairs to wall-breaching devices

---

68   Neil Davison and Nick Lewer, 'Bradford Non-Lethal Weapons Research Project (BNLWRP)', research report no. 8, Centre for Conflict Resolution, Department of Peace Studies, 2006, 33.

69   Xeni Jardin, 'Focused Sound 'Laser' for Crowd Control', *Day to Day*, National Public Radio, 21 September 2005, available at *www.npr.org*.

70   Steven Morris, 'Police Clamp Down on Beach "Snob Yobs"', *Guardian*, 26 June 2008.

for urban combat, gear invented for Israel's anti-terror wars in Gaza and the West Bank are increasingly being put in the hands of US warfighters'.[71] At the event, Major A. P. Graves-Buckingham of the US Marine Corps Warfighting Laboratory's Technology Division in Quantico stated that 'the Israelis are way ahead of the others in some very interesting, niche fields'.[72] Such purchases are also leading to joint R&D by US and Israeli companies. Rafael and General Dynamics, for example, are jointly developing a range of hand-held missiles designed specifically to destroy urban buildings, as well as new protection systems for vehicles fighting in cities.[73]

The most dramatic and widely noticed US purchase of urban-warfare equipment, however, was for twelve of the very same D9 Caterpillar bulldozers that have wrought such havoc at the heart of Jenin and other Palestinian cities since the mid-1990s (and which famously killed peace protestor Rachel Corrie in Gaza in March 2003). The decision to buy D9s from Israel – or perhaps, more properly, to buy them back, as the basic machine is made in the US by Caterpillar – reportedly came after a series of training exercises by US forces at the IDF Adam base near Modi'in.[74]

US forces have so far eschewed Jenin-style mass demolitions by D9s in Iraq, conscious of the possible PR impact of uncomfortable parallels with Israeli practice. Instead, as in Fallujah in 2004, they basically cordoned off the symbolic centre of resistance and leveled the whole city through mass artillery bombardment and bombing. Some US military commentators, however, regret the failure to exploit the power of D9s during major urban battles. 'Even though bulldozers worked well in close urban combat', comments Thomas Henriksen, writing for a US Joint Special Operations publication in 2007, 'US forces in Iraq did not resort to using them in the attack on Fallujah (November 2004) or other urban assaults. In the course of the Falluja assault, US forces instead relied on artillery and heavy air strikes on militant positions thereby leveling whole neighborhoods. This bombing-induced tabula-rasa strategy later resulted in recriminations and reevaluation'.[75]

71 Barbara Opall-Rome, 'Israeli arms, gear aid US Troops', Defense News.com, 29 March 2004.

72 Such US purchases have included 'Simon' door breeching grenades, helicopter rocket launchers, an automatic system to locate and target snipers in cities, Hunter and Pioneer unmanned surveillance drones, new radio systems designed to overcome urban interference, and a set of 'kits' designed to protect armoured vehicles when operating in urban environments. See Opall-Rome, 'Israeli Arms, Gear Aid US Troops'.

73 Defense Update.com, 'Trophy Active Protection System', undated.

74 Margot Dudkevitch, 'IDF Teaches US Soldiers Guerrilla Response', Jerusalem Post, 18 August 2004.

75 Henriksen, The Israeli Approach to Irregular Warfare.

Instead, D9s have been used mainly to clear security 'buffer zones', obstacles and roadside bombs – a task essential for enabling US patrols to penetrate huge, dense suburbs like Baghdad's Sadr City (Figure 7.4). Occasionally, however, tactics reminiscent of Gaza or the West Bank have become evident.[76]

7.4   Israeli-modified D9 bulldozer, at work for the V
Corps Combat Engineers in Baghdad.

DRONESPACE

> The effectiveness [of Israel's aerial assassination policy] is amazing. The State of Israel has brought preventive assassination to the level of a real art. When a Palestinian child draws a sky nowadays, he will not draw it without a helicopter.[77]

The development by the CIA and US special-operations forces of targeted assassination programmes in the War on Terror has also been a direct imitation of the Israeli policy of 'pre-emption' by extrajudicial state killing, usually by

---

76   Ed Blanche, 'West Bank East: Americans in Iraq Make War the Israeli Way', *Lebanon Wire.com*, 6 December 2003.
77   Avi Dichter, Israel Security Agency, quoted in Jon Elmer, 'Maple Flag, the Israeli Air Force, and "the new type of battle we are being asked to fight" *Briarpatch Magazine*, 3 December 2005.

helicopters or unmanned, remotely piloted drones armed with missiles.[78] 'In the post-9/11 security environment', writes Graham Turbiville in the aforementioned 2007 report, 'the targeting of terrorist and insurgent leaders and cadres by U.S. military and intelligence resources has advanced in many ways – some publicly reported and visible – and has been accompanied by notable successes'.[79] Among US special-ops theorists, Israeli practice is lauded as worthy of imitation, especially as US assassination raids are rolled out across the territory of supposed allies like Pakistan, as well as over enemy territory. 'Certainly, Israeli [assassination] action against Palestinian, Hezbollah, and other terrorist leaders and support infrastructure since independence', Turbiville writes, 'constitutes the gold standard for the systematic conceptual and operational consideration it has received from the Israeli Government and military and security bodies'[80]

Whilst assassinations had been explicitly prohibited by a US executive orders since 1977, the US began employing this tactic again in November 2002.[81] Israeli-style arguments were invoked to justify the assassination of the first target, Ali Qaed Sinan al-Harithi, in Yemen by a Predator drone, an attack which killed five other people as well. Even though the attack occurred within a country not at war with the US (i.e., Yemen), officials argued that extrajudicial assassination was legitimate because Harithi was allegedly a member of al-Qaeda and it was impossible to arrest him.[82]

By December 2003, US assassinations via drone had been combined with aggressive actions by special-operations forces inside Syria, which were attempts to kill jihadists ostensibly on their way to fight in Iraq. IDF urban-warfare specialists helped train these forces at Fort Bragg in North Carolina.[83] As well as a robust response from anti-war campaigners and humanitarian-law specialists, some US intelligence officials decried both the policy and the direct imitation of Israel. 'This is basically an assassination programme', a former senior US intelligence official argued to Julian Borger of the *Guardian*. 'That is what is being conceptualized here.

---

78 For a brilliant analysis of the Israeli shift towards aerial assassination, see Weizman's *Hollow Land*, 237–58.

79 Graham Turbiville, *Hunting Leadership Targets in Counterinsurgency and Counterterrorist Operations, Selected Perspectives*, Joint Special Operations University Report 07-6, Hurlburt Field, FL: The Joint Special Operations University Press, 2007, available at jsoupublic.socom.mil, 8.

80 Ibid., 11.

81 Hajjar, 'International Humanitarian Law and "Wars On Terror"'.

82 Ibid.

83 Julian Borger, 'Israel Trains US Assassination Squads in Iraq', *Guardian*, 9 December 2003.

It is bonkers, insane. Here we are – we're already being compared to [then Israeli president] Sharon in the Arab world, and we've just confirmed it by bringing in the Israelis and setting up assassination teams'.[84] Nevertheless, by 2008 US forces were regularly launching similar assassination raids into Pakistani and Syrian territory.

Again, Israeli practice in Gaza has been a key exemplar. Following Israel's withdrawal from Gaza in 2005, drone-based assassinations became a primary mechanism for the new model of 'external control' without the occupation of permanent armies, a model that has significantly influenced US policy. Such tactics have been 'positively correlated with territorial isolation and segregation'.[85]

However, aerial assassinations have been but one element of a much broader strategy of what Israeli planners term 'urban area domination' – another influential doctrine.[86] Indeed, although rarely publicized, US and Israeli efforts to perfect the armed unmanned drone are now very closely integrated. Israeli Aircraft Industries (IAI), for example, is now making Pioneer drones for the US Army and Navy, and assists US companies such as TRW Avionics and Surveillance Group in the manufacture of other drones for the US military.[87]

By 2007, new Israeli missiles designed specifically for drone raids had already were being bought to equip France's new generation of armed drones.[88] The US, British and Singaporean militaries had ordered Hermes armed drones, made by the Israeli arms corporation Elbit. Most controversially, Elbit had been awarded a major contract by the US Department of Homeland Security to patrol the US–Mexico border and to target immigrants passing through this increasingly militarized zone.[89] By 20 July 2004, the US border patrol was claiming that there had been '42 apprehensions [of immigrants] directly attributable to UAV surveillance'.[90] It was already being envisaged by 2004 that such patrols would also be extended to the US Canadian border.

84   Ibid.

85   Li, 'The Gaza Strip as Laboratory', 34.

86   Ralph Sanders, 'Israel Practice New Concepts for Airborne, Urban Area Domination; an Israeli Military Innovation', Defense Update.com, undated.

87   Ibid.

88   Pierre Tran and Barbara Opall-Rome, 'French UAV to Carry Israeli Missiles', Rafael Corporation, undated, available at www.rafael.co.il.

89   Israeli Weapons.Com, 'Hermes 450 in US Service,' 2004.

90   Ibid.

RAIDS AT A DISTANCE FOR THE 'LONG WAR'

The shift from occupation – a horizontal activity – to vertical surveillance and assassinations within both Israeli and US practice brings with it a new geometry of occupation and othering. 'The geography of occupation has thus completed a 90-degree turn', writes Eyal Weizman. 'The imaginary "orient" – the exotic object of colonization – was no longer beyond the horizon, but now under the vertical tyranny of Western airborne civilization that remotely managed its most sophisticated and advanced technological platforms, sensors and munitions above'.[91]

Influenced by Israeli practice, such vertical and special-ops forces raids are an important emerging element of both US strategy and tactics. They are seen to be perfectly suited to the US military as it seeks to develop doctrine for what the Pentagon has, since 2005, called 'the Long War' – the more or less permanent, global use of pre-emptive raids and armed drones against purported adversaries, such as those launched into Pakistan and Syria in late 2008. Arguments for a shift towards 'control at a distance' through raids, targeted killings and persistent surveillance by unmanned drones and satellites have been significantly bolstered by the disastrous failure of the full military invasion of Iraq.

According to Henriksen of the Hoover Institution, writing in 2007, 'denied areas' and 'ungovernable spaces' – where 'American counterinsurgency strategies' cannot be utilized – now 'lend themselves to the Israeli way of war'.[92] He predicts that 'the United States might find that it . . . must dispatch commando raids, capture terrorists for intelligence, assassinate diabolical masterminds, and target insurgent strongholds with airpower, missiles, or Special Operations Forces from bases around the globe rather than undertaking enormous pacification programs and nation-building endeavors in inhospitable lands'.[93]

Here Henriksen suggest that both Israel and the US would do well to turn to continuous warfare through long-distance 'preventive' aerial raids and assassination programmes, rather than full-scale invasions. The US, he argues, must thus strive increasingly to model its strategy on that of Israel. Both 'Israeli and American societies are better at sustaining low-profile counterattacks that

---

91 Eyal Weizman, 'Thanotactics', in Michael Sorkin, ed., *Indefensible Space: The Architecture of the National Security State*, New York: Routledge, 2007, 325.

92 Thomas Henriksen, 'Security Lessons from the Israeli Trenches', *Policy Review* 141, 2007.

93 Ibid.

are launched in the name of prevention, deterrence, and retribution', he writes, 'than full-blown offensive wars such as Israel's 1982 Lebanon intervention or America's Iraq and Afghanistan invasions'.[94]

SELLING THE SECURITY STATE

It is no coincidence that the emergence of Israel as the global laboratory of urban militarism and securitization has been closely associated with a dramatic resurgence in its national economy. Between 2000 and 2003, the Israeli economy experienced a major recession. This was due both to the impacts of the global collapse of Internet stocks and to the al-Aqsa, or second, Intifada, which started in September 2000 and was marked by devastating suicide attacks against Israeli cities and other civilian spaces. Imri Tov, writing in 2003 in *Strategic Assessment*, the journal of the pro-Israel Jaffa Centre for Strategic Studies, characterizes the early 2000s as 'one of the worst economic periods in the country's history' and asserts that as of 2003 'the conflict has reached its current peak, at which the two sides are trying to exhaust each other'. Tov believed that the Intifada played a major role in producing the 2003 recession, not least because it had directly caused fifty to sixty billion shekels' ($10–13 billion) worth of material damage by that date.[95]

Since that recession, however, Israel's increasingly high-tech economy has been marshalled towards the challenges of selling state-of-the-art security systems and urban-warfare machinery to a rapidly growing global market, using its 'combat-proven' status to advantage. This approach has been so successful that, according to *Jane's Defence Weekly*, Israel made more than $3.5 billion in arms sales in 2003 alone and was exporting arms and security equipment on a par with Russia.[96] In 2004, *Business Week* magazine labelled Israel one of the world's 'rising innovation hotspots' because of its strengths in high-tech communications, chips, software and sensors – all of which derive heavily from military research and development. Between the 2002 downturn and 2005, foreign industrial investment in Israel rose from $1.8 billion to $6.1 billion.[97]

If after-sales services are included, Israel is now the world's fourth biggest

94   Thomas H. Henriksen , *The Israeli Approach to Irregular Warfare*, 40.

95   Imri Tov, 'Economy in a Prolonged Conflict: Israel 2000–2003', *Strategic Assessment* 6: 1, 2003, available at www.tau.ac.il.

96   *USA Today*, 'US Military Employs Israeli Technology in Iraq War', 24 March 2003.

97   Bernel Goldberg, 'Introduction to WTCTA Breakfast Series: Israeli Investment and Trade Opportunities with the Pacific Northwest', 4 May 2007, Tacoma, WA.

arms and security equipment exporter (if not, it is the fifth). Israel now sells $1.2 billion worth of defence and security products to the US every year.[98] The rapid integration of US and Israeli security-technology sectors has been powerfully assisted by considerable cross-investment and cross-ownership between high-tech industries in the two nations. Israel, for example, now lists more companies on the Nasdaq stock exchange than do any of the advanced countries of Europe. By January 2008, more than seventy-five Israeli companies, worth a total of $60 billion, were so listed.[99]

Since the 9/11 attacks, and the concomitant deepening integration of Israeli strategy into urban-warfare aspects of the War on Terror, Israeli capital, with considerable support from the US and Israeli governments, has taken its skills, expertise and products beyond the more obvious markets surrounding urban warfare, and expertly projected them towards the much broader and ever-extensible arena of global securitization, securocratic war, 'homeland security' and counterterrorism. It is a distinctly advantageous strategy. Such are the infinite variety of ways in which the everyday spaces and infrastructures of cities can be deemed insecure in the contemporary world that virtually any high-tech company – biotechnology, computing, telecommunications, electronics, new materials – can easily project itself as a 'security' company.

Speaking in May 2007 at a business breakfast in Tacoma, Washington, designed to forge US–Israeli links in high-tech security industries, Bernel Goldberg, the executive director of the Washington Israel Business Council, was unequivocal on this point. 'As a top national priority, Homeland Security in Israel is more than just an exportable commodity', he said. 'Israel's self-reliance has created a diversified and cutting edge security industry, adding innovation to existing technologies as well as developing new ones'. He further claimed that 'Israel today has earned its worldwide reputation for providing leading security solutions and continues to successfully partner with key world players to protect airports, seaports, government offices, financial institutions, recreational centers, international events and more'.[100]

Israeli firms have been able to use this context and reputation to rebrand themselves better and faster than other nations' firms in the post-9/11 context. Their systems, standards and practices are fast emerging as global exemplars, to be imitated, copied, or bought up outright. As a result, 'Israel's long history of government spending on the war on terror has produced

98   Naomi Klein, 'Laboratory for a Fortressed World', *The Nation*, 14 June 2007.

99   Donald Snyder, 'Israel's Technology Creates an Investment Goliath', Fox Business. com, 16 January 2008.

100   Goldberg, 'Israeli Investment and Trade Opportunities with the Pacific Northwest'.

standards, methodologies and concepts that are only now emerging around the world.'[101]

These trends have dramatically improved the profitability of Israeli technology and defence industries.[102] By February 2008, the Israel High-Tech Investment Report was able to report that 'in the aftermath of the war in Lebanon in 2006, Israel has experienced one of its best economic years. Venture capital investments flowed in and could reach $1.7 billion. Foreign investments were strong. The Tel-Aviv Stock Exchange gained nearly 30 per cent. 2007 marked the year that Israel became the world's fourth largest defence supplier.'[103]

A GLOBAL EXEMPLAR

Indeed, the very Israeli identity and branding of the new techniques and technologies of urban militarization have been a major selling point. 'Many of the country's most successful entrepreneurs', observes Naomi Klein, '[are now] using Israel's status as a fortressed state, surrounded by furious enemies, as a kind of twenty-four-hour-a-day showroom – a living example of how to enjoy relative safety amid constant war'.[104]

To visitors, this 'showroom' is the essence of hypermilitarized urbanism – a vision of urban life in which every movement, every action, requires scrutiny and the negotiation of architectural or electronic passage-points to prove one's right to passage. In effect, the whole of Israeli urban society has taken the sorts of security architectures and intense profiling practices more normally reserved to airports and generalized them to an entire system of cities and everyday infrastructures. A US report from the US Air Force's Future Warfare Series, assessing the lessons that the US might learn from Israel, points out that, in Israel, 'nearly every upscale restaurant has private security at the door, including metal detectors and bomb sniffing sensors. All public buildings, including shopping malls and bus and train stations, have armed guards and metal detectors at their gates'.[105]

101   Fairfax County Ecibiomic Development Authority, 'Special Event: United States-Israel HLS Technologies Conference and B2B (Business to Business) Meetings between Israeli and US Companies', 16–18 January 2007, available at www.fairfaxcountyeda.org.

102   Naomi Klein, 'Laboratory for a Fortressed World'.

103   Israel High-Tech Investment Report, February 2008, available at www.ishitech. co.il.

104   Klein, 'Laboratory for a Fortressed World'.

105   Jeffrey Larsen and Tasha Pravecek, 'Comparative US–Israeli Homeland Security', *The Counterproliferation Papers, Future Warfare Series no. 34*, Air University, Maxwell Air Force Base, AL: United States Air Force Counterproliferation Center.

An Israeli government promotional brochure on the homeland security (HLS) industry argues that this experience places Israel 'at the forefront of the global security and HLS industries'. It argues that these industries 'were developed to serve a nation forced to fight for its existence and remain vigilant against continued threats', and so 'Israeli-made security systems and solutions have been tested time and time again'. The result, continues the spiel, is that 'from their unique perspective, the country's HLS and security manufacturers have gained unparallelled expertise and a worldwide reputation for developing leading-edge security solutions'.[106]

Thus, Israel has been able to marshal its techniques of hypermilitarization to match and exploit global trends towards the militarization of everyday spaces, infrastructures, and sites. The key markets here are not merely the more formal technologies of control and killing: militarized borders, unmanned drones, weapons designed for use in dense urban areas, missiles for pre-emptive assassination. Rather, they include the whole gamut of urban surveillance and securocratic war – passenger-profiling software, biometrics, 'intelligent' street cameras, check-point systems – 'precisely the tools and technologies Israel has used to lock in the occupied territories'.[107]

Israeli companies such as Rafael stress that everyday urban systems are now sites of 'low intensity conflict' (LIC) which require radical securitization (using their expertise and technology, of course). 'In wartime conditions', goes the spiel in their 'anti-terror homeland security solutions' marketing brochure, 'Rafael systems provide defense against intruding military forces, intelligence and terrorist units. In times of peace, these systems prevent the border crossing of illegal immigrants, smugglers, drug traffickers and terrorists.' During LIC, Rafael argues, its 'technologies serve as shields against intruding intelligence or terrorist units. They also provide smart screening of pedestrians, vehicles and cargo at border check points'.[108]

In 2006, for the first time, Israeli firms exported more than $1 billion worth of equipment and services specifically tailored for homeland security needs – 20 per cent up on the 2005 figure. David Arziof, director of the Israeli Exports Institute (IEE), an Israeli government body – estimated that exports would increase a further 15 per cent in 2007.[109] The $39 billion US Homeland Security

---

106   See Israeli Export and Economic Cooperation Institute, undated, at www.export. gov.il.

107   Klein, 'Laboratory for a Fortressed World'.

108   Rafael Corporation, 'Anti-Terror Homeland Security Solutions', brochure, undated, available at www.rafael.co.il.

109   Ali Kravitz, 'US Homeland Security Market Beckons', *Jerusalem Post,* 18 January 2007.

market loomed large in these growing exports, as did the projected global growth of homeland security markets from $46 billion in 2005 to $178 billion by 2015 (with the US accounting for half the global market).[110]

JOINT VENTURES

Complex joint ventures between US and Israeli companies and central and local governments are now arising. The aim is to further the integration between US and Israeli security companies and profitably generalize Israeli experience. Driven by the perception that 'the United States, as well as the entire international community, can learn much from Israel's efforts in the homeland security arena',[111] HR 3871 – the joint US–Israel Homeland Security Foundation Act – was introduced in March 2004 in the US House of Representatives. This bill proposed to 'set aside $25 million for research and development of new homeland security technologies conducted jointly by American and Israeli companies'.[112] Major goals of the act are the development of new security products for US and Israeli markets, as well as the pump-priming of US and Israeli security companies to help them address global markets and achieve 'positive economic effects in both states'.[113]

Another, related effort emerged from the US-Israel Science and Technology Foundation (USISTF), a joint American-Israeli organization founded to promote high-tech development. In 2004 it set up an initiative to encourage US and Israeli firms to develop new comprehensive security systems to protect key buildings and infrastructures.[114]

US local governments also see the enrolment of Israeli security firms as a way to bolster their own economic development as hotbeds of R&D in the burgeoning, and lucrative, security industries. In January 2008, for example, the local economic development authority for Fairfax County, Virginia – an area within the huge concentration of high-tech US defence and security

110   James Carafano, Jonah Czerwinski, and Richard Weitz, 'Homeland Security Technology, Global Partnerships, and Winning the Long War', *The Heritage Foundation*, 5 October 2006, available at www.heritage.org.

111   Consuella Pockett, 'The United States and Israeli Homeland Security: A Comparative Analysis of Emergency Preparedness Efforts', Counterproliferation Papers Future Warfare Series no. 33, Air University, Maxwell Air Force Base, AL: United States Air Force Counterproliferation Center, 150.

112   Ibid., 147.

113   State of Israel Ministry of Public Security, 'Israel–USA Homeland Security Cooperation', undated, available at www.mops.gov.il.

114   Joe Charlaff, 'Joint Israeli–American Initiative to Streamline Homeland Security Management', *Israel 21c*, 28 November 2004, available at www.usistf.org.

capital around Washington, DC – hosted a senior delegation of representatives from major Israeli security and defence corporations. This 'matchmaking' event, funded in part by the Israel Exports Institute, was 'a conference designed to showcase Israeli technologies and the opportunities for partnering with US systems integrators, contractors, investors, and other prospective partners'.[115] Similar events took place in 2007 at the University of Southern California in Los Angeles and in Maryland.

The declared aim of the Fairfax conference was to convince major Israeli companies to set up US offices in the area (to add to the sixty-five that, by 2007, already had offices in and around Washington, DC) and to entice them to work on joint ventures with US firms based there. Gerald Gordon, president and CEO of the Fairfax authority, described the rationale clearly: 'Homeland security covers such an enormous range of services given the need to protect our air, land and water borders', he explained. 'We don't have the sufficient experience to cover everything [in the US,] and Israel has to be the first place to look for these. Because of the close alliances the US has with Israel, the conference takes on a second layer in how to tap into government contracts'.[116]

The Israeli firms present at the Fairfax event demonstrate the extent to which the detailed experience of securitization and repression in the Occupied Territories lies at the heart of Israel's global push to be the planetary exemplar of military urbanism. DefenSoft™ Planning Systems, for example, boast of their unrivalled experience in 'buffer zone protection planning'. A recent contract covering 'airports, seaports, industrial campuses, urban zones, and other strategic infrastructure sites' has involved planning for the deployment of new sensors around the Gaza Strip.[117] MATE-CCTV, which received grants from the Israel–US Binational Industrial Research and Development Foundation (BIRD), offers 'intelligent video surveillance', including an automated 'behaviour watch' function. Suspect Detection Systems' specialty is a system that, the makers claim, automatically 'identifies malicious intent at border control and other checkpoints'.[118]

These joint ventures are already garnering major contracts in US and global securitization. The Israeli firm Elbit, for example, is working with Boeing under a controversial Department of Homeland Security contract to build a high-tech surveillance system along the rapidly militarizing US–Mexico border, using

115   Fairfax County Economic Development Authority conference.
116   Ali Kravitz, 'US Homeland Security Market Beckons'.
117   Defensoft.com press release.
118   Fairfax County Economic Development Authority conference.

their expertise in 'protecting Israel's borders' as a path to 'keep Americans safe'.[119] Elbit's president, Tim Taylor, has claimed that 'the strategic and technological strengths that we bring to the project will help restore the safety and security that Americans have known for so long. Detecting threats along 6,000 miles of border in the US is not the place for experimentation'.

SHOOT-TO-KILL GOES GLOBAL

Alongside the global diffusion of Israeli equipment and services for urban securitization and militarization, another imitation of Israeli counterterror doctrine is underway. In 2005 it emerged that the US Capitol Police in Washington, DC, had become the first police department in the country to adopt a 'shoot-to-kill' policy for dealing with suspected suicide bombers. Associated with this was the doctrine of 'behavior pattern recognition', intended as a means to 'identify and isolate the type of behavior that might precede an attack'.[120] Both shoot-to-kill policies and behavior pattern recognition techniques have a long history in Israel, and since 2001, Israeli experts have trained law enforcement and security personnel from across the world on their implementation.

The International Association of Chiefs of Police (IACP), a global organization that supports training of and co-operation among police, has been instrumental in this rapid international diffusion of Israeli doctrine regarding shoot-to-kill and behavior pattern recognition. The day after the devastating suicide bombing attacks on London's tubes and buses, the IACP released its guidelines for dealing with potential suicide bombers, instructing 'police officers to look for certain behavioral and physical characteristics, similar to those identified in behavior pattern recognition guidelines'. They also promoted 'the use of lethal force, encouraging officers to aim for the suspect's head and shoot-to-kill'. The IACP has held a number of training events in Israel to enable US and UK law enforcement officers to learn these policies.[121]

The implications of such imitation emerged during the investigations that followed the killing of a young Brazilian man, Jean Charles de Menezes, in London's Stockwell tube station by anti-terrorist British police on 22 July

---

119 Laura Goldman, 'Israeli Technology to Keep US Borders Safe', Israel21c.org, 15 Oct 2006.

120 *Irreversible Consequences: Racial Profiling and Lethal Force in the 'War on Terror'*, briefing paper, New York University School of Law, Center for Human Rights and Global Justice, 2006, 5.

121 Ibid., 13.

2005. In the scandal that followed, the extent to which Israeli shoot-to-kill counterterrorist policy had diffused to other states became starkly evident.

In addressing the new threat of suicide bombing after the 9/11 attacks, London's Metropolitan Police quickly introduced into civilian policing practices a highly militarized notion of pre-emptive lethal force. Barbara Wilding, then deputy assistant commissioner and chair of the Met's suicide-bomber working party, revealed that, after 9/11, the group 'quickly visited Israel, Sri Lanka, and Russia' in search of policies to imitate. The Met's anti-terrorist branch then developed its own policy response, 'based primarily upon the experiences of the Israeli police who are told to shoot to the head if there is [a perceived] imminent danger to life'. This policy was labelled Kratos, meaning 'strength' or 'force', after the mythical Spartan hero. Without debate, the British Parliament signed off on the policy on 22 January 2005.[122]

PERMANENT WAR ECONOMIES

> Clearly, Israel no longer has reason to fear war.[123]

As this chapter has demonstrated, integration is underway between the security–industrial complexes and the military–industrial complexes of Israel and the United States. Even more than this, the emerging security–military–industrial complexes of the two nations are becoming umbilically connected, so much so that it might now be reasonable to consider them as a single diversified, transnational entity.

Fuelled by the two states' similar ideologies of permanent war – within the infinitely flexible and extensible notions of counterterror war – the processes of exemplification, experimentation, imitation and justification are, in turn, further consolidating the permanent war economies of Israel and the US. The military–industrial–security complexes of both countries now centre on extending corporate economic dominance through the permanent targeting of civilians and of everyday urban and infrastructural sites. Meanwhile, widespread privatization, neoliberalization, and social fracturing are radically reducing the social benefits of citizens and soldiers alike.[124]

The US–Israeli security-industrial bubble – a rare point of growth within a global economic downturn – is firmly based on the generalization of doctrines

---

122   Nick Vaughan-Williams, 'The Shooting of Jean Charles de Menezes: New Border Politics?', *Alternatives* 32, 2007, 185.

123   Klein, *Shock Doctrine*, 440.

124   Jonathan Nitzan and Shimshon Bichler, 'Cheap Wars', www.tikkun.org.

and technologies forged during the long-standing lockdown and repression of Palestinian cities by Israeli military and security forces. There is thus a danger of Israeli urban hypermilitarism being normalized across transnational scales, carried along by the US War on Terror as it targets cities and quotidian city life at home and abroad. In the end, the Israeli economy benefits massively, as Israel acquires the status of unequalled exemplar within the global trend towards urban securitization and militarization.

Three points deserve emphasis here. First, the Israeli exemplars being offered, sold and mobilized – not only physical but also architectural technologies of control; new means of electronic sensing, surveillance, targeting, bordering, incarceration and killing; as well as the telling instances of their deployment adduced here – show what happens when a military defines its adversaries and targets as the mainstream civilian population of cities, and when it permanently mobilizes against them, spurred by ideologies encapsulated in such terms as 'asymmetric', 'low intensity', or 'fourth generation' warfare, or 'military operations other than war'. Inevitably, the result is the ratcheting-up of militarization, and, most importantly, the systematic denial or elimination of possibilities, responses, and policies that do not involve action, control and expansion by security and military forces.

Second, counter to the rhetoric of both Israel and the US, these exemplars of new military urbanism are not being mobilized to win a war. Rather, as Naomi Klein argues, their generalization and circulation serve primarily to underpin a new political-economic structure she labels the 'disaster capitalism complex'.[125] Such a constellation thrives on rendering everything and everybody a target – perpetually. It profits from the clean geographical tabula rasa and the political-economic tableaux which result from urbicidal colonialism and war. It sustains massive profits and massive exploitation of resources, enabled by wars and social catastrophe.

'This recipe for endless worldwide war is the same one that the Bush Administration offered as a business prospectus to the nascent disaster capitalism complex after September 11', writes Klein. 'It is not a war that can be won by any country but winning it is not the point. The point is to create "security" inside fortress states bolstered by endless low-level conflict outside their walls'.[126]

Klein's concern is that 'Baghdad, New Orleans and Sandy Springs provide glimpses of the kind of gated future built and run by the disaster capitalism

---

125 Klein, *Shock Doctrine*, 440–441.
126 Ibid.

complex' – that these new militarized urban complexes might become yet further generalized. But as this chapter has demonstrated, and as Klein herself seems to agree, it is Israel-Palestine that provides the ultimate exemplars, models and ideas underpinning the new military urbanism, for it is there that 'an entire country has turned itself into a fortified gated community, surrounded by locked-out people living in permanently excluded red zones . . . In South Africa, Russia and New Orleans the rich build walls around themselves. Israel has taken this disposal process [of the urban poor] a step further: it has built walls around the dangerous poor'.[127]

Yet the deep and reciprocal connections between Israel's disaster-capitalism complex and that of the United States mean that, however extreme, Israel does not stand alone. Rather, as we have seen, a whole gamut of joint ventures, overseas trade missions, training exchanges, exercises, and legal, political and military imitations mean that the 'extreme case' of national lockdown in Israel-Palestine is in the process of being exported and rendered normal. Indeed, the danger is that Israel's security and military complex is losing its distinctiveness, as it becomes absorbed within transnational circuits of investment, ownership, exemplification and economic partnership.

The third point involves the consequences of the central role performed by Israeli military, technological and political experience within the global shift towards the new military urbanism. We must dwell on this because of the key force sustaining the global spread of Israeli models of military urbanism: the entrenched, unmatched power of the Israel lobby in the shaping of US foreign policy. To John Mearsheimer of the University of Chicago and his colleague Stephen Walt of Harvard University's Kennedy School of Government, the Israel lobby within the United States was a key factor in the disastrous foreign policy of the Bush administration. 'The overall thrust of U.S. policy in the region', they wrote in 2006, 'is due almost entirely to U.S. domestic politics, and especially to the activities of the "Israel Lobby" '.[128] The resulting 'attempt to transform the region into a community of democracies has helped produce a resilient insurgency in Iraq, a sharp rise in world oil prices, and [by 2006] terrorist bombings in Madrid, London, and Amman'.[129]

Mearsheimer and Walt also stress that, far from facing a unified set of 'evil' enemies, Israel and the US actually face very different terrorist threats. 'The

---

127   Ibid., 441–2.
128   John Mearsheimer and Stephen Walt, 'The Israel Lobby and US Foreign Policy', working paper no. RWP06-011, Harvard University, John F. Kennedy School of Government, March 2006, 1.
129   Ibid., 5.

terrorist organizations that threaten Israel (e.g., Hamas or Hezbollah) do not threaten the United States, except when it intervenes against them (as in Lebanon in 1982)'. Above all, they assert, 'Palestinian terrorism is not random violence directed against Israel or "the West"; it is largely a response to Israel's prolonged campaign to colonize the West Bank and Gaza Strip'.[130]

Finally, there is little doubt that US treatment of Israel is a powerful, possibly even the most powerful, catalyst for Islamist recruitment. 'Unconditional US support for Israel makes it easier for extremists like bin Laden to rally popular support and to attract recruits', contend Mearsheimer and Walt.[131] In making the United States inescapably complicit in the crimes perpetrated against Palestinian civilians through the Israeli colonial lockdowns in the West Bank and Gaza, the US also faces an unwinnable public-opinion battle in the Arab world.

130 Ibid.
131 Ibid.

CHAPTER EIGHT

Switching Cities Off

City-dwellers are particularly at risk when their complex and sophisticated infrastructure systems are destroyed and rendered inoperable, or when they become isolated from external contacts.[1]

If you want to destroy someone nowadays, you go after their infrastructure. You don't have to be a nation-state to do it, and if they retain any capacity for retaliation then it's probably better if you're not.[2]

URBAN ACHILLES

On our rapidly urbanizing planet, the everyday life of the world's swelling population of urbanites is increasingly sustained by vast, unknowably complex systems of infrastructure and technology. Although often taken for granted – at least when they work – these systems allow modern urban life to exist. Their pipes, ducts, servers, wires, and tunnels sustain the flows, connections, and metabolisms that are intrinsic to contemporary cities. Through their endless technological agency, these systems continually help to transform the natural into the cultural, the social, and the urban, thus supplying the hidden background to everyday modern urban life. They fundamentally underpin the *processes* of city life.

By sustaining the flows of water, waste, energy, information, people, commodities, and signs, contemporary urban infrastructures embody Enlightenment dreams of the social control of nature. They are a prerequisite to any notion of modern civilization. And yet, at the same time, the continuous reliance of urban dwellers on huge and complex systems of infrastructure creates inevitable vulnerabilities. Paradoxically, it is the moment when the blackout occurs, when the server is down, when the subway workers strike or the water pipe ceases to function, that the dependence of cities on infrastructure becomes most visible. 'For most of us', writes Bruce Mau, 'design is invisible. Until it fails.'[3] This applies most strikingly in wealthy, technologically advanced

---

1 Sultan Barakat, 'City War Zones', *The Urban Age*, Spring 1998, 12.

2 Phil Agre, 'Imagining the Next War: Infrastructural Warfare and the Conditions of Democracy', *Radical Urban Theory*, 14 September 2001, available at www.rut.com.

3 Bruce Mau, *Massive Change*, London: Phaidon, 2003, 3.

cities. In much of the so-called developing world, by contrast, the interruption of infrastructure is the norm, rather than a special event.

The potential for catastrophic violence against cities and urban life proceeds in tandem with the shift of urban life towards ever greater reliance on modern urban infrastructures – highways, subways, computer networks, water and sanitation systems, electricity grids, air transport. These systems may be easily assaulted and turned into agents of instantaneous terror, or debilitating disruption, or even de-modernization. Increasingly, then, in high-tech societies dominated by socially abstract interconnections and circulations, both high-tech warfare and terrorism target what John Hinkson characterizes as 'the means of life, not combatants'.[4] And as John Robb puts it, 'most of the networks that we rely on for city life – communications, electricity, transportation, water – are extremely vulnerable to intentional disruptions. In practice, this means that a very small number of attacks on the critical hubs of an [infrastructure] network can collapse the entire network'.[5]

Disruption or destruction of one point in a water, transport, communications or energy grid tends to move quickly through the whole system, and because these systems work together – engineers say they are 'tightly coupled' – disruption in one tends to rapidly 'cascade' to the others. In addition, because all the 'big systems' that sustain advanced urban societies are profoundly electrical, city residents quickly become 'hostages to electricity'.[6] In an electrical blackout, it is not just electric lighting that fails. Electrically powered water and sewerage systems generally grind to a halt: public transportation often stops; food processing and distribution are disabled; health care becomes almost impossible; the Internet ceases to function; some buildings even become effectively uninhabitable, so wired are they with electrified gadgets and aids.

In a 24/7, always-on, intensively networked urban society, urbanites – especially those who live in the advanced industrial world – are so reliant on infrastructural and computerized networked systems that the disruption does not merely inconvenience them. Rather, they creep ever closer to the point where, as Bill Joy famously put it, 'turning off becomes suicide'.[7] The processes of economic globalization, which string out sites of production, research, data entry, consumption, trans-shipment, capitalization and waste disposal across the world, merely tighten the already tight coupling, because of the reliance on ever more complex combinations of logistical, information and infrastructural

---

4   John Hinkson, 'After the London Bombings', *Arena Journal* 24, 2005, 145–6.
5   John Robb, 'The Coming Urban Terror', *City Journal*, Summer 2007.
6   John Leslie, 'Powerless', *Wired* 7: 4, 1999, 119–83.
7   Bill Joy, 'Why the Future Doesn't Need Us', *Wired* 8: 4, 2000, 239.

systems, working 'just-in-time', in intimate synchrony, simply in order to function.

One must remember, though, that the absolute dependence of human life on networked infrastructures exists in modern cities everywhere on the planet, not just in 'high-tech' cities. This is revealed in horrifying detail when states, conducting their 'air power' campaigns, deliberately de-electrify entire urban societies as a putative means of coercing leaders and forcing entire populations into the sudden abandonment of resistance. Strategic bombing rarely, if ever, has had such an effect. As we shall see, the effects of urban de-electrification are both more ghastly and more prosaic: the mass death of the young, the weak, the ill, and the old, over protracted periods of time and extended geographies, as water systems and sanitation collapse and water-borne diseases run rampant. No wonder such a strategy has been called a 'war on public health', an assault which amounts to 'bomb now, die later'.

Everyday urban life everywhere is thus stalked by the threat of interruption: the blackout, the gridlock, the severed connection, the technical malfunction, the inhibited flow, the network-unavailable notice. During such moments, fairly normal in cities of the global South but much less so in cities of the global North, the vast edifices of infrastructure become so much useless junk – temporary (or perhaps not) ruins of the dreams of Enlightenment and Modernity. The daily life of cities turns into a massive struggle against darkness, cold, immobility, hunger, isolation, fear of crime and violence, and – if water-borne diseases threaten – a catastrophic and rapid degeneration in public health. The perpetual technical flux of modern cities is suspended. Improvization, repair, and the search for alternative means of keeping warm and safe, of drinking clean water, of eating, of moving about and disposing of wastes, swiftly become the overriding imperatives. All of a sudden, the normally hidden background of everyday urban life becomes palpably clear to all.

Obviously, 'tremendous lethal capabilities can be created simply by contra-functioning the everyday applications' of a number of ordinary urban infrastructures.[8] The act of using systems and technologies normally taken for granted, ignored, or viewed as banal artifacts of daily life thus becomes charged with anxiety and geopolitical imaginaries. Unknowable risks associated with international geopolitical conflicts infuse everyday technology. Post–Cold War 'asymmetric' conflict transforms components of urban material culture into potential weapons capable of causing death, destruction, disruption, or economic collapse.

---

8   Timothy Luke, 'Everyday Technics as Extraordinary Threats: Urban Technostructures and Nonplaces in Terrorist Actions', in Graham, ed., *Cities, War and Terrorism*, 120–136.

The intensification of global interconnections, however, means that states also wield massive power through the threat, or the implementation, of infrastructure disruption. Russia's status as a resurgent power under Putin is due less to its territorial ambitions or military might than to the way it continually threatens to interrupt, and occasionally does interrupt, energy supplies to South Asia and Europe, both of which rely increasingly on its massive reserves.

Of course, anxieties surrounding the risks of infrastructure disruption, destruction, or weaponization are not new. Since the very origins of urban life, warfare and political violence have targeted the technological and ecological support systems of cities. Indeed, that was a main thrust of medieval siege warfare. During the Second World War, bombing planners sought to achieve 'strategic paralysis' through the destruction of transport systems, water infrastructures, and electricity and communications grids. Then, of course, there are car bombs – a staple of every insurgency and terrorist campaign for at least the past four decades. But urban assault has dramatically escalated. Today, states and non-states alike attack and exploit everyday urban infrastructures with considerable sophistication and lethal power.

INFRASTRUCTURE AND TERRORISM

Technology calls into being its own kind of terrorists.[9]

Most attention, so far, has centred on how non-state insurgents and terrorists can dramatically boost their destructive potential by appropriating or targeting the embedded systems which sustain modern urban life. As political theorist Tim Luke suggests, 'the operational architectures of modern urbanism by their own necessities design, deploy, and dedicate what ironically are tremendous assets for destruction as part and parcel of mobilizing materiel for economic production'.[10] In such cases, writes John Hinkson, it is '"technological civilization" that is the target ... and the contradiction is that it is this civilization's technology that will be used against it'.[11]

Along with iconic urban buildings, today's ultimate terrorist targets are the infrastructures of 'fast capitalism'. As the material foundations of global circulation, contemporary infrastructures 'repudiate fixed territories, sacred spaces, and hard boundaries in favour of unstable flows, the non-places used

---

9   Hinkson, 'After the London Bombings', 145.
10   Luke, 'Everyday Technics as Extraordinary Threats'.
11   Hinkson, 'After the London Bombings', 146.

to stage consumer practices, and permeable borders'.[12] Such 'big systems', however, are always open to asymmetric violence from non-state actors who could never hope to counter conventional Western military might. It is the particular ways in which big systems of infrastructure intersect with global cities that seem to dominate the targeting strategies of contemporary terrorists. And it is this sort of setting, writes Hinkson, that needs 'to be understood in relation to the socially thinned-out and increasingly poverty-stricken modes of life in regions, and among certain social sectors, that are stage by stage being turned into dependent, dysfunctional satellites of the metropolitan centres'.[13]

The most obvious examples here, of course, were the devastating airline suicide attacks of 9/11. In effect, the attackers fashioned massive, kamikaze-style, fuel-laden cruise missiles out of just four of the several thousand airliners flying above and between US cities at that hour of the day. Four aircraft – of the forty thousand or so flights that carry about two million people per day above US territory – were appropriated and translated into catastrophic weapons with the aid of a few box-cutters. But in fact the attacks were facilitated by a wide range of the technological circuits associated with Western, globalized modernity: electronic finance, stock market speculation, computers, media networks, aeronautic technologies. And what these facilitated attacks aimed at was the destruction of those circuits.[14]

Strategic and symbolic targets at the metropolitan heart of US military and economic power were devastated in the 9/11 attacks. Thousands of people were murdered in just a few hours. These effects far outstrip the power of the entire Nazi or Japanese régime during the entire Second World War. As the World Trade Center towers collapsed, destruction approximating the power of a small nuclear bomb reversed the gravitational and architectural hubris of modernist skyscrapers. Using a few specific elements of everyday infrastructure as weapons produced general infrastructure failures and disruptions across large parts of Manhattan, the Eastern seaboard, and the world. The visual circuits of the media, however, remained functional: a global infrastructure bearing witness to the deployment of global infrastructure as urbicidal weapon.

Other powerful examples include the later Madrid and London train, bus and subway attacks of 2003 and 2005, and the numerous and horrifying Palestinian

---

12   Luke, 'Everyday Technics as Extraordinary Threats'.
13   Hinkson, 'After the London Bombings', 149.
14   Leonie Ansems de Vries, '(The War on) Terrorism: Destruction, Collapse, Mixture, Re-enforcement, Construction', *Cultural Politics* 4: 2, 185.

suicide attacks on crowded Israeli buses between 2000 and 2002. The bombing of Moscow metro cars by Chechen terrorists in February 2004 and the gassing of Tokyo's underground railways by the Aum Shinrikyo group in March 1995 also exploited everyday mobility systems to murderous effect. In India, meanwhile, as part of a recent spate of urban atrocities, terrorists have sometimes deliberately targeted the electricity systems that supply the high-tech enclaves which house the city's well-known global software and call-centre industries.[15]

Such attacks have raised widespread anxiety about the vulnerabilities of all manner of basic infrastructures that, by definition, pervade the everyday life of every modern urbanite (Figure 8.1). The mailings of anthrax spores, for example, were acts perpetrated through the US postal system in the wake of the 9/11 attacks and killed five people. Or consider the case of the Washington snipers who turned ordinary highways and gas stations in and around the Beltway suburbs into killing fields in October 2002, murdering ten people. Or the possibility that there could be misuse of nuclear material, or – as the 2008 Chinese baby milk scandal demonstrated – mass poisoning or contamination of the food-production systems upon which urban societies so utterly rely. Consider, too, the widespread fears that the computerized nature of advanced societies could become their Achilles' heel as remote and unknowable 'cyberterrorists' launch malign code into crucial systems at the flick of a distant keystroke, bringing on some type of 'electronic Pearl Harbor' in the process.

Responding to these sorts of threats by formulating policies regarding 'critical infrastructure', nation-states and city governments face almost insurmountable problems in trying to move beyond purely symbolic gestures such as armed police at airports or Jersey barriers around railway stations. For they face the inevitable fact that, in order actually to function as infrastructure, today's big technical systems necessarily must be open to a massive flux of use and exchange which can never be controlled, even with the most sophisticated surveillance and information technologies. 'Because most mechanisms, structures, and links in world capitalism must be essentially insecure to operate optimally', writes Luke, 'defence against the insecurities of all who now live amidst these linked assemblies in big market-driven systems is neither certain nor final'.[16] Ultimately, the costs, delays and reductions in capacity that accompany infrastructural security initiatives hurt the bottom-line: Big Business, which in many ways is now constituted *through* transnational infrastructure systems for moving raw materials, commodities, capital, information, media and

---

15   Vyjayanthi Rao, 'How to Read a Bomb: Scenes from Bombay's Black Friday', *Public Culture* 19: 3, 567–92.
16   Timothy Luke, 'Everyday Technics as Extraordinary Threats'.

8.1   Anxiety and Infrastructure: Exploiting fear in a series of magazine ads.

labour power quickly and efficiently across the planet. Totally securitizing infrastructure and its circulations would, writes Luke, add 'tremendous cost at the corporate bottom line that few companies are willing to pay'.[17]

Clearly, non-state insurgents and terrorists are fully aware of the costs of disruption. In many ways, as John Robb illustrates in his influential 'Global Guerrillas' blog,[18] their greatest political and economic leverage in an

---

17 Ibid.

18 See Global Guerrillas.typepad.com, 'Networked Tribes, Infrastructure Disruption, and the Emerging Bazaar of Violence, an open notebook on the first epochal war of the 21st Century'.

interconnected world comes from the manipulation, destruction, or disruption of the tightly coupled infrastructure networks that sustain global, urbanized capitalism. Robb catalogues a growing incidence of what he calls 'open source warfare' – a multitude of attacks by insurgents and terrorists aimed at generating massive system disruptions by targeting key bottlenecks and supply facilities, especially in oil supply and electricity generation.

Robb points to the devastating efforts by a wide variety of insurgent groups in Iraq to cut supplies of power and oil in Baghdad as a means of undermining the legitimacy of the US-appointed government. Such groups regularly 'destroy multiple towers in series and remove the copper wire for resale to fund the operation; they ambush repair crews in order to slow repairs radically; they [also] attack the natural gas and water pipelines that feed the power plants'.[19] Similar tactics show up elsewhere. In Afghanistan in 2008, the Taliban threatened to detroy the country's mobile phone towers unless operators deactivated them at night – a means of preventing informers from telling occupation forces about night-time activities.[20] In the Niger Delta, gangs and insurgent groups, some protesting the catastrophic conditions faced by indigenous inhabitants of the region, have successfully targeted Western oil transnationals. According to Robb, the group commanded by Henry Ok, who was arrested in February 2008, 'was able to orchestrate the shutdown of over a half a million barrels a day of Nigerian/Shell oil production for over two years, with a total market value of $29 billion'.[21]

DEMODERNIZING BY DESIGN: US AIR POWER

We need to study how to degrade and destroy our adversaries' abilities to transmit their military, political, and economic goods, services and information . . . Infrastructures, defining both traditional and emerging lines of communication, present increasingly lucrative targets for airpower. [The vision of] airmen should focus on lines of communication that will increasingly define modern societies.[22]

Insufficiently recognized as a factor in state military doctrine is the emphasis on the systematic demodernization and immobilization of entire societies classified

---

19 Ibid.

20 Noah Shachtman, 'Taliban Threatens Cell Towers', *Wired Danger Room*, 25 February 2008, available at blog.wired.com/defense.

21 See Global Guerrillas, 'Networked Tribes'.

22 Edward Felker, 'Airpower, Chaos and Infrastructure: Lords of the Rings', paper, Maxwell Air Force Base, Maxwell, AL: United States Air War College, Air University, 1998, 14.

as adversaries. This strategy, in fact, has a greater impact than infrastructural terrorism. The destruction of everyday urban infrastructures across the world derives overwhelmingly from the formal violence of nation-states.

Befitting its current (albeit teetering) hegemonic status, a single nation-state – the United States – dominates infrastructural warfare. US doctrine on this matter derives from the military's quest for globe-spanning dominance via verticalized, information-based power, combined with a preoccupation with minimizing US casualties, regardless of the losses thereby visited on opposing forces and societies. This is the dream of 'full spectrum dominance', achieved through the high-tech fruits of the so-called revolution in military affairs – stealth bombing, GPS targeting, 'precision' bombs. To systematically paralyse adversary societies by destroying or disrupting civilian telecommunications, energy and transport grids is intended both to incapacitate military resistance and to psychologically coerce urban civilians.[23]

MODERNIZATION'S SHADOW

Underpinning US targeting of civilian infrastructure is the belief that subjecting societies to systematic aerial bombing is a form of demodernization – the exact reversal of post–Second World War theories of modernization. Just as those theories see 'development' as enabling societies to 'progress' through successive ages, defined by their infrastructure – from the coal age to the electricity age and onwards to the nuclear age, the information age, and so on – so bombing is seen to lead societies 'backwards', reversing this chain of economic stages. By the same token, just as late-twentieth-century development programmes for 'developing' nations have usually employed economists and civil engineers, so bombing programmes have also widely employed such experts to ensure that destruction succeeds in realizing the desired reversals. 'Working from satellite photos and other intelligence', noted one civil engineer who gave advice regarding US bombing targets during the 2003 invasion of Iraq, we 'supplied pilots with very specific coordinates for the best place to bomb [Iraqi bridges], from a strategically structural point of view'.[24]

One who takes the simple linear view that new technology and infrastructure deterministically yield the fruits of a new economic age for whole societies is likely to see the systematic devastation of technology and infrastructure as a simple reversal of such processes, a reversal that quickly brings adversaries to

---

23 Mike Davis, 'Slouching toward Baghdad', Zmag.org, 26 March 2004.

24 Andrew Wright, 'Structural Engineers Guide Infrastructure Bombing', *Engineering News Record*, 3 April 2003.

their knees. If technology can usher societies towards the future, its devastation can thrust them back into the past.

One cannot miss seeing the close connection between modernization and development theory, on the one hand, and demodernization and infrastructure-bombing theory, on the other, when one learns that the very same experts sometimes preside over both. Most notorious here is the figure of Walt Rostow, perhaps the most influential US economist of the Cold War. On the modernization hand, his seminal book *The Stages of Economic Growth* outlined the most important development model of the late twentieth century: a linear, one-way model through which 'traditional' societies managed to achieve the 'pre-conditions for economic take-off' and then enjoyed the fruits of modernization through the 'drive to maturity' and, finally, an 'age of mass consumption'.[25]

Yet Rostow also played a key part in demodernization. He participated in the US strategic bombing surveys of Japan and Germany and between 1961 and 1968 was the influential national security advisor to both the John F. Kennedy and Lyndon B. Johnson administrations.[26] Rostow's incessant lobbying in that latter role was crucial to the gradually extension and increase of the systematic bombing of North Vietnamese civilian infrastructure, in the campaign called Rolling Thunder. As well as 'bombing . . . countries back through several "stages of growth"'[27] within his development model, this was seen as a means of undermining the Communist challenge to US power.[28] Rostow, a rabid anti-Communist, regarded the eradication of Communism as necessary because he saw it as a repellent form of modernization. Rostow argued that 'communism is best understood as a disease of the transition to modernization'.[29]

This wider notion – that bombing, as a form of punitive demodernization, can inaugurate a straightforward reversal of conventional, liberal economic models of linear economic and technological progress – is now so wide-spread as to be a cliché. Curtis LeMay, the force behind the systematic fire-bombing of urban

---

25   Walter Rostow, *The Stages of Economic Growth: A Non-Communist Manifesto*, Cambridge: Cambridge University Press, 1960.

26   David Milne, 'Our Equivalent of Guerrilla Warfare: Walt Rostow and the Bombing of North Vietnam, 1961–1968', *The Journal of Military History* 71, 2007, 169–203.

27   Nils Gilman, *Mandarins of the Future: Modernization Theory in Cold War America*, Baltimore: Johns Hopkins University Press, 2003, 199.

28   As is generally the case, of course, the increasingly intense aerial annihilation only strengthened the resolve of the North Vietnamese civilians, so bolstering Viet Cong power in the process.

29   Cited in Milne, 'Our Equivalent of Guerrilla Warfare'.

Japan in the Second World War, famously urged that the US Air Force, which he led at the time, should 'bomb North Vietnam back into the Stone Age'. He added the USAF needed to 'destroy . . . every work of man in North Vietnam'.

Despite the waning fashionability of the modernization theories, its dark shadow, demodernization theory remains as popular as ever among the US military. Le Mayesque and Rostowian imperatives have tripped as well from the lips of many a Dr. Strangelove-style US politician, US Air Force commander and hawkish US commentator since the 1960s. Influential celebrant of neoliberal globalization Thomas Friedman, for example, deployed such arguments as NATO cranked up its bombing campaign against Serbia in 1999. Picking up a variety of historic dates that could mirror the post-bombing future of Serbian society, Friedman urged that the movements and mobilities sustaining life in Serbian cities be brought to a grinding halt. 'It should be lights out in Belgrade', he wrote. 'Every power grid, water pipe, bridge, road and war-related factory has to be targeted . . . We will set your country back by pulverizing you. You want 1950? We can do 1950. You want 1389? We can do that, too!'[30] In Friedman's scenario, the precise reversal of time that the adversary society is to be bombed back into is presumably a matter of selecting the correct weapon for the target.

Three years later, as US aircraft pummeled Afghanistan in 2002, Donald Rumsfeld famously quipped, with his usual sensitivity, that the US military were 'not running out of targets. Afghanistan is.'[31] Such humour reveals much about the mentality of the USAF and the importance of modern infrastructure as optimal sites of devastation. Indeed, it shows that *without* a web of modern infrastructures to blast to kingdom come, the Air Force literally doesn't know what to destroy. One Afghan replied to the claim that the USAF would bomb Afghanistan 'back into the Stone Age' with the caustic rejoinder 'You can't . . . We're already there.'[32]

The politics of bombing infrastructure as a form of reverse modernization plays an even wider discursive role. It bolsters the depiction of countries deemed 'less developed' as being backward, barbarian. Aerial bombing aimed at demodernization thus reinforces Orientalist notions which relegate 'the "savage," colonized target population to an "other" time and space'.[33] Indeed,

30   Thomas Friedman, *New York Times*, columnist 23 April 1999, cited by I. Skoric, 'On not killing civilians', posted at amsterdam.nettime.org, 6 May 1999.

31   Donald Rumsfeld, transcript, US Department of Defense, Office of the Assistant Secretary of Defense (Public Affairs), 22 March 2004, available at www.defenselink.mil.

32   Tamim Ansary, 'An Afghan-American Speaks', Salon.Com, 14 September 2001.

33   Deer, 'The Ends Of War And The Limits Of War Culture'.

Nils Gilman has argued that 'as long as modernization was conceived as a unitary and unidirectional process of economic expansion,' one could explain backwardness and insurgency 'only in terms of deviance and pathology'.[34]

THE ENEMY AS A SYSTEM

The central idea shaping the frequent US devastation of urban infrastructure by aerial bombing during the past two decades has been the notion of the 'enemy as a system'. A modification of Second World War ideas of targeting the 'industrial webs' of Germany and Japan to create 'strategic paralysis' in war production, this notion originated within the 'strategic ring theory' devised by a leading USAF strategist, John Warden.[35] This systematic view of adversary societies has served to justify and sustain the rapid extension of US infrastructural warfare capability and has been used as the explicit basis for all major US air operations since the late 1990s.

The latest USAF document on targeting doctrine, for example, speaks of 'useful target sets' and encourages planners to bomb 'infrastructure targets across a whole region or nation (like electrical power or petroleum, oil, and lubricants production) . . . non-infrastructure systems such as financial networks [and] nodes common to more than one system'.[36] To increase the effectiveness with which civilian infrastructure is destroyed, the Air Force has funded the development of specialized weaponry. Prime amongst these are the 'soft' or 'blackout' bombs, which critics have labelled the 'finger on the switch' of a targeted country.[37] These bombs rain down thousands of spools of graphite string onto electric transmission and power systems, creating catastrophic short circuits.[38] As part of the mythology of humanitarianism that has pervaded post–Cold War discussions about 'precision strikes', these weapons have regularly been lauded in the military press as 'non-lethal', creating 'minimal risk of collateral damage' (i.e., dead civilians).[39]

---

34   Nils Gilman, *Mandarins of the Future*, 199.

35   John Warden, 'The Enemy as a System', *Airpower Journal* 9: 1, 1995, 41–55.

36   United States Air Force, *Targeting Air Force Doctrine*, document 2-1.9, 8 June 2006, 22–33.

37   Patrick Barriot and Chantal Bismuth, 'Ambiguous Concepts and Porous Borders', in *Treating Victims of Weapons of Mass Destruction: Medical, Legal and Strategic Aspects*, Patrick Barriot and Chantal Bismuth, eds., London: Wiley, 2008.

38   The only such weapons that have been made public are the CBU-94 'Blackout Bomb' and the BLU-114/B 'Soft-Bomb'.

39   See Federation of American Scientists, 'CBU-94 "Blackout Bomb" and BLU-114/B "Soft-Bomb"', available at www.fas.org.

'At the strategic level', writes Warden, 'we [the US military] attain our objectives by causing such changes to one or more parts of the enemy's physical system'.⁴⁰ This system is seen to have five 'rings', or parts: the political leadership at the center; organic essentials (food, energy); infrastructure (vital connections such as roads, electricity, telecommunications, and water); the civilian population; and, finally and least important, the fighting forces (see Figure 8.2). Rejecting the direct targeting of enemy civilians, Warden instead argues that only indirect attacks on civilians are legitimate, and that these should operate through the targeting of societal infrastructures. This strategy is seen as a means of bringing intolerable pressures to bear on the nation's political leaders, even though such attacks contravene a host of the key statutes of international humanitarian law.⁴¹

The doctrine of 'shock and awe' which shaped the US bombing onslaught against Iraq in 2003 represents an extreme extension of Warden's ideas. It advocated the rapid and complete paralysis of an entire society, visiting upon its urban populations psychological shocks commensurate with those of a nuclear attack. 'Shutting the country down', write the doctrine's authors, Harlan Ullman and James Wade, 'would entail both the physical destruction of appropriate infrastructure and the shutdown and control of the flow of all vital information and associated commerce [that would] achieve a level of national shock akin to the effect that dropping nuclear weapons on Hiroshima and Nagasaki had on the Japanese'.⁴²

US air-power strategists are no doubt well aware that, in highly urbanized societies, the destruction of civilian infrastructure is likely to lead to major public health crises and mass civilian deaths. In a telling example, published in 2001 in the official US Air Force journal *Air and Space Power Chronicles*,⁴³

---

40 Warden, 'The Enemy as a System', 41–55.

41 As the MADRE human rights organization point out, 'Attacks on civilians and civilian infrastructure are grave breaches of international law, including: Article 33 of the Fourth Geneva Conventions, Article 48 of the Protocol 1 Additional to the Geneva Conventions, and Article 50 of the Hague Convention. Further, the Rome Statute of the International Criminal Court (ICC) includes as war crimes: "Intentionally directing attacks against the civilian population as such or against individual civilians not taking direct part in hostilities," and "Intentionally directing attacks against civilian objects" (Article 8 2 (b) (i) and (ii)).' MADRE.org, 'War on Civilians: A MADRE Guide to the Middle East Crisis', 19 July 2006.

42 Harlan Ullman and James Wade, *Shock and Awe: Achieving Rapid Dominance*, Institute for Strategic Studies, National Defense University, 1996.

43 Kenneth Rizer, 'Bombing Dual-Use Targets: Legal, ethical, and doctrinal perspectives', *Air and Space Power Chronicles*, 1 May 2001, available at www.airpower. maxwell.af.mil/airchronicles.

8.2   John Warden's 1995 Five-Ring Model illustrating the
strategic composition of contemporary societies central
to US Air Force strategy.

Kenneth Rizer sought to justify the US strategy of direct destruction of so-
called dual-use targets (civilian infrastructures) by contending that, in
international law, the legality of attacking such targets 'is very much a matter
of interpretation'. The US military applied Warden's ideas in the 1991 air war in
Iraq with 'amazing results', claimed Rizer. 'Despite dropping 88,000 tons in the
forty-three-day campaign, only three thousand civilians died directly as a result
of the attacks, the lowest number of deaths from a major bombing campaign
in the history of warfare'. He openly admits, however, that the systematic
destruction of Iraq's electrical system in 1991 'shut down water purification

and sewage treatment plants, resulting in epidemics of gastro-enteritis, cholera, and typhoid, leading to perhaps as many as 100,000 civilian deaths and the doubling of infant mortality rates'.[44]

Such large numbers of indirect civilian deaths seem of little concern to US Air Force strategists, though. Rizer states that 'the [US] Air Force does not consider the long-term, indirect effects of such attacks when it applies proportionality [ideas] to the expected military gain'. More tellingly still, he goes on to examine the connection between carpet-bombing and the morale of the bombed population. 'How does the Air Force intend to undermine civilian morale without having an intent to injure, kill, or destroy civilian lives?' he asks. 'Perhaps the real answer is that by declaring dual-use targets legitimate military objectives, the Air Force can directly target civilian morale. In sum, so long as the Air Force includes civilian morale as a legitimate military target, it will aggressively maintain a right to attack dual-use targets'.[45]

In 1998 another air-power theorist, Edward Felker, based at the US Air War College, Air University, proposed a further development of Warden's model[46] (Figure 8.3). Felker's was based on the experiences of the 1991 war with Iraq (code-named Desert Storm) and presented the idea that infrastructure, rather than being a separate ring of the enemy as a system, in fact pervaded and connected all the others – that it actually 'constitute[s] the society as a whole'. 'If infrastructure links the subsystems of a society', he wondered, 'might it be the most important target?'[47]

By modelling the ripple effects that result from destruction of key parts of an adversary society's infrastructure, US military planners have started to develop a more complex doctrine for extending US infrastructural warfare. It centers on systematic demodernization, not just of the military forces of enemy nations but of their civil societies as well. Indeed, US military analysts are now concentrating on finding the tipping points in critical infrastructure systems that will lead to first-, second- and third-order effects capable of rapidly inducing complete societal chaos (Figure 8.4).[48]

---

44 Ibid.
45 Ibid.
46 Felker, *Airpower, Chaos and Infrastructure*, 1–20.
47 Ibid.
48 Christina Patterson, 'Lights Out and Gridlock: The Impact of Urban Infrastructure Disruptions on Military Operations and Non-Combatants', Washington, DC: Institute for Defense Analyses, 2000.

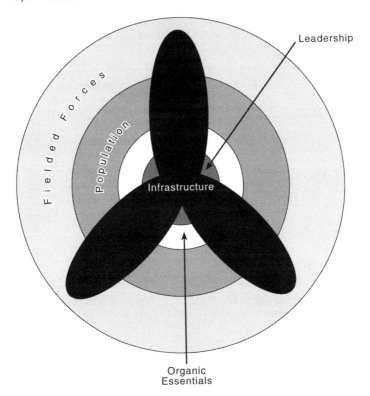

Leadership

Fielded Forces

Population

Infrastructure

Organic
Essentials

8.3   'A New Model for Societal Structure': Edward Felker's
adaptation of Warden's Five-Ring Model (Figure
8.2), stressing the centrality of infrastructural warfare
to post–Cold War US air-power doctrine.

'BOMB NOW, DIE LATER': IRAQ, 1991

If strategic paralysis is to attain quick victory by applying technologically superior
air power, planners must identify important, vulnerable targets. Such targets are
readily found in a modern, industrialized society that relies on a fixed and vulnerable
infrastructure. For example, because Iraq's bridges, communication centers, power
production stations, and water plants were strategically important and extremely
vulnerable to air attack, they were nearly ideal targets for a strategic paralysis campaign.[49]

---

49   Jason Barlow, 'Strategic Paralysis: An Air Power Strategy For The Present', *Airpower
Journal* 7: 4, 1993, available at www.airpower.maxwell.af.mil/airchronicles.

First order effects	Second order effects	Third order effects
No light after dark or in building interiors	Erosion of command and control capabilities	Greater logistics complexity
No refrigeration	Increased requirement for power generating equipment	Decreased mobility
Some stoves / ovens non operable	Increased requirement for night vision devices	Decreased situational awareness
Inoperable hospital electronic equipment	Increased reliance on battery-powered items for news, broadcasts, etc.	Rising disease rates
No electronic access to bank accounts / money	Shortage of clean water for drinking, cleaning and preparing food	Rising rates of malnutrition
Disruption in some transportation and communication services	Hygeine problems	Increased numbers of non-combatants required assistance
Disruption to water supply; treatment facilities and sanitation	Inability to operate and process some foods	Difficulty in communicating with non-combatants

8.4 Patterson's analysis of the first-second-and third-order 'ripple' effects of US forces disrupting electrical power grids during urban warfare in an 'adversary country'.

An exploration of the experience of war, sanctions, and more war in Iraq between 1991 and 2004 helps replace the abstract pontifications of 'air power theorists' with the facts of what happens to real cities, and real people, when theories shape actual wars against highly urbanized societies.

The 1991 Desert Storm bombing campaign, targeted heavily against dual-use urban infrastructure systems, relied on a strategy that Ruth Blakeley has termed 'bomb now, die later'.[50] It has become clear that the wholesale demodernization of metropolitan life in Iraq, a profoundly urbanized nation, in 1991 – followed by the sanctions imposed between 1991 and 2003, making it impossible to reconstruct life-sustaining infrastructures – created one of the largest engineered public-health catastrophes of the late twentieth century. Even USAF papers admit that the public-health disaster created by the bombing of

50 Ruth Blakeley, 'Bomb Now, Die Later', Bristol University Department of Politics, 2003, 25.

Iraq's electricity infrastructure killed at least thirty times as many civilians as did the actual fighting.[51]

Because Iraq's true military targets were so easily annihilated, what happened in Desert Storm was that a very large percentage of strategic aerial missions were targeted against industry, power generation, roads, and bridges, rather than against military assets. Along with military and communication networks, urban infrastructures received the bulk of the bombing. One US air war planner, Lt Col David Deptula, passed a message to Iraqi civilians via the world's media as the planes started going in: 'hey, your lights will come back on as soon as you get rid of Saddam!'[52] Another Wardenian thinker, Brig. Gen. Buster Glosson, explained that infrastructure was the main target because the US military wanted to 'put every household in an autonomous mode and make them feel they were isolated . . . We wanted to play with their psyche'.[53] As Colin Rowat suggests, for perhaps 110,000 Iraqis, this 'playing' ultimately proved fatal.[54]

Chris Bolkcom and John Pike, in a major analysis of the 2001 Gulf War, recall the centrality of targeting dual-use infrastructures in the planning of Desert Storm. 'From the beginning of the campaign', they write, 'Desert Storm decision makers planned to bomb heavily the Iraqi military-related industrial sites and infrastructure, while leaving the most basic economic infrastructures of the country intact. What was not apparent or what was ignored, was that the military and civilian infrastructures were inextricably interwoven'.[55]

The political rationale of 'turning off the lights' generated much debate amongst Gulf War bombing planners.[56] Apparently, some predicted that the 'loss of electricity in Baghdad and other cities would have little effect on popular morale'. Others argued that 'the affluence created by petro-dollars had made the city's population psychologically dependent on the amenities associated with electric power'.[57]

Whatever the disagreements, the prime target of the air assault was in fact

---

51   Ellwood Hinman, 'The Politics of Coercion, Toward a Theory of Coercive Airpower for Post–Cold War Conflict', CADRE paper no. 14, Maxwell Air Force Base, AL: Air University Press, 11.

52   Cited in Colin Rowat, 'Iraq - Potential Consequences of War', Campaign Against Sanctions in Iraq Discussion List, 8 November 2002, available at www.casi.org.uk.

53   Ibid.

54   Ibid.

55   Chris Bolkcom and John Pike, *Attack Aircraft Proliferation: Issues for Concern*, Federation of American Scientists, 1993, available at www.fas.org/spp/aircraft, 2.

56   Blakeley, 'Bomb Now, Die Later', 25.

57   Thomas Keaney and Elliot Cohen, *Gulf War Air Power Surveys* (GWAPS), vol. 2: 2, Washington, DC: Johns Hopkins University and the US Air Force, 1993, 23 n53.

Iraq's system of electricity generation. Destroying the means of producing electricity was deemed 'particularly attractive because it can not be stockpiled'.[58] During Desert Storm, the coalition forces flew more than two hundred sorties against electrical plants. The destruction was devastatingly effective. A major post-war assessment found that 'almost 88 per cent of Iraq's installed generation capacity was sufficiently damaged or destroyed by direct attack, or else isolated from the national grid through strikes on associated transformers and switching facilities, to render it unavailable'.[59] In addition, 'more than half of the 20 electrical generator sites were 100 percent destroyed'. At the end of the first week of the air war, 'the Iraqis shut down what remained of the national power grid. It was useless'.[60]

At war's end, Iraq had a mere 4 per cent of the pre-war electricity supply. Four months later, only 20–25 per cent of the pre-war level had been attained – 'roughly analogous to that of the 1920s before Iraq had access to refrigeration and sewage treatment'.[61]

The UN Under-Secretary General Martti Ahtisaari, reporting on his visit to Iraq in March 1991, was clearly shaken by what he had witnessed. 'Nothing that we had seen or read had quite prepared us for the particular form of devastation that has now befallen the country', he wrote. 'The recent conflict has wrought near-apocalyptic results upon an economically mechanized society. Now, most means of modern life-support have been destroyed or rendered tenuous. Iraq has, for some time to come, been relegated to a pre-industrial age, but with all the disabilities of post-industrial dependency on an intensive use of energy and technology'.[62]

The most devastating impact of mass de-electrification was indirect, however. Iraq's water and sewage systems, which relied entirely on electrical pumping stations, ground to a halt. As with the electricity-generation system, prospects of repair sank to near-zero because of the coalition's punitive sanctions – introduced, with the help of UN resolutions, just before the war. As a result, virtually any item or supply required for infrastructural repair was classified, and prohibited, as a dual-use item with military potential. Ironically, it was an exploitation of the selfsame slippery legal jargon that had legitimized the massive infrastructural destruction in the first place. Here, then, the rhetoric of

58 Bolkcom and Pike, *Attack Aircraft Proliferation* 2.
59 Keaney and Cohen, *Gulf War Air Power Surveys*.
60 Bolkcom and Pike, *Attack Aircraft Proliferation* 5.
61 Ibid., 20.
62 Perez De Cueller, Report S/22366 to the United Nations Security Council. New York: UN Office of the Iraq programme, 1991.

'dual use', initially invoked to target infrastructures, took an additional perverse and murderous twist by preventing its repair.

As with the evident culpability of US bombing theorists regarding the massive civilian death toll in Iraq, it is clear that the humanitarian catastrophe triggered by the punitive sanctions was fully known at the time by the US Department of Defense (DoD). Now-declassified documents from the Defense Intelligence Agency (DIA), for example, demonstrate the DoD's distinct awareness of the terrible impacts of aerial demodernization followed by public health–related sanctions in post-war Iraq. Thomas Nagy has demonstrated that DIA memos in early 1991 clearly predicted what they called 'a full degradation of Iraq's water system'.[63] These memos stated that a failure to acquire embargoed water-treatment equipment would inevitably lead to massive food and water shortages, a collapse of preventive medicine, an inability to dispose of waste, and epidemics of diseases such as cholera, diarrhea, meningitis, and typhoid.

These, in turn, it was predicted, would lead to huge casualty rates, 'particularly amongst children, as no adequate solution exists for Iraq's water purification dilemma [under the sanctions régime]'.[64] The memo, titled 'Disease Outbreaks in Iraq' and dated 21 February 1991,[65] stated that 'conditions are favorable for communicable disease outbreaks, particularly in major urban areas affected by coalition bombing'. Despite all this, planners went ahead with the imposition of sanctions.

By 1999, these predictions had come true. The availability of drinkable water had fallen to 50 per cent of 1990 levels.[66] 'The number of Iraqis who died in 1991 from the effects of the Gulf war or the postwar turmoil approximates 205,500', calculates Colin Rowat of the Oxford Research Group. 'There were relatively few deaths (approximately 56,000 military personnel and 3,500 civilian) from direct war effects. The largest component of deaths derives from the 111,000 attributable to postwar adverse health effects'.[67]

Using a longer time-frame, UNICEF estimates that between 1991 and 1998 there were, statistically, more than five hundred thousand excess deaths amongst Iraqi children less than five years of age; a sixfold increase in death rates for this

---

63   Thomas Nagy, 'The Secret Behind the Sanctions: How the US Intentionally Destroyed Iraq's Water Supply', *Progressive,* September 2001.

64   Ibid.

65   Defense Intelligence Agency memo to Centcom, 'Iraq Water Treatment Vulnerabilities', filename 511rept.91, 18 January 1991.

66   Ruth Blakeley, 'Targeting Water Treatment Facilities', posted on Campaign Against Sanctions in Iraq Discussion List, 24 January 2003, available at www.casi.org.uk, 2.

67   Rowat, 'Iraq – Potential Consequences of War'.

group occurred between 1990 and 1994.[68] Such figures mean that 'in most parts of the Islamic world, the sanctions campaign is considered genocidal'.[69]

THE SECOND GULF WAR, 2003–

Not surprisingly, the second and even more savage onslaught of shock-and-awe aerial bombing to which Iraq was subjected in 2003 – having already undergone twelve years of systematic demodernization and impoverishment, caused by sanctions and continued bombing – led to an even more complete demodernization of everyday urban life in the country, even though key centralized infrastructure nodes were targeted less extensively than in 1991. This time, the bombing strategy, with a view to the needs of post-war reconstruction and oil extraction, was ostensibly designed to 'avoid power plants, public water facilities, refineries, bridges, and other civilian structures'.[70] Yet new weapons, including electromagnetic pulse (EMP) cruise missiles, were used for the first time not merely to attack but to completely fry dual-use communications and control equipment.

Nevertheless, a substantial proportion of dual-use systems such as electrical and power transmission grids, media networks, and telecommunications infrastructures were still targeted and destroyed in 2003. Media installations and antennae were destroyed by new CBU-107 'passive attack weapons' – non-explosive cluster bombs, nicknamed 'rods from God' by the US Air Force, which rain metal rods onto sensitive electrical systems.

In addition, more traditional bombs were used to destroy Al Jazeera's office in Baghdad on April 8, killing several journalists – an action taken because the Pentagon, bent on information dominance, considered that the highly successful independent channel's coverage of civilian deaths caused by the bombing was undermining its own propaganda (or PSYOPS) campaign. As David Miller suggests, in current US geopolitical strategy 'the collapse of distinctions between independent news media and psychological operations is striking'.[71]

Finally, as in the 1991 Iraq assault and the 1999 NATO intervention in Kosovo, carbon 'soft' bombs were widely used on electricity distribution systems. The resulting fires completely ruined many newly repaired

68   United Nations Children's Fund (UNICEF), Annex II of S/1999/356, Section 18. 1999, available at www.un.org/Depts/oip/reports.

69   Thomas Smith, 'The New Law of War: Legitimizing Hi-Tech and Infrastructural Violence', *International Studies Quarterly* 46, 2002, 365.

70   Human Rights Watch, *Off Target: The Conduct of the War and Civilian Casualties in Iraq*, Washington DC, 2003, available at www.hrw.org.

71   David. Miller, 'The DominationEffect', *Guardian*, 8 January 2004.

transformer stations, creating, once again, a serious crisis of water distribution because of the resulting power blackouts.[72] In addition, the old and decayed water pipes in Iraq's main cities often fractured simply from the seismic shocks of near- explosions. In al-Nasiriyya, Human Rights Watch researchers found that 'in many places people had dug up water and sewage pipes outside their homes in a vain attempt to get drinking water'.[73] Not surprisingly, large numbers of water-borne intestinal infections were once again reported after the war, a direct result of the targeting of electrical distribution systems. By December 2007, cholera epidemics were occurring in Baghdad, reflecting the fact that 70 per cent of Iraqis still did not have access to clean water.[74]

SWITCHING OFF THE OCCUPIED TERRITORIES

As we saw in Chapter 7, criticisms of Israeli policies of besieging the West Bank and Gaza have concentrated mostly on civilian deaths caused by air and tank raids; on mass house demolitions and the bulldozing of settlements with massive D9 Caterpillar bulldozers[75]; on the drawing of extremely tight limits on Palestinian enclaves and the construction of brutal apartheid-style walls, check-points, registers, laws and databases; and on the construction of a parallel world of generously proportioned, expanding Jewish-only settlements, linked together with their own private infrastructures and cleared, free-fire 'buffer zones'.[76]

Much less reported has been a systematic and continuous programme by Israeli forces which adds a new twist to the geographies and politics of contemporary siege warfare against urban civilians: the targeting and destruction of modern infrastructure systems. In May 2001, for example, Ben Azri, then Israel's minister of labour, called for the dismantling of Palestinian roads, utilities and cultural institutions as a way of 'making the Palestinians' lives hell'.[77] In 2002, Operation Defensive Shield put his words into action. As well as the battles, raids, abductions and mass demolitions, its central feature – perpetuated in all subsequent Israeli operations – was the deliberate destruction of any symbol of urban modernity or a proto-Palestinian state.

72   Human Rights Watch, *Off Target*.
73   Ibid.
74   David Smith, 'Cholera Crisis Hits Baghdad', *Observer*, 2 December 2007.
75   See Chapter 7.
76   See Weizmann, *Hollow Land*.
77   See Graham, 'Lessons in Urbicide', 63–73.

Financial damage to infrastructure from the first major offensive alone has been estimated by donors at some $360 million.[78]

During the 2002 operations, water tanks were regularly riddled with bullets. Electronic communications were bombed and jammed. Roads and street furniture were widely bulldozed and destroyed. Computers were smashed, and hard discs stolen. Electricity transformers were destroyed. Any cultural or bureaucratic symbol of a would-be Palestinian state was ransacked. Touring the West Bank in April 2002, Amira Hass described the wreckage: 'Smashed, burned and broken computer terminals heaped in piles and thrown in yards, server cables cut, hard disks missing, disks and diskettes scattered and broken, printers and scanners broken and missing, laptops gone, telephone exchanges disappeared or vandalized, and paper files burned, torn, scattered or defaced – if not taken'. 'Such destruction', she wrote, 'was not a whim, or crazed vengeance. Let's not deceive ourselves – this was not a mission to search and destroy the "terrorist infrastructure"'.[79]

The main damage to the physical infrastructure of Palestinian cities, roads, water systems and electricity grids was done using massive, sixty-tonne D9 armoured bulldozers. As Mark Zeitoun remarked in August 2002, the behemoth D9s were retrofitted with 'special blades and buckets optimized for concrete demolition and a powerful asphalt-ripper in the rear. The resultant power house machinery . . . is the tool of choice for destroying electrical grids, digging up buried water and sewerage services, taking out shop fronts and demolishing cars'.[80]

Like the US bombing of Iraq, such actions are a direct reflection of changes in Israeli military doctrine. The systematic targeting of civilian infrastructure has come to be seen as a means of coercing adversaries in the 'non-traditional' wars against insurgents, and supportive civilian populations, in cities. Israeli doctrine here has clearly been heavily influenced by US doctrine surrounding John Warden's work, in which adversary societies are seen as 'systems of systems' and the targeting of urban infrastructure is one means of launching 'effects-based operations' to psychologically coerce entire populations. Israeli military theorists now talk of targeting infrastructure as the key means of undertaking 'diffused warfare', where there are no obvious front-lines. 'Rather

---

78 'Israeli Official Calls for Striking Palestinian Infrastructure', *Arabic News*, 6 May 2001; Rita Giacaman and Abdullatif Husseini, 'Life and Health During the Israeli Invasion of the West Bank: The Town of Jenin', *Indymedia Israel*, 22 May 2002.

79 Amira Hass, 'Operation Destroy the Data', *Ha'aretz*, 24 April 2002.

80 Mark Zeitoun, 'IDF Infrastructure Destruction by Bulldozer', *Electronic Intifada*, 2 August 2002.

than being defined by parameters of front-lines and home fronts', retired Israeli admiral Yedidia Groll-Yaari and Haim Assa recently wrote, 'the nature of future conflicts for nation states will be determined by legitimate objectives and desired effects in a *multitude of contact points* – be they military or civilian, infrastructure'.[81] Thus, as in US doctrine, destroying civilian infrastructure is seen by Israeli military planners as one of the few ways of bringing pressure to bear on the actions of stealthy insurgents.

STRANGLING GAZA

> It could, rightfully, be a cause of shame to the world. But the world, besieged by violence and injustice, hardly notices it.[82]

Though Lebanon's urban infrastructure was devastated in 2006 as part of Israel's new strategy of launching diffused warfare (against Hezbollah, in this case), it is the Gaza Strip that provides perhaps the most startling example of the effects of this new Israeli doctrine.[83] For it is within Gaza that Israel has pushed to extremes this strategy for the Occupied Territories. 'Diffused warfare' combines physical, hermetic closure;[84] the prevention of circulation; intensive aerial surveillance; continual air raids; the devastation of modern infrastructure; and overpowering incursions by squadrons of tanks, backed by artillery assaults. The idea is to combine withdrawal and maximum at-a-distance military control with a complete absolution of political, legal, social, or moral responsibility for the fate of Gaza's 1.4 million inhabitants.[85] The Gaza Strip, writes Darryl Li, is thus a 'space where Israel tests and refines various techniques of management, continuously experimenting in search of an optimal balance between *maximum control* over the territory and *minimum responsibility* for its non-Jewish population'. The strip

---

81   Yedidia Groll-Yaari and Haim Assa, *Diffused Warfare, The Concept of Virtual Mass*, Haifa: University of Haifa, 2007, 23.

82   The 'Strangling Gaza' subtitle, and the quote are drawn from from César Chelala, 'Strangling Gaza', Common Dreams.org, 15 December 2007.

83   Gaza is an extended and densely populated city-strip roughly the size, at twenty-five miles long by six miles wide, of England's Isle of Wight. As of 2006, the Strip was inhabited by 1.4 million people. Of these, 840,000 were children. The density of the population in Gaza is one of the highest in the world. For example, in the Jabalya refugee camp, there are approximately 28,571 people per square mile. See Li, 'The Gaza Strip as Laboratory', 40.

84   As Li puts it, '"Closure" is a broad term that includes various restrictions on the circulation of people and goods, ranging from prohibition on international travel to mass house arrest ("curfew")'. 'Li, The Gaza Strip as Laboratory', 40.

85   Ibid.

provides a kind of dystopian proving ground for practices that could become increasingly relevant in the West Bank as Palestinian life becomes increasingly fragmented across an archipelago of isolated Gaza-like strips.[86]

Israel's new strategy has transformed what had been, in effect, a giant open-air prison into a massive, besieged city-strip where there are no apparent prospects for the lifting of the demographically inspired siege. The strangulation of Gaza has dramatically intensified following the evacuation of Jewish settlements there in the late summer of 2005 and the election of a Hamas government in January 2006.[87] The prime cause of the present crisis was that 'the Palestinian people went to the polls, participated in free, fair, and transparent democratic elections unmatched in the Arab world, but voted for the *wrong party*'[88] – Hamas. Israel, the EU, the US and other aid donors then decided to apply economic, tax and aid sanctions against what was immediately cast as a 'terrorist state'. Israel also declared that Gaza was, from then on, a 'hostile territory' with which it was 'at war'.[89] Such a designation was the basis for the 2006 invasion and the much larger twenty-two-day invasion in 2008–9 labelled 'Operation Cast Lead'.

Two days after Corporal Gilad Shalit was taken prisoner by Palestinian fighters in Rafah on 25 June 2006, Israel launched its Summer Rain offensive against Gaza. At the outset of the attacks, Israeli Prime Minister Ehud Olmert claimed that the operations were not aimed 'to mete out punishment but rather to apply pressure so that the abducted soldier will be freed'.[90] During the Summer Rain attacks, the IDF also claimed that 'the goals of the operations were "to stop the terrorist organizations that relentlessly fire [home-made Kassam] rockets" over the border into Israel, and that the operations were "tailored to avoid civilian casualties"'.

The latter claim seems particularly ridiculous, since the use of artillery and bombing in one of the world's most densely populated urban environments will inevitably maim and kill large numbers of civilians. This result is neither accidental nor 'collateral', in that those who take these actions are fully aware of this inevitability. Between 28 June and 13 September 2006,

---

86   Ibid., 38–43.

87   It has aso emerged that the later Hamas take-over of the strip in June 2007 was their attempt to forestall a US-funded coup attempt by the rival Fatwa organisation – an attempt to reverse the result of the democratic election. See Seumas Milne, 'To Blame the Victims for this Killing Spree Defies both Morality and Sense', *Guardian,* 5 March 2008.

88   Jennifer Loewenstein, 'Notes from the Field: Return to the Ruin that is Gaza', *Journal of Palestine Studies* 36: 3, 2007, 23–35.

89   Karen Koning-AbuZayd, 'This Brutal Siege of Gaza can only Breed Violence in Gaza City', *Guardian*, 23 January 2008.

90   Electronic Intifada, 'Israel Invades Gaza: "Operation Summer Rain"', 27 June 2006.

290 people, mostly civilians, were killed in Gaza by Israeli actions. Of the 290, 135 were children.[91] In addition, 750 people sustained injuries that left them permanently disabled. Israeli incursions in 2008, ostensibly designed to stop the firing of homemade rockets, killed another 323 Palestinians, as compared with the deaths of seven Israelis, only two of whom were civilians. (All told, between 2001 and 2008, the rockets caused seven Israeli civilian deaths.)[92]

Despite Israeli press releases, it is hard not to conclude that these operations, along with the later 'Cast Lead' invasion which killed over 1,200 Gazans including over 300 children,[93] were designed as a massive exercise in the collective punishment of Gazans. These revealing releases stressed that 'it must . . . be recalled that the Palestinian people themselves elected a government led by Hamas, a murderous terrorist organization'. Some of Israel's policies, such as the deliberate creation of sonic booms low over Gaza by aircraft at night – causing particularly traumatic effects on children – were unmistakably designed to terrorize the population. Nevertheless, the tightening of the infrastructural siege and destruction as part of the 'Summer Rain' attacks proved far more devastating. Food imports were curtailed, a calamitous action in a city that relies heavily on food imports and food aid for survival.[94] Fuel and power supplies were also cut off. Bombing left bridges and roads impassable. Gaza's main electricity generating facilities were also bombed (Figure 8.5), resulting in the dwindling of pumped water and sewerage services.[95] Even prior to the ground invasion of Rafah, the Israeli air force bombed a power station, disrupting both the electricity supply and the water supply for large areas of Gaza. Finally, the parts needed to make crucial repairs to the devastated infrastructure were subject to sanctions.[96]

---

91   Imogen Kimber, 'What Happened to the Gaza Strip?', *IMEMC News*, 13 October 2006, available at www.imemc.org.

92   Milne, 'To Blame the Victims'.

93   Tim McGirk, 'Could Israelis Face War Crimes Charges Over Gaza?', *Time*, 23 January 2009.

94   At the time the UN was feeding 735,000 Gazans, more than half the territory's population.

95   Palestinian Medical Relief Society, 'Public Health Disaster in Gaza Strip: Urgent Appeal for Support to Avert Public Health Disaster in the Gaza Strip', 27 June 2007, available at www.pmrs.ps.

96   Association of Civil Rights in Israel, Letter to Israeli Minister of Defense, undated, available at www.phr.org.il.

8.5   The Gaza electricity generation facility destroyed
by an Israeli air strike on 26 June 2006.

In the aftermath of the 2006 attacks, Karen AbuZayd, United Nations Relief Works Agency (UNRWA) Commissioner-General in Gaza, stated that the strip was 'on the threshold of becoming the first territory to be intentionally reduced to a state of abject destitution, with the knowledge, acquiescence and – some would say – encouragement of the international community'.[97] She added that 'the decision to limit fuel and potentially electricity to the general population constitutes a form of collective punishment which directly contravenes international humanitarian law'.[98] Imogen Kimber of the International Middle East Media Center meanwhile called the attacks a 'sick madness', in which 'power cuts caused by the deliberate bombing of the electricity supply by the Israeli air force leave doctors with a near impossible task in attempting to treat the injuries and ill health'.[99]

As a result of Summer Rain, many of Gaza's health facilities ceased to function,

97   Koning-AbuZayd, 'This Brutal Siege of Gaza Can Only Breed Violence in Gaza City'.

98   Kirsten Zaat, 'Isolation of Gaza must end', Norwegian Refugee Council, AlertNet. org, 29 November 2007.

99   Kimber, 'What happened to the Gaza Strip?'.

as they had no generators (which, in any case, were often useless because of fuel shortages). The public health effects soon became clear. The World Health Organization (WHO) reported that 'the total number of cases of watery and bloody diarrhoea amongst refugees for the last week in June and the first week in July [2006] increased by 163 per cent and 140 per cent compared to the same period last year'.[100] Rates of anaemia amongst children skyrocketed,[101] and the already high rates of children's malnutrition and stunted growth increased yet further.[102]

Within a few months, the public health system of Gaza was on the verge of complete meltdown. Extremely ill patients were no longer able to travel to Israel for care. Dialysis patients started dying because of the lowered frequency of dialysis sessions, a state of affairs necessitated by electricity blackouts resulting from the bombing of a generating station.[103] At the end of March 2007, in perhaps the ultimate indication of the Gaza Strip's strangulation, so much raw sewage backed up that retaining banks collapsed and some neighbourhoods were flooded with human waste. Five people drowned in one such incident. Thus did Gazans become a people literally drowning in their own shit.[104]

And all this *before* Israel's much larger and even more brutal twenty-two-day assault on Gaza in December 2008 which centred on the now familiiar discursive trick of labelling the entire urban fabric of Gazan society a mere 'terrorist infrastructure' to be destroyed *in toto*. Whilst it is crucial here to stress the agency of Gazans and Palestinians in dealing with the strangulation and destruction of their modern means of survival, under such conditions their strategies to cope with and resist mass infrastructural warfare can surely have only marginal effects.

STATE CYBERWARFARE

According to William Church, former director of the now-defunct Center for Infrastructural Warfare Studies, the next frontier of state infrastructural warfare will involve the development of capacities to undertake co-ordinated

---

100   Canadian Health Professionals, 'Statement of Concern for the Public Health Situation in Gaza', open letter, 31 July 2006, available at electronicintifada.net.

101   Care International, 'Crisis in Gaza', available at www.care-international.org.

102   'Malnutrition Common for Gaza Kids', *Jerusalem Post*, 11 April 2007.

103   Canadian Health Professionals, 'Statement of Concern for the Public Health Situation in Gaza'.

104   Associated Press, 'Four Dead, Thousands Evacuated in Gaza Sewage Flood', *International Herald Tribune*, 27 March 2007.

cyberterror attacks.[105] 'The challenge here', he writes, 'is to break into the computer systems that control a country's infrastructure, with the result that the civilian infrastructure of a nation would be held hostage'.[106] Church states that, in 1999, NATO considered cutting Yugoslavia's Internet connections but that the idea was rejected. Now, however, a dedicated capacity to use software systems to attack opponent's critical infrastructures is rapidly being developed in consonance with the emerging US doctrine of 'integrated information operations' and infrastructural warfare – encompassing everything from dropping leaflets to disabling web sites, destroying electric plants, dropping electromagnetic pulse (EMP) bombs that destroy all electrical equipment within a wide area, and developing globe-spanning surveillance systems such as Echelon.

Deliberately manipulating computer systems to disable opponents' civilian infrastructure is widely seen as a powerful new weapon, an element of the wider US strategy of 'full spectrum dominance'.[107] The military calls it CNA, or computer network attack. Whilst the precise details of this emerging capability remain classified, some of its elements are becoming clear.

First, it is apparent that a major R&D program is underway at the Joint Warfare Analysis Center at Dahlgren, Virginia, focused on the computational and software systems that sustain the critical infrastructures of real or potential adversary nations. Major General Bruce Wright, deputy director of information operations at the centre, revealed in 2002 that 'a team at the Center can tell you not just how a power plant or rail system [within an adversary country] is built, but what exactly is involved in keeping that system up and making that system efficient'.[108]

Second, it is evident that during the 2003 invasion of Iraq, US forces undertook certain offensive, though as yet unspecified, CNAs.[109] Richard Myers, commander in chief of US Space Command, the body tasked with CNA, admitted in January 2000 that 'the US has already undertaken computer networked attacks on a case-by-case basis'.[110] Finally, the shift from blue-sky

---

105   Gregory Rattray, *Strategic Warfare in Cyberspace*, Cambridge, MA: MIT Press, 2001.

106   William Church, 'Information Warfare', *International Review of the Red Cross* 837, 2001, 205–16.

107   US Department of Defense, *Joint Vision 2020*, Washington, DC, 2000.

108   Cited in Church, 'Information Warfare', 205–16.

109   Daniel Onley, 'US Aims to Make War on Iraq's Networks', *Missouri Freedom of Information Center*, 2003, available at foi.missouri.edu.

110   Paul Stone, 'Space Command Plans for Computer Network Attack Mission', US Department of Defense, 14 January 2003, available at www.defenselink.mil.

research to explicit doctrine in this area is embodied in the National Security Presidential Directive 16 on computer network attacks, signed by George W. Bush in July 2003.

In 2007 it was announced that the USAF had established a unit named the Cyber Command, located at Barksdale Air Force Base, Louisiana. Cyber Command was tasked with both 'cybernetwork defense' for the US homeland and 'cyberstrike' (CNAs) against adversary societies.[111] In effect, this five-year programme sought to militarize the world's global electronic infrastructures; its stated aim is to 'gain access to, and control over, any and all networked computers, anywhere on Earth'.[112] Lani Kass – a former major in the Israel Defence Force, former head of the Air Force's Cyberspace Task Force, and now a special assistant to the Air Force chief of staff – reveals that these latest doctrines of cyberattack are seen as a mere continuation of the history of striking societal infrastructure with air power. 'If you're defending in cyber [space]', she writes, 'you're already too late. Cyber delivers on the original promise of air power. If you don't dominate in cyber, you cannot dominate in other domains'.[113] Whilst the Air Force Cyber Command initiative was suspended in August 2008, due to inter-service rivalry, similar capabilities are being developed within the US military, spread out between the Army, Navy and Air Force.

These efforts to bolster US cyberwar capabilities were significantly bolstered by developments elsewhere, including a series of massive 'denial-of-service attacks' against Estonia in the spring of 2007, apparently in revenge for the moving of a statue commemorating, the Soviet war dead in Talinn.[114] These attacks – at least partly the work of hackers linked to the Russian state, it seems – crippled the web sites of Estonia's prime minister and Estonian banks. US strategic planners are also closely monitoring the growing ability of China's armed forces to launch sophisticated and continuous cyberwarfare attacks as part of Chinese doctrine of 'unrestricted' or asymmetric warfare. Such risks led NATO leaders to say, in 2008, that cyberwarfare attacks are as serious a risk as a missile strike.[115]

The concern of US military planners is that the proliferation of cyberwarfare

---

111   Barry Rosenberg, 'Cyber Warriors: USAF Cyber Command Grapples with New Frontier Challenges', *C4ISR Journal*, 1 August 2007.

112   William J. Astore, 'Attention Geeks and Hackers: Uncle Sam's Cyber Force Wants You!', *Tom Dispatch*, 5 June 2008.

113   Ibid.

114   A 'denial-of-service attack' aims to disable a communications network with a deluge of useless information.

115   Bobbie Johnson, 'NATO Says Cyberwarfare Posses as Great a Threat as a Missile Attack', *Guardian*, 6 March 2008.

might jeopardize advanced and high-tech economies, which rely on extremely interdependent, dense, and computerized infrastructure systems – making them vulnerable to attack from a wide range of state and non-state organizations operating at a diversity of scales. If state or terrorist cyberattacks were to become common, argues Steven Metz of the US Strategic Studies Institute, 'the traditional advantage large and rich states hold in armed conflict might erode. Cyberattacks require much-less-expensive equipment than traditional ones. The necessary skills can be directly extrapolated from the civilian world . . . If it becomes possible to wage war using a handful of computers with Internet connections, a vast array of organizations may choose to join the fray'.[116] Metz even suggests that these transformations could lead to such scenarios as non-state groups attaining power equivalent to that of nation-states; commercial organizations waging cyberattacks on each other; and cyber 'gang wars' being played out on servers around the world rather than in the alleys of ghettos.[117]

In an interconnected world, however, where infrastructure systems tightly connect both with others in the same area and with other geographical areas, the effects of cyberwarfare attacks may be profoundly unpredictable. While attacking Iraq in 2003, for instance, it is now clear that the USAF's CNA staff contemplated the complete disablement of Iraq's financial systems. Apparently they rejected the idea, however, because the Iraqi network was so closely linked to the French network, which meant that an attack on Iraq, for example, might easily have led to the collapse of Europe's ATM machines.[118] 'We don't have many friends in Paris right now', quipped one US intelligence officer, commenting on this decision. 'There is no need to make more trouble if [then French president] Chirac won't be able to get any euros out of his ATM!'[119]

WAR IN A WEIRDLY PERVIOUS WORLD

This chapter has asserted the central place of everyday urban infrastructure within contemporary spaces of war and terror in the context of what computer scientist Philip Agre has called our 'weirdly pervious' world.[120] Neglected and taken for granted – as long as they continue to work – the everyday infrastructures sustaining urban life are increasingly at the heart of contemporary political

---

116 Steven Metz, 'The Next Twist of the RMA', *Parameters* 30: 3, 2000.
117 Ibid.
118 Cited in Colin Smith, 'US Wrestles with New Weapons', NewsMax.Com, 13 March 2003.
119 Ibid.
120 Agre, 'Imagining the Next War'.

violence and military doctrine. As we have seen, in our rapidly urbanizing world they have become the main targets for catastrophic terror attacks; they are increasingly central to the doctrines of advanced Western and non-Western militaries, and lie at the heart of contemporary means for projecting what can only be called state terror. There is also increasing evidence that nation-states are already actively engaging in low-level computer network attacks on a more or less continual basis – an activity that blurs the boundary separating warfare from economic competition.

Moreover, the sorts of on-the-ground realities that result from attacks on ordinary civilian infrastructure are far from the abstract niceties portrayed in military theory. Rather, the experiences of Iraq and Gaza forcefully remind us that the euphemisms of theory distract from the hard fact that targeting essential infrastructure in highly urbanized societies kills the weak, the old, and the ill just as surely as carpet bombing. The difference, of course, is that the deaths are displaced in time and space from the capricious gaze of mainstream media. So often, members of the media are seduced by the geek-speak of military press conferences about 'effects based operations', the minimization of 'collateral damage', 'non-lethal weapons', the targeting of 'terrorist infrastructure', or the application of 'psychological pressure' on adversary régimes. In this context, I would like to close this chapter by stressing three crucial points.

NEW NOTIONS OF WAR

> How civilizing can war indeed be, if it kills thousands of people and destroys the very infrastructure of civilization?[121]

The first point to stress is that strategies of forced demodernization and cyberattack require us to reconsider prevailing notions of war. Contemporary intersections of political violence and infrastructure blur traditional binaries of war and peace, the local and the global, the civil sphere and the military sphere, the inside and the outside of nation-states. As everyday urban infrastructures fall victim to state (and non-state) violence, potentially boundless, continuous landscapes of conflict, risk, and unpredictable – even undetectable – attack are emerging. Many contemporary military theories and doctrines now hold that, in Agre's words, 'war, in this sense, is everywhere and everything. It is large and small. It has no boundaries in time and space. Life itself is war.'[122]

---

121   Andreas Behnke, 'The Re-enchantment of War in Popular Culture', *Millennium: Journal of International Studies* 34: 3, 2006, 937.
122   Agre, 'Imagining the Next War'.

Such an unrestricted notion of warfare is finding favour outside the terrorist and insurgent groups, and the US and Israeli militaries, that have been our main focus here. The Chinese state, for example, is investing heavily in developing doctrine and capabilities in infrastructural warfare. A 1999 People's Liberation Army publication contends, 'There is reason for us to maintain that the [1997] financial attacks by George Soros on East Asia, the [1998] terrorist attack on the [Kenyan] US embassy by Osama bin Laden, the [1995] gas attack on the Tokyo subway by the disciples of Aum Shinri Kyo, and the havoc wreaked by the likes of Morris Jnr. [a computer hacker] on the Internet, in which the degree of destruction is by no means second to that of war, represent semi-warfare, quasi-warfare, and sub-warfare'. Such examples represent 'the embryonic form of another kind of war'. War, it goes on to say, 'has . . . re-invaded human society in a more complex, more extensive, more concealed, and more subtle manner'.[123]

Such notions of war as being literally unleashed from the boundaries of time and space – what Paul James has termed 'metawar'[124] – push a two-pronged doctrine to the centre of US geopolitical strategy in particular. On the one hand, as we saw in Chapter 4, the US emphasizes the defence of both the homeland's everyday urban infrastructures and the key strategic connections to the other parts of the world that sustain global capitalism.[125] On the other hand, the US strives to develop the capability to systematically degrade, or at least control from afar, the infrastructural connectivity, modernity, and geopolitical potential of the supposed enemy. Such a strategy is, Agre argues, 'what defense intellectuals call infrastructural war, and is war in the most general possible sense; war that reaches into the tiniest details of daily life, reengineering the most basic arrangements of travel and communications in a time when everyday life, in a mobile and interconnected society, is increasingly organised around these very arrangements'.[126]

When the object of political violence is to use the vulnerable, crucial urban infrastructure networks to project spectacle, terror, and coercion, another curious development emerges. Often, these strategies are hidden. Increasingly, they blur with the 'normal' world, in which systems break down, services stall, and infrastructures require continual repair. It is less and less clear, in other words, where accidental failures stop and deliberately induced failures begin. When a

123   Qiao Liang and Wang Xiangsui, *Unrestricted Warfare*, Panama: Pan American Publishing, 2002, 2.

124   Paul James, 'The Age of Meta-War', *Arena Magazine* 64, 2003, 4–8.

125   See Wood and Coaffee, 'Security is Coming Home'.

126   Phil Agre, 'Imagining the Next War'.

subway, water, Internet or electricity system fails in an advanced industrial city, speculation often runs rampant that it is the doing of far-off, shadowy terrorists lurking within the global infrastructure networks infrastructure, rather than a prosaic technical malfunction or human error. 'Networked technology', writes James Der Derian, thus 'provides new global actors the means to traverse political, economic, religious, and cultural boundaries'. This new accessibility transforms 'not only how war is fought and peace is made, but mak[es] it ever more difficult to maintain the very distinction of not only accidental, incidental, and intentional acts but war and peace itself'.[127]

The problem with these new imaginaries of war, of course – as has been made clear in earlier chapters of this book – is that they encourage a deepening militarization of all aspects of contemporary urban societies. Questions of security come home with a vengeance; elements of militarization further pervade the everyday practices, architectures and politics of urban life. In the process, the politics of security become less and less concerned with territorial, state-versus-state conflicts that result in formalized battles, and focus instead 'on the civic, urban, domestic and personal realms' within a boundless universe of unending risk.[128] War in this broadest sense, suggests Phil Agre, becomes a continuous, distanciated event, without geographical limits, that is replayed live, 24/7, on TV and the Internet. [129]

Certainly, many political and military officials currently perpetuate a discourse of endless war as part of the construction and perpetuation of post-9/11 states of emergency.[130] By continually invoking malign, unmodern lurking Others, ready to plunge advanced industrial society into pre-modern immobility at the flick of a keystroke, they seek to legitimize their own much more devastating efforts to demodernize entire populations in the poor cities of the majority world, in the name of 'minimizing collateral damage', shifting to 'non-lethal' or 'non-kinetic' weapons, or targeting 'terrorist infrastructure'.

In the most powerful of ironies, the strategy of 'switching cities off' makes a mockery of the broader neoconservative ideology of permanent war. It casts pre-emptive military violence as a means to help *connect* the societies of the Middle East and the developing world to the fruits of a US-led neoliberal capitalism, through the agency of continuous imperial war. As part of his

---

127 James Der Derian, 'Network Pathologies', *InfoTechWarPeace*, 2003, available at www.watsoninstitute.org/infopeace/911.

128 Murakami Wood and Coaffee, 'Security is Coming Home', 503–517.

129 Agre, 'Imagining the next war: Infrastructural warfare and the conditions of democracy'.

130 See Agamben, 'Security and Terror', 1–2.

bellicose call for the 2003 US invasion of Iraq, for example, Thomas Barnett,[131] the neocon geopolitical theorist we encounterd in Chapter 2, declared that he 'believe[s] the new security paradigm that shapes this age [is] *Disconnectedness defines danger*'.[132] 'Show me where globalization is thick with network connectivity, financial transactions, liberal media flows, and collective security', Barnett wrote, 'and I will show you regions featuring stable governments, rising standards of living, and more deaths by suicide than murder'. To Barnett, the role of imperial, expeditionary, permanent war was to forcibly connect societies beyond a Manichaean geographical line separating the supposed 'functioning core' of neoliberal capitalist states and the 'non-integrating gap' of central American, African, Middle Eastern, Central Asian and South-East Asian states which have supposedly remained disconnected from the global neoliberal economy. How ironic, then, that the doctrine which underlies contemporary US warfare emphasizes the devastation of the very architectures and infrastructures that make connection to the world possible.[133]

Interestingly, as the effects of the devastation visited upon the infrastructures of purported adversaries have begun to filter home to the US, there has been a shift in emphasis from complete physical devastation to more temporary and reversible disruption. In 2003, for example, some care was taken not to annihilate Iraq's entire electrical systems, as had been done in 1991 – not out of humanitarian concern for the survival of urbanites but rather to smooth the way for the installation of client régimes. Certainly, intact infrastructures greatly facilitate the imposition of what Naomi Klein calls the 'shock doctrine', now so central to neoliberal capitalism: a political economy which preys on and consumes geographies, resources and countries in the aftermath of natural or manufactured disasters.[134]

In such circumstances, of course, resilient infrastructures are essential. They are the main foci of the imposition of wholesale neoliberal privatization, as financialized capital appropriates the sunken capital of preyed-upon spaces and nations. They are also fundamental to a swift transition to the predatory resource exploitation associated with a key tenet of the new imperialism: capital accumulation through dispossession.[135] As the case of post-2003 Iraq demonstrates, this process is generally a massive engine of instability and violence, never a simple switch-over. Resistances, insurgencies, criminal gangs,

---

131 See Chapter 2.
132 Thomas Barnett, 'The Pentagon's New Map'.
133 Ibid.
134 Klein, *Shock Doctrine*.
135 See Harvey, *The New Imperialism*.

and corrupt political groups of various sorts tend to spring up. Soon, within the new context, they themselves concentrate on the targeting or appropriation of urban infrastructure and the fruits of resource exploitation.

EVERYTHING IS NOT WAR

My second point is that the goal of securitizing urban societies against the endless, sourceless, boundless threat of infrastructural war risks becoming such an overpowering obsession that it is used as a basis for re-engineering the common systems that are now exposed to threat. Two concerns loom particularly large.

First, the very construction of boundless threats and limitless war might legitimize the wholesale hollowing-out, or even the eradication, of democratic societies. 'The military intellectuals' new concept of war is flawed because it starts from the military and simply follows the logic of interconnection until the military domain encloses everything else', warns Philip Agre.[136] In this scenario, everything is viewed as an element of warfare. Indeed, nothing remains outside the boundless war. To accept such a view is to provide ripe conditions for profoundly anti-democratic tendencies, as right and far-right political coalitions demand the suspension of due process, legal norms, and democratic rights while, at the same time, scapegoating a wide range of threats which lurk, invisibly and ubiquitously, within the technical and urban interstices of everyday life.

A dominant characteristic of the War on Terror, certainly, has been its endless portrayal of the everyday sites, spaces and systems of the city as domains where Others might jump out at any time, raising existential threats to cities and civilizations 'from within'. In portraying the risks of terrorism both as acts of war and as existential societal threats, rather than as international crimes that pose massive risks to public safety, it is easy to justify unending global war, extended imperialism, racialized state violence, pre-emptive incarceration, authoritarian legislation and the radical suspension of legal and juridical norms. All these elements of securocratic war are consistent with recent trends, in societies such as the US and UK, towards what some commentators regard as 'soft' or 'incipient' fascism.

Given such a context, state responses which extend the securitization of everyday life serve also to extend feelings of vague insecurity, potentially establishing a self-perpetuating circle. Always the focus is on what *might* be;

---

136   Agre, 'Imagining the Next War'.

on the infinite possibilities of the *next* terrorist appropriation of infrastructure; on the need for yet *more* pre-emptive or anticipatory surveillance systems. 'As the state machine acts stealthily to prevent things happening', Richard Sennett writes, 'as its technologies become built into the fabric of everyday business practice, there can be no defining moment when an ordinary citizen could declare, "now I am more secure"'.[137]

This impossibility is compounded by the fact that it is basically futile to try to turn the infrastructures of everyday life – which, by definition, attain usefulness only through their openness – into truly secure systems which cannot be attacked or appropriated by terrorists. It would be much more effective in the long run, as sociologist Langdon Winner argues, to work towards designing and developing infrastructures 'that are loosely coupled and forgiving, structured in ways that make disruptions easily borne, quickly repaired'.[138] Urban planner Matt Hidek points out, however, that centralized command-and-control military paradigms have been creeping into the management of US civil infrastructures, owing to the efforts of the Department of Homeland Security and the new US Northern Command, or NORTHCOM.[139]

The danger here, of course, is the chipping away of democratic rights and liberties, and the progressive expansion towards globe-spanning surveillance, which, as discussed in Chapter 4, in their attempt to parallel global circulations, become as boundless as the purported threat. These trends are driven by the construction of a series of (real or chimeric) infrastructural terror threats, fanned by the flames of sensationalist, voyeuristic, and jingoistic media. Fundamentally, 'war in the new sense – war with no beginning or end, no front or rear, and no distinction between military and civilian – is incompatible with democracy', writes Phil Agre.[140]

Ultimately, then, ideas of security must be radically re-thought so that the human, social and bodily security of subjects within cities, infrastructural systems, biospheres and social worlds is the central object of governance. This human-centred vision of security must be counterposed to notions of national security based on permanent war and hypermilitarization, on the retreat into militarized enclaves, and on the application of military paradigms to all avenues of life and governance. Agre is right to argue that 'the important thing is to

---

137   Richard Sennett, 'The Age of Anxiety', *Guardian*, 23 October 2004.
138   Langdon Winner, 'Technology, Trust and Terror', in *Shaping Technologies: The Sarai Reader*, ed., Sarai Collective, Delhi: CSDS, 2003, available at www.sarai.net.
139   Matt Hidek, 'Networked Security in the City: A Call to Action for Planners', *Progressive Planner*, Fall 2007, available at www.plannersnetwork.org.
140   Agre, 'Imagining the Next War'.

draw a distinction between military action, as the exercise within a framework of international law of the power of a legitimate democratic state, and war, as the imposition of a total social order that is the antithesis of democracy, and that, in the current technological conditions of war, has no end in sight'.[141]

BARING LIFE

My final point is that efforts by state militaries to systematically destroy the essential infrastructures of adversary urban societies require much discursive work. Indeed, such work is just as important as efforts to 'put steel on the target', as Captain John Bellflower of the US Army put it.[142] Most often, of course, water, sewerage, electricity, transport, and communications infrastructures are targeted as a putative means of destroying the infrastructure of terrorism. Both Israel and the US have long legitimized their systematic demodernization of whole societies in this way, while urban dwellers in Palestine, Lebanon and Iraq, among others, have suffered the spiral of consequences: death, disease, poverty and economic collapse.

Yet terrorists' attacks against Western or Israeli cities do not actually rely on basic modern services in Iraqi, Palestinian or Lebanese cities in order to launch their attacks. Rather, they depend on Western bus systems, airline networks, tube and subway trains, mobile phones, finance and Internet infrastructures, and so on. The means through which rich countries launch their wars against so-called terrorist infrastructures within poor countries thus serves mainly to radicalize and immiserate entire urban societies, dramatically adding to the pool of recruits willing to launch or support further terrorist attacks against the West. 'The phrases "defeating terrorist states" and "destroying the infrastructures of terrorism"', writes Tamim Ansary, in practice 'turn out to mean, simply, "defeating states" and "destroying infrastructure"'.[143]

At its heart, then, the systematic demodernization of whole societies in the name of 'fighting terror' involves a dark, ironic, and self-fulfilling prophecy. As Derek Gregory[144] has argued, drawing on the ideas of Giorgio Agamben, the demodernization of entire Middle Eastern cities and societies, whether through Israeli wars against Lebanon and the Palestinians or through the US War on Terror, is fuelled by a similar Orientalist discourse. It revivifies well-established

---

141   Ibid.
142   John W. Bellflow, 'The Indirect Approach', *Armed Forces Journal*, January 2007.
143   Tamim Ansary, 'A War Won't End Terrorism', *San Francisco Chronicle*, 19 October 2002.
144   Gregory, *The Colonial Present*.

tropes and casts out ordinary civilians and their cities – Kabul, Baghdad, Nablus, Gaza – 'so that they are placed beyond the privileges and protections of the law so that their lives (and deaths) [are] rendered of no account'.[145] Thus, beyond the increasingly fortified homeland, 'sovereignty works by *abandoning* subjects, reducing them to bare life'.[146]

As a consequence, in the forcible creation of a chaotic urban hell – through switching off cities and subjecting them to demodernization – state violence, perversely, produces the very thing depicted by the Orientalists: a chaotic and disconnected urban world 'outside of the modern, figuratively as well as physically'.[147] Because Western culture has long been predicated on the anti-modern figure of the Oriental, Western warfare can easily be modeled as the means to demodernize Orientalized cities and societies – all in the name of defending the homeland's infrastructures. The result is another self-perpetuating cycle, since, not surprisingly, the anger and despair of those living in switched-off cities can readily be exploited and radicalized, turning into a willingness to launch terroristic violence against the perpetrators of their plight.

---

145 Derek Gregory, 'Defiled Cities', *Singapore Journal of Tropical Geography* 24: 3, 2003, 311.
146 Bülent Diken and Carsten Laustsen, 'Camping as a contemporary strategy: From refugee camps to gated communities', *AMID Working Paper Series no.* 32, Aalborg: Aalborg University. 2002.
147 Gregory, 'Defiled Cities', 313.

CHAPTER NINE

Car Wars

WHERE FOREIGN POLICY MEETS THE ROAD

The United States' response to the events of 9/11 have configured the automobile as a new site for the conduct of warfare.[1]

Few aspects of everyday urban life so fully exemplify the deep connections between security and militarism in wealthy, technologically advanced cities and in developing cities than the ubiquitous automobile and its use. The link between the global geopolitics of oil and US urban life are particularly acute; suburban and exurban lifestyles generate an unrivalled dependence on the automobile – a dependence that continues to grow as cities sprawl into the distant countryside. Indeed, transportation accounts for fully two-thirds of US petroleum use, and 40 per cent of that is by automobiles.[2] Given the rapid global increase of automobilization, air travel, shipping and logistics, and the wide-ranging export and imitation of extravagant US models of urbanism and mobility, it has been estimated that by 2020, transportation will account for fully 57 per cent of global petroleum demand.[3]

The construction of US society as the archetypal hyper-automobilized society since before the Second World War has been fuelled – literally – by cheap and plentiful oil supplies. These supplies have been sustained over the course of more than five decades by US military intervention combined with political support for a range of dubious and authoritarian proxy regimes in the Middle East, notably in Saudi Arabia. The brutality of the historical record is inescapable. 'Right from the start', write the Retort collective, 'commercial oil extraction has been accompanied by ruthless and undistinguished imperial violence, by repeated warfare and genocide, and by a cynical lawlessness characteristic of the corporate frontier.'[4] The history of imperial acquisitiveness

---

1 Jeremy Packer, 'Automobility and the Driving Force of Warfare: From Public Safety to National Security' in *Architectures of Fear*, Barcelona: Centre for Contemporary Culture, 107.

2 David Campbell, 'The Biopolitics of Security: Oil, Empire, and the Sports Utility Vehicle', *American Quarterly* 57: 3, 2005, 952.

3 National Energy Information Center, 'Transportation Energy Use', *International Energy Outlook*, 2001, available www.eia.doe.gov, 148.

4 Boal, Clark, Matthews, and Watts, *Afflicted Powers*, 55.

regarding oil is a bloody tale, too rarely told, of militarized dispossession and primitive capital accumulation.[5]

Recent chapters in this ongoing saga of oil imperialism have involved the design of a system producing what the Retort group calls 'organized scarcity'.[6] This strategy balances the need to keep oil prices low enough for the continued growth of highly automobilized capitalist societies with the need to keep them high enough for the profitability of the oil cartels and OPEC (Organization of Petroleum Exporting Countries) nations, especially 'high absorbers' such as Nigeria and Venezuela.[7] This system, now reeling from the oil surges and financial collapses of 2006–9, worked in the 1990s to allow US (as well as many other) consumers to move towards ever larger vehicles and to drive them over ever larger distances within ever more dispersed cities and personal geographies. Between 1990 and 2001, for example, the number of miles travelled on American shopping trips rose by 40 per cent.[8] By 2003 the average American was spending 450 hours a year behind the wheel.[9]

The vehicular icon dominating the interface between all these relations in recent years has been the sports utility vehicle, or SUV. From a base of only 7 per cent of the US car market in 1997, SUVs started to outsell conventional automobiles in the US by 2002.[10] 'In 2003, SUV or "light truck" sales in the US hit an all-time high of 8,865,894 pickups, vans, and SUVs. That worked out to 53.2 per cent of all new-vehicle sales, another all-time high. In the first month of 2004, the 70 or more SUV models' share of the market grew even more, to 54.6 per cent' of the total market, we learn from an Air War College publication.[11]

SUV sales declined rapidly in 2007–8 as a result of the US credit crunch and the hike in oil prices. As a result, many car-makers, accustomed to the SUV's profitability, were now struggling to survive. But the skyrocketing, and hugely profitable, US SUV sales, which exploited massive loop-holes in both emissions regulation and taxation, provides a dramatic parallel to the increasingly

---

5 Ibid., 76.

6 Ibid., 60.

7 'High absorbers' are OPEC members such as Iran, Iraq, Indonesia, Algeria, Venezuela, and Nigeria, who have relatively high populations, low per-capital incomes, and other resources who have no problem expending their vast oil incomes on consumption and investment. Ibid., 60.

8 Julian Borger, 'Half of Global Car Exhaust Produced by US Vehicles', *Guardian*, 29 June 2006.

9 'Big, Not Clever', *Guardian*, 22 April 2003.

10 Andrew Garnar, 'Portable Civilizations and Urban Assault Vehicles', *Techné* 5: 2, 2000.

11 John M. Amidon, *America's Strategic Imperative: A National Energy Policy Manhattan Project*, US Air Force Air War College, Air University, 25 February 2005, available at research.au.af.mil, 35.

aggressive US military incursions in the Persian Gulf between 1991 and 2010. Exemplifying the links between US and other western cities and colonial frontiers, the design and marketing of SUVs grew increasingly militarized as the US military's imperial wars proliferated. 'With names like Tracker, Equinox, Freestyle, Escape, Defender, Trail Blazer, Navigator, Pathfinder, and Warrior', suggests David Campbell, 'SUVs populate the crowded urban routes of daily life with representations of the militarized frontier'.[12] And even though sales of SUVs are currently declining, these vehicles embody a broader shift in the material culture of automobile marketing and use. Steve Macek points out that 'automobile manufacturers – who for decades have marketed cars as a source of fun and youthfulness, or as symbols of technological progress and modernity – have increasingly now turned to promises of "safety", "security", and protection for the imperiled urban "family" as selling points'.[13]

The remarkable popularity of explicitly militarized SUVs between the early 1990s and 2007–8 managed to worsen US fuel-economy levels; exacerbate US oil dependence at a time of decreasing supply levels; provoke a major backlash in US cities because of their perceived embodiment of selfish, anti-urban and aggressively hyperindividualistic values; and exaggerate the already high levels of greenhouse gas emissions caused by US auto use.

By 2006 it was clear that 'the fuel economy of US vehicles has been declining since 1988, which means the CO_2 emissions have been increasing, associated with a shift to large [SUV] trucks'.[14] Also by 2006, and largely as a result of the US SUV boom, the US – with about 5 per cent of the world's population – was estimated to be using about 25 per cent of the world's oil supply (twenty-one million barrels per day out of eighty-four million, up from slightly more than seventeen million as the OPEC oil crisis hit home in 1973).[15] In addition, Americans were driving almost a third of the world's cars (202 million of the 683 million cars). With the average US vehicle getting less than twenty miles per gallon – a twenty-year low[16] – and producing, on average, 15 per cent more CO_2 than vehicles elsewhere in the world, fully half of the planet's car exhaust fumes were thus coming from US vehicles.[17] SUVs became faster and heavier,

12   Campbell, 'The Biopolitics of Security', 958.

13   Macek, *Urban Nightmares*, 273.

14   Quoted in Borger, 'Half of Global Car Exhaust Produced by US Vehicles'.

15   Thomas Kraemer, *Addicted To Oil: Strategic Implications Of American Oil Policy*, US Army Strategic Studies Institute, May 2006, 2.

16   National Energy Information Center, 'Transportation Energy Use', *International Energy Outlook*, 148.

17   Borger, 'Half of Global Car Exhaust Produced by US Vehicles'.

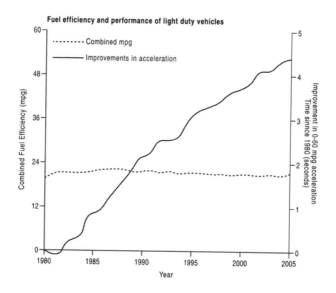

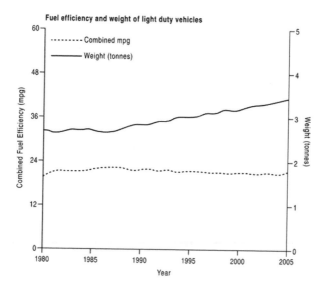

9.1 US automobiles 1980–2005: Dramatic increases in weight
and acceleration, without improvement in fuel efficiency.

and their booming sales meant that US auto-makers had thus completely failed to take advantage of massive contemporary technological advances to improve fuel efficiency (Figure 9.1).

The US possesses less than 3 per cent of the world's proven oil reserves.[18] At the same time, a significant proportion of US oil imports have derived from volatile regions such as the Middle East, regions where the volatility relates directly to the global geopolitics of oil exploitation. Thus the massive growth of SUV sales, creating ever more reliance on imported oil imports, had a very direct impact on the global geographies of war, (in)security, and imperial power. Indeed, one of the ironies of the War on Terror has been that, throughout it, the US has purchased billions of dollars of oil from nations that are sponsors of, or allied with, radical Islamists who foment hatred of America.[19] David Campbell points out that, perversely, 'as the country was preparing to go to war with Iraq, the United States was importing half of all Iraqi exports (which satisfied only 8 per cent of America's needs), even though this indirectly funded the regime of Saddam Hussein'.[20]

Given that a modest increase of about 2.7 miles per gallon in the average fuel efficiency of US vehicles would completely remove the need for the 15–20 per cent of US oil supplies which come from the Middle East,[21] one could contend, as has George Monbiot, that 'arguably, the war with Iraq was a war for 4x4s'.[22] Hence, in Todd Gitlin's memorable phrase, the SUV phenomenon is perhaps best undertood as 'the place where foreign policy meets the road'.[23]

CAPSULES FOR THE URBAN BORDERLANDS

> Why should the rest of the world be held hostage by the energy budget of the three-car American suburban home?[24]

Disentangling the multiple Foucauldian boomerangs associated with the SUV within the framework of the new urban militarism – our task here – involves tracing the connections which fuse contemporary automobility with broader

---

18   National Commission on Energy Policy, *Oil Shockwave: Oil Crisis Executive Simulation*, Washington: National Commission on Energy Policy, 2005, available at www. secureenergy.org.

19   Philip K. Verleger, Jr. *US Energy Policy: In Conflict with the War on Terrorism*, Institute for International Economics, January 2004, 1, available at www.pkverlegerllc.com; Kraemer, *Addicted To Oil*, 13.

20   Campbell, 'The Biopolitics of Security', 952.

21   Paul Salopek, 'A Tank of Gas, a World of Trouble', *Chicago Tribune*, 29 July 2006.

22   George Monbiot, 'Driving into the Abyss', *Guardian*, 6 July 2004.

23   Quoted in Campbell, 'The Biopolitics of Security'.

24   Ross, 'Duct Tape Nation', 2.

circuits of popular culture, geopolitical power, military strategy, energy (in) security, resource wars, and deeply militarized discourses and technologies. Clearly, the manufacture, marketing, celebration and (mostly American) use of SUVs mesh with the practice of state warfare and violence. This situation goes way beyond the defence of sovereignty. Instead, its focus is the sustenance and securitization of willfully profligate styles of urban life, and the dominant processes of capital accumulation associated with them[25] – all of which, as we shall see, become coded and celebrated as patriotic.

'It is this centering of the life of the population rather than the safety of the sovereign or the security of territory', writes David Campbell, 'that is the hallmark of biopolitical power and that distinguishes it from sovereign power'.[26] In oil wars, as in many other spheres of contemporary state activity, state violence – organized to defend the oil-dependent life of Western populations – operates in legal grey zones. In the name of this Western manner of life, norms of state sovereignty are often suspended, with the result that 'the geopolitical pursuit of energy security is likely to produce new and intensive forms of insecurity for those in the new resource zones'.[27] Oil wars, and the resultant deaths, should thus be understood in terms of Agamben's notion of 'bare life' – life that can be extinguished with sovereign impunity.

Urban automobile cultures tend to materialize and territorialize the separation between the domestic city, situated within the home space of the Western nation, and the borderlands, cursed with the ongoing resource wars which surround oil exploitation. Such borderlands, Campbell proposes, 'are conventionally understood as distant, wild places of insecurity where foreign intervention will be necessary to ensure domestic interests are secured'. Far from enriching local populations, the dominant forms of organizing exploitation and pipelines further marginalize impoverished indigenous communities, ratcheting up insecurity and violence in the process. The destiny of such people and places, Campbell continues, is thus violently 'subsumed by the privilege accorded a resource (oil) that is central to the American way of life, the security of which is regarded as a fundamental strategic issue'.[28]

The convenient separation between the home urban spaces of automobile use and the colonial frontiers of oil exploitation are illusory, however. Complex networks of technology, social practices of driving and consumption, and

25 Shimshon Bichler and Jonathan Nitzan, 'Dominant Capital and the New Wars', *Journal Of World-Systems Research* 10: 2, 2004, 255–327.
26 Campbell, 'The Biopolitics of Security', 945.
27 Ibid.
28 Ibid.

BECAUSE *driving* ISN'T ALWAYS
A WALK IN THE PARK.

The harshest roads aren't necessarily located out in the boonies. And they're not
tamed by cowboys named Hoss and Jake. But by people named Tony and Susan on the way
home from the firm. And when the road resembles craters on the moon,
the Blazer® Driver Control System makes the trip a lot easier and more comfortable.
Just because the road is paved doesn't mean it's smooth.

CHEVY BLAZER
LIKE A ROCK

9.2   A typical SUV advert, depicting a dark, threatening urban
exterior surrounding the cocoon of speed, power and safety.

the politics of resources and identity formation give rise to intimate bonds
between the domains of home and frontier. These are forged through violence;
war; attempted control; calculation and financialization; and the destabilizing,
profoundly unpredictable, and global effects of petroleum pollution, climate
change, biofuels production, and the insecurities created by amalgams of these
processes. War has had such special prominence in constructing the political
order of liberal Western societies because it underlines, as Michael Hardt and
Antonio Negri suggest, that the biopolitics of the globe 'operates as a strategic

game in which the principle of war is assimilated into the very weft and warp of the socio-economic and cultural networks of biopolitical relations'.[29]

Of course, SUVs also materialize another, much more obvious, separation of 'inside' and 'outside': that between the cocooned, air-conditioned, high-tech interior of the vehicle itself, and the city that lies beyond the 'extrahard exoskeleton' of the SUV body, to use Daniel Miller's term[30]. As Lieven De Cauter has shown, SUVs can be understood as mobile 'capsular' technologies, designed to offer autonomous neoliberal subjects the fantasy of complete individual control and total libertarian secession from the social and public spaces of city life – spaces which, because they exist beyond the cocoon of the interior, become residualized.[31]

Along with the other proliferating capsular spaces and technologies in contemporary cities – gated communities, private condominiums, malls, theme parks, airports, privatized public spaces and plazas – SUVs are, De Cauter argues, inherently suburbanized 'inner-directed spaces, closed in on themselves, which are supposed to represent security, shelter and hygiene (without being really safe)'.[32] Radically ignoring their wider surroundings, they attain usefulness only by relying on huge and complex networks of highways, road facilities, and communications and GPS systems, becoming, in the process what De Cauter calls 'capsules on networks'.[33]

In 'capsular civilizations' like ours, he suggests, the contrast between the interior of a capsule, such as an SUV, and the residualized urban outside tends to grow (Figure 9.2). 'The grimmer and uglier reality on the outside becomes', he writes, 'the more hyper-reality will dominate the inside of the capsular civilization'.[34] Thus, as Shane Gunster has argued, the 'incessant celebrations of a luxurious [SUV] interior defended by an armored shell champion the mobile and aggressive privatization of public space in which those with wealth and resources can use and enjoy the commons while maintaining complete control over their own personal environment'.[35]

29   Michael Hardt and Antonio Negri, *Empire*, Cambridge, MA: Harvard University Press, 2000, 22.

30   Daniel Miller, 'Forward: Getting Behind the Wheel', in Elaine Cardenas and Ellen Gorman, eds, *The Hummer: Myths of Consumer Culture*, Lanham, MD: Lexington Books, 2007, vii–x, ix.

31   Lieven De Cauter, *The Capsular Civilization: On the City in the Age of Fear*, Rotterdam: Nai Publishers, 2004.

32   Ibid., 81.

33   Ibid.

34   Ibid., 83.

35   Shane Gunster, '"You Belong Outside": Advertising, Nature, and the SUV', *Ethics & The Environment* 9: 2, 2004, 4–32.

Similarly, Gunster points out that the cycles of withdrawal, capsularization and militarization which surround the proliferation of SUVs, gated communities, and other hardened urban spaces tend to be self-perpetuating. The very process of removal and fortressing feeds the fear of the ever-more-distant central city. 'As the fear of crime, however irrational, has risen in lockstep with the intensification of violence in the mass media', he writes, 'the SUV offers itself as an ideal technology for armoring the self against the perceived dangers that lurk outside'.[36] As an icon of neoliberal subjecthood, the SUV helps reconfigure urban life as an interlinked series of mobile built capsules, withdrawn from the wider social environment, whilst selective connectivity is maintained through new control and surveillance technologies.[37]

SUV users' perceptions of increased security are both paradoxical and illusory, however. For such vehicles merely promote increased oil consumption and dependence, which will only deepen current and future crises and insecurities.[38] With suburbanization and sprawl – a project so critical to the mass adoption of SUVs – now threatened by oil depletion, the paradox is pronounced indeed. One influential critic of urban sprawl, Jim Kunstler, is convinced that 'the grand meta-cycle of the suburban project as a whole', within which SUVs now play such a major role, is 'at the end of the cycle'. To him, 'the remaining things under construction are the last twitchings of a dying organism' – a process accelerated by the US recession, brought on by a credit crunch generated largely by criminally lax lending of largely fictitious capital to fuel yet another massive round of sprawl and exurbanization.[39] Kunstler argues that US suburban history, climaxing in mass SUV ownership and hypersprawl, must be interpreted through the lens of oil geopolitics:

> The suburban expansion has been based entirely on cheap-and-abundant supplies of oil. It was not an accident that the suburban project faltered briefly in the 1970s, when America's oil production entered its long decline, OPEC seized the moment, and oil prices shot up. Notice that the final suburban blowout occurred after 1990, when the North Sea and Prudhoe Bay oil strikes came into full production . . . That ushered in the climactic phase of suburbia, as represented by things like the standard 4000-square-foot Toll Brother's McMansion and the heyday of the super-gigantic SUV to go with it.[40]

---

36 Ibid., 15.
37 De Cauter, *The Capsular Civilization*.
38 Campbell, 'The Biopolitics of Security', 943.
39 Jim Kunstler, 'Clusterfuck Nation', 25 June 2007, available at jameshowardkunstler.typepad.com/clusterfuck_nation.
40 Ibid.

THE $230 FILL-UP

As John Amidon, a lieutenant colonel with the USAF's Air University, puts it, 'imported oil dependence has become the proverbial elephant in the [US] foreign policy living-room: an over-riding strategic consideration in a multitude of issues'. Since 2001, he cautions, US energy policy has both overestimated available supply and dramatically underestimated the social and political instability caused by US attempts to manage 'the major oil producing countries diplomatically and militarily'. Amidon lambasts the Bush administration in particular for its dramatical understatement of the military costs associated with preservation of access to oil.[41]

Amidon estimates that, with US domestic reserves dwindling fast – despite the controversial decision by the Bush administration to drill in the wildlife reserves of northern Alaska, and the 2008 Republican vice presidential candidate Sarah Palin having made much political capital out of her similar promise – by 2025, fully two-thirds of all US oil supplies will need to come from overseas. More specifically, they would need to come from highly unstable and conflict-ridden areas of the Middle East, Africa and South America. With the world's existing oil supplies likely to be largely extinguished within twenty-two to thirty years, and with the massive growth in consumption underway in India and China, a militarized scramble to secure the remaining reserves looks increasingly likely (Figure 9.3).

The US Department of Energy, which has projected global oil supply and demand up to 2025, suggests that world oil demand will continue to rise at a rate of about 2 per cent per year, and that much of the projected growth will centre on emerging economies like China and India, with energy use in these regions more than doubling by 2025.[42] A major driver of this doubling will be the rapid growth of automobile use in India and China. By 2001 the world had half a billion cars; by 2030 it will likely have more than one billion.[43]

Regarding the United States, the US Army's Strategic Studies Institute predicts that oil imports from the Middle East will rise by 268 per cent, from 2.3 million barrels a day in 2002 to 5.8 million in 2025. Total oil imports for the same period are likely to rise from 11.3 million to 21.1 million barrels a day within an overall US consumption growth of 67 per cent (from 19.7 million to 32.9 million barrels a day).[44] Of this projected growth, two-thirds will occur within the transportation sector.

---

41 Amidon, *America's Strategic Imperative.*
42 Kraemer, *Addicted To Oil*, 8.
43 Jonathon Bell, ed., *Carchitecture: When the Car and the City Collide*, Basel: Birkhäuser, 2001.
44 Kraemer, *Addicted To Oil.*

	2002		2025	
	U.S.A.	**Emerging Asia** (primarily China, India, S. Korea)	**U.S.A.**	**Emerging Asia** (primarily China, India, S. Korea)
Middle East Imports (million barrels per day)	2.3	4.1	5.8	15.1
Total Imports (million barrels per day)	11.3	11.0	21.1	27.4
Total Consumption (million barrels per day)	19.7	15.1	32.9	33.6

Source: U.S. Department of Energy (Energy Information Agency)

9.3   US and 'Emerging Asian' (Chinese, Indian and South Korean) reliance on Middle Eastern oil imports, 2002 and 2025 (projected).

To understand the full costs of this growing dependence, we must look far beyond the rising prices at the petrol pump. Rather, we must disentangle the whole gamut of direct and indirect costs associated with oil exploitation, gluttonous energy use, and the wars and military operations associated with it. Perhaps surprisingly, right-of-centre economists have been among the most penetrating here. In a recent pioneering study for the National Defense Council Foundation, for example, Milton Copulos attempts to assess such economic costs directly.[45] He includes the costs of supporting 18,000 injured US troops at $1.5 million each; the economic losses caused by the rising oil prices resulting from the war; and the massive direct costs of the Iraq and Afghan wars, which he cites as totalling $137 billion a year. Copulos concludes that if all these costs were borne by consumers at the moment they fill up their vehicles, Middle East petrol should fetch $11 a gallon, and a fill-up for the average SUV or Jeep would cost at least $230. 'Gas isn't too expensive', he argues. 'It's way, way too cheap'.[46]

Of course, US consumers don't dodge the indirect costs. They merely confront them indirectly – through higher taxes, spiralling national debt floated largely by Asian nations, and the extreme financial vulnerabilities that have become so obvious with the recent US financial meltdown. Yet, 'unaware

45   Cited in Salopek, 'A Tank of Gas, a World of Trouble'.
46   Ibid.

of the true costs of their oil habit, US motorists see no obvious reason to curb their energy gluttony'[47] – at least until actual costs start to show up in the price at the pump.

An even more comprehensive study of the full economic implications of the Iraq debacle has been undertaken by Nobel Prize-winning economist Joseph Stiglitz.[48] His conservative estimate of the total costs of the Iraq war to the US by the start of 2008 is merely $3 trillion. He argues that the rest of the world, too, will probably have to cover a similar figure. Stiglitz's breakdown of the costs to the US includes $16 billion per month in running costs; $1 trillion to pay interest on money borrowed for the war (through 2017); $25 billion per year for the spikes in oil prices actually caused by the war; and $19.3 billion paid to Halliburton, a private military corporation. Per US household, the monthly costs amount to $138.[49]

In mid-2008, as oil prices spiked to unprecedented levels, and analysts talked seriously about price rises to $200 a barrel by 2010 – a tenfold increase within a single decade – some of the potential political fallout was beginning to become apparent.[50] Leading oil commentator Michael Klare even predicted that when combined with other factors – the credit crunch; rising oil imports; the shift away from the dollar as the global currency standard; increasing reliance on foreign capital; catastrophic balance-of-payments deficits (exacerbated by those very same rising oil prices) – the exponential rise in the cost of oil might even usher in the end of the United States' status as a superpower. 'The fact is, America's wealth and power have long rested on the abundance of cheap petroleum', Klare observed. 'As a result of our addiction to increasingly costly imported oil, we have become a different country, weaker and less prosperous. Whether we know it or not, the energy Berlin Wall has already fallen and the United States is an ex-superpower-in-the-making'.[51]

SUV CITIZEN

The radical individualism and aggressive, militarized libertarianism that has dominated SUV culture has still wider urban implications, however. Worryingly, such cultural norms are being used as a model for the legal redrawing of concepts way beyond the roadscape. Don Mitchell has shown that

---

47 Ibid.
48 Aida Edemariam, 'The True Cost of War', *Guardian*, 28 February 2008.
49 Ibid.
50 Michael Klare, 'America Out of Gas', *Tom Dispatch*, 8 May 2008.
51 Ibid.

what he calls the 'SUV model of citizenship' has been a prototype for a new type of urban citizenship, as set forth in recent US legal rulings about social encounters on streets and sidewalks. These rulings have emphasized the 'purely atomic' nature of the individual in the city and have suggested that there is a legal need to insulate this individual from the wider contaminations of urban life – panhandling and political agitation, for example – through the idea of personal 'bubbles' or floating 'buffer zones' on city streets.[52]

Such a trend means that both the US Supreme Court and lower courts are now ruling that individuals have rights to be 'left alone' on city streets, rights that previously applied only to private property. Such a model of citizenship – 'based on, and protective of, the fully privatized juridical individual' – is, contends Mitchell, 'quite at odds with the cosmopolitan, associational citizenship theorized and promoted by many political theorists'.[53] Such a transformation is crucial because, traditionally, 'city spaces are those places where the public comes together in its diversity, and where, presumably, the interaction of difference helps create the possibility for democratic transformation'.[54]

Legally enshrining a person's body on a street as an analogue of the fortified capsule or bubble of an SUV is thus a deeply anti-democratic and anti-urban proposition. 'Purely atomic social relations mark the eclipse of the civic', Mitchell argues. 'Civic space becomes an illusion, little more than a representation of public life that no longer exists. Purely atomic relations, reinforced through bubble laws, represent the apotheosis of the individual'.[55]

ARMOURED CARS FOR THE URBAN BATTLEFIELD

> It is eerie to drive up next to a big bright yellow H2 [Hummer] on a highway at night and see the DVD player reflecting *Finding Nemo* onto the faces of the children safely strapped onto the back seats of a compact version of the US military vehicle you have just seen on your own television screen moving American soldiers into Tikrit and out of Fallujah.[56]

---

52 Don Mitchell, 'The SUV Model of Citizenship: Floating Bubbles, Buffer Zones, and the Rise of the "Purely Atomic" Individual', *Political Geography* 24, 2005, 77–100.

53 Ibid., 80.

54 Ibid., 84.

55 Ibid., 80.

56 Ellen Gorman, 'The "stop and stare" aesthetics of the Hummer: Aesthetic illusion as an independent function', in Cardenas and Gorman, eds, *The Hummer: Myths of Consumer Culture*, 87.

To understand why SUVs became the most popular vehicle choice in the US, it is necessary to explore how their meaning has been manufactured and consumed within the context of an increasingly militarized US urban culture. SUVs were fashioned and marketed after the first Gulf War as quasi-military 'urban assault luxury vehicles' – armoured 'capsules' or 'exo-skleteons' designed to separate fearful inhabitants from the uncertain, dangerous city outside.[57] 'For the sub- and exurban middle classes', notes Andrew Garnar, 'the SUV is interpreted culturally as strong and invincible, yet civilized'.[58]

SUVs acquired this meaning within the context of US suburbanites removing themselves far from the cores of American cities and becoming part of a culture which often demonizes the (racialized) places left behind. Setha Low captures how fear of poor or racialized Others, beyond the assemblage of gated community and fortified SUV, often pervades suburbanites' journeys downtown. One respondent in her research, 'Felicia', says that when she leaves her gated community and goes downtown, she feels 'threatened, just being outside in normal urban areas'. Moreover, she admits that her daughter now 'feels very threatened when she sees poor people. We were driving next to a truck with some day laborers . . . and we were parked beside them at a light. [My daughter] wanted to move because she was afraid those people were going to come and get her. They looked scary to her'.[59]

The widening anxieties surrounding urban life within the context of the War on Terror add to moral panics over crime, social unrest, and the need to fortress oneself and one's family against all manner of incursions and risks. Enter the SUV, carefully designed and marketed to exploit and perpetuate fears of the Other, the ghetto, while at the same time providing reassurance and patriotic symbolism for 'homeland' suburbanites who find themselves experiencing a new kind of war, in which vague and unknowable threats might lurk everywhere and anywhere, threatening to strike at any time. Added to this, SUVs have been shaped to tap powerfully into American cultural tropes of rugged individualism, the frontier existence, and the mastery of nature through technology.

These three parallel discourses – racialized anti-urbanism, War on Terror-induced insecurity, and frontier mythology[60] – have produced an especially

---

57 Cauter, *The Capsular Civilization.*

58 Garnar, 'Portable Civilizations and Urban Assault Vehicles', 7.

59 Setha Low, 'The new emotions of home: Fear, insecurity and paranoia', in Michael Sorkin, ed., *Indefensible Space: The Architecture of the National Insecurity State*, New York: Routledge, 2007, 233–257.

60 Gunster, '"You Belong Outside": Advertising, Nature, and the SUV', 4–32.

potent cultural mix. 'In the case of the middle class alienation from the inner city', Garnar writes, 'the SUV is an urban assault vehicle. The driver is transformed into a trooper, combating an increasingly dangerous world . . . As the middle class comes to see this country as an increasingly dangerous place, the SUV becomes a portable civilization, a way to stabilize the meaning of the suburban self-sign'.[61]

Tellingly, much of the rhetoric of the users, dealers and commentators clustered around SUVs draws on military analogies suggesting that urban life itself amounts to a socially Darwinian 'war' requiring the right sort of militarized vehicle if one is to stand any chance of survival. 'Not only is it a jungle out there, it's also a war: in the promotional field of the SUV the two flow into one another and become one and the same', in Gunster's words.[62] Thus, the SUV driver's relation to the city emerges as 'an encounter with a hostile and inscrutable Otherness'.[63] The city outside is rendered as a brutal, Hobbesian space of threat and fear, while the cocoon within is a safe, civilized, portable refuge. 'As armored nomads', writes Gunster, SUV drivers 'confront . . . urban alienation, crumbling infrastructure, and the erosion of community as the incarnation of a new "uncivilized" frontier in which one (seemingly) has little choice but to carve out mobile zones of comfort and security'.[64]

Far from being isolated, however, the SUV cocoon is equipped with the latest, military-derived visioning, control, communications and navigation technologies, further reducing the need for visual, let alone bodily, engagement with the city outside. (Visual engagement, in any case, is an increasingly asymmetric process, as one-way glass is becoming *de rigueur*). An ad for the Infiniti QX4, for example, depicts the hulking vehicle emerging unscathed from a huge concrete maze. The strapline declares: 'A network of 24 highly calibrated global-positioning satellites to guide you. 3 million miles of US roadways to explore. This way to the future.'[65]

The SUV, then, is 'pitted against the city in advertisements'.[66] The menacing cityscapes depicted in ads suggest that risk, hazard and evil are 'uniquely (though perhaps not exclusively) urban phenomena, a notion that a certain segment of [US] suburbia seems to accept wholeheartedly'.[67] Indeed, SUV

61 Garnar, 'Portable Civilizations and Urban Assault Vehicles', 7.
62 Gunster, "You Belong Outside': Advertising, Nature, and the SUV', 20.
63 Ibid., 25–6.
64 Ibid., 12.
65 Ibid., 25–6.
66 Garnar, 'Portable Civilizations and Urban Assault Vehicles', 7.
67 Macek, *Urban Nightmares*, 276.

ads echo widespread discussions about the US military's Humvees not having adequate armour to protect their passengers against mines and rocket-propelled grenades on the streets of Baghdad.[68] The ads present their vehicles as quasi-military weapons in the struggle to dominate road space. Meanwhile, the spaces and occupants of US cities become mere obstacles to be brushed aside or dominated. 'I need a car that no matter what happens in this town-earthquake, civil unrest, fire, flood – I can get through it, under it or over it', one LA entertainment manager and Hummer H2 owner reported in 2003.[69]

Thus do natural disasters merge with imminent urban social chaos. The resulting blend of scenarios 'constructs a fierce tableau in which one has little choice but to brace oneself against the perils of a hostile world'.[70] The SUV buyer automatically becomes 'apocalyptic cool'. Journalistic reviews of SUVs regularly tap into *Mad Max* and millennial fantasies, asking, for instance, which SUV is best equipped 'for the apocalypse'. In an article titled 'If the end is nigh, what to drive?' Jared Holstein of *Car and Van Magazine* writes that 'when the apocalypse comes . . . the best vehicle to have parked in your post-apocalyptic driveway is an M1A2 Abrams tank. If you don't live close enough to a National Guard armory to crack a hatch and drive off, however, consider these ten other [SUV] vehicles'.[71]

HUMMER MANIA: THE CAR IN UNIFORM

> In search of understanding contemporary America, a good place to start might well be behind the wheel of a Hummer.[72]

No SUV has symbolized the dynamics of 'retrenched nationalism'[73] and anti-urban hyper-individualism quite as powerfully as the GM Hummer and its two slightly lighter derivatives, the H2 and H3 (Figure 9.4). The original Hummer was a derivative of the thoroughly military Humvees that have been so iconic during the various US incursions and invasions in the Middle East since the

---

68   Garnar, 'Portable Civilizations and Urban Assault Vehicles', 7.

69   Paul Wilborn, 'Hummer Mania: SUV Backlash? Not For Owners Of Oversized Hummers', *CBS News*, 3 Febuary 2003.

70   Gunster, '"You Belong Outside": Advertising, Nature, and the SUV', 20.

71   Jared Holstein, 'If the End Is Nigh, What Are You Going to Drive?' CarandDriver. com, June 2007.

72   Daniel Miller, 'Foreward: Getting Behind the Wheel', in Cardenas and Gorman, eds, *The Hummer*, vii–x.

73   Ibid., vii–x, viii.

early 1990s. The Hummer became a cult vehicle after body-builder and film star – and, subsequently, California's governor – Arnold Schwarzenegger convinced the manufacturers to make a $100,000 civilian model in 1992 following the first Gulf War. At that time, the vehicle, in effect, 'had 24-hour-a-day unpaid advertising', courtesy of the ultra-patriotic mainstream news channels.[74] To one magazine writer, the Hummer remained 'the ultimate SUV, even without machine gun mounts'.[75]

Weighing in excess of ten thousand pounds, costing a minimum of $50,000, and averaging eight to ten miles per gallon, H1 Hummers are gargantuan and profligate even by SUV standards. In 2002 General Motors sold 18,861 of the slightly smaller Hummer H2s in the US, making it the best-selling 'large SUV'. By April 2003, at the start of the second Gulf War, sales had risen to 3,0000 a month.[76] Sales collapsed dramatically with the oil price hike of 2007–8, however, to the extent that GM even attempted to sell off the brand, which had switched from hyper-profitable to hyper-unprofitable almost overnight.

Nonetheless, the cultural potency of the Hummer as icon perseveres. From the start, the Hummer H2 was associated quite closely with a post-9/11 urban culture of fear and the wider politics of Bush's globe-spanning War on Terror. GM bought the brand in 1999, and employed Schwarzenegger to unveil the new H2 in downtown Manhattan on the three-month anniversary of the 9/11 attacks.[77] Adverts featured the vehicles in Desert Storm–style arid environments, with tag lines such as 'When the asteroid hits and civilization crumbles, you'll be ready'.[78] The message was clear: 'For a world full of danger, the H2 girds you in armor', wrote a *New York Times* reviewer. 'Driving a Hummer makes a unilateral personal statement in sync with a unilateral foreign policy'.[79]

---

74 Garnar, 'Portable Civilizations and Urban Assault Vehicles'.

75 Steve Finlay, 'Military Vehicles Are Now Cool', *Ward's Dealer Business*, 1 Aug 2002, available at wardsdealer.com.

76 Danny Hakim, 'In their Hummers, Right Beside Uncle Sam', *New York Times*, 5 April 2003.

77 By 2003 Schwarzenegger owned at least seven Hummers. Once elected Governor of California, he began a policy to support the development of 'Green' Hummers and SUVs compatible with alternative fuels such as hydrogen. This policy was widely lampooned as oxymoronic by environmental campaigners. See Amanda Griscom, 'The Beat of a Different Hummer: Schwarzenegger's "Green Hummer" Plan Sparks Cultish Following', Grist.org, 29 April 2004.

78 Gunster, '"You Belong Outside"', 4–32.

79 James Cobb, '2003 Hummer H2: An Army of One', *New York Times*, 6 April 2003.

9.4   A Hummer H2 on the streets of Tokyo.

The rhetoric of Hummer owners has often blended hyper-patriotic fervour and libertarian individualism with an aggressive desire to insulate oneself against the risks and threats of the contemporary city. 'When I turn on the TV', Hummer owner Sam Bernstein told the *New York Times* in April 2003, at the height of the US invasion of Iraq, 'I see wall-to-wall Humvees, and I'm proud. They're not out there in Audi A4s,' he said of the troops. 'I'm proud of my country, and I'm proud to be driving a product that is making a significant contribution. If I could get an A1 Abrams, I would,' he added, 'but I don't know if California would allow it.'[80] And in the view of Rick Schmidt, founder of IHOG (International Hummer Owners Group), 'those who deface a Hummer in words or deed . . . deface the American flag and what it stands for'.[81]

The patriotic fervour surrounding the Hummer has been performed as well as manufactured. Clotaire Rapaille, a notorious consumer psychologist and automobile design consultant who has worked for GM and other car makers, has indicated that vehicles like the Hummer were hyper-militarized so as to exploit the wider cultural context. The Iraq war 'definitely help[ed]'

---

80   Quoted in Danny Hakim, 'In their Hummers, Right Beside Uncle Sam'.
81   Ibid.

to sell Hummers, he reported. 'I told them in Detroit, "Put four stars on the shoulder of the Hummer and it will sell better." The Hummer is a car in uniform. Right now we are in a time of uncertainty, and people like strong brands with basic emotions'.[82] To Rapaille, the Hummer's design is an unequivocal materialization of Social Darwinism, sending out a clear signal: 'Don't mess with me because I can crush you, I can kill you right away, so don't approach me, hah?'[83]

Rapaille speaks of designing and selling deliberately 'reptilian' vehicles – a term he uses to refer to the consumer's primitive desires for survival and reproduction, which become exaggerated in times of war.[84] 'We are at war', he contended in a CBS interview in 2003. 'You don't go to war in a [Ford] Pinto or in a little Volkswagen. You want a tank, you want, you know, and I told the people there in Detroit, you know, SUVs – you put a machine gun on the top, you're going to sell them better'.[85] Gunster summarizes Rapaille's view on the SUV thus: SUVs are 'the most reptilian vehicles of all because their imposing, even menacing appearance appeals to people's deep-seated desires for survival and reproduction . . . [He] believes that "we're going back to medieval times," and you can see that in that we live in ghettos with gates and private armies. SUVs are exactly that, they are armored cars for the battlefield'.[86]

Such invocations of a new and deeply insecure medievalism within the militarized borderland of the domestic US city fit with the more general suggestions of right-wing foreign policy commentators such as Robert Kaplan, who speaks of the 'coming anarchy' on a planetary scale, which will reduce our world to an assortment of lawless 'feral cities',[87] where only the strongest – and the most aggressively militarized – will survive or prosper. [88] Here again, deeply anti-urban rhetoric blends into geopolitical imaginations, with the SUV linking the two. As George Monbiot quipped in the *Guardian*, perhaps the Hummer patriots, as they lumbered around US cities in their massive vehicles, 'should also have been demonstrating their love for their country by machine-gunning passers-by'.[89]

---

82   Ibid.
83   CBS News, 'The Thrill of the SUV: Owners Believe Bigger Is Always Better', 13 July 2003.
84   Shane Gunster, '"You Belong Outside": Advertising, Nature, and the SUV', 15.
85   CBS News, 'The Thrill of the SUV'.
86   Cited in Gunster, '"You Belong Outside": Advertising, Nature, and the SUV', 15.
87   Richard J. Norton, 'Feral Cities'.
88   Robert Kaplan, 'The Coming Anarchy', *Atlantic Monthly*, February 1994.
89   Monbiot, 'Driving into the Abyss'.

THE PENTAGON PIMPS OUT

Given this general backdrop, it is not surprising to discover that, in addition to using familiar recruiting tactics such as air shows and car races, the US military has exploited the Hummer. Backed by a veritable army of specialized PR consultants – and focused on impoverished young Latino and African-American men, by far the likeliest new recruits, since recruitment among other segments of society is collapsing – the iconic Hummer is presented as the ultimate embodiment of the new military urbanism. Modified Hummer H2s have been mobilized as quasi-military urban fashion statements to tour US car and racing shows, soccer games, and Latino music festivals as part of the roving recruitment initiatives. As Nick Turse puts it, these 'pimped-out rides' are meant to attract 'minority cannon fodder'.[90]

The Army, for example, has developed a fleet of modified H2s bearing the Army's Spanish-language slogan 'Yo Soy El Army' (I Am the Army) (Figure 9.5). Designed to tap into styles of Latino auto modification, based on *Lowrider* Magazine and video games, these H2s are 'chrome laden, custom painted [vehicles with] custom leather interior[s] and souped-up entertainment systems'. The latter includes a full fifteen TV screens.[91]

Meanwhile, the Army has modified other Hummers to appeal to African-American youths as part of its 'Takin' It to the Streets' recruitment campaign. Exploiting every cliché, such Hummers even have a regulation-height basketball hoop attached to the rear. Clearly these Hummers are an explicit attempt to appropriate messages and codes of inner-city violence and hip-hop consumption, for the purpose of selling the imperatives of a nation at war.[92]

Not to be outdone, the US Air Force has thirty-two 'enhanced marketing vehicles' in the form of GMC Yukon SUVs, modified into so-called Raptor SUVs,[93] named after the USAF's $400 million F-22 fighter plane. These vehicles are 'custom painted in blue, white, and gray, replete in Air Force logos, backlit grills, custom rims, leather interiors, entertainment centers featuring 42-inch plasma screen TV, DVD player, full-range sound system and even a Sony PS2 thrown in for good measure'.[94] Like the modified Hummers, the Raptor SUVs tour sporting and entertainment events – in this case, accompanied by high-tech flight simulators on massive 'pimped out' trucks.

90 Nick Turse, *The Complex: How the Military Invades Our Everyday Lives*, New York: Metropolitan Books, 2008, 143.

91 Ibid.

92 Julie Sze, 'The Hummer: Race, Military and Consumption Politics', in Cardenas and Gorman, eds, *The Hummer*, 229.

93 The US air force web site reveals that 'RAPTOR stands for Reaching America's Public To Optimize Recruiting'. Source: *events.airforce.com*.

94 Turse, *The Complex*, 144.

9.5   The customized 'Yo Soy El Army' [I Am the Army] Hummer H2
designed to extend recruitment among US Hispanic communities.

MAD MAX 3: BAGHDAD ON THE HUDSON

Our fashion accessories . . . are mowing down the people of Iraq.[95]

Hummers, then, modified and marketed to suit the circumstances, traverse a range
of urban realities from suburb to war zone. Once one of these glitzy and glamorous
examples of 'tricked-out' automobilia helps recruit a few young persons to the cause
of war, the recruits will soon find themselves, writes Nick Turse, in 'less flashy, non-
tricked-out vehicles – unless of course you count the scavenged scrap metal armor
plating that soldiers were forced to weld onto their unarmoured Humvees in Iraq'.[96]

Moving beyond the Hummer–Humvee nexus, US car makers became almost
playful in tapping into, and amplifying, cultures of modification and capsularization.[97]
Prototype and concept vehicles which emerged after the onset of the War on Terror
became ever more militarized and armoured while simultaneously becoming
equipped with ever more lavish and self-sufficient technological interiors. A look at

95 Monbiot, 'Driving into the Abyss'.
96 Turse, *The Complex*, 146.
97 Monbiot, 'Driving into the Abyss'.

their design and marketing campaigns shows, once again, 'how the foreign is folded back into the domestic by reference to the border zones of contemporary urban life.'[98]

In the 2005 Las Vegas Car Show, for example, Ford radically blurred the line between car manufacture and dystopian and militarized urban cyberpunk when it revealed its SynUS Concept SUV (Figure 9.6). The vehicle mixed 1950s styling with pessimistic, apocalyptic messages about contemporary and future urban life,[99] providing startling parallels with the emergence of *Mad Max*–style armed SUVs among Blackwater mercenaries on the streets of Iraqi cities. The *New York Times* called the SynUS 'the boldest, most honest rhetoric' at the show.[100] Ford's press release described it as an armoured 'techno sanctuary' with 'intimidating styling'. More than this, the release invoked an imaginary geography of US cities, with fast-gentrifying, largely white upscale neighbourhoods in the central cores, surrounded by minority ghettos brimming with resentment. 'As the population shifts back to the big cities', Ford declared, 'you'll need a rolling urban command center.'[101]

9.6   The Ford Synus, a concept SUV.

98   Campbell, 'The Biopolitics of Security', 943.

99   Aaron Naparstek, 'The Ford Blade Runner', 22 January 2005, available at www.naparstek.com.

100   Phil Patton, 'Sports Cars with Promises to Keep', *New York Times*, 16 January 2005.

101   Quoted in Naparstek, 'The Ford Blade Runner'.

The release went on to describe the gun turret-style openings on the SynUS's sides as 'non-opening and bullet-resistant'. When parking the SynUS, drivers would be able to 'deploy' the vehicle's protective shutters over the windshield and the side windows, turn on its outdoor video cameras, and transform the womblike interior 'into a mini-home theater with multi-configuration seating and multi-media work station', using the forty-five-inch flat-panel TV screen with Internet access, located where the rear windscreen would normally be.

'In the end, this car is the logical extension of SUV marketing', suggested blogger Aaron Naparstek. At its heart, the vehicle reflected a cycle of fear, hyper-inequality and aggravated militarization. 'The more intimidating and aggressive vehicles there are out on the road', wrote Naparstek, 'the more you need one too, lest you be squashed. It's an arms race and the Ford SynUS is the latest weapon you need to defend yourself'. He wondered, though, whether this rolling urban command center was 'designed for urbanites fearful of terrorism, or for the terrorists themselves'.[102]

Predictably, much of the response to the SynUS invoked its resemblance to the influential vehicles used for post-apocalyptic nomadism in the 1980s *Mad Max* movies. This is where we see another connection between images of militarized automobility at home and abroad. Sometimes the connection is made indirectly, via the very real uses of large numbers of modified and armed SUVs on the streets of Iraqi cities by private military corporations such as Blackwater.[103] The James Hom blog, for example, considered that the Ford SynUS was 'kind of reminiscent of the *Mad Max* trucks that mercenaries were [then] using in Iraq, except with a bit more OEM [original equipment from the manufacturer] style. Betcha it'll be just a few years until miniguns and ceramic armor show up at the [biggest US car show] in Las Vegas!'[104]

Much of the controversy surrounding the role of Bush's private armies in Iraq has arisen in regard to instances of these private forces driving around Iraq's cities in armed and armoured SUVs, killing Iraqi civilians – either as a by-product of their efforts to defend themselves and the convoys they were escorting, or for simple entertainment. The latter was demonstrated by videos posted on YouTube which showed mercenaries laughing and joking as they shot civilians from their armed SUVs.[105] In September 2007, Blackwater was forced to leave Iraq after an incident in which, while protecting a diplomatic convoy in Baghdad, they killed eight Iraqi civilians.[106]

---

102   Ibid.
103   Peter W. Singer, *Corporate Warriors: The Rise of the Privatized Military Industry*, Ithaca, NY: Cornell University Press, 2003.
104   James Hom blog, 28 November 2006.
105   National Public Radio, 'Iraq Cancels Blackwater's Operating License', 17 August 2007, available at www.npr.org.
106   Ibid.

9.7   Armoured and armed SUVs used by military contractors in Iraq.

Some of the responses to images circulated of the modified SUVs used for such patrols have been interesting. In June 2006, for example, Todd Lappin posted some images on his blog (Figure 9.7).[107] 'There's a soldier in Iraq who's been posting some crazy pictures of American SUVs and pickup trucks that have been modified by civilian security contractors for use as gun trucks', he wrote. 'They're insane, in a "*Mad Max* at the Wal-Mart parking lot" kind of way'.[108]

The many readers' responses to Lappin's posting were a mixture of, on the one hand, technical discussions with serving US soldiers about how they modified their own poorly armoured Humvees in Iraq and, on the other hand, fantasies of transplanting these vehicles to their everyday urban encounters in the US. One reader enthused, 'This could be the ultimate ride for [American football team] Raider Nation fans headed to the Oakland Coliseum!' Another asked, 'How come you never see the commercials for these?' Still others quipped that such vehicles 'should alleviate traffic jams' in US cities' or 'scare the heck out of some American commuters', or that the vehicles were 'definitely not your average Soccer Mom's SUV'.[109]

ROAD-PRICING ROBOWAR

The freeway is not only imagined as a track on which cars are guided and moved along, but it is turned into a surveillant recognition machine in a broad control network.[110]

A paradox marks automobile culture in urban borderlands at home and abroad. On one side, there is the celebration of militarized SUV drivers as hyper-individual subjects, completely divorced from engagement with or obligations to their wider city, society, or planet. On the other side, something quite different is emerging: the effort to forge multitudes of cars into collectively organized and controlled units within a new culture of orchestrated, even robotized, automobility.

'The imagined future of the automobile has a long history', writes Jeremy Packer. 'And it is dominated by one feature: Automobiles will be made to drive

---

107   Mark Frauenfelder, 'Amazing *Mad Max* Vehicles in Iraq', BoingBoing.net, 1 June 2006.

108   Todd Lappin, 'Amazing *Mad Max* Vehicles in Iraq', available at digg.com/mods/Amazing_Mad_Max_vehicles_in_Iraq_.

109   See '*Mad Max* at the Walmart parking lot', http://digg.com/d11W1D.

110   Jeremy Packer, 'Becoming Bombs: Mobilizing Mobility in The War Of Terror', *Cultural Studies* 20: 4–5, 2006, 385.

themselves'.[111] At the same time, unfettered and free automobility is being seen as a problem in a society targeted by terrorists – especially those armed with the ubiquitous car bomb.[112] Increasingly, as part of the shift towards ubiquitous borders discussed in Chapter 4, the right to move by car is becoming provisional – acceptable only under new security and 'safety' regimes based on the digital tracking, profiling, anticipation and governing at a distance that are now so familiar in air travel. 'Under these changes, rather than being treated as one to be protected from an exterior force and one's self, the citizen is now treated as an always potential threat' within the urban borderlands of the homeland, warns Packer.[113]

This shift relies on the use of military-style command and control technologies.[114] An intensification of what we might call a 'techno-militaristic controlled society',[115] it is widely seen as a means to improve road safety, to reduce traffic congestion, and increase the security of a highly automobilized homeland – and to achieve all this without having to build a new system of roads. Yet it is also a means of building a hugely profitable set of civil/military markets for the rapidly converging industries of defence, security, media, automobility, entertainment and electronics.[116]

The attempt to integrate cars through new sensors and new navigation and communications systems is as militarized as SUV culture, if in a different way. For the world of 'intelligent' transportation increasingly crosses over into military projects such as the army's huge Future Combat Systems initiative. As we saw in Chapter 5, this initiative utilizes GPS, radar, and new computing technologies to fully robotize a third of all US military ground vehicles by 2015.[117] DARPA's project Combat Zones That See, an initiative to track all vehicles in an occupied city (also see Chapter 5), is another Foucauldian boomerang. 'Will it come as

111   Ibid., 386.
112   Mike Davis, *Buda's Wagon: A Brief History of the Car Bomb*, London: Verso, 2007.
113   Packer, 'Becoming Bombs', 380.
114   Ibid.
115   Peter Weibel, 'Jordan Crandall: Art and the Cinematographic Imaginary in the Age of Panoptic Data Processing', in Jordan Crandall, ed., *Drive*, Graz: Neue Gallerie am Landesmuseum Joanneum, 2000, 8.
116   Here we confront the latest in a long-standing series of attempts to remodel car and road cultures to address the alleged imperatives of national security. The most famous examples here include the deliberate planning of Germany's autobahn network as a means of national military mobilization, and the imitation of this strategy in the enormous US interstate construction of 41,000 miles of 'defense highways' from 1956. This latter project was shaped heavily by concern that roads allow for the speedy evacuation of urban centres in the event of nuclear war.
117   Packer, 'Becoming Bombs', 385; see also IHS Aero and Defense, *Future Combat Systems (FCS)*, white paper, March 2007, available at aerodefense.ihs.com.

any surprise that after [Combat Zones That See] is battle tested abroad', asks Packer, 'it may very well be implemented in the US?'[118]

Anticipatory vigilance and surveillance which are targeted to car use in homeland cities will be much easier to implement when those cities are already building the large surveillance systems necessary for road-pricing and congestion-charging initiatives. In London, for example, a highly successful congestion charge has done much to reduce car traffic, promote cycling, and improve air quality and the quality of urban life in central London. On the 'polluter pays' principle, it is also being used as a mechanism to penalize SUV drivers. Simultaneously, however, some 'mission creep' is going on: the surveillance infrastructure that makes road pricing in London possible has now been drafted into the UK's apparently insatiable appetite for new means of digital surveillance by the state. Indeed, it is striking how often 'road pricing zones' – which, by definition, tend to be in strategic city cores – morph into 'security zones'. The paradigms which drive this process draw on classic military doctrines of 'network centric operations' and 'command and control.' Thus, computer algorithms continually undertake 'data fusion' between all manner of civilian databases as an attempt to locate and track 'targets' within the mass of the electronic 'clutter' of the city.

In March 2008, for example, it was announced that the digital tracks of moving vehicles and digitally sensed number plates, which enable London's congestion charge to work, would in future be accessed by MI5 and police counterterrorism officers. UK police and MI5 are also linking a multitude of CCTV systems, originally established for general traffic management, to their Hendon headquarters in order to establish a national system of vehicle tracking based on number plate recognition. True to its reputation as the ultimate 'surveillance society', the UK is the first nation to allow this.[119]

According to Frank Whiteley, leader of the initiative, 'what the data centre should be able to tell you is where a vehicle was in the past and where it is now, whether it was or wasn't at a particular location, and the routes taken to and from those crime scenes'.[120] This project places particular emphasis on highlighting 'associated vehicles': those that associate with one other on the roads). With the possibility of ubiquitous road-pricing in the UK and EU being actively considered, the tracking of entire societies' patterns of mobility seems set to radically intensify.

---

118   Ibid.
119   See Steve Conner, 'Britain Will Be First Country to Monitor Every Car Journey', *Independent,* 22 December 2005.
120   Ibid.

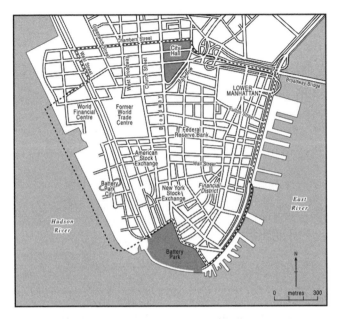

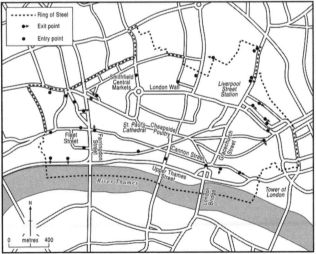

9.8   The Boundaries of the 'Lower Manhattan Security Initiative' and the 'Ring of Steel', established around London's financial centre to stop IRA bombers in the 1990s.

Similar efforts to build security tracking into 'smart' transport projects are underway in the US. In 2002, as we saw in Chapter 4, the well-established E-ZPass system, which facilitates access to faster lanes on highways in the US and Canada, was extended as a means of biometrically checking people crossing the border.[121] Also in 2002, ITS America, a group of US corporations which designs and builds 'intelligent transport' equipment, set up its own homeland security task force to oversee the computerization of transport in ways that supported increased securitization of US urban life.[122] In 2007 New York City announced a $100 million plan to turn Lower Manhattan into a 'ring of steel' – a much more advanced version of what was built around London's financial centre in response to IRA bombings there in the 1990s (Figure 9.8). At the same time, New York City proposes to instigate a road-pricing scheme for all vehicles entering Manhattan below Eighty-sixth Street. This so-called Lower Manhattan Security Initiative aims to 'provide the most sophisticated armor of any major urban area in the world'.[123] It would involve a series of roadblocks and more than a hundred automated number-plate recognition CCTV cameras, designed to track all vehicle movements in and around the area, and do real-time comparisons with criminal-records databases in Washington, DC. [124]

As in London, the New York cameras would check the vehicles' number plates and issue alerts for suspect vehicles.[125] More than three thousand public and private sidewalk security cameras, equipped with software which scans for 'suspicious' patterns of activity, would also be integrated into the scheme. Law Professor Jeffrey Rosen stresses that, in both London and New York, 'there's really a form of mission creep, and cameras that are accepted for one purpose are used for another'.[126]

Incremental experiments like those in London, New York, and on the US-Canadian border prefigure a much more substantial and systematic move towards intelligent automobility based on militarized robotic navigation technologies. For example, in an attempt to stimulate further development of

121   Maureen Sirhal, 'Homeland Security Chief Touts Benefits of "E-Z-Pass" System', *National Journal's Technology Daily*, 13 February 2002.

122   Henry Peyrebrune and Allison L. C. de Cerreño, 'Security Applications of Intelligent Transportation Systems: Reflections on September 11 and Implications for New York State', report to the New York state legislature by the NYU Wagner Rudin Center for Transportation Policy and Management, 16 July 2002.

123   Noah Shachtman, 'NYC is Getting a New High-Tech Defense Perimeter. Let's Hope it Works', *Wired* 16: 5, 2008.

124   See Cara Buckley, 'New York Plans Surveillance Veil for Downtown', *New York Times*, 9 July 2007.

125   Ibid.

126   Steven Josselson, 'New York's "Ring of Steel"', *Gotham Gazette*, 4 September 2007.

9.9   DARPA's 'Urban Challenge' competition in November 2007.
Eleven fully robotized SUVs and other cars had to navigate a
simulated urban course completely autonomously.

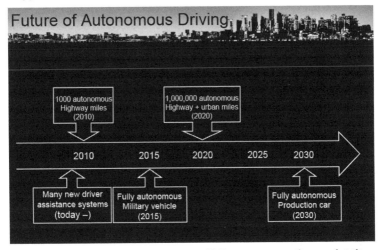

9.10   Estimates for the future introduction of fully autonomous military and civilian vehicles from the Urban Challenge presentations of Stanford University's entry.

robotic ground vehicles for use in both the US military and on the streets of US cities, the Pentagon's high-tech R&D arm, the Defense Advanced Research Projects Agency (DARPA), has initiated a series of high-profile robotic-vehicle competitions. The agency stressed that the aim of the 2007 competition, called 'Urban Challenge', was to develop 'technology that will keep warfighters off the battlefield and out of harm's way'.[127] It was 'the first time in history that truly autonomous vehicles met and (mostly) avoided each other on the open road'.[128] The event required that competing teams build vehicles capable of driving autonomously in traffic, relying entirely on on-board sensors, cameras, radars, computers and GPS systems. These vehicles had to perform turns, mergers, overtaking, and passing, and had to negotiate junctions within a cordoned-off sixty-mile 'urban' course in and around a former military base in Victorville, California. To ramp up the challenge, thirty manned vehicles also roamed the course. Urban Challenge was truly groundbreaking, declared DARPA, as it was 'the first time autonomous vehicles have interacted with both manned and unmanned vehicle traffic in an urban environment'.[129] Thirty-five teams

---

127   Defense Advanced Research and Projects Agency, 'What Is Grand Challenge?', available at www.darpa.mil.
128   Don Jewell, 'Victory in Victorville', *GPS World*, 15 November 2007, available at mg.gpsworld.com/gpsmg.
129   Ibid.

from twenty-two US states entered the competition, involving consortia linked to every major high-tech US university, defence company, and computing corporation. European and Israeli corporations and research teams were also heavily involved. On the first Saturday of November, eleven finalists took to the course.[130] (Figure 9.9). After a close contest, with six finishers, the Tartan team, an alliance of General Motors and Pittsburgh's Carnegie Mellon University, was declared the victor – gaining the $2 million first prize in part because their vehicle had not only finished the course but also complied with California traffic rules.

Whilst driverless cars are unlikely to become available to consumers until 2030 at the earliest, the Urban Challenge robocars are already being displayed at car shows, billed as a way to 'fortify road safety and eliminate driver error as the most common cause of crashes'.[131] The already strong links between militarized robotic combat vehicles (Figure 9.10) and an increasingly militarized society where cars become increasingly automated and surveilled, will likely intensify. One team of Italian military scientists working on these cross-overs said in 2006 that 'the Urban Challenge will provide some feel of how long it will be before we sit in our own automatic cars'.[132]

It is also becoming clear that Urban Challenge is a way for the Pentagon to capture the latest civilian technology in robotic vehicles and apply it to its own huge Future Combat Systems programme for the partial robotization of US Army vehicles within urban operating environments. As the manager of Future Combat himself remarked, 'We use many of the same sorts of technology for autonomous navigation as the DARPA vehicles'.[133]

OIL SHOCKWAVE

Military force and energy security are inseparable twins.[134]

Another aspect of the SUV, and of the broader culture of automobility, that must be examined in connection with the new urban militarism relates to the combination of rapidly rising oil demand and rapidly diminishing oil supply. Obviously, this presents major challenges for Western military doctrine. In light

---

130   Ibid.
131   American National Standards Institute, 'Unmanned Vehicle Drives Progress in Transportation Safety', press release, 8 January 2008, available at www.ansi.org.
132   Massimo Bertozzi, Alberto Broggi and Alessandra Fascoli, 'VisLab and the Evolution of Vision-Based UGVs, *IEEE Computer Magazine*, December 2006, 38.
133   See Joseph Ogando, 'Military MULE', DesignNews.com, 11 December 2007.
134   Michael Klare, 'The Pentagon as Energy Insecurity Inc', *Tom Dispatch*, 12 June 2008.

of the growing reliance on volatile supplies from the Middle East, Africa and Latin America, how can Western and US military forces support energy security – given the increasing military and economic strength of major competitors like China and India, which are struggling to meet their own exploding oil demand? How, in short, must military and political strategy respond to what has been widely called 'peak oil', and to the scarcity and dramatic increasing oil prices that it will inevitably bring (Figure 9.11)?

The strategic imperative is underlined by simulation exercises suggesting that even relatively modest disruptions in the global oil supply might have broad and cascading implications. One especially high-profile simulation, named Oil Shockwave, was undertaken in mid-2005 by a group of senior US national security officials for the National Commission on Energy Policy. Its director, Robert M. Gates, pointed out that the simulation's main conclusion was that 'it only requires a relatively small amount of oil to be taken out of the system to have huge economic and security implications'.[135] A 4 per cent global shortfall in daily supply, for example – generated, in their hypothetical scenario, by violent unrest in the Niger delta, combined with simultaneous terrorist attacks on oil ports and infrastructures in Alaska and Saudi Arabia – was enough to result in an immediate 177 per cent increase in the price of oil.

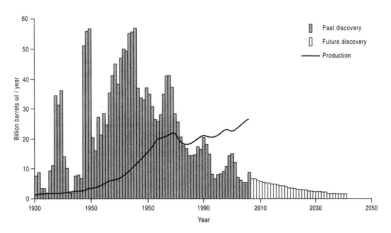

9.11   Peak Oil and the growing gap between discovery and production.

135   National Commission on Energy Policy, *Oil Shockwave*.

Since the days of Jimmy Carter, US foreign and military policy has been organized around the imperative of using, as he famously put it, 'any means necessary, including military force', to safeguard the supply and flow of Persian Gulf oil.[136] The invasion of Iraq was the direct result of the imposition of a new, pre-emptive warfare strategy, developed by a group of neoconservatives and designed, in part, to secure US control over the rapidly diminishing strategic oil reserves in both the Middle East and the Caspian basin. As former deputy secretary of defence Paul Wolfowitz – a key co-author, along with Donald Rumsfeld and Dick Cheney, of the pivotal Project for a New American Century report in 2000, 'Rebuilding America's Defenses' – once put it, Iraq 'floats on a sea of oil'.[137] Even though the exploitation of Iraqi oil since the 2003 invasion has occasioned much violence and disruption, the cartel of major Western oil companies had managed, by early 2008, to regain the massive oil concessions that they had lost in 1972 when Iraq nationalized the country's reserves.[138]

The decision to remove Saddam Hussein – made, at the very latest, in January 2001, well before the 9/11 attacks[139] – was a result of a new and aggressive policy of reshaping Middle East geopolitics using the unassailable military firepower of the US, with a view to attaining hegemonic control over the world's major remaining oil reserves. In 2007 Alan Greenspan, former chairman of the Federal Reserve, became one of the few senior politicians associated with the Bush administration to utter what everyone knew: 'The Iraq war is largely about oil'.[140]

The invasion of Iraq is thus a key element within a new Great Game, in which the major powers – principally the US, Russia, China and, to a lesser extent, India – are struggling to control the largely untapped Caspian basin reserves. These massive reserves hold an estimated 110 billion to 243 billion barrels of crude oil and are worth as much as $4 trillion.[141] In other words, one of the world's last oil frontiers lies in and around the Caspian Sea.[142] Each power is pushing to install its own military bases, pipelines and giant oil firms in the region and, in the process, is forging proxy rivalries and alliances

136 Then president, Jimmy Carter, 1980, cited in Michael Schwartz, 'Why Did We Invade Iraq Anyway? Putting a Country in Your Tank', CommonDreams.org, 31 October 2007.
137 Ibid.
138 Tom Engelhardt, 'No Blood for . . . er . . . um . . . The Oil Majors Take a Little Sip of the Ol' Patrimony', Tom Dispatch, 22 June 2008.
139 Schwartz, 'Why Did We Invade Iraq Anyway?'
140 Ibid.
141 Lutz Kleveman, 'The New Great Game', Guardian, 20 October 2003.
142 Amidon, America's Strategic Imperative, 72.

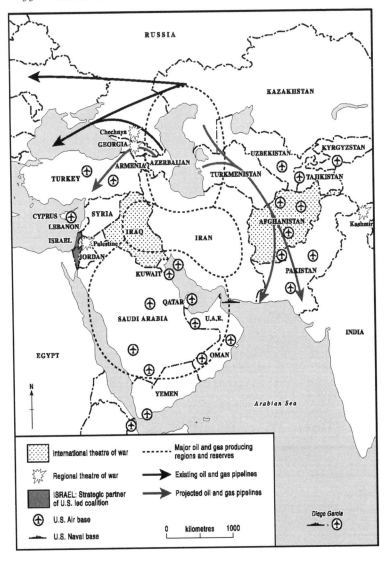

9.12   The Iraq and Afghanistan wars within a wider perspective of US military strategy centring on the world's most important energy resources in the Middle East and Caspian Basin.

with many a dubious regime. The map in Figure 9.12 presents a particularly revealing picture of the centrality of the Caspian Basin's oil and gas reserves within the geopolitics of recent US military strategy in the Middle East.[143]

A similarly tawdry scramble is also taking place in the oil-rich regions of Africa as the major powers seek to diversify their supply beyond OPEC countries.[144] Michael Klare notes that AFRICOM, the new US Africa Command, is being established with the explicit goal of dealing with 'oil disruption' in Nigeria and West Africa.[145]

Klare argues that the rampant reorganization of the US military (and those of other countries as well) to pursue and protect contesting claims on the world's remaining oil reserves could have catastrophic effects, ushering in what he calls 'Energo-fascism' – a switch from the military neoliberalism of the past two decades to a full-scale fascism organized around control of fossil fuels.[146] He suggests that the US military is already being transformed into 'a global oil protection service whose primary mission is to defend America's overseas sources of oil and natural gas, while patrolling the world's major pipelines and supply routes'. Klare sees a bleak future as military force becomes the option of choice amid dwindling and unstable supply, rocketing demand, volatile price, disruption by insurgency, and an increased shift towards remaining supplies in the global South. As a result, he predicts, the world will see recurring US military interventions, characterized by 'the constant installation and replacement of client regimes, systemic corruption and repression, and the continued impoverishment of the great majority of those who have the misfortune to inhabit such energy-rich regions'.

There is little doubt that the US military is putting much thought into the military and geopolitical imperatives associated with rapidly growing crises in energy security. Ironically, this is driven in part by the need to secure oil

143   Michel Chossudovsky points out that 'In March 1999, the US Congress adopted the Silk Road Strategy Act, which defined America's broad economic and strategic interests in a region extending from the Eastern Mediterranean to Central Asia. The Silk Road Strategy (SRS) outlines a framework for the development of America's business empire along an extensive geographical corridor.' See Michel Chossudovsky, *America's 'War on Terrorism'*, Pincourt, Québec: Center for Research on Globalization, 2005.

144   Michael Watts, 'Empire of Oil: Capitalist Dispossession and the Scramble for Africa', *Monthly Review* 58: 4, 2006.

145   Michael Klare, 'The Pentagon as Energy Insecurity Inc.', *Tom Dispatch*, 12 June 2008.

146   See Michael Klare's books, *Blood and Oil*, London: Penguin, 2004; and *Rising Powers, Shrinking Planet: The New Geopolitics of Energy*, New York: Metropolitan Books, 2008.

to supply its own stupendous appetite for oil: the US military itself consumed 134 million barrels of oil in 2005, as much as the entire population of Sweden. 'Every day', notes Klare, 'the average G.I. in Iraq uses approximately 27 gallons of petroleum-based fuels.'[147]

In 2000 the Center for Strategic and International Studies (CSIS) in Washington argued that 'the United States, as the world's only superpower, must accept its special responsibilities for preserving access to the worldwide energy supply'.[148] Between 2001 and 2009, through the US Central Command, or CENTCOM, the Bush administration exploited the War on Terror discourse to push highly controversial plans to build a formidable series of bases in Azerbaijan, Kyrgyzstan, Georgia, Kazakhstan and Uzbekistan (Figure 9.12). It has offered support to the Nigerian military in suppressing rebels in and around the Niger delta – rebels who are fighting against the systematic impoverishment and devastation of their region created by the exploitation of oil. And in 2007, the Bush administration helped establish a 35,000-strong 'oil facilities protection force' in Saudi Arabia – the latest US act in its fifty-year effort to protect the Saudi royal family in exchange for securing access to the kingdom's estimated 264 billion barrels of oil. This last initiative was a response to the proliferation of sabotage attempts within the kingdom by terrorists and insurgents loyal to al-Qaeda (see Chapter 8).

The Bush administration also built up the military infrastructure of fourteen huge bases within Iraq so that a more or less permanent presence of between fifty thousand and seventy-five thousand heavily armed US troops (along with a similar number of contractors) could remain there to protect oil supplies even after a wider US 'withdrawal' from Iraq.[149] As Ann Wright has argued, 'the Iraqi parliament knows that an "enduring security" relationship with the US is a codeword for an "enduring profit" relationship for US oil companies' – whose rights and control have been privileged, since the 2003 invasion, through 'shock doctrine' techniques of legal re-engineering and the privatization of Iraqi oil fields and infrastructure. In the words of 'geopolitical intelligence' consultants Stratfor, the invasion presented US oil capital with a 'sublime' opportunity to 'scoop up cheap assets'.[150]

---

147   Klare, 'America Out of Gas'.
148   Klare, 'The Pentagon as Energy Insecurity Inc.'.
149   Ann Wright, 'An "Enduring" Relationship for Security and Enduring an Occupation for Oil', truthout.org, 5 December 2007.
150   See stratfor.com; cited in Boal, Clark, Matthews, and Watts, *Afflicted Powers*, 47.

Year	Europe	Asia	United States
2010 - 2020		2010: Border skirmishes and conflict in Bangladesh, India and China as mass migration occurs toward Burma	2010: Disagreements with Canada and Mexico over water increase tension
	2012: Severe drought and cold push Scandinavian populations southward, push back from EU	2012: Regional instability leads Japan to develop force projection capability	2012: Flood of refugees to southeast U.S. and Mexico from Caribbean islands
	2015: Conflict within the EU over food and water supply leads to skirmishes and strained relations	2015: Strategic agreement between Japan and Russia for Siberia and Sakhalin energy resources	2015: European migration to United States (mostly Wealthy)
			2016: Conflict with European countries over fishing rights
	2018: Russia joins EU, providing energy resources	2018: China intervenes in Kazakhstan to protect pipelines regularly disrupted by rebels and criminals	2018: Securing North America, U.S. form integrated security alliance with Canada and Mexico
	2020: Migration from northern countries such as Holland and Spain towards Spain and Italy		2020: Department of Defence manages borders and refugees from Caribbean and Europe
2020 - 2030	2020: Increasing skirmishes over water and immigration	2020: Persistent conflict in South East Asia; Burma, Laos, Vietnam, India and China	2020: Oil prices increase as security of supply is threatened by conflicts in Persian Gulf and Caspian Sea
	2025: EU nears collapse	2025: Internal conditions in China deteriorate dramatically leading to civil war and border wars	2025: Internal struggle in Saudi Arabia brings Chinese and U.S. naval forces to Gulf in direct confrontation
	2027: Increasing migration to Mediterranean countries such as Algeria, Morocco, Egypt and Israel		
	2030: Nearly 10% of European population moves to a different country	2030: Tension growing between China and Japan over Russian energy	

9.13   Potential Military Implications of Climate Change: The View of the 2003 Pentagon report by Peter Schwartz and Doug Randall.

The costs of such a strategy – in human life, infrastructure, dollars, manpower, environmental devastation, pollution, and the rampant insecurity generated in oil-rich regions – are astronomical. Such costs, warns Klare, threaten to 'throw an ever darkening shadow of Energo-fascism over our world'.[151] Even elements

151   Klare, 'The Pentagon as Energy Insecurity Inc.'.

of the US military and security sectors are starting to question why radical energy conservation and the replanning of US cities in more sustainable ways can't be adopted as a much cheaper and less bloody alternative.

More strategically, the Pentagon and other Western militaries have begun to put serious thought into the medium- and long-term implications of climate change, which is generated in part, as rational people acknowledge, by emissions from spiralling global automobile and SUV use. It's a paradoxical development, given that Bush spent most of his two terms denying its existence.[152] One 2003 Pentagon report, for example, was titled 'An Abrupt Climate Change Scenario and Its Implications for United States National Security' (Figure 9.13).[153] It predicted massive flooding, storms, forced migration, food shortages, starvation, water crises, and – as a result of the diminished carrying capacity of many regions – a dramatic growth in violent political and social unrest over dwindling resources. 'According to the International Energy Agency', the authors write, 'global demand for oil will grow by 66 per cent in the next 30 years, but it's unclear where the supply will come from'.[154]

The report's authors, Peter Schwartz and Doug Randall, predict disturbing boom-times for militarized security, as those who have food, water, energy and other resources mobilize the high-tech techniques of the new military urbanism to try to separate themselves from the masses outside their geographical, urban, or technological borders. By 2025–30, predict Schwartz and Randall, 'the United States and Australia are likely to build defensive fortresses around their countries because they have the resources and reserves to achieve self-sufficiency. . . . Borders will be strengthened around the [US] to hold back unwanted starving immigrants from the Caribbean islands (an especially severe problem), Mexico, and South America'.[155]

---

152   Dave Webb, 'Thinking the Worst: The Pentagon Report', in David Cromwell and Mark Levene, eds, *Surviving Climate Change: The Struggle to Avert Global Catastrophe*, London: Pluto Press, 2007.

153   Peter Schwartz and Doug Randall, 'An Abrupt Climate Change Scenario and Its Implications for United States National Security', report to the Pentagon, October 2003, available at www.gbn.com.

154   Ibid.

155   Ibid., 18.

FEEDING THE CAR

> What biofuels do is undeniable: they take food out of the mouths of starving people
> and divert them to be burned as fuel in the car engines of the world's rich consumers.[156]

By 2008, it was already quite clear that the radical global discrepancy between the extraordinary growth in the number of cars; the continued rapid rise in the population of humans; but declining and increasingly expensive oil supplies was a major generator of insecurity. In particular, as the shortage of fossil fuels led to massive investment in purportedly renewable and sustainable biofuels, grown agriculturally, it began to have a direct and considerable effect on global hunger. As part of their 'green' measures, many governments commited themselves to the introduction – and heavy subsidy – of such fuels as a certain percentage of the overall supply. On the surface, these commitments appeared to be a way not only of reducing the political instabilities caused by fossil-fuel extraction but perhaps also of chipping away at greenhouse gas emissions. Surely a win-win siutation.

But the realities of the global biofuel surge are astonishing in their dark absurdity. In effect, it represents the appropriation of scarce agricultural land and labour, on a planet with a rapidly burgeoning population level,[157] by the automobile and its associated political–economic complex and drivers. It involves the redirection of the world's abundant harvests – at 2.1 billion tonnes in 2007, the global harvest of grain broke all records – to feed the world's booming population of 800 million cars rather than its booming population of people (its poorest people, at any rate).[158]

As the *Guardian*'s Simon Jenkins points out, 'one [SUV] tank of bio petrol needs as much grain as it takes to feed an African for a year'. By April 2008, a third of the grain production in the US, one of the world's foremost breadbaskets, was being subsidized for conversion into biofuel. The World Bank has estimated that, for instance, maize production increased globally by more than fifty million tonnes between 2004 and 2007; however, during that same period, the use of maize-based biofuels in the US alone grew by fifty million tonnes, meaning that one country single-handedly used up nearly the world's entire increase. By 2009, moreover, it was predicted that use of US maize for ethanol

---

156   Mark Lynas, 'Food Crisis: How the Rich Starved the World', RedOrbit.Com, 22 April 2008.

157   As Mark Lynas points out in 'Food Crisis', in the 2007–8 period, the world population was growing by 78 million a year.

158   George Monbiot, 'Credit Crunch? The Real Crisis is Global Hunger. And if You Care, Eat Less', *Guardian*, 15 April 2008.

would rise to 114 million tonnes – nearly a third of the projected US crop for that year.[159]

These increases, along with the negative impact of climate change on agriculture, and the knock-on effects of rising oil prices throughout oil-intensive cash-crop markets, played a major role in generating massive price hikes in staple foods in 2007–8. Food crises, mass hunger, and riots in more than forty countries were the direct result.[160] At a stroke, more than a hundred million people were shoved below the poverty line.[161] Even a report from the typically sober and economistic World Bank estimated that the biofuel push was responsible for fully 75 per cent of the global food-price spike of 140 per cent between 2002 and early 2008.[162] Jacques Diouf, director general of the UN Food and Agriculture Organization, reported at an emergency summit in June 2008 that Western, and especially US, biofuel policies were mainly to blame for the crisis. 'Nobody understands', he said, 'how 11 to 12 billion dollars a year [of US biofuel] subsidies in 2006 and protective [US] tariff polices have had the effect of diverting 100m tonnes of cereals from human consumption, mostly to satisfy a thirst for fuel for vehicles'.[163]

Worse still, state-supported biofuel expansion programmes in countries such as India and Indonesia were bringing about wide-scale deforestation (which sparked major bursts of greenhouse gases); an extension in the power of corporate agribusiness; and the forcible removal of indigenous and poor communities from their lands (which governments often class as 'wastelands'). 'Tens of millions of hectares worldwide have been converted to grow biofuels', writes Almuth Ernsting. 'Hundreds of millions of hectares are being eyed by biofuel corporations and lobbyists. The land-grab now underway has devastating impacts on food sovereignty and food security'.[164]

In response, mass evictions and mass protests have become common.

---

159 Lynas, 'Food Crisis'.

160 In 2008, major food riots occurred in Egypt, Haiti (at least four people were killed in the southern city of Les Cayes), Cote d'Ivoire, Cameroon (at least 40 deaths), Mozambique (at least four people killed), Senegal, Mauritania, Bolivia, Indonesia, Mexico, India, Burkina Faso, and Uzbekistan. See Lynas, 'Food Crisis'. It is important to stress that one of the consequences of urbanization is that people are removed from direct involvement in growing their own food and so rely on food markets instead. These are becoming increasingly global and are organized by major corporate and agribusiness. See Monbiot, 'Credit Crunch?'.

161 Aditya Chakrabortty, 'Secret Report: Biofuel Caused Food Crisis', *Guardian,* 4 July 2008.

162 Ibid.

163 Julian Borger, 'US Attacked at Food Summit over Biofuels', *Guardian,* 4 June 2008.

164 Almuth Ernsting, 'Biofuels or Biofools?', *Chain Reaction: The National Magazine of Friends of the Earth Australia,* April 2008, 10–11.

Indonesia's indigenous Orang Rimba community, for example, has held demonstrations against the deforestation of the Sumatran rain forest – which had sustained their semi-nomadic livelihoods for centuries – for biofuel palm-oil monoculture (Figure 9.14). As a result, many Orang Rimba 'are [now] forced to beg or take food from plantations where they are vulnerable to violence, and they suffer from hunger and malnutrition'.[165]

9.14   Orang Rimba indigenous groups protesting against the takeover of their lands by biofuel plantations in Indonesia's Jambi province.

But here is the ultimate absurdity: some of the countries pushing biofuel programmes to earn hard currency were the very same countries experiencing food riots and mass hunger. 'It doesn't get madder than this', George Monbiot observed in November 2007. 'Swaziland is in the grip of a famine and receiving emergency food aid. Forty per cent of its people are facing acute food shortages. So what has the government decided to export? Biofuel made from one of its staple crops, cassava.'[166]

It is difficult to avoid the conclusion that, beyond the greenwash, what the deliberate shift to biofuels represents is, in the words of Jean Ziegler,

---

165 Ibid.

166 George Monbiot, 'An Agricultural Crime against Humanity', *Conservation Magazine* 9: 1, 2008, available at www.conbio.org.

the UN's special rapporteur on the right to food, nothing less than a 'crime against humanity'.[167] The global peasant network La Via Campesina draws an obvious but powerful conclusion. 'To avoid a major food crisis', they say, 'governments and public institutions have to adopt specific policies aimed at protecting the production of the most important energy in the world: food!'[168]

FOSSIL FUEL FREEDOM

The events of 9/11, in their own way, reflect and symbolize the deep connections between everyday urban life in the United States, on the one side, and the violence spawned by geopolitical conflict and imperialist aggression, revolving around access to and control of oil, on the other. Tim Watson writes that, since 9/11, he has been haunted by images of the hundreds of vehicles abandoned at railway stations in New York, Connecticut, and New Jersey by commuters to the Twin Towers – vehicles never to be recovered. In one day, 'these symbols of mobility', he writes, became 'images of immobility and death. But these forlorn, expensive cars and SUVs also represent a nodal point between the US domestic economy and a global oil market in which Saudi, Kuwaiti, and Iraqi production is still so important'.[169]

Just under four years later, as another even more devastating catastrophe ravaged a major US city – this time it was New Orleans – a second indelible image momentarily linked the apparent banality of urban automobile use to global circuits and flows pregnant with symbolic power. In 2005, survivors of Hurricane Katrina, isolated, powerless, and virtually abandoned by the US state in the searing heat of their city's flooding streets, kept themselves cool by sitting in air-conditioned cars with their engines running – until, of course, their gas tanks ran dry. In the middle of a storm probably made more intense by global warming, cars thus provided temporary islands of cool whilst throwing out more heat and more greenhouse gases.

As with the SUVs abandoned at commuter rail stations in New England and New Jersey after 9/11, crises in metropolitan America, as well as the rest of the urbanized world, all too readily connect, through the automobilized landscapes of sprawl, to the global geopolitics of oil. This happens as consumers reach the peak of world oil supplies, and the intensification of global warming

---

167   Cited in Lynas, 'Food Crisis'.
168   Almuth Ernsting, *'Biofuels or Biofools?'*, 10–11.
169   Tim Watson, 'Introduction: Critical Infrastructures after 9/11', *Postcolonial Studies* 6: 1, 2003, 110.

is paralleled by the highly militarized transnational scramble to exploit and control the remaining oil – at almost any cost, apparently.

We thus find ourselves confronting large practical, ethical, political and philosophical questions as we ponder how our oil-driven, modern urban civilization might deal with potentially rapid and catastrophic collapses in the oil supply in the near or medium term. These questions move far beyond the media obsession with how steep rises in the price of oil have led to rapid declines in the sales of SUVs, a process that is threatening the very existence of iconic vehicles such as the Hummer.[170] For, in reality, it is mass and expanding automobility that is the overriding problem, not just the rise and possible fall of SUV culture. A stylistic shift to less militarized, less gargantuan vehicles ultimately provides only marginal reductions in oil consumption and greenhouse gas emissions. It fails to provide the systemic shifts necessary to address global warming, peak oil, and the depredations and insecurities generated by oil wars and the biofuel campaign.

Systemic shifts produce pressing questions. How, for example, might a rapid decline in oil supplies be managed so that catastrophic economic collapse and devastating food crises might be averted, and more sustainable urban ways of life be introduced without generating high levels of political and social violence? How might sprawling cities and globalized production systems and lifestyles – all of which depend, every step of the way, on personal automobile use and fossil-fuel dependence – be radically replanned and reimagined for life after fossil fuels?

If contemporary politicians were focused on the most important insecurities that face our world, instead of obsessed with fighting terrorism, they would wage a global war on fossil-fuel dependence. That war would, simultaneously and radically, reduce levels of global hunger, of ecological, human and food insecurity, and of greenhouse gas emissions. One useful component of this war would be to concentrate on the almost invisible global scourge of road deaths, for on a global scale, cars kill and maim far more effectively than terrorist attacks. And these numbers are soaring. The UN, for example, predicts that globally, between 2000 and 2015, twenty million people will die and two hundred million will be seriously injured in car accidents.[171]

Embedded deep within the enormous challenges of a transition to a post-fossil-fuel culture lie yet more fundamental philosophical questions

---

170 See Andrew Clark, 'End of the Road for Hummer after Sales of "World's Most Anti-environmental Car" dive', *Guardian*, 4 June 2008.

171 See Juliette Jowit, 'UN Says Road Deaths Kills as Many as Aids', *Observer*, 23 March 2008.

– for instance, regarding the meaning of 'freedom' within Western urban civilization. Now being exported in modified form to a diverse assortment of the world's cities, this concept seems predicated on the freedom to rely utterly on the profligate use of presumably almost limitless fossil fuels. It also depends on, though almost completely ignores, the global systems of political violence and militarization necessary to extract the ever-diminishing supplies. So again, in such a context, surely we must revisit the meaning of 'freedom'. Indeed, many environmental activists are now arguing such a position as they work to 'jam' the norms and axioms of fossil-fuel culture (Figure 9.15).

Drawing on Hegelian concepts, the philosopher of education Nigel Tubbs writes that 'my identity as a person . . . consists in my having fossil fuel culture relieve me of all social and political relations [and] from a totality which I no longer see as absent but view as not mine'. He believes that, currently, the idea of freedom is effectively destroying itself. The riots and wars which it perpetuates suggest that 'in fossil fuel culture, destruction *is* freedom'. Political states of emergency mobilized in its name demonstrate that fossil-fuel freedom is ultimately best understood as what Tubbs calls an 'absolute godless spirituality'. Chillingly – and echoing Klare's predictions of Energo-facism, discussed above – Tubbs predicts that in the major societal crashes likely to surround oil depletion, 'fascism will carry the crisis'.[172] The daunting challenge, then, is to find ways to rapidly construct new political economies, state systems, urban geographies, and styles of mobility and consumption, so that oil dependence can be unravelled before it is too late, and without appropriating the world's food or agricultural land. It is to these interrelated projects that states of emergency should be directed, not to the militarized scramble over the world's fast-dwindling oil reserves.

---

172   Nigel Tubbs, 'Fossil Fuel Culture', *Parallax* 11: 4, 2005, 111.

9.15 A environmentalist 'jam' of corporate oil advertising. The tag-
line reads 'WARNING: Oil Addiction – causes climate change,
funds violent extremism, damages health, reduces wealth!'

CHAPTER TEN

Countergeographies

THE NEW ANTI-MILITARY URBANISM

It's time to draw new maps.[1]

How, then, to confront the new military urbanism? Focusing on the United States, with forays primarily into Israel and the UK, the present book offers a starting point.

Cities Under Siege has first sought to expose and undermine how Manichaean renderings of our urbanizing world demonize cities as instrinsically threatening places. It has explored in detail how the latest military ways of thinking colonize the everyday spaces and sites of city life, imposing paradigms that project life itself as war, within a boundless battlespace. Such thinking – xenophobic, deeply anti-urban, and technophilic – translates difference into othering, othering into targeting, and targeting into violence. This logic pervades popular culture, from automobility to video games, film, and science fiction, and onwards to a melding of entertainment, war, and weapons design. Finally, this book has examined dreams of ubiquitous bordering and omniscient surveillance within and beyond nation-states; the systematic demodernization of cities and societies deemed to be adversaries; fantasies of robotized warriors; and efforts to project Israeli experience and expertise as exemplars worthy of wide imitation.

The critical perspective employed here seeks to (re)populate targeted cities, revealing them to be lived and embodied places intimately linked to 'our' cities and places. In so doing, we reveal the complex ways in which the techniques, technologies and imaginations of the new military urbanism gain their purchase through innumerable 'Foucauldian boomerangs'. It is through the exploitation of such circuits that the new military urbanism colonizes the norms of everyday life and the means of projecting war or force against demonised Others, and, through burgeoning global military-security complexes, becomes a basis for wealth creation. We thus insist, as Simon Dalby puts it, 'that real people live in the gap/wild zones, people who might be better served by political action and the insistence that peace comes by peaceful means rather than the extension of war as the fundamental social relation of our time'.[2]

---

1 noborder.org/nolager.
2 Simon Dalby, 'The Pentagon's New Imperial Cartography', in Derek Gregory and Allan Pred, eds, *Violent Geographies*, New York: Routledge, 2007, 306.

We now go one step further. In what follows, we consider how 'countergeographies' might be mobilized to contest and disrupt the circuits and logics of the new military urbanism, with its normalized separation of 'us' and 'them'; its crumbling market fundamentalism; its invocation of permanent securocratic war and ubiquitous bordering; its imperative of accumulation through dispossession; its blurring of the military, entertainment and security industries; and its mobilization of states of emergency and exception, the goal being to break through the grey zones of legality and to circumvent geography.

Given that the new military urbanism is predicated on Manichaean and Orientalist imaginations of geography, what can be done to subvert its logic? Within civil society, especially the multiple media circuits circling the globe, there has been much recent experimentation to address this question. Though scattered and often ephemeral, these experiments yield useful lessons in countering urban militarization. They present an important complement to more traditional methods of resistance and political mobilization – street protests, social movements, grassroots organizations, and formal political organizing aimed at, for instance, the re-regulation of economies or the redirection of state power. As a start, the architectures and discourses which sustain the new military urbanism must be countered in the crucial realms of public discourse and public spectacle, which, in an urban setting, can take advantage of the presence of transnational media.

NEW PUBLIC DOMAINS

> The modern state . . . has come to need weak citizenship. It depends more and more on maintaining an impoverished and hygienized public realm, in which only the ghosts of an older, more idiosyncratic civil society live on.[3]

Where the very circuits of the new military urbanism pre-emptively re-engineer traditional urban public and media realms in the name of 'security', what are the possibilities for building new and effective public domains through which countergeographies can be mobilized? Moreover, how can this be done in a world of extraordinary technological convergence, as well as concentration of control, within digital media?

In these times of war and empire, the idea of the 'public domain' must move beyond the traditional notion that it encompasses media content and geographical space exempt from proprietary control, which combine to 'form

---

3   Boal, Clark, Matthews, and Watts, *Afflicted Powers*, 21.

our common aesthetic, cultural and intellectual landscape'.[4] Rather than being permanent, protected zones of urbanity or 'publicness', organized hierarchically by key gate-keepers, public domains in contemporary transnational urban life are continually emergent, highly fluid, pluralized, and organized by interactions among many producers and consumers. The new public domains through which countergeographies can be sustained must forge collaborations and connections across distance and difference. They must materialize new publics, and create new countergeographic spaces, using the very same control technologies that militaries and security states are using to forge ubiquitous borders.

Patricia Zimmerman notes that such collaborations across difference and nations can 'mobilize larger transnational goals and solidarities, and very frequently combine analog, digital, and embodied practices that are multi-platformed and migratory'.[5] The 'embodied' bit is the crucial one here: to expose, challenge and reverse the creeping architectures of national security states, new countergeographies necessarily involve the massing and swarming of the insurgent bodies of citizens – and their electronic avatars. Usually this happens in cities, and usually it is done against the edifices of corporate, military and state power; always it must ripple through the multiple digital circuits so central to contemporary urban life. Only then might a raucous assemblage of blogs, independent video, subversive video games, and locative or ambient media help reinvent public domains across multiple geographical scales.

Experimentation and collaboration are necessary because of the concentration in transnational media ownership – a concentration that locks down the possibility, offered by many traditional media domains, of serving as a base for oppositional voices or renderings. 'Our era of empire, infinite war and massive media consolidation', writes Zimmerman, 'poses enormous obstacles to imagination, freedom and collectivity. The public spaces for an interventionist, argumentative public media shrink daily. Public domains seem elusive, theoretical, phantasmatic, lost'.[6] Intead, constellations of spectacle, simulacra, commodity fetishism and celebrity culture provide wider media constructs within which war blends into electronic entertainment.

Mainstream US TV news, for example – now concentrated in the hands

---

4   Patricia Zimmermann, 'Public Domains: Engaging Iraq Through Experimental Digitalities', *Framework: The Journal of Cinema and Media* 48: 2, 2007, 66–83.

5   Ibid.

6   Ibid.

of a few global media corporations – was absolutely central to the cultural mobilization of the Manichaean geographies which have underpinned the War on Terror. Such traditional media are, Zimmerman suggests, 'now in the manufacturing business'. They produce 'endless product lines of panic, amnesia, and anaesthesia . . . They enact and inscribe power through the production of panic', which produces a 'systematic incarceration of imagination and mobility'.[7] As a result, she argues, the classical public sphere of the nation or the city is not merely challenged or threatened: it has 'become a fantasy, a chimera, a collective hallucination concocted by theory to enforce the science fiction of democracy'.[8] Certainly, the efforts to embed reporters, to control satellite imagery, to censor photography, to plant military representatives within TV studios, and to demonize 'unpatriotic' critics, all of which were so central to the 'information operations' of the War on Terror, have been greatly facilitated by the growing consolidation of media.[9]

To Zimmerman, such a context demands a response which involves 'decentring the white male unities of empire and mobilizing the polyvocalities of multiple others that can dismantle it'.[10] Though that's a tall order, requiring extremely strong political and cultural mobilizations which are not currently in evidence, I propose six overlapping avenues of countergeographic experimentation that could help pave the way.

EXPOSURE

> Try to see what is not easily visible. Rethink invisibility; rethink as overt the covert realms of power that are not being named.[11]

First, and most obviously, countergeographies must work to render the invisible visible: to map, visualize and represent the hidden geographies of the new military urbanism. Once the hidden is unhidden, its seductive and ubiquitous mythologies can be confronted and potentially reversed. War might then not seem immutable or inevitable – and cultures which celebrate virtualized and stylized death within a hyperpatriotic frame, which violently obfuscate the fates of real bodies, might be confronted and exposed.

Patrick Deer argues that 'by charting the genealogy, construction, and

---

7   Ibid.
8   Ibid.
9   Deer, 'The Ends Of War', 5.
10   Zimmermann, 'Public Domains'.
11   Zillah Eisenstein, 'Feminisms in the Aftermath of September 11', *Social Text* 20: 3, 2002, 79.

buried histories of a "postmodern" war culture, we can challenge its seductive mythology'.[12] Such efforts can reveal that the "'cultural tradition" that seeks to make war a permanent and natural way of life' is actually contingent and constructed.[13] The task of exposure must confront the fact that the new military urbanism relies on violence to obfuscate what is often taboo or invisible.[14] To have any effect, however, the work of exposure must confront the thorny issue of the construction, maintainence and performance of the states of social denial which act so powerfully to obfuscate reality.[15]

Ironically, the mass circulation of digital imaging technologies can bring unintended effects which can do much to expose the new military urbanism's violence: the most powerful acts of exposure are now often inadvertent, caused by leaks from the practitioners of war themselves. The infamous Abu Ghraib torture photos which so de-legitimated the War on Terror, were, as Patrick Deer reminds us, 'produced by the guards themselves as a kind of war-porn designed to document their own everyday lives, as screen savers, as amateur reality TV or a horrifying mutation of *America's Funniest Home Videos*'.[16]

Imperatives of exposure extend across art, activism, documentary-making, and cartography. Exposure demands geographies that, in Derek Gregory's words, 'affirm the materiality and corporeality of places' targeted by the many violences of the War on Terror and the Long War, and 'attend to the voices (and the silences) of those who inhabit them'.[17] In this way, cities might become much more than verticalized targets viewed on maps, feral trouble spots within geopolitical abstractions, stylized videoscapes where murderous rampage is presented as entertainment. Instead, they might emerge as fully lived places, seen and inhabited from the ground rather than through the distancing gaze of the video targeting screen, satellite imaging device, geopolitical map or games console. In the process, the bodies and voices of the living, as well as the bodies of the dead – perhaps including the erased faces and lives of the dead and maimed soldiers of the West – might be made central to the frame.

---

12 Deer, 'The Ends Of War', 7.

13 Ibid.

14 Ibid., 2.

15 Stanley Cohen, *States of Denial: Knowing About Atrocities and Suffering*, Polity, Cambridge, 2000.

16 Deer, 'The Ends Of War', 2.

17 Derek Gregory, 'Geographies, Publics and Politics', essay derived from contribution to the Presidential Plenary, 'Raising Geography's Profile in the Public Debate', annual meeting of the Association of American Geographers, Philadelphia, PA, March 2004, available at geography.berkeley.edu.

Derek Gregory wonders what might have happened had effective countergeographies, rendering Iraq's cities as lived places full of ordinary urban lives, been mobilized as energetically as the relentless drum-beats of war and the fake intelligence dossiers had been to support the US-UK invasion back in 2002. 'How', he asks. 'might the public have viewed the war then?'[18] What might have been possible if we had been able to 'refuse the brutal reduction of other places and other people to counters in a calculus of self-interest and opportunism, and instead to affirm the importance of a *care*ful geography of engagement and understanding?'[19]

A related challenge is to make connections and interdependencies visible – those webs of exploitation, affiliation, dependence and hospitality which bind urban life in Western cities with that of cities elsewhere in the world much more tightly than cultures of war-mongering can ever do. [20]

The challenge, then, is to employ all and any strategies of representation, art, cartography, witnessing and activism to make visible 'the lives of distant strangers, people whom [viewers] don't know but without whom their own lives would be impossible'.[21] The wider, perhaps earlier, challenge is how – in the wake of the anti-globalization campaigns of the 1990s, and the widespread precariousness created by neoliberal globalization – to conceive of solidarities and dependencies that attain global scales and stretch across global peripheries and global cores.[22] Success at such tasks will make it difficult indeed to render entire populations as barbarian Others who require highly militarized 'assistance' (read 'invasion') from the West in the name of 'freedom' and 'democracy'. Binary geographies of 'us' and 'them' will become mixed-up and disrupted, a salutary process that most urban dwellers will recognize as indispensable to the warp and weft of urban life.

Some excellent work is already emerging on the geographies of commodity chains, on the new international divisions of labour, on offshore services, as well as on questions of resource wars, the dumping of waste, biofuels, biopiracy, the militarization of immigration controls, the global financial crisis, genetically modified crops, and the global construction of agribusiness agriculture. Simply mapping the militarization of borders, and the resulting deaths of 'illegal' immigrants, is a powerful example of this work (Figure 10.1).

---

18   Ibid.

19   Ibid. This, of course, is a major challenge, given that critical Middle Eastern studies have been systematically repressed in the United States since 2001.

20   Ibid.

21   Ibid.

22   Robby Herbst, 'Hinting at Ways to Work in Current Contexts; an Interview with Brian Holmes', *Journal of Aesthetics and Protest* 1: 4, 2007.

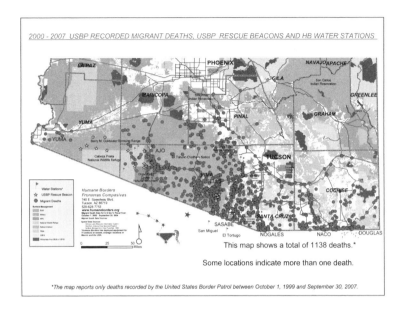

10.1   Humane Borders map of migrant deaths around
Tucson, Arizona, 1 Oct. 1999–30 Sept. 2007.

Another is addressing the totally different experiences of borders for kinetic élites and kinetic underclasses, under a state of securocratic war. Stefano Boeri, for example, videoed two different journeys within the militarized West Bank, between the same two cities: one journey, rapid and privileged, took place along a Jewish-only highway; the other through the interminable delays, immobility and humiliations of the Israeli check-point system imposed on Palestinians (Figure 10.2).

Possibly the ultimate challenge is to expose global divisions of labour. As Brian Holmes puts it: 'Who works, at what kind of production, under which financial system, for whose consumption – and who doesn't even get the chance to work, whose territory remains tragically undeveloped and destitute, or is destroyed by invasive technologies and pollutants?'[23] Such exposure is quite difficult, however, for the new international divisions of labour associated with

---

23   Herbst , 'Hinting at Ways to Work in Current Contexts'.

10.2 Part of Stefano Boeri's 'Solid Seas' Project, 2003: Video recordings of parallel journeys between two cities through the apartheid architectures of the West Bank on a Jewish-only highway (left), and through the humiliating check-points for Palestinians (right).

neoliberalization thrive on the systematic production of invisibility through geographical distanciation.[24]

Some of the complex transnational geographies of the War on Terror and its antecedents have been brilliantly exposed, in imaginative and provocative ways, by the recent work of artists, activists and cartographers. Artist Elin O'Hara Slavick, for example, has completed the potent but straightforward task of rendering visible – on more than fifty artistic maps of the world – all the places bombed by the United States (Figure 10.3).[25] Her drawings, she writes, 'are manifestations of self-education on the subjects of US military interventions, geography, politics, history, cartography, and the language of war'.[26]

24 Gregory, 'Geographies, Publics and Politics'.

25 Elin O'Hara Slavick, *Protesting Cartography or Places the United States has Bombed*, art exhibition, see www.unc.edu/~eoslavic.

26 Ibid.

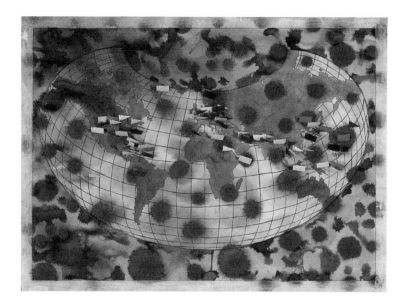

10.3   Elin O'Hara Slavick's 'World Map, Protesting Cartography:
Places the United States has Bombed', 2002–ongoing. Pins mark each
bombed site for which there is a corresponding drawing.

An especially productive area of new work is the use of complex graphic design and 'cognitive mapping'[27] to visually capture the dynamics of transnational neoliberalism and militarism. Ashley Hunt's startling *New World Map: In Which We See*[28] – a state-of-the-art visualization of global circuits of neoliberal restructuring, exploitation, social polarization, incarceration and militarization – is an example (Figure 10.4). Rarely have the latest social theorizations of our world been rendered in such a striking, visual manner.

---

27   This term invokes Fredric Jameson's classic argument that 'postmodern' urban life requires new 'cognitive maps' to make sense of the landscapes of globalization. See Fredric Jameson, 'Postmodernism or the Cultural Logic of Late Capitalism', *New Left Review* 1: 146, 1984, 53–92.

28   See *An Atlas of Radical Cartography*, available at www.an-atlas.com.

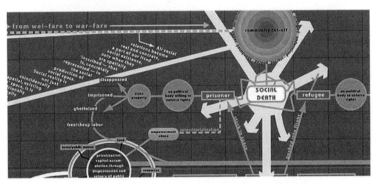

10.4   Ashley Hunt's 'New World Map: In Which We See'
(above) and a detail from the same (below).

The French collective Bureau d'Études has also published a series of brilliant cognitive maps that capture the élite political, economic, technological and military institutions which jointly orchestrate neoliberal capitalism. Their map 'infowar/psychic war' (Figure 10.5), for example, explicitly maps the concentration of control and privatization in transnational corporate media, and links it to doctrines of information warfare. The collective's *refusal of the biopolice* project, meanwhile, does a similar job mapping transnational circuits in the extension of surveillance and control technologies.

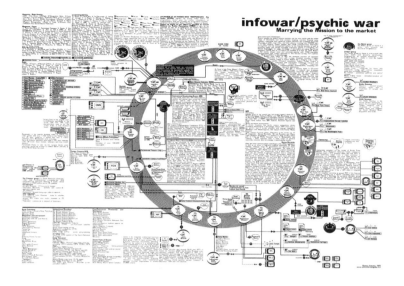

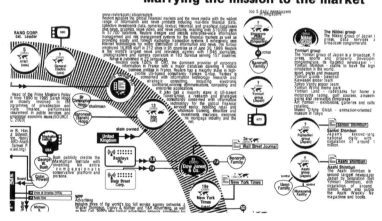

10.5   Bureau d'Étude's 'infowar/psychic war' (detail,
at top; expanded detail at bottom).

The maps by Bureau d'Études present 'an excess of information, shattering subjective certainties and demanding reflection, demanding a new gaze on the world that we really live in.'[29] In so doing, they help reveal the abstract and usually invisible architectures of power that operate beyond democratic control and scrutiny as state, corporate, security and military players cross-fertilize across global circuits of neoliberal governance.[30]

Another example of the forceful new cartographies of exposure comes from geographer Trevor Paglen and activist-designer John Emerson, who have produced compelling maps of the CIA's global system of abduction, extraordinary rendition, incarceration and torture. 'Selected CIA Aircraft Routes and Rendition Flights, 2001–2006'[31] (Figure 10.6) used flight data provided by the Federal Aviation Administration and Eurocontrol to map the flights linking the CIA's global carceral archipelago. These maps have been publicly displayed on ordinary, existing ad billboards erected along the sides of major roads around Los Angeles.

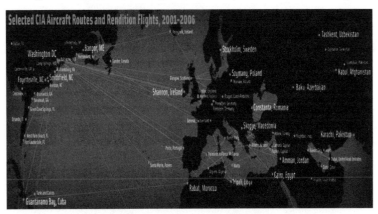

10.6   Trevor Paglan and John Emerson's project 'CIA Rendition
Flights 2001–2006' in map and billboard form.

Mexican artist Marcos Ramirez's 2003 'Road to Perdition' billboard – installed alongside a major street in Reading, Pennsylvania, and eventually banned – underlines the continuity between recent US urban bombing campaigns against far-off cities in Afghanistan and Iraq, and those conducted elsewhere in

29   Brian Holmes, 'Maps for the Outside: Bureau d'Études, or the Revenge of the Concept', message board post, *InterActivist Info Exchange,* available at info.interactivist.net/node/2398.
30   Ibid.
31   See clockshop.org.

the previous two centuries (Figure 10.7).[32] Billboards like this, and other public installations of subversive or critical art, gain their power from the very way 'they intervene in our mundane routines and trivial everyday journeys'.[33] As unavoidably visible, they bring attention to the unseen circuits through which the new military urbanism operates.

Ciudad de Mexico	3.202 km.	1847
Veracruz	3.040 km.	1914
Hiroshima	11.194 km.	1945
Dresden	4.837 km.	1945
Hanoi	13.206 km.	1972
Ciudad de Panama	3.497 km.	1989
Kabul	10.979 km.	2001
Bagdad	9.897 km.	2003

10.7   Marcos Ramirez's 2003 'Road to Perdition' billboard campaign in Reading, Pennsylvania.

JUXTAPOSITION

The second avenue – an obvious one, in a world of Manichaean geographies – is the act of juxtaposition. Though simple, it is an extremely effective way to bring renderings of 'them' or the 'Other' that help manufacture enmity and war and legitimize state killing, into the domestic spaces at the metropolitan cores of power where 'we' live. The tactic here, with the aim of debunking the binaries of the Manichaean geographical imagination, is to assert, once again and very clearly, that targeted cities are not demonic or abstract spaces of enmity but lived, embodied civil worlds much like the urban places inhabited by Westerners.

As the Republican National Convention rolled into New York City in August 2004 – on the eve of the third anniversary of the 9/11 attacks, which it shamelessly exploited – hundreds of protests took place. One stood out: artist Anne-Marie Schleiner and a colleague, decked out in Robocop outfits reminiscent of countless futuristic science fiction films, toured Manhattan while projecting scenes from the US military's video games onto the city's streets and buildings (Figure 10.8). The procedings were broadcast simultaneously on the Web.

Taking its name directly from the military term 'military operations on urban terrain', or MOUT, the performance was titled *Operation Urban Terrain*,

---

32 See Mike Davis, 'Reading (PA.) by Bomb Light', *Tom Dispatch*.

33 Louise Amoore, 'Vigilant Visualities: The Watchful Politics of the War on Terror', *Security Dialogue* 38: 2, 2007.

or OUT. Schleiner declared that the project was a challenge to 'an endless spiral war of terror [in a context where] a government is at war with its own citizens, with soldiers in the midst of the fabric of ordinary life'. OUT, she said, was 'an artistic intervention in the public space of online games and cities'.[34]

Welcome to OPERATION URBAN TERRAIN
Public Americas Army Ops
Powered by

10.8   Anne-Marie Schleiner's 'OUT of the closet'.

Cartographic juxtaposition offers considerable potential for the subversion of the binaried geographies which sustain the War on Terror and the Long War. Most influential here has been the 'You Are Not Here' project (Figure 10.9).[35] Calling itself an 'urban tourism mash-up', the project supplies maps of New York and Tel Aviv that are co-ordinated with maps of Baghdad and Gaza City, so that it becomes possible, when navigating the 'homeland' city, to be vicariously and imaginatively present within the 'enemy' city. Detailed information about sites in Baghdad and Gaza where war has actually been experienced are delivered, via mobile phone, to people touring New York and Tel Aviv, with sites marked in the latter cities by 'You Are Not Here' stickers. The organizers of the project want their maps to allow navigation in 'the streets of one city' whilst inviting people 'to become meta-tourists of another city … Through investigation of these points and with or without the aid of a downloadable map, local pedestrians are transformed into tourists of foreign places'.[36]

A final example of artistic juxtaposition is Paula Levine's 'Shadows From Another Place: Baghdad < – > San Francisco' project, which superimposed maps of the two cities as the 2003 invasion rolled into Iraq (Figure 10.10). 'The invasion was a distant simultaneous event', she wrote. 'In spite of connections

34   See www.opensorcery.net/OUT.
35   See youarenothere.org.
36   Ibid.

Welcome to
Baghdad

*You Are Not Here (.org) is an urban tourism mash-up.
This persistent game takes place in the streets of New
York City and invites participants to become
meta-tourists on an excursion through the city of
Baghdad. Passers-by stumble across the curious You Are
Not Here signs in the street. The YANH street-signs
provide the telephone number for the Tourist Hotline, a
portal for audio-guided tours of present day Baghdad
destinations in NYC. Through investigation of these
points and with or without the aid of a downloadable
map, New Yorkers are transformed into tourists of
contemporary Baghdad.*

YOU ARE NOT HERE.org

Home | Print the map | About | Contact

10.9   The 'You Are Not Here' project, which allows tourists in New York and
Tel Aviv to navigate virtual versions of Baghdad and Gaza City respectively
while receiving detailed information about the 'enemy' city over a mobile.

through media that reinforced my own expectation of proximity and simultaneity, the physical space between San Francisco and Baghdad remained fixed and sufficient to buffer the impact of the invasion taking place there'.

Levine's Web- and GPS-based maps were set up to help viewers 'imagine the impact of political or cultural changes taking place in one location upon another'. They worked by 'shadowing distant events, overlaying the impact of political and cultural traumas, such as wars or shifts in borders or boundaries, upon local landscapes'. In the process, Levine aimed to collapse the binaries of 'foreign' and 'domestic', to 'bridge local and global', and to 'allow walkers/viewers to experience spatial and narrative contiguity between separate and distant locations'.

First, satellite images and maps of the two cities were superimposed. Then the individual bombing attacks on Baghdad by US warplanes during the first wave of Shock and Awe were transposed though GPS coordinates onto equivalent sites in San Francisco. Each site 'hit' in San Francisco was then physically furnished with a container which included information about Levine's project and a list of the latest war dead within the US military.[37]

---

37   Paula Levine, 'Shadows from Another Place: Transposed Space', review paper, San Francisco: San Francisco State University.

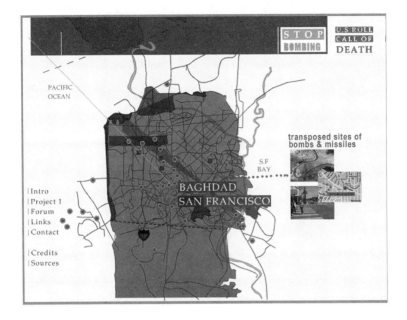

10.10   'Shadows from Another Place': Transposed spaces by Paula Levine.

APPROPRIATION

A third strategy for the building of countergeographies involves the very technologies of control that are so central to the new military urbanism and that offer excellent potential for appropriation and reverse engineering. Indeed, a whole universe of experiments in what are called 'locative' or 'ambient' media seek to challenge contemporary cultures of militarized urbanism by exploring new uses of infrastructures and technologies such as GPS, radio frequency (RFID) chips, unmanned drones, digital mapping, satellite surveillance, video simulation, data mining, Internet communications and wireless communications – all of which more or less originated through military research.

The emphasis here is first to demystify and make visible the invisible technologies of control, tracking, and surveillance which now thoroughly permeate everyday objects, architectures, environments and infrastructures, and then to redeploy them in counter-hegemonic ways. A key starting point is to assert the limits of control technologies – the fact that they never work with the effectiveness sought, and claimed, in the technophilic fantasies of omnipotent power we have encountered throughout this book. This unavoidable fact confirms the crucial political point that, as Brian Holmes has said, 'an entire society cannot be controlled by individualized stimulation and surveillance – much less an entire world'.[38]

'Even in our critiques', argues Peter Baker of the *Washington Post*, 'we tend to replicate the birds-eye perspective of the press and impute too much power to the war machine', which tends to make us swallow technophilic dreams at face value. 'If we are to challenge successfully the official efforts to make high-tech war an acceptable foreign policy option', he suggests, 'we need to get more intimate, get in close and witness how, from the micro- to the macro-level, fog, friction, and general screw-ups regularly operate in war games as well as in war'.[39]

'Getting in close' is crucial to building a politics of transgressing, resisting, reverse-engineering and even dismantling the vast systems of intensified digital control – that is to say, *attempted* control – on which the new military urbanism depends. The locative media movement is especially interesting in this respect, because it centres on the current convergence between digital media and geographical places as such media merge into the geographical background to facilitate digital urban life. Locative media artists and activists thus 'marshal portable, networked computing devices like GPS, mobile phones, RFID as well as wearable technologies to map space and intervene into data streams, [and they] focus on horizontal, user-led and collaborative projects to interrupt and interrogate a powerful system of observation and control'.[40]

A related stream of experimentation centres on the reverse engineering of control technologies. The aim of these experiments is to take apart the architectures of technology and control so that they can be creatively remodelled and redeployed. 'Reverse engineering needs to be added to the tactics of pirating, pranks, collage, culture jamming, and copyleft', writes Patricia Zimmerman, 'as strategies for resistance and intervention into transnational capital and empire'.[41] Here we encounter ideas of 'full spectrum resistance', designed to reappropriate militarized media and control

---

38 Herbst, 'Hinting at Ways to Work in Current Contexts'.

39 Peter Baker, in *Under Fire.2*, 57–8. For a good example of such micro-level studies of how military forces actually use new control, media and targeting technologies, see Caroline Crosser, 'Networking Security in the Space of the City: Event-ful Battlespaces and the Contingency of the Encounter', *Theory and Event* 10: 2, 2007.

40 Zimmermann, 'Public Domains'.

41 Ibid.

technologies as a way to counter military ideas of 'full spectrum dominance' through the very same technologies.[42]

The most well known examples include the reverse engineering of militarized video games.[43] More startlingly, however, Chris Csikszentmihalyi of MIT has built a reverse-engineered unmanned roaming vehicle – Afghan Explorer – to be deployed to the killing zones of the War on Terror to act as global witness and to overcome restrictions on the press. This vehicle is an 'autonomous robot for remote cruising and imaging of rural and urban geopolitical hotspots to gather news for the public in the face of Pentagon press controls of war zones'.[44]

In Austria, meanwhile, the System-77 Civil Counter-Reconnaissance group, led by artist Marko Peljhan, has reverse-engineered military surveillance drones and built their own drone system using a vehicle bought off the Internet (Figure 10.11).[45] Its task, they say, is a form of countersurveillance[46] – it will work as a 'tactical urban countersurveillance system [to] monitor public space'. Motivated by the sense that in contemporary politics 'the real issues are above your heads', the group's drone is explicitly designed to counteract state violence against legitimate demonstrations and urban activism.[47] 'Just look at the precision of the computerized city plans, the high-resolution detail of the surging crowds, the instantaneous breadth of perspective and control afforded by the drone's eye view', writes Brian Holmes. 'And imagine the exhilarating sense of mission on the morning of the big demo, when *you* get to be the mobile operator of a 1.8 metre-long AeroVironment Pointer [unmanned drone]'.[48]

System-77 explicitly locates their initiative within the new military urbanism, with its pervasive low-intensity conflicts and privatized high-tech security. 'The violence of classical theatres of battle', they write, 'is overshadowed by the rise of low intensity conflicts in highly developed societies of capitalist democracies. The increasing privatization of security in this all-pervading omni directional new style of confrontation asks for solutions towards transparency and a

---

42 Ibid.

43 Zimmerman notes that 'one of the most famous is Velvet Strike, an antiwar modification to Counter-Strike, a multiplayer game where players join terrorists or counter-terrorists', Zimmermann, 'Public Domains'.

44 Ibid.

45 See s-77ccr.org.

46 See Torin Monahan, 'Countersurveillance as Political Intervention?', *Social Semiotics* 16: 4, 2006, 515–34.

47 Brian Holmes, 'Top-down Surveillance for Grassroots Initiatives!', available at s-77ccr.org.

48 Ibid.

10.11　'They See Streets, We See Concentrations': System-77's public displays in Vienna in 2004 (bottom) and a mock-up of their reverse-engineered drone (top).

balance of power'.[49] They see their project as a means of creating a 'fluid gaze for top view assessment of structural social conflicts'. The drone could perhaps enable groups which launch civil protests to protect themselves from violence and other abuses by the state, because they can summon independent media testimony to events in question. In addition, 'the observation of police forces or riot control units can give a tactical advantage in mass demonstrations and acts of civil disobedience'.[50] In 2004 the drone was deployed in Vienna.

To what extent, then, is it possible to appropriate infrastructure and technology designed to sustain imperial and military gain? With the infrastructures and technologies of control now interwoven through the cultures of leisure, play, consumption, mobility and tourism, this is an especially important question. When one factors in the palpable eroticization of military control, simulation, and targeting technologies within contemporary mainstream culture, this question becomes even more vital. 'It is extremely uncomfortable', writes media artist Jordan Crandall, 'for audiences to confront their own libidinous investments in violence and they can find in my work a difficult positioning of the dynamics behind their own voyeuristic pleasure'.[51] Peter Weibel, writing about Crandall's work, challenges art and activism to 'give . . . us a vision of this geometry' that links desire, anxiety, fear and techno-military control and violence, so as to yield 'insight into a dark zone of new pleasures and pains within the techno-military controlled society'.[52]

Holmes thinks it important to conceive of worldwide systems of communications technology as, in effect, 'Imperial infrastructure' – systems which have strictly military origins but have been rapidly liberalized, so that broad sectors of civil society are integrated into the basic architecture.[53] Any use of, or reliance on, GPS, for example, involves connecting to three of the twenty-four satellites launched and controlled by the US military. Much less recognized, however, is the fact that such positioning also relies on global geodetic mapping projects organized by the US Department of Defense since 1984 and atomic clocks run by the US military. 'When you use the locating

---

49   Jordan Crandall, 'Envisioning the Homefront: Militarization, Tracking and Security', *Journal of Visual Culture* 4: 1, 2005, 19.

50   Ibid.

51   Ibid.

52   Weibel, 'Jordan Crandall: Art and the Cinematographic Imaginary in the Age of Panoptic Data Processing', 7.

53   Brian Holmes, 'Drifting Through the Grid: Psychogeography and Imperial Infrastructure', available at www.springerin.at.

device you respond to the call', writes Holmes. 'You are interpolated into Imperial ideology'.[54]

What does this mean for countergeographic or other projects which attempt to appropriate GPS and other tracking technologies to render city lives and urban cultures visible in new ways? Too often, Holmes argues, such projects represent over-aestheticised interventions, mere 'politics as décor'.[55] They also fail to tackle their own reliance on imperial infrastructure designed to sustain global surveillance, targeting, and killing. 'Can we still make any distinction', he asks, 'between a planetary civil society articulated by global infrastructure, and the military perspective that [Jordan] Crandall calls "armed vision"?'[56] For Holmes, in a world where digital media and military architecture have become so totally conflated, the social subversion of imperial infrastructure remains an open question.

JAMMING

Fourth, we need to see widespread efforts to 'jam' the new military urbanism by problematizing and undermining its performances, spectacles, circuits, rituals and obfuscations. These efforts must address not only the sites of military recruitment, militarizing education, and militarized simulation/entertainment, but also the sites where armaments and control technologies are developed and produced.

Karen Fiorito's 2005 billboard campaign on Sepulveda Boulevard in Santa Monica, California – our hard-hitting first example – drew public attention to the convergence of military information operations and supine corporate media – notably News Corporation's Fox News – in sustaining the War on Terror (Figure 10.12).

Widespread campaigns, drawing on a long history of such activism, have targeted the militarized R&D that is carried on in US universities and so firmly underpins securocratic war, ubiquitous bordering, and the Long War.[57] Two of the main centres for work on the robotization of weapons – the Robotics Institute and its commercial arm, the National Robotics Engineering Center (NREC) – are at Carnegie Mellon University in Pittsburgh, and both have been the target of a jamming campaign (Figure 10.13). (In Chapter 9 we already encountered

---

54   Ibid.
55   Ibid.
56   Ibid.
57   See Giroux, *University in Chains*.

10.12   Karen Fiorito's 2005 billboard campaign, Santa Monica,
LA: An attempt to expose and jam the seamless blurring of
corporate TV news and military 'information operations'.

NREC: its 'robocar' was the winner of DARPA's 2007 Urban Challenge
competition.) The Carnegie Mellon campaign, labelled 'Barricade the War
Machine', is challenging the take-over of engineering sciences in the university
and the local economy by military-robotics research in the service of the
military-industrial-academic complex. It is also raising the key ethical question
forced by the shift to fully autonomous weapons systems (see Chapter 5): 'Who
bears moral responsibility for outcomes that are caused by autonomous robotic
systems?'[58]

Highly successful jamming campaigns have also dramatically undermined
efforts by the US military to undertake recruitment in certain secondary schools
in the country. The National Network Opposing Militarization of Youth has been
especially effective here, as have the counter-propaganda campaigns of 'An Army

58   See David Meieran, 'CMU and the Development of Warfare Robotics', February
2007, available at www.organizepittsburgh.org.

DON'T BE A COG
IN CMU'S WAR MACHINE

10.13　Counter-propaganda from the 'Barricade the War Machine' campaign at Carnegie Mellon University, Pittsburgh.

of None' (Figure 10.14).[59] Many urban recruitment stations in the US continue to be picketed. Such initiatives are closely linked to efforts by radicalized US military veterans of the wars in Iraq and Afghanistan to mobilize against war and occupation.

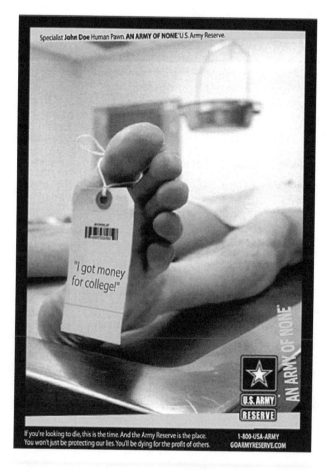

10.14   The counter-propaganda campaigns of 'An Army of None' initiative, aiming to undermine the penetration of the US education system by military recruiters.

59   See www.nnomy.org and also Aime Allison and David Solnit, *Army of None: Strategies to Counter Military Recruitment*, New York: Seven Stories Press, 2007.

Another jammer artist is Micah Ian Wright, who has reworked a wide range of US Second World War-style propaganda posters to hammer home powerful messages about the War on Terror. Among the topics he addresses are the links between SUV use and imperial aggression; the post-9/11surveillance surge; corporate war-profiteering; the robotization of killing; and the establishment of extra-territorial torture camps (Figure 10.15).[60]

Our final examples of jamming challenge the way the new military urbanism colonizes popular culture. In 2005, for instance, a globally orchestrated campaign led to sixty thousand people working simultaneously to disturb the electronic operations of the Minuteman Border Fence right-wing militia group, whose supporters were then patrolling the US–Mexico border on behalf of the US state in search of 'illegal' civilian invaders.[61]

Other jams have challenged the enactment of Manichaean geography and the sanitized killing of virtual Others for entertainment that take place within the US Army's *America's Army* video game. By participating in a multiplayer version of the game on the Internet, the artist Joseph DeLappe – a professor in the art department at the University of Nevada, Reno – has turned participation in the game into both a protest and a memorial for the US soldiers killed in Iraq.[62] As part of his 'Dead in Iraq' project, DeLappe entered across the game's screen the names of US soldiers recently killed on duty. As Rebecca Clarren described his activity on Salon.com, 'he logs on to the game and does nothing. While other online players around him simulate war – and eventually shoot him – he types into the program's chat interface – typically used for gamers to strategize with one another – the name of each service person killed in Iraq'.[63]

Within a somewhat different context – what Gilbert Achcar has called the 'clash of barbarisms'[64] – jamming is also a relevant response to the efforts of radical Islamists to breed fear and anxiety through spectacular and murderous terrorist attacks on the basic infrastructures and circulations of contemporary cities. The 'We're Not Afraid' group, for example, have launched campaigns in various cities targeted by such attacks, as a means both of resisting these attacks and resisting the cycles of securitization they generate. Stressing a strong sense of global cosmopolitanism, rooted in cities, the campaign's message is that 'we who are not afraid will continue to live our lives the best way we know how.

---

60 See ministryofhomelandsecurity.blogspot.com.
61 See www.swarmtheminutemen.com.
62 See Rebecca Clarren, 'Virtually dead in Iraq', Salon.com, 16 September 2006.
63 Ibid.
64 Gilbert Achcar, *Clash of Barbarisms*.

10.15   Micah Ian Wright's influential 'remixed propaganda'.

We will work, we will play, we will laugh, we will live. We will not waste one moment, nor sacrifice one bit of our freedom, because of fear'.[65]

SATIRE

Subverting militarization and neoliberalization through satire is part of a long tradition and offers rich possibilities. Inherently moralizing, such interventions are especially successful at exposing the pretensions and absurdities of power and authority. The Yes Men, for example, engage in what they call 'identity correction'. One or another of them have successfully passed themselves off as corporate or WTO spokesmen, appearing on BBC and other news channels, as a way of inducing 'tactical embarrassment' and highlighting the excesses of military and corporate corruption and violence.[66] A striking example of this approach was a live four-minute interview on the BBC World News on December 3, 2004, in which Andy Bichlbaum impersonated a spokesman from Dow Chemicals on the twentieth anniversary of the deadly industrial accident at the Dow plant in Bhopal, India.[67]

Notable efforts to satirize the painful absurdities of the War on Terror have emerged from the work of the widely read *Onion*, a satirical newspaper published in the US (Figure 10.16), and responses in the UK to a series of anti-terror adverts (Figures 10.17 and 10.18).

One of the best-known acts of subversive satire against the War on Terror addressed the inseparable linkages that exist between military control technologies and electronic entertainment. In 2004, in the wake of global outrage at the newly circulating pictures of torture at Abu Ghraib prison, a street artist whose pseudonym was 'Copper Greene' placed mock adverts on the streets of LA and New York (Figure 10.19). At first glance, these seemed to be merely a few more examples of Apple's ubiquitous efforts to market its latest generation of iPods. On closer, inspection, however, it became clear that these 'ads' were a subtle and powerful piece of guerrilla art attacking the US invasion of Iraq.

Among the three images used in the ads is the infamous silhouette of the hooded Iraqi prisoner undergoing 'mock electrocution' at Abu Ghraib. On

---

65 Cited in Cynthia Weber, 'An Aesthetics of Fear: The 7/7 London Bombings, the Sublime, andWerenotafraid.com', *Millennium: Journal of International Studies* 34: 3, 2006. See also www.werenotafraid.com.

66 See Stephen Wright, 'Spy Art: Infiltrating the Real', *Afterimage* 34: 1–2, 2006.

67 Ibid.

Orange Alert Sirens To Blow 24 Hours A Day In Major Cities

FEBRUARY 26, 2003 | ISSUE 39•07

WASHINGTON, DC—As an additional reminder that the U.S. is on high alert for terrorist attacks, Secretary of Homeland Security Tom Ridge announced Tuesday that Orange Alert klaxons will blare 24 hours a day in all major cities.

"These 130-decibel sirens, which, beginning Friday, will scream all day and night in the nation's 50 largest metro areas, will serve as a helpful reminder to citizens to stay on the lookout for suspicious activity and be ready for emergency action," Ridge said. "Please note, though, that this is merely a precautionary measure, so go about your lives as normal."

The sirens, Ridge said, will be strategically positioned throughout each city and will be audible within a three-mile radius. The noise will be loud

ARTICLE TOOLS

⊕ Share This

✉ Email This

🖶 Print This

Sponsored by **WHAT JUST HAPPENED**

RELATED ARTICLES
EPA Warns Of Rise In Gl Heartwarming
OCTOBER 28, 1998

Energy Secretary Just Assumed Cabinet Knew I Did Porn Films In The '80
NOVEMBER 5, 2003

10.16   The *Onion*'s satirical treatment of the US Department of Homeland Security's colour-coded alert system.

10.17   The London Metropolitan Police's 2007 public information campaign targeting purportedly threatening street photography in the City.

MILLIONS OF PEOPLE
TAKE PHOTOS EVERY DAY.

SOME OF THEM ARE BROWN.

PLEASE DO NOT SHOOT THEM.

FASCISM. IF YOU SUSPECT IT, REPORT IT.
CALL 0800 789 321 CONFIDENTIAL ANTI-**FASCIST** HOTLINE

10.18   One of the many satirical responses to the Met's posters. This (anonymous) version alludes to the killing of Brazilian Jean Charles de Menezes in Stockwell Tube Station in 2005 by counter-terrorist police.

this, as Gene Ray describes it, 'the white iPod wires are wittily re-functioned as shoulder straps, fuse, or conduits of simulated electrocution'.[68] Echoing the strapline on the iPod ad, the message reads, 'iRaq – 10,000 volts in your pocket, guilty or innocent'. The posters received a good deal of mainstream media coverage, and are an excellent example of how 'images of dissent had been introduced into the spectacle machine and had multiplied like a virus'.[69]

Perhaps the bravest satirical effort, though, must be the work of Danish artist Jakob Boeskov and his pseudo arms company, Empire North ('The Logical Solution').[70] In 2002 Boeskov managed to worm his way into the first major arms and security fair in China to display a product called ID Sniper™. Next to the 'weapon' at the unmanned stall was a poster explaining its purpose:

> What is the ID Sniper™ rifle? It is used to implant a GPS-microchip in the body of a human being, using a high powered sniper rifle as the long distance injector . . . At the same time, a digital camcorder with a zoom lens fitted within the scope will take a high-resolution picture of the target. This picture will be stored on a memory card for

---

68   Gene Ray, 'Tactical Media and the End of the End of History', *Afterimage* 34: 1, 2006.
69   Ibid.
70   See www.backfire.dk/empirenorth.

10.19   '10,000 volts in your pocket, guilty or innocent': street artist Copper Greene's 2004 posters, mimicking Apple's adverts for its iPod (bottom).

later image-analysis. GPS microchip technology is already being used for tracking millions of pets in various countries, and the logical solution is to use it on humans as well, when the situation demands it.

Boeskov described his satire thus: 'Fictionism is a brand new art style. The goal of Fictionism is to create fresh reality and to give people a taste of the future, today'[71] By satirizing the obsession to saturate the mass and flux of urban life with the means to identify and track human targets, the ID Sniper™ goes straight to the heart of the technophilic fantasies that drive the new military urbanism. That the Empire North display was accepted as normal within the context of the fair is telling indeed. One computer magazine ran an in-depth article about the Sniper.[72] A delegate tried to purchase the product. And a Chinese company apparently offered venture capital and a manufacturing location to Empire North during the event.

Given the context, in which subcutaneous chip implants for workplace and consumption surveillance are rapidly increasing, satire seems almost prosaic. The journalist suckered into writing the serious article about the the ID Sniper™ later said that 'while the device I wrote about is an undoubted fake, similar technologies are almost certainly being researched or developed'.[73] And as Holmes suggests, what is disturbing is the very ease with which 'such invasive technologies are accepted and made into norms. Under these conditions, the work of an artist like Boeskov becomes a rare chance to actually play the governance game, by opening up a public space for refusing, contesting and challenging these new tracking and recording regimes'.[74]

COLLABORATION

Finally, and perhaps most important, countergeographic strategies which attempt to undermine the new military urbanism must work beyond new assertions of cosmopolitanism or democracy.[75] They must engage and collaborate with, rather than merely speaking on behalf of, those on the receiving end of urbicidal violence, the ruthless imposition of neoliberal fundamentalism, and the spread of mass incarceration.[76]

71   Quoted in Julian Bajkowski, 'Journalist Suckered by RFID Sniper Rifle "Fictionism"', ComputerWorld.com, 3 May 2004.
72   Ibid.
73   Ibid.
74   See Holmes, 'Signals, Statistics and Social Experiments'.
75   See Esref Aksu, 'Locating Cosmopolitan Democracy in the Theory-Praxis Nexus', Alternatives 32: 3, 2007, 275–94.
76   See Kipfer and Goonewardena, 'Colonization and the New Imperialism'.

It is necessary to work against the habitual silencing of the non-Western Other because, as we have seen in this book, acts of silencing are often combined with representations that legitimatize the power to penetrate and re-order societies en masse, from afar, through war, through 'modernization' (or, indeed, demodernization), or through the violent imposition of 'democracy' or 'civilization'. Denying the Other a voice leads directly to conceiving of the global South as an abstract or pathological 'space ready to be penetrated, worked over, restructured and transformed'[77] from afar, using the superior military or technological power of the West. Bringing visibility to the non-Western voice and acknowledging the agency of the Other are means of counteracting the tendency to deny non-Western societies what David Slater calls 'the legitimate symbols of independent identity and authority' – a tendency that allows the act of representation 'to be frozen around the negative attributes of lack, backwardness, inertia and violence'.[78]

Urban theorists Stefan Kipfer and Kanishka Goonewardena argue for what they call an 'urbanization of anti-imperialism' in the contemporary world. Most anti-imperialism, they write, 'falls on the shoulders of the very slum populations who bear the brunt of neo-colonial strategies and urbicidal attacks'. An urbanized anti-imperialism, however, would work across the Manichaean divisions of North and South by linking postcolonial urban peripheries – 'internal colonies' – in Paris, London, and elsewhere with the strategies of the urban poor of the global South. 'As the uprisings in French cities in late 2005 showed', they contend, 'anti-imperial struggles in the "far" peripheries of our urbanizing world may resonate with "anti-colonial" aspirations in "our own" cities'.[79]

Brady Thomas Heiner, similarly, wonders how the growing numbers of the imprisoned within what he calls 'the global circuit of carcerality', whether in the US, Iraq, Afghanistan, or elsewhere, might gain a direct voice rather than continue being spoken for by activists in the global North. 'Only when the voices of the incarcerated pass through the iron curtain of silence and reverberate through the streets and halls of public discourse', argues Heiner, "will it be possible for the geography of globalization to be *justly* reconfigured. Only then will we be in a position to construct a civil society that does not require an archipelago of carceral institutions to provide the "sewage disposal" for its life'.[80]

The collaborative elements of the emerging urban anti-militarism are part of

---

77 David Slater, *Geopolitics and the Post-Colonial: Rethinking North-South Relations*, Oxford: Blackwell, 2004, 222.
78 Slater, *Geopolitics and the Post-Colonial*, 222.
79 Ibid.
80 Heiner, 'The American Archipelago', 112.

a much large mobilization of transnational movements calling for global justice on a wide range of issues. Rejecting the 'globalization from above' embodied in neoliberalism's relentless commodification, privatization, standardization and mililitarization of social life, such movements are 'associated with heterogeneiety, diversity and bottom-up participatory politics'.[81] Transnational coalitions of social movements in the Americas, for example, have done much to expose the violence, poverty, insecurity and militarization perpetuated by 'free trade' agreements. The swarming of such movements around global political summits in the 1990s played a major role in exposing the savage inequities and insecurities perpetuated by global neoliberalization.[82]

Urban collaborations that transcend the North-South divide are already particularly advanced in cities that transcend the global political equator that separates North from South. In San Diego–Tijuana, for instance, the architect Teddy Cruz has developed a range of art, media, and architectural projects designed to cross-fertilize the 'two urbanisms' of the joined cities. This he sees as a means of disrupting the emergence of gated communities, militarized check-points and 'the barricade[s] against complexity and contradiction" which stand as the 'dominant paradigm for a post-9/11 fortified city'.[83]

WHERE NEXT?

The continued and relentless militarization and colonization of everyday life can be resisted, but this takes more than simple demystification.[84]

Political weakness is not the lack of opposition but, rather, the disorganization of dissent.[85]

The many countergeographies discussed above, then, can each play a part in exposing, debunking or eroding the entrenchment of the new military urbanism around the globe. The artists' clever and caustic projects show us that it is possible to undermine prevalent Manichaean geographies which fold distance into difference, and thereby justify murderous violence, hatred and

---

81   Slater, *Geopolitics and the Post-Colonial*, 219.
82   See Donatella della Porta, *Transnational Protest and Global Activism*, New York: Rowman & Littlefield Publishers, 2004.
83   Teddy Cruz, 'Border Postcard: Chronicles from the Edge', American Institute of Architects, 2005.
84   Deer, 'The Ends Of War and the Limits of War Culture', 7.
85   Susan Buck-Morss in *Under Fire.1*, 60.

war. Elements of what Hardt and Negri call the resistance of the 'multitude',[86] such projects are often playful, celebratory and cosmopolitan, working through urban lived experience and the very same techno-cultural circuits of transnational connection that sustain their target, the new military urbanism. In the process, these initiatives undercut the possibility of living an ordinary, peaceful life at the heart of metropolitan complexes in which the economy and politics are sustained by military atrocities against far-off cities.[87]

Perhaps most important, though, the new anti-military urbanism demonstrates that there is an urgent need for radical new concepts of 'security', capable of serving as the conceptual basis of countergeographies. These must be based on addressing the fundamentals of urban, human, social, biospheric, hydro and ecological security within the context of intensifying global interconnections, rapid urbanization, extreme financial volatility, increasing demographic pressure and resource depletion, and startling environmental crises.[88] To reimagine security makes it possible to remodel the relation between difference and globalization so that it does not depend on launching boundless and perpetual colonial war against continually targeted Others within and through architectures of hyperinequality.

Huge challenges await, but the starting-points are clear. First, we must stress the legitimacy and the urgency of countergeographies, and their radical or critical politics of security. By providing channels for addressing the causes of war, hyperinequality, and insecurity, countergeographies can be powerful means of challenging the legitimacy of violent, fundamentalist ideologies of resistance. 'A non-orthodox, non-nostalgic, non-rejectionist, non-apocalyptic critique of the modern', write the Retort collective. 'That ought now to be the task of Left politics. Otherwise, the ground of opposition to the present will be permanently ceded to one or another [Christian or Islamist] fundamentalism.'[89] Indeed, they are concerned that the weakness and confusion of the Left means that fundamentalist terrorism might come to constitute more powerful ideologies of resistance in many cases than legitimate social and political movements organised through global civil society.

Second, state provision and control must no longer be anathema. We must see to it that socialized infrastructure, housing and urbanism once again

86 Michael Hardt and Antonio Negri, *Multitude: War and Democracy in an Age of Empire*, London: Penguin, 2006.

87 Ghassan Hage, '"Comes a time when we are all enthusiasm": Understanding Palestinian Suicide Bombers in Times of Exighophobia', *Public Culture* 15: 1, 2003, 68.

88 Humansecurity-cities.org. *Human Security for an Urban Century*, Vancouver, 2004.

89 Boal, Clark, Matthews, and Watts, *Afflicted Powers*, 177.

become axiomatic within a resurgent conception of Keynesian state politics, organized through multiple scales of intervention to match the contexts of accelerating globalization.

Third, neoliberal economics must go – *in toto*.

Fourth, progressive redistribution; social and environmental justice; a positive politics of diversity; an idea of difference which resists being violently transposed into otherness[90] – these must become foundational concepts rather than political dirty words confined to the political margins.

Finally, the temporal horizons of politics must reach well beyond the speculative advantages, the sound-bite opportunities, of the 'long now'. Consider, after all, that the human shaping of the earth has become so dominant that an entirely new geological era – the Anthropocene – has been introduced to address it.[91] Surely, cultural, technological and environmental politics must be re-forged to match the force of the Anthropocene. With fossil-fuel extinction looming, and water and food security rapidly deteriorating, a radical new politics of security must be both local and transnational. A 'low-energy cosmopolitanism'[92] demands a revitalized, democratic public sphere at every level. At the same time, of course, we face the thorny problem of re-regulating globalized finance and capital based on a new politics of security.

Although it is the harbinger of chaos and of worsening conditions for the world's already-poor, the current global financial meltdown might possibly also serve as an opportunity, especially because it is combined with the beacon of hope offered by Barack Obama's new presidency. At the very least, these events open up important spaces within which to politically contest the taken-for-granted assemblage of concepts, mythologies, imaginaries and norms that have sustained both the new military urbanism and its central place within neoliberalizing capitalism over the past few decades.

The shift towards renewed state control of the world's financial system that has emerged as a result of the meltdown must not, however, be allowed to occur without a fundamental reworking of our planet's economic and political architectures. The problem, of course, is that states are now so woven into the circuits of dominant capital, so complicit in their own politics of public

90   Thanks to David Campbell for stressing this crucial point. See William Connolly, *Identity/Difference: Democratic Negotiations of Political Paradox*, Minneapolis, MN; University of Minnesota Press, 2002.

91   See Simon Dalby, 'Ecological Intervention and Anthropocene Ethics', *Ethics & International Affairs* 21: 3, 2007.

92   Andrew Dobson and David Hayes, 'A Politics of Crisis: Low-Energy Cosmopolitanism', OpenDemocracy.net, 22 October 2008.

spectacle and private secrecy, that such a reworking is unlikely to come from them. Meanwhile, emergent forms of globalized civil society, linking a myriad of a subaltern groups and social movements, do not yet have the purchase to threaten these arrangements or to challenge dominant party politics and economic regulation – even amidst this crisis.[93] It remains to be seen whether an Obama presidency will have both the commitment and the power to substantially address the deep-set political economies of militarization, hyperinequality and violence.

However a radical politics of security is mobilized, I would argue the importance of maintaining an analytical focus on cities, urbanization and urban life, given our rapidly urbanizing planet. This is an excellent starting-point for the reimagining of globalization, difference and security – and the links among them. This would force a stronger understanding of the continually deepening transnational and cosmopolitan connections that so mark our age, in all their complexity and ambivalence. A radical politics of security requires an appreciation of the demographic pressures and the insecurities created by extreme social polarization, and a grasp of the fact that such polarization is an inevitable hallmark of societies founded on market fundamentalism. While the standard security discourses remain preoccupied with national or supranational governance, a radical politics of security – focused on cities – necessitates a profound recognition of the fundamental reliance of human life on biospheric processes. Cities and urban life are vicerally related to climate change, floods, disasters, wars, and crises of migration; supranational governance and finance are more abstract, more virtual realms which tend, by contrast, to systematically obfuscate everyday life as it is actually lived.

To be meaningful for our own time, new concepts of 'security' must forcefully reject traditional notions of 'national security'.[94] Those who are dependent on the dictates of an acquisitive, colonial and violent neoliberalism, forged within the contemporary national and supranational state system, must be at the centre of critique and intellectual reconstruction.[95] The language of 'security' and 'humanitarianism' has all too often cloaked killing, plunder and dispossession, while complexes of military, corporate, agribusiness,

93 See Leonie Ansems de Vries, '(The war on) terrorism: Destruction, Collapse, Mixture, Re-enforcement, Construction', *Cultural Politics* 4: 2, 183–98.
94 See Keith Krause and Michael Williams, eds, *Critical Security Studies: Concepts and Cases,* New York: Routledge, 1997.
95 See Willem de Lint and Sirpa Virta, 'Security in Ambiguity: Towards a Radical Security Politics', *Theoretical Criminology* 8: 4, 2004, 465–89.

technological, academic, and/or petrochemical capital have generated massive insecurity at home and abroad. Indeed, by feeding at the trough of the fears and anxieties felt by the powerful when surrounded by the marginalized masses, 'security' industries sell anything but. As the debacle in New Orleans in 2005 demonstrates, hypermilitarized discourses about the need to launch 'war' against the existential security threats of 'terrorism' swiftly lead to radical denial of the ultimately far more pressing threats and risks surrounding global climate change, environmental degradation, racialized hyperinequality, and state urbicidal violence.[96]

A cautionary note, however. Though they illustrate the breadth of emergent possibilities, the countergeographic initiatives discussed above have very real limitations. Many are, of necessity, highly ephemeral. Many reach relatively small audiences of already-committed activists and artists. With some notable exceptions,[97] most have a tendency to speak on behalf of those who bear the brunt, at the receiving end, of the new military urbanism, rather than collaborating with these receivers and their own resistances. In addition, virtually all the initiatives explored here confine themselves to the circuits of artists and activists, and do not cohere into the kind of broader political coalitions necessary to the forging of concerted political challenges.

These new, tentative public domains are thus, as we have seen, highly multiple, multiscaled and fluid, and this very characteristic raises a group of major questions: How can the multiple media circuits, locations and themes of activism, protest, and resistance amount to more than the sum of their parts? How can this fluid and pluralized assemblage help bring about the radical security politics that its constituent elements seek? How might a loose and mobile, yet effectual, totality be forged from diverse and multiple countergeographies, to challenge and to parallel the multiple sites, circuits and spectacles so characteristic of the new military urbanism? How, in other words, can we name the enemy?[98]

---

96 See Stephen Graham, '"Homeland" Insecurities? Katrina and the Politics of Security in Metropolitan America', *Space and Culture* 9: 1, 63–7, 2006.

97 The collaborative resistance projects linking Palestinian and Israeli antiwar movements are a good example here. See Adi Louria-Hayon, 'Existence and the other: borders of identity in light of the Israeli/Palestinian conflict', *Afterimage* 34: 1–2, 2006, and 'The School of Panamerican Unrest' (2006) organized by New York–based Mexican artist Pablo Helguera. According to Stephen Wright, this exists in 'the hope of generating connections between the different regions of the Americas through a variety of events – discussions, performances, screenings, and collaborations – by means of a nomadic forum that will cross the hemisphere by land, from Alaska to Argentina', Stephen Wright, 'Spy Art: Infiltrating the real', *Afterimage* 34: 1–2, 2006.

98 Boal, Clark, Matthews, and Watts, *Afflicted Powers*, 191.

I suggest that if we can encompass the plethora of activist projects within broader political coalitions and movements, then insurgent styles of activism and citizenship would gain the power to make higher-level political demands, thus increasing the possibility that radical ideas of security may be implemented to a meaningful degree. But such suggestions, as well as the foregoing questions, lie beyond the concern of this book, whose effort has been to map the new militarism that works so perniciously by rendering urban civilian life as its primary target. I hope it has succeeded in delineating the scale of the challenge that a diversified movement will need to face.[99]

---

99 Quoted in Brian Holmes, 'Signals, Statistics and Social Experiments: The governance conflicts of electronic media arts', available at www.aec.at/en.

Sources and Acknowledgements

Every effort has been made to contact the copyright holders of the images used in this book. Verso and the author would like to extend their gratitude to all of those who have given permission for their work to be reproduced here. The following is a partial list of illustration sources for researchers.

1.1 World total population, and urban population, 1600–2000. 'A World of Cities, an Urbanized World', State of the World, Nairobi: UN Habitat, 2000.

1.2 World's largest thirty cities in 1980, 1990, 2000 and (projected) 2010. 'A World of Cities, an Urbanized World'.

1.3 Radical growth in income inequality in the UK between 1961 and 2002/3. 'Inequality and Poverty', Jonathan Shaw, Institute of Fiscal studies, at www.ifs. org.uk/lectures/jonathans_2005.

3.1 The convergence of state, corporate and civilian sectors to create global 'security' industries. Peter Gill, 'Not Just Joining the Dots but Crossing the Borders and Bridging the Voids: Constructing Security Networks after 11 September 2002', Policing and Society 16, 1 (2006), pp. 27, 49, 30.

4.2 The burgeoning worlds of private security across Europe (above) and a detailed picture from Germany (below). Source, Volker Eick, 'Disciplining the Urban Poor', at http://www.policing-crowds.org/speaker/2006/volker-eick.html.

4.4 Green zones and passage-point urbanism. Images reproduced courtesy of Jeremy Németh.

4.5 7 World Trade Center. Reproduced courtesy of Ben Colebrook, James Carpenter Design Associates Inc.

4.7 Post-apartheid road closures organized by middle and upper classes in post-apartheid Johannesburg. Claire Bénit-Gbaffou (2008), 'Unbundled Security Services and Urban Fragmentation in Post-Apartheid Johannesburg', Geoforum (forthcoming).

4.8 Population incarcerated in US Federal jails, 1910–2004 and the geographic proliferation of such prisons between 1950 and 2005. US Department of Justice Bureau of Justice Statistics.

4.10 Notice announcing the use of DNA testing to deter anti-social behaviour on public transport in Sheffield, UK. Reproduced courtesy of Clive Norris.

4.11 Teddy Cruz's 'Global political equator' and its architectural manifestation on the San Diego/Tijuana border (the San Ysidro checkpoint). Courtesy of Bryan Finoki, 2008.

4.12 Anti-globalization protests at the 2003 World Economic Forum in Cancun, Mexico. Found at http://italy.indymedia.org/uploads/2003/09/picto851.jpg.

4.13 The 'Protest Zoning State'. Found at http://www.digital-photo.com.au/tag/apec.

4.14 Legal, spatial and intimidation tactics used by US Police in dealing with major urban protests, 1999–2005. Gan Golan, 'Closing the Gateways of Democracy: Cities and the Militarization of Protest Policing', Masters degree essay, submitted at MIT.

4.15 Security ring and roadblock around stadium for the 2008 European Soccer Championship. Reproduced courtesy of Francisco Klauser.

4.16   'Identity dominance'. John D. Woodward, 'Using Biometrics in the Global War on Terrorism', Department of Defense Biometrics Management Office, West Virginia University Biometric Studies Program, 7 April 2005.

4.17   Data-mining 'fusion' centres being established in the US. Order code RL34070, Todd Masse, Siobhan O'Neil, John Rollins, 'CRS Report for Congress Fusion Centers: Issues and Options for Congress', 6 July 2007.

4.19   The 'World City Network'. Loughborough University's Globalization and World Cities research centre.

4.20   The 'global homeland', Frankfurt airport, Germany. Image found at http://everystockphoto.com/photo.php?imageId=3722286.

4.21   The fifty-three pieces of information required, at point of reservation, from 2007 for anyone entering or leaving the UK as part of the UK's 2007 e-Borders strategy. Image found at http://www.melonfarmers.co.uk.

4.23   The NSA's global Internet surveillance. Map courtesy of Telegeography; Ryan Singel 'NSA's Lucky Break: How the US Became Switchboard to the World', 10 October 2007, Wired.com.

5.1   The US Military's 'Revolution in Military Affairs'. Brian D. Graves, 'Remote Sensing and Military Transformation: Lifting the Fog of War', http://www.emporia.edu/earthsci/student/graves1/project.html.

5.4   Global South urbanization and the diminishing size of the US military. Randy Steeb, 'Appendix H: Preemption for Mout', www.rand.org/pubs/conf_proceedings/CF148/CF148.apph.pdf.

5.5   DARPA's Visibuilding Programme. Found at www.darpa.mil/sto/smallunitops/visibuilding.html.

5.6   Data-mining a city for 'advanced target acquisition'. Edward J. Baranoski, Urban Operations, The New Frontier for Radar DARPA.

6.2   Mock Iraqi villages at the National Joint Readiness Training Center at Fort Irwin, California. Beth Reece, Soldiers, September 2005; see www.soldiersmagazine.com.

6.3   The Baladia mock Palestinian city. Top: US Army Corps of Engineers, Engineering in Europe, Summer 2007, www.nau.usace.army.mil. Middle: URIEL SINAI / GETTY IMAGES. Middle and bottom: Reproduced courtesy of Adam Broomberg and Oliver Chanarin, 2006.

6.4   Ghost town in Playas, New Mexico. Photographs reproduced courtesy of Steve Rowell/the CLUI Photographic Archive.

6.5   Third World urban simulation. Image found at http://www.defenselink.mil/dodcmsshare/homepagephoto/2008-02/hires_080219-N-0696M-289.JPG.

6.6   Officers in the US Air Force operate an airborne tracking laser in a computer simulation. Image found at United States Joint Forces Command, http://www.jfcom.mil/newslink/storyarchive/2006/pa102406.html.

6.7   Orientalized cityscapes of 'America's Army'. http://www.americasarmy.com/media/index.php?type=mission.

6.8   The reasoning behind the US military's development of urban warfare video games. Tim Lenoir, 'Taming a Disruptive Technology', open source, Stanford University.

6.9   Participants at an 'America's Army Experience' roadshow. Hannah M. Hayner, 'Virtual Experience Lets Civilians Act as Soldiers', 27 February 2007, http://www.army.mil/-news/2007/02/27/2005-virtual-experience-lets-civilians-act-as-soldiers/.

6.10   Playground at Kadena Air Base, Okinawa, Japan; Patriot missile battery at overseas US base. Photographs reproduced courtesy of Mark Gillem.

6.11   An air force 'Pilot' controlling an armed Predator drone. AP photo by Maya Alleruzzo.

6.12   Sim City: The concentration of military, academic, simulation and security complexes, bases and research parks in Suffolk, Virginia.

7.1   Total military and economic aid to Israel from the US, 1949–2006. Shirl McArthur, 'A Conservative Estimate of Total Direct US Aid to Israel: $108 Billion', Washington Report on Middle East Affairs, July 2006, at http://www.wrmea.com/archives/July_2006/0607016.html.

7.2   Captive societies: The West Bank and Baghdad. Found at http://s3.amazonaws.com/estock/fspid10/19/36/58/4/israele-israel-gerusalemme-1936584-0.jpgandhttp://www.everystockphoto.com/photo.php?imageId=2546508.

7.4   Israeli-modified D9 bulldozer. Gregg F. Martin and Captain David E. Johnson, 'Victory Sappers: V Corps Engineers in Operation Iraqi Freedom. Part 1: The Attack on Baghdad and Beyond", Engineer, July–September 2003.

8.2   John Warden's 1995 'Five-Ring Model'. Re-drawn from Edward Felker, Airpower, 'Chaos and Infrastructure: Lords of the Rings', US Air War College Air University, Maxwell Air Force Base, Alabama, Maxwell paper 14, 1998, 12.

8.3   'A New Model for Societal Structure'. Redrawn from Edward Felker, Airpower, 'Chaos and Infrastructure: Lords of the Rings', US Air War College Air University, Maxwell Air Force Base, Alabama, Maxwell paper 14, 1998, 12.

8.4   Patterson's analysis of the first, second and third order 'ripple' effects of US forces disrupting electrical power grids during urban warfare in an 'adversary country'. Christina Patterson, Lights Out and Gridlock: The Impact of Urban Infrastructure Disruptions on Military Operations and Non-Combatants, Washington: Institute for Defense Analyses, 2000.

9.1   US automobiles 1980–2005. Reproduced courtesy of Energy Security Leadership Council, Recommendations to the Nation on Reducing US Oil Dependence, Washington DC, December 2006.

9.3   US and 'Emerging Asian' (Chinese, Indian and South Korean) reliance on Middle Eastern oil imports, 2002 and 2025 (projected). Data sourced from Thomas D. Kraemer, 'Addicted to Oil: Strategic Implications of American Oil Policy', US Department of Energy, May 2006, 13.

9.5   The customised 'Yo soy El Army' Hummer H2. Found at http://www.goarmy.com/assets/images/downloads/wallpapers/h2_800x600.jpg.

9.6   The FORD SYNUS. Found at http://www.desktopcar.net/wallpaper/27101-2/Ford-SYNus-03.jpg.

9.7   Armoured and armed SUVs. Found at http://www.flickr.com/photos/defensorfortis/143322630/and http://www.flickr.com/photos/defensorfortis/128826897/in/set-72157594152852804/.

9.9   DARPA's 'Urban Challenge'. Found at http://www.darpa.mil/GRANDCHALLENGE/gallery.asp.

9.10   Estimates for the future introduction of fully autonomous military and civilian vehicles from the Urban Challenge presentations of Stanford University's entry Sebastian Thrun, 'Stanford Racing Team', at http://mediax.stanford.edu/conference_07/speakers/thrun/thrun,%20sebastian%20-%20urban%20challenge.pdf.

9.11   Peak Oil and the growing gap between discovery and production. Redrawn from Cameron Leckie, 'Peak Oil and the Australian Army', The Australian Army Journal, 4: 3, 23.

9.13   'Potential Military Implications of Climate Change'. Peter Schwartz and Doug Randall, An Abrupt Climate Change Scenario and Its Implications for United States National Security, report to the Pentagon, October 2003, http://www.gbn.com/GBNDocumentDisplayServlet.srv?aid=26231&url=/UploadDocumentDisplayServlet.srv?id=28566.

10.1   Humane Borders map. Found at http://www.humaneborders.org/.

10.2   Stefano Boeri's 'Solid Seas' Project, 2003. Found at http://www.attitudes.ch/expos/multiplicity/road%20map_gb.htm.

10.3   Elin O'Hara Slavick's 'World Map, Protesting Cartography'. Found at http://www.unc.edu/~eoslavic/projects/bombsites/index.html.

10.4   Ashley Hunt's 'New World map: In Which We See'. Found at http://www.an-atlas.com/contents/hunt_gordon.html and full size display in a Los Angeles gallery. Sources http://www.an-atlas.com/contents/hunt_gordon.html and http://publik.dk/public_address/participants.html.

10.5   Bureau D'etude's 'infowar/psychic war' (detail). Found at http://utangente.free.fr/index2.html.

10.8   Anne-Marie Schleiner's 'OUT of the Closet', the OUT Project, New York, 2004. Reproduced courtesy of Anne-Marie Schleiner.

10.10   'Shadows from Another Place': Transposed spaces by Paula Levine. Republished courtesy of the artist.

10.12   Karen Fiorito's 2005 billboard campaign. Found at http://www.woostercollective.com/2005/06/shox_news_billboard_from_karen.html.

10.15   Micah Ian Wright's influential 'remixed propaganda'. Found at http://homepage.mac.com/leperous/PhotoAlbum1.html.

10.16   *The Onion*. Found at http://www.theonion.com/content/node/27924.

10.17   The London Metropolitan Police's 2007 public information campaign. Found at http://www.met.police.uk/campaigns/campaign_ct_2008.htm.

10.18   Poster found at http://www.flickr.com/photos/illegalphotos/.

Index

Page numbers in *italics* indicate images